On the Front Lines

On the Front Lines

Following America's Foreign Correspondents across the Twentieth Century

Michael Emery

THE AMERICAN UNIVERSITY PRESS
JOURNALISM HISTORY SERIES

Sanford J. Ungar, *Editor*

THE AMERICAN UNIVERSITY PRESS

Washington, D.C., 1995

Copyright © 1995 by
The American University Press
4400 Massachusetts Avenue, N.W.
Washington, D.C. 20016

Distributed by arrangement with
University Publishing Associates
4720 Boston Way
Lanham, M.D. 20706

3 Henrietta Street
London WC2E 8LU England

Library of Congress Cataloging-in-Publication Data

Emery, Michael C.
On the front lines: following America's foreign correspondents across
the twentieth century / Michael Emery.
p.   cm.
1. Emery, Michael C.   2. Journalists--United States--Biography.
3. War correspondents.   4. War in the press.   I. Title.
PN4874.E4A3   1995
070.4'332.0922--dc20   95-4254 CIP

ISBN 1-879383-36-5 (cloth: alk. paper)

#32167661

Contents

Dedication

For my father, Edwin Emery—a keen observer of international news gathering who could write and edit with the best, a world-traveling journalism educator who left his mark from the University of Minnesota to Beijing—and for my mother, Mary McNevin Emery, his partner of 58 years who, from her children's earliest days, stressed the need for practicing tolerance and fairness, in our neighborhood as well as overseas.

Acknowledgments

My interests in foreign correspondence and world history coincided at Murphy Hall, the University of Minnesota's School of Journalism and Mass Communication, home of the *Minnesota Daily*—the training ground for future giants like Harrison E. Salisbury and CBS's Eric Sevareid. As an undergraduate, apparently hoping to be inspired, I felt secure sitting in a classroom chair under an autographed photo sent by World War II correspondent Sevareid to Dr. Ralph Casey, the School's director. Professors Hage, Emery, Nixon, and others taught me about writing, journalism history, and international communications. Professors Berman, Loehr, and Deutsch shared their love of U.S. and world history.

I have particularly warm recollections of meeting a number of professional journalists in the field and thank each of them for taking valuable time to share their ideas and experiences. Thanks also to those former correspondents who consented to long interviews. A special tip of the hat to Phil Otis, Roberto Ceniceros, Jim Lukoski, Judith Gabriel, Kent Kirkton, Ibrahim Dawud, Marc Cooper, Martha Honey, and Tony Avirgan—freelance colleagues during various unforgettable experiences in Central America, the Middle East, and Yugoslavia—and to Dan Bishoff, my *Village Voice* editor, for his contagious enthusiasm; his boss, Jon Larsen, who authorized my stories; Amy Virshup of the *Voice*, for her sensitivity; Bruce Brugmann of the *San Francisco Bay Guardian*, who encouraged my early freelance reporting efforts; George Krimsky, executive director of the Center for Foreign Journalists, for his interest and repeated assistance; former UPI chief H. L. Stevenson for his encouragement; and a host of friends who continually showed deep interest in my travels.

The author wishes to acknowledge the uncounted volumes of books and articles that aided this research, including work done by members of the Association for Education in Journalism and Mass Communication and their students. This is reflected in an extensive bibliography and extended notes. My own students, particularly those in my senior tutorial on foreign correspondents, raised my spirits by asking how to become one of them. They also shared library books with me. My hope is that some of them will get their own front-row seats. Graduate students Eric Swanson and Ezra Shapiro provided lifesaving computer assistance in the final stages of manuscript preparation, along with Allen Lin, our department's computer technician.

Special thanks for unusual patience are due to the people at American University who finalized this project, especially the editor of this series, Sanford Ungar, Dean of the School of Communication. Christopher Kelaher, Richard Rowson, and Kim Kinne of The American University Press suffered through the various phases with good humor. Greg Pearson's insightful comments and Jeanne Pinault's scrupulous editing helped to bring the project to a successful conclusion. Then there is my family, particularly my wife, Lulu, who tolerated many hours of closed-door work over a number of years. Thanks to everyone, from start to finish—but it is obvious that I am solely responsible for the findings and judgments in this book, including the selection of the time periods for study and the focus on certain journalists.

Michael Emery
Woodland Hills, California
November 1994

About the Author

Michael Emery, a former United Press International reporter, earned his Ph.D. in Mass Communications at the University of Minnesota. He has been on the journalism faculty at California State University, Northridge, since 1968, serving as Department Chair for five years. He has worked overseas, particularly in the Middle East and Central America, as a freelance foreign correspondent and media analyst. His work has appeared in New York's *Village Voice*, the *Los Angeles Times* and other newspapers, and in many academic journals. In 1978 he joined his father, the late Edwin Emery, as co-author of *The Press and America*, the popular journalism history textbook (8th edition, 1995). He is co-editor with Ted Curtis Smythe of *Readings in Mass Communication* (12th edition, 1995) and co-editor of *America's Front Page News, 1690–1970*.

INTRODUCTION

One goal of this book is to create a deeper public appreciation of our nation's foreign correspondents, the men and women who sit on the edge of history and bring us the flow of words and images that shape our view of the world. Only a few of those currently active will win major awards. Most move from one assignment to the next in relative anonymity, recognized by colleagues and news sources more than by readers or viewers. In doing so they follow in the footsteps of the thousands of other American journalists who personally witnessed the faraway events of this century that affected every family in this land.

Another purpose is to reinforce the professional demand for heavier financial commitments to overseas coverage by major news organizations. While most serious observers of foreign news agree on the need for increased quantity and substance, the prevailing tendency of news managers is to cut back on overseas material unless it is sensational or trendy: gossip about Prince Charles, the caning of a young American student in Singapore, the success of a McDonald's restaurant in Moscow.

As the post–Cold War world splits into north versus south, or perhaps Western civilization versus a half-dozen other civilizations, we need to enhance the foreign news product. It is crucial for our survival in the twenty-first century to insist on better information about the people and governments of other nations, and about our own government's ambitions. In writing this book, I posit that the best hope of improvement lies in an analysis of past performance—to determine how well the public was served at those junctures and to learn from those experiences.

But above all, this book is written for the reader who likes a good story. That's what journalism is all about, telling truthful and compelling stories, as Theodore H. White did in his 1978 treasure, *In Search of History,* or as Harrison E. Salisbury did in his books about the Soviet Union and China. White's personal adventure as a journalist seeking the truth is the intellectual model for this series of tales about the men and women of the U.S. overseas press corps who covered selected events in the twentieth century. White, with his matchless literary style, analytical force, and admirable integrity, demonstrated the mental and physical discipline necessary for success as a foreign correspondent.

Salisbury's style and achievements model for all journalists the characteristics of the ideal field correspondent. One of the greatest all-around journal-

ists of the century, he was a prolific writer and enthusiastic foreign correspondent whose iron will, enormous stamina, and broad world view took
him to the ends of the earth for the United Press, the *New York Times*, and
himself. Fueled by his "Minnesota spirit," he was a tough, skeptical man
who often demonstrated unusual courage in writing contrary to the conventional wisdom.

On the practical level, the core of this book was inspired by Robert
Desmond's series of books on world news reporting and John Hohenberg's
1964 classic, *Foreign Correspondence,* where he neatly and clearly told us
who was on the scene and what happened to them and their copy. When
Desmond published his landmark *The Press and World Affairs* in 1937, he
listed the pitfalls for all overseas journalists and subsequently their readers:
censorship, personal danger, inadequate education, and hasty editing by
provincials on the home desk. The handfuls of American correspondents
clustered today in the comfort of London-Paris-Bonn-Tokyo assignments or
reporting from one of the Third World brushfire areas are confronted with
these basic problems as well as more complex pressures that Desmond could
not have contemplated.

The research challenge was to discover the contributions of reporters other
than the prize winners and to cut through the stereotypical images brought
to us by novels and film in such masterpieces as British writer Evelyn Waugh's
Scoop (1937), with its early twentieth-century setting, Alfred Hitchcock's
World War II movie thriller, *Foreign Correspondent* (1940), featuring Joel
McCrea as the star-spangled hero, and the film *Under Fire* (1983), where
Nick Nolte's photography influenced the Nicaraguan revolution. The writing challenge was to recount some of the nation's most crucial moments
through news stories and the correspondents' recollections. In addition to
seeing who was on the story, it was important to include as often as possible
how the journalists felt about themselves and their work.

Given this strong focus on the correspondents and factors that influenced
their reportage, it is natural that this book is sympathetic toward these men
and women in the field. They were not perfect, of course, and there is plenty
of criticism to pass on. In general, however, the sharpest criticism of journalists is reserved for those home-desk editors and broadcast producers who
short-circuited stories because they were ignorant of a rapidly changing world
or were in political agreement with official sources, or both. Those journalists differed little from some Washington officials and foreign embassy officers who at various times conspired against journalists and the public. It is
recognized that journalists and government officials have different goals and
that those officials who sometimes distort the truth are not necessarily evil
characters. Nevertheless, it is argued strongly in these pages that unquestion-

ing reporters and editors who accept false stories deserve the same condemnation as officials who engage in systematic patterns of deceit designed to protect corrupt allies.

The historical underpinning of these chapters—placing the journalistic efforts into a global context—is vital to an analysis of the news media's performance. It is hoped that the reader with a love of history who enjoys the anecdotal pages and the many sidelights tucked into an extensive notes section also will appreciate a serious attempt to determine why at crucial times the U.S. audience did not get enough information about overseas events required to make intelligent decisions. It will be apparent to readers that this happened often enough to raise concern about the future.

The following pages introduce hundreds of characters who offer us valuable lessons about journalism—and about life. We struggle with Walter Duranty as he tries and, in the eyes of modern critics, fails to cover the depth of brutality in Stalin's Russia. Talented writers—Edward R. Murrow (the Munich Crisis of 1938) and Peter Arnett (Baghdad, 1990)—thrill us with their broadcasts. We move down back roads and into poverty-stricken villages with Maggie Higgins in Korea and Stephen Kinzer in Nicaragua. Scarring arguments with government officials are part of the story, as was discovered by David Halberstam in Vietnam and Raymond Bonner in El Salvador.

Foreign news gathering is part of a proud tradition. Americans have received news from overseas since Colonial days, when it largely was in the form of rewritten accounts from foreign newspapers. The development of foreign correspondence included these "firsts": The famed James Gordon Bennett Sr. of the *New York Herald* saw the need for direct foreign correspondence in the late 1830s and hired a half-dozen European correspondents. The Mexican War of 1946–48 was the first conflict to be covered by American foreign correspondents as editors effectively used the newly established telegraph system, the Pony Express, trains, and ships to get news to their readers. Horace Greeley of the *New York Tribune* sent Margaret Fuller to Europe in 1846 as the first U.S. woman foreign reporter. Later, George W. Smalley established an office in Europe for the *Tribune*, the first U.S. bureau. James Gordon Bennett Jr., by then in charge of the *Herald*, caused a furor when he sent reporter Henry M. Stanley to Africa where in 1871 he discovered the "missing" explorer David Livingstone. But this aggressive coverage was the exception. For example, during the Russo-Turkish War of 1877–78, only a few of the 80 correspondents wrote for U.S. papers, most notably John P. Jackson of the *Herald*. Jackson was the only American present among a horde of journalists who arrived in Moscow for the 1883 coronation of Czar Alexander III. A possible reason for the dearth of Americans overseas is that from 1867 to the early 1890s dozens of U.S. journalists covered the Indian Wars in the Western states and territories.

The U.S. press remained largely dependent on others for foreign news, principally the British, until the late 1890s. In addition, the Associated Press was locked into a cartel agreement with European news agencies for the distribution of foreign news and provided limited original foreign coverage. On the positive side, the opening of the Atlantic Cable in 1866 accelerated foreign news reporting, and by the turn of the century the use of "wireless" reports was another factor in drawing attention to events thousands of miles away. In 1898 Victor F. Lawson established the first regular European news service, which became the famed *Chicago Daily News* organization. Meanwhile the steady influx of immigrants added to the number of those interested in keeping track of overseas news. As the world began to shrink and American foreign interests became more pronounced, U.S. journalists began to assume responsibility for providing an increased volume of coverage.

The first full-scale attempt by Americans in the twentieth century to bring home tales of a major foreign story was the coverage of the Russo-Japanese War of 1904–05. This began in Korea and then spread into Manchuria and down the Liaotung Peninsula. The news was fed by a hardy corps of writers representing large newspapers and magazines, including those who had chased the Spanish in Cuba during the Spanish-American War (1898), spent time in South Africa during the Boer War (1899–1902), or sailed to the Philippines to cover the rebellion there against U.S. annexation of the islands (1899–1901). A few were veterans of the Sino-Japanese War (1894) and the Boxer Rebellion in China (1900). The news flow was enhanced because Melville E. Stone, general manager of the Associated Press, negotiated a temporary end to censorship of news from Russia in 1904.

The reporters who covered the Russo-Japanese War—and who battled a sophisticated Japanese censorship—formed an experienced, somewhat rough, intelligent press corps. The American reader was fortunate that writers like Frederick Palmer, Jack London, Richard Harding Davis, and photojournalist Jimmy Hare were of this era. These famous adventurers, and about 80 others, were the link between the story and home. This was America's first exposure to Japanese imperialism, with its unmistakable sense of power and order—all part of the history of U.S.-Japanese relations necessary for Americans trying to understand modern Japan in the 1990s.

The war ended on a dramatic note in May 1905 when Carr Van Anda, the legendary managing editor of the *New York Times,* scooped rivals by holding his printing presses until 5 A.M. so that he could publish the most definitive Associated Press bulletin confirming the Japanese naval victory over the Czar's fleet. That excitement of 90 years ago has not ceased.

Despite (or because of) the progress from the age of steamships and undersea cables to fax machines and portable satellite dishes, the correspondent's job remains extremely difficult. World events that demand interpretation tumble one after another. And unlike the reporting of earlier years, when major stories were scrutinized by partisan government officials and a few political critics, today's journalists are open targets for members of every conceivable interest group. One thing has not changed, however. At any single moment, the journalist witnessing a desperate fight for food in Africa or the signing of a treaty by the world's heads of state is as close to history as the U.N. aid worker at the site or the President. It is the correspondents' job to tell us what it was like, even when facing life-threatening odds against survival. The Committee to Protect Journalists reported that 56 journalists were killed worldwide in 1993, most of them nationals working in their home country, and 124 were in jail. In the most notable episode four journalists working for Western media were killed by a mob in Somalia, where a month earlier Tina Susman of the Associated Press was kidnapped and held for three weeks.

The opening of the Great War in 1914—the topic for the first chapter—permits an examination of how U.S. journalists reacted at a moment when war hung in the balance. As Barbara Tuchman wrote in her celebrated *Guns of August*: "The nations were caught in a trap, a trap made during the first thirty days out of battles that failed to be decisive, a trap from which there was and has been no exit." Overnight there was a shocking transformation for U.S. diplomatic reporters living in Europe, from writing stories spawned in fancy restaurants to passing on ugly tales told in field hospitals. For the American public the days of romantic innocence were numbered, to be replaced by a lingering cynicism and disillusionment after war's end. British journalist Philip Knightley ascribed this in part to the world's first scientific use of propaganda, organized by each major power to further national interests and to deceive the home audience. He said in his *The First Casualty* that correspondents were "victimized" by propaganda.

The Soviet Union grew from the rubble of that first war, and while ignored early on its story colored every aspect of U.S. life for more than 70 years. Thus a pivotal and relatively unexplored period—Stalin's consolidation of power in the cruel winter of 1928–29—is the subject of the second chapter. Studying this coverage assumes special value in light of the fall of Communism and retrospective looks at the Stalin years. A small group of hardy American journalists was there that winter, facing censorship, language problems, and the bitter cold. Few Americans realized in the 1920s and 1930s how important the Soviet story would become. Most of them, including newspaper editors, had been inoculated with the fear of Bolshevism during the domestic "Red Scare" years of 1918–20, and this greatly affected the treatment of stories for years to come.

A decade later the world was on the verge of a greater war and a new technology was available for journalistic use. Edward R. Murrow, William L. Shirer, and others on radio brought home to America the dangers of Nazism during the Munich Crisis of 1938. For the first time journalists in different capitals used a multiple hookup to talk back and forth. The world, and journalism, would never be the same. Those who marvel at live CNN and *Nightline* intercontinental exchanges need only read of this first miracle. While the book's focus is on print journalists who provided the essential continuous stream of stories, their broadcast colleagues are mentioned whenever appropriate, particularly in the final chapters. The events of the Munich chapter show the contributions of the radio journalists overshadowing their newspaper counterparts, although some reported for both media. Just as the Spanish Civil War (1936–39) and the Nazi takeovers of Austria and Czechoslovakia (1938–39) were Fascist training exercises for World War II, these events provided radio journalists with their own training, which paid off when war broke out.

The reader will find the roots of World War II developing in each of the preceding chapters, particularly the ones dealing with U.S. coverage of Japan's rise to world prominence and the Munich Crisis story. The effects of the 1939–45 fighting and its journalism ripple through the final chapters, covering years in which Cold War thinking dominated. It is acknowledged that a reader raised in the 1940s and 1950s, hoping to find a case study dealing with some aspect of World War II that shaped his or her perceptions of good and evil and America's role as a world power, will be disappointed. Certainly, Ernie Pyle, Cecil Brown, George Hicks, Leland Stowe, Frank Tremaine, Bob Considine, Wes Gallagher, William L. Laurence, and a host of others deserve another round of applause. However, so many volumes have been written about that war's coverage and its star reporters that it seemed more useful to concentrate on events less well explored.

The story continues, therefore, with the first months of the war in Korea, where some of the WWII writers, like the great Homer Bigart, were in the field again along with many U.S. fighting personnel who were recalled into service. The Korean fighting of 1950–53 was a miserable experience for Americans, dismayed to see another war so soon after V-E and V-J days. In recent years the Korean War has emerged as a topic for revisionism by authors who argue that American anti-Soviet policies and a domestic exploitation of Communism caused events like the Korean War, the Berlin and Cuban crises, and other numbing situations. That aside, this chapter offers some understanding of how reporters reacted to the shock of the 1950 invasion from North Korea and how their reports were received at home.

The Vietnam War flowed directly from our Korean experience and has continued to affect American life. The lessons of Vietnam were with us throughout the Gulf War, the 1992 presidential campaign, and discussions of possible intervention in Bosnia. The focus here is on the Kennedy years, with a look at government deception, self-censorship by media organizations, and partisanship by some veteran journalists. Examination of the 1962–63 reports from Saigon is crucial because, during those days, there was still a chance to avoid a long-term U.S. commitment and all-out war. But, we learned later, the odds were slim. As the story examples in this chapter make clear, the United States and its South Vietnamese allies faced almost certain defeat by Ho Chi Minh's forces.

The chapter on U.S. policies in Nicaragua and El Salvador deals with a history closer to home but unfamiliar to most North Americans—a history of more than a century of attempts to control the economic life of Central America through such acts as a U.S. Marine occupation of Nicaragua from 1912 to 1933. The topic is essential, particularly because U.S. aggression against the Nicaraguan government from 1979 to 1990 and extensive involvement on behalf of the right wing in El Salvador during those same years was condemned by most of the world. Yet the Reagan and Bush administrations were able to continue their actions because they dominated lopsided domestic debates.

An analysis of the coverage in Nicaragua from the days of the dictator Anastasio Somoza in the 1970s to Violetta Chamorro's 1990 election—and a separate analysis of coverage of El Salvador—shows how Washington was able to "set the agenda" for much of the discussion. The embassy people were accomplished at this, as those in the field found out. Both the Central America chapter and the Middle East chapter that follows it include discussions of how government sources dominated the flow of news, minimizing the impact of some of the stories coming from the field correspondents. They demonstrate how coverage ebbed and flowed, depending on the pressure of other events, and serve to predict how future events would be covered.

The Middle East story begins in 1948 with the creation of the State of Israel. The highlights of this torrid time include the subsequent wars (1948, 1956, 1967, 1973, and 1982), and the events of the Palestinian *Intifada*, which began in 1987. The book closes with descriptions of the Tanker War and the Gulf War itself, where many of the names from preceding pages appear once again—old hands like Peter Arnett, who saw the opening and ending of the Vietnam War and then recorded the bombing of Baghdad for CNN. The core of the Middle East chapter is the Israeli-Palestinian conflict, because of the old axiom that as long as there is no peace for Palestinians, there will be no peace in the Middle East.

What conclusions might evolve from this recitation of events and their coverage by U.S. foreign correspondents in terms of today's crisis coverage? We have reached the point where it often is impossible to separate the reality of one of those rare penetrating foreign reports—print or broadcast—from the flood of self-interested government and corporate tracts designed to confuse. More than ever before, what happens overseas today is directly linked to the political and economic bases of this nation's élite, including media owners. The vast majority of foreign news and related opinion pieces is influenced by a smothering corporate mindset. Unhappily, in today's world of professional "agenda-setters," the impact of the foreign journalist's work is affected here and abroad by the greatly increased sophistication of government propagandists who proudly create "disinformation," and corporate lobbyists, image-makers, and others skilled in avoiding the truth. Veteran journalist James McCartney, in a 1994 analysis of the 1962 Cuban missile crisis, said, "The fact is that in such situations the press consistently has joined in supporting whatever policy, misguided though it may be, the reigning administration tried to sell—from the early stages of the Vietnam War through the Persian Gulf War. For the most part, in foreign policy crises the critical faculties of the news media shut down."[1]

Adding to the problems, in today's mad rush to cheaply package and deliver news to the widest possible print or broadcast audience, it is convenient for corporate-minded news managers to overlook the importance of the foreign segment, especially in a depersonalized era of mergers and "downsizing." Local news is king, just as it was in the 1880s when the philosophy of the tight-fisted William Rockhill Nelson's *Kansas City Star* was: "The further it's from Kansas City the less it's news."

Television footage of starving Somalians and massacred Bosnians prompted outrage from pundits, politicians, and religious leaders, but there was no more public enthusiasm for intervention in those miserable situations than there was to send troops to France when war broke out in 1914. Americans saturated by bad economic news and stories of violent crime sympathetically nodded their heads but felt no connection to the people on the screen. The historic isolation of the average American is the final barrier facing any foreign correspondent trying to make a statement. There is a desperate need for more and better foreign news presentations to overcome this isolation, as part of a national effort, beginning with early schooling, to merge our society's goals and needs with a global perspective.

Major foreign stories continued to break while this manuscript was in its final stages of preparation. Most reflected a worldwide uneasiness about the ability of the so-called Great Powers and the United Nations to deal with regional chaos that so often spills over into international politics. The news included genocide in Rwanda, another standoff with Fidel Castro, the sending of U.S. troops to Haiti and Kuwait, and a unified Germany faltering in the face of new responsibilities. Mexico survived the assassination of a presidential candidate and held peaceful albeit fraudulent national elections, but drug lords sent a shiver through the region by warning a new government not to cross the line. On the positive side, the Irish Republican Army (IRA) and Great Britain negotiated for the first time, Nelson Mandela brought some hope to South Africa despite continued violence, Russian troops left Berlin after a 49-year stay, and German troops joined a Bastille Day parade on the Champs Élysées in Paris.

Interestingly, a number of these headlines and broadcast bulletins merely continued the stories traced in this book. For example: The Balkans were in chaos, as were Russia and the former Soviet Republics so tightly controlled by Stalin. Dangerous zealots like the Bosnian Serb leader Radovan Karadzic and Russia's Vladimir Zhirinovsky defied reason. The United States and South Korea were in a showdown with North Korea, but there were signs of cooperation between South and North Korean leaders for the first time since their peninsula was divided in 1945. The death of North Korean dictator Kim Il Sung focused attention on his son and successor, Kim Jong Il. Nicaragua was ripe for renewed violence, while El Salvador struggled through a national election that included former antigovernment guerrillas. Leaders in Iran and Iraq mocked the West, with another major crisis possible at any minute. A right-wing settler's murder of Palestinians at a mosque in Hebron in the Occupied West Bank increased pressure to end the Israeli-Palestinian standoff before it disrupted the next step toward the formation of an independent Palestinian state. The Palestinian National Authority gradually assumed responsibilities in Gaza and the West Bank, but the future was a question mark because of attacks against Israelis by Hamas (the Islamic Resistance Movement), rifts within the Palestinian ranks, arguments between the PLO, Jordan, and Israel over the final status of Jerusalem, and the lack of a comprehensive Arab-Israeli peace treaty.

We look ahead with both excitement and trepidation, not only because of the fragility of world leadership, but also because of cutbacks in news media resources, an alarming decline in U.S. literacy, and a growing overdependence on skimpy television news bites. It is amazing that fewer than a thousand U.S. nationals, about half of them working for press associations, are given responsibility for covering the world for our population of more than 250 million persons. For better or worse, the men and women of the foreign press corps are America's scouts in the battle for truthful information about the other 96 percent of this globe's people.

Chapter One

The Coming of the Great War:

That Last Quiet Summer, 1914

Wythe Williams (left) of the *New York Times* and Floyd Gibbons (right) of the *Chicago Tribune*, two of America's most influential correspondents during the First World War period. UPI/Bettmann

INTRODUCTION

Bismarck said it. "Some damned foolish thing in the Balkans," he predicted, would trigger the next war. That foolish thing happened June 28, 1914, at the Bosnian town of Sarajevo: Archduke Francis (Franz) Ferdinand of Austria was assassinated and suddenly the future of Europe was at stake. Ahead lay the outbreak of a world war, a reluctant American commitment to defend its allies, the futile postwar attempts to create an effective League of Nations, and eventually more sacrifices in a second great war. No one could have known during that sleepy pleasant summer of 1914 that America was about to come of age while the Russian, Austro-Hungarian, Turkish, and German empires would disappear.

This chapter will consider how well American correspondents in Europe covered this breaking story for U.S. newspaper readers, who glanced with no warning and little background at those first large headlines proclaiming "Austrian Archduke Assassinated." Did they probe the possible repercussions during the days following the assassination? What were the barriers in the communication process?

Prior to the outbreak of modern war, the world takes one last deep breath and the atmosphere becomes almost festive for the young and romantic. This was the mood in June 1914—tense, uneasy, but at the same time exciting, because people tend to forget what the "last war" was really like. The 1914 generation had this disadvantage. The last major European war had been the Franco-Prussian war of 1870–71 and the Germans had taken Paris so easily that the rigors of battle had not been experienced by a majority of the population. After that bitter quarrel, which unified the German nation, the Continent enjoyed the final years of the Victorian peace period. Between Victoria's death in 1901 and Sarajevo, the arms race between England, France, and Germany accelerated. The Czar's enslaved revolted in 1905 in a prelude to the 1917 revolution, and the following year France and Germany sparred over interests in Morocco. But these were war scares, not wars.

The major obstacle to long-term peace was the Austrian-German determination to stop Serbia from forming a Pan-Slavic state in the Balkans. The treaty following the Russo-Turkish War, signed in Berlin in 1878, gave Serbia independence from the Turks. In Vienna, the Hapsburg rulers of the Austro-Hungarian empire saw things differently. Croatia and Slovenia had become Hungarian provinces, and there was fierce resistance to the Serb plan to pull them into union with Serbia, Montenegro, Bosnia, and Herzegovina. In 1908 Austria used force to annex Bosnia and Herzegovina. Then between 1911 and 1913 there were three minor wars, beginning with the Italo-Turkish War of 1911–12 by which Italy gained power in Libya and the Mediterranean.

The First Balkan War of 1912–13 was sparked by Turkish repression in the region and a demand by Bulgaria (independent since 1908) that Turkey grant similar status to Macedonia. Greece, Serbia, Montenegro, and Bulgaria fought Turkey, bringing threats of intervention from Austria. One provision of an armistice signed in 1913 called for Turkey to withdraw from the Balkans and achieved nothing but more arguing. The Second Balkan War of 1913 broke out after Austria and Italy protested planned Serbian use of the Adriatic port of Scutari. At the same time Bulgaria decided not to cooperate with Serbia on a plan to annex part of Macedonia in order to gain access to the Aegean. As tensions built, Bulgaria attacked Serbia and its ally, Greece. A peace settlement was signed in August, but not before Turkey and Rumania had joined against Bulgaria and Albania had tangled with Serbia. That latter action brought an ultimatum from Austria, demanding Serbian evacuation from Albania.

Given this background it is understandable that the Austrian Archduke Ferdinand would be seen as an enemy of Slavic peoples, making him a target for assassination. His visit to Sarajevo symbolized Austrian determination to keep the Slavic peoples fragmented. It also is understandable that, following the shootings of the Archduke and his wife, the Austrians would hold Serbia, the leaders of the Pan-Slavic movement, responsible. It took the Austrians a month to declare war, supported by Germany. The Russians, British, and French moved into the other camp, and full mobilizations led to a series of war declarations worldwide that climaxed with the U.S. declaration against Germany on April 6, 1917.

The two Balkan wars had left the region in chaos, but despite the flurry of storm signals there had been a high degree of optimism that the alliance systems and individual strengths of the great empires would offset the threat of total war. U.S. readers were not prepared for Sarajevo and the eruption that had barely been avoided in 1912–13. Among the few Americans covering the Balkan conflicts were two veterans of the Russo-Japanese War, Frederick Palmer (then with the *New York Times*) and *Collier's Weekly* photographer Jimmy Hare. Otherwise the British correspondents dominated the coverage.

Mark Sullivan, then editor of *Collier's Weekly*, offered a memorable description of the fateful assassination day in his *Our Times* series, in a chapter entitled "Just Another Sunday." The peacefulness of the American scene, as contrasted to the underlying currents of intrigue in Europe, is brought home in this poignant recollection:

> America, still asleep on the Pacific Coast, or beginning to arise in mid-West and East is unaware of the tragic act of a political maniac seven thousand miles away, has no dream of the consequences to America that are to flow from that mad deed.
>
> At that time, the day was merely one in the flow of eventless diurnities. Months later, some who cast their memories back could recall it vaguely as a Sunday in mid-summer, associated with newly reaped wheat stacked in fields, cattle knee-deep in shaded pools, hay drying in the sun. Those who tried to remember what they were doing on the day that was a dividing point in history could identify only their accustomed routine of pursuit and diversion.[1]

SARAJEVO: SCENE OF THE CRIME

Paul Scott Mowrer of the *Chicago Daily News* was walking down New York's Sixth Avenue with a friend on June 28, 1914, when he spotted a newsboy waving an afternoon "extra." His companion read the headline and shrugged. "What is it?" Mowrer asked. "Nothing. Some Austrian archduke killed." "Wait a minute, this may be important," Mowrer said, only to have his friend argue back, "Why? Who gives a damn?" Speculating for a moment, Mowrer said, "If they can pin it on the Serbs this might be the very pretext Austria has been waiting for."[2] Mowrer, in New York awaiting European passage to continue his assignment for the *Daily News,* was filled with excitement.

The handful of U.S. diplomatic correspondents in Europe probably shared Mowrer's reaction when they saw the headlines in local newspapers. The original news came from a telegraph station in Sarajevo. The guard at the dispatch center was Lieutenant Emil Vadnay of the Imperial Guards, who earlier in the day had been helping conduct army maneuvers designed to impress or intimidate Bosnians recently included in the shelter of the Austro-Hungarian empire. When he noticed crowds of people hurrying away toward their villages he marched his own men to Sarajevo.

It was stifling hot that Sunday afternoon as he sat in the telegraph room, allowing only military dispatches to be sent to the world. This Associated Press report made it through to Vienna, where it was edited and cabled onward by the AP's Robert Atter:

> Sarajevo (Bosnia) June 28—Archduke Ferdinand, heir to the Austro-Hungarian throne, and the Princess of Hohenberg, his morganatic wife, were shot dead today by a student in the main street of the Bosnian capital, a short time after they had escaped death from a bomb hurled at the royal automobile. They were slain while passing through the city on their annual visit to the annexed provinces of Bosnia and Herzegovina.[3]

Suddenly the 22–year-old Vadnay was selected for a job that no one else wanted. Led to a small stone building, he entered nervously and knelt to make the sign of the cross. Before him were the bodies of Ferdinand and his wife; he was to be commander of the guard for the first night. Years later Vadnay became the *New York Times* correspondent in Vienna, and he told Wythe Williams of how he saw "the raising of the curtain on Armageddon."[4]

Historian Edmond Taylor, in his *The Fall of the Dynasties*, put the assassination in broad perspective:

One of the last known photographs of the Archduke Francis Ferdinand of Hapsburg, heir to the throne of his uncle, the octogenarian Emperor Francis Joseph of Austria-Hungary, shows him coming down the steps in Sarajevo a few minutes after eleven on the morning of June 28, 1914 . . . in five minutes Ferdinand and Sophie will be lying unconscious in their speeding car bleeding to death from an assassin's bullets: an ancient dynasty—and with it a whole way of life—will start to topple; then another and another and another. Close to nine million men fell in World War I as a direct result of those two shots fired in a dusky Balkan town roughly a half-century ago; then 15,000,000 more in a second, greater conflict implicit in the ending of the first one. The visit of the Hapsburg heir and wife paid to Sarajevo lasted only a little more than an hour— not quite the length of a normal feature film—but the drama of those 60 or 70 minutes has literally revolutionized the whole course of modern history; reconstructing it helps to understand many of the tragic dramas that humanity has witnessed since.[5]

America's papers carried every detail of Gavrilo Princip's deed. The stories in the *New York World*, the *New York Times*, *New York Herald*, and *Chicago Daily News* read like history texts, with precise details from an unknown AP stringer which have stood the test of time. No one reporter's byline graced a front page that day; no one was in Sarajevo to cover this seemingly insignificant visit. During the following few days the major papers carried items about European reaction, the Kaiser not being welcome at the funeral, arguments between Austrian court officials over whether the royal couple was given a proper funeral, anti-Serbian demonstrations in Vienna, and details of Princip's confession.

But after July 6 the story from Europe was forgotten. On July 7 the *New York World* began to expand its coverage of the Carmen murder case; on July 9 Mrs. Carmen was arrested and charged with the slaying of Mrs. Louise Bailey in the office of her husband, medical doctor Edwin Carmen. She shared headlines with Ulster Unionists, anarchist Alexander Berkman, Pancho Villa and Dictator Huerta, directors of the New Haven Railroad accused of illegal combinations, the Mme. Caillaux trial in Paris, the New York Giants, and Theodore Roosevelt. The sensational Carmen trial eventually was delayed until fall but in the meantime had taken precious space for nearly two weeks. Then came almost immediately the publicity about Mme. Caillaux, the second wife of the former Premier Joseph Caillaux, who was on trial for killing Gaston Calmette, the editor of the Paris daily *Figaro*, on March 16. The trial was linked to the highest figures in French politics.

The *New York Herald* offered the best overall foreign coverage during this early period and yet, between a story about the "third class funeral" of the Archduke on July 7 and the ultimatum news on July 24, the *Herald* carried only two items, totaling five paragraphs, relating directly to the possibility of future trouble in Europe. For reasons to be examined later, there was a news blackout of sorts. On July 19 a Vienna dispatch maintained that despite vitriolic editorials in Austrian newspapers, neither Francis Joseph nor Minister of Foreign Affairs Count Berchtold would take "coercive action" against Serbia.[6] The other, on July 22, from the Paris *Herald* office, quoted a *London Daily Telegraph* reporter as believing that the "real danger" was found in the tendency of the Austrians to try to lower the prestige of Serbia, whose attraction was strong in the southern sections of the Austro-Hungarian empire. The reporter said if the Austrians tried to regain lost prestige then the situation could become quite serious.[7]

The *Herald's* correspondence network did pick up several other interesting items which were somewhat related to the crisis, one appearing on June 28 itself. That brief article, based on an interview with a St. Louis editor just home from Europe, said Serbia and Rumania were boycotting Hungarian trade in retaliation for past abuses.[8] "Past abuses," of course, were piling up. Three stories detailed a dispute between French and German reporters about the "rights of German correspondents" in Paris.[9] It was hinted that this could lead to strained French-German relations. And one short item mentioned that French Socialists led by Jean Jaures, soon to be assassinated, were protesting Poincaré's trip to Russia because of the expense and because the Russian Duma no longer had any influence on Russian foreign policy. That last point was important because the Czar eventually mobilized his troops on the advice of military and not political leaders.

But the *Herald* was no more aware than the other papers, as demonstrated by this editorial published while armies were mobilizing:

> There is no exaggeration in the assertion that interest in the Caillaux trial is truly world-wide. Here in the United States every phase of the proceedings in Paris is being followed with just as keen interest as throughout France. This is proved by the press comment the *Herald* published today in connection with its reports of the trial.[10]

The *Herald* then devoted the good part of a page to comments from other U.S. newspapers, leaving the impression that Mme. Caillaux was the most popular French woman since the Maid of Orleans. She was popular. William Philip Simms of the United Press Paris bureau received a cable from New York in July that stopped him cold:

Simms down hold warscare upplay Caillaux[11]

William Randolph Hearst's *New York American* received foreign news from Hearst's International News Service, the Associated Press, and from many official and semi-official correspondents. These sources provided only four stories even indirectly related to the crisis after the first week in July. The most direct story came on July 14. A Vienna dispatch said Austria was determined to destroy the dangerous "Greater Servia" propaganda and prevent the union of Serbia and Montenegro, adding that Germany was prepared to back Austria with all her resources.[12] The Kaiser's message to German author Lieutenant-Colonel Frobinus, who had just completed his *The German Empire's Hour of Fate*, made an interesting story two days later. It is known, however, that French dailies like *Le Journal* carried some aspect of the Austro-Serbian tensions nearly every day in July along with reports from other nations. Apparently, as often has been the case in the history of foreign correspondence, these stories were not picked up by the U.S. or British correspondents.[13]

Frobinus said France's thirst for revenge and Russia's hatred of Austria meant that Germany would be engaged in a massive defensive war by 1915. The Kaiser's telegram expressed his desire to have all Germans read the book, and the *American's* interpretative headline read, "Crown Prince Sees Germany at War in 1915."[14] The two other items were on Poincaré's trip to St. Petersburg, one stating that the French-Russian alliance provided irritations for Germany.

SECRET DIPLOMACY AND HOMETOWN IGNORANCE

Following the assassination the chief European correspondents were handed a tremendous responsibility, to search for anything that might shed more light on the disturbing incident. Frederick William Wile began covering Berlin for the *New York Times* and *London Daily Mail* in 1906. By 1914 he was an expert at climbing the stairs of the Wilhelmstrasse to play an "unabashed hide-and-seek game" with the German Foreign Office. But chief complaint was not in being frustrated by the antics of press chief Otto Hammann but rather by the unexplained refusal of American editors and readers to become interested in European affairs:

> The difficulty of foreign newspaper correspondents in Berlin was not in obtaining and reporting news of the Fatherland's far-flung plans for *Weltmacht oder Niedergang*, the prophetic title of General von Bernhardi's book prognosticating that Germany must either achieve world power or go under. Correspondents' problems, rather, were those of per-

suading readers abroad, particularly British and American readers, that the Germany of William II was consciously bent on conquest by the blood and iron method bequeathed and sanctified by Bismarck, the Empire-builder.[15]

Mowrer of the *Chicago Daily News*, who had covered the earlier fighting in 1911–13, noticed that the longer the Italo-Turkish War went on the less attention the newspapers at home gave it. This tendency of American editors and readers or viewers to fall into disinterest remains a major liability. In 1914 it affected this nation's knowledge of the prewar maneuvering. It was a dangerous habit and one that only a few journalists were able to perceive. Mowrer's first impression was that Americans were not greatly concerned because there were few American correspondents in Europe. Being firm in the credo that the more detailed, precise, and complete a story is, the more the reader will be drawn into the reality of the situation, Mowrer made an intensive effort to write in this fashion. He realized that many European dispatches were brief, vague versions which meant little and thus were relegated to inside pages if only for their shortness. To his dismay he found his careful writing made no difference, or at least not to the deskmen for the *Daily News*.

In one attempt he tried, without editorializing, to indicate the gravity of the general European situation. A few days after he predicted more turmoil would break out, it did. But his story was placed on the editorial page, "as if it were a bit of philosophy." The Taft-Wilson presidential battle was on, but Mowrer felt strongly that Americans should not be allowed to relax after Turkey and Italy signed a treaty in London. However, in America he said, "Interest was no sooner kindled than it died out."[16]

Will Irwin, the old *New York Sun* reporter who covered the war's start for *Collier's,* was one of the few American magazine correspondents with wide experience in Continental affairs. He spared little when he criticized newspaper reporting:

> By 1914, the foreign correspondence of our American newspapers had fallen to its nadir. In the period of the Dreyfus case, whose personal note gave it interest for the man in the street, such first class reporters as Wilbur Chamberlin, Henry R. Chamberlain, Julian Ralph and Arthur Brisbane gave us proportionate accounts of social and political events and trends in Europe. But after the Boer War and the Dreyfus case the reading public went isolationist.[17]

A few men had made themselves quite knowledgeable in European affairs, among them Edward Price Bell of the *Chicago Daily News* London bureau, and freelancer Herbert Adams Gibbons. But most American newspaper editors, Irwin said, held to the illusion that U.S. interest in any foreign war would last no more than a few months. Following the outbreak of hostilities he praised Ellery Sedgwick of the *Atlantic Monthly* for being the one magazine editor who perceived the truth that "this was one of the periodic upheavals of the world which would affect the destinies of all nations."[18] If the outbreak of war did not mean much to many American journalists, what did the dispatches prior to the outbreak hold for them? Shocking statements come from oldtimers who were present when these tide-turning events were occurring. "Most of the American newspapers and newspapermen considered the European war a colossal bore. In New York it played havoc with the lucrative 'space' [pay by words] system, except for the lads who covered the Liberty Loan drives . . . probably most of us didn't realize that the golden era, which reached its climax in 1912, was going forever."[19]

Irwin took a poke at correspondents in general, saying, "The foreign correspondent [by 1914] became mainly a purveyor of gossip about Americans abroad. A Pittsburgh playboy who broke the bank at Monte Carlo, or a young blood of the Four Hundred who entangled himself with a showgirl in London, was worth more space in Chicago and New York than Asquith's social legislation or the rise of Social Democracy in Germany."[20] Let's not forget that the home office often made assignments.

Both Irwin and E. Alexander Powell of the *New York World* complained that few of the regular correspondents were men of distinction or, to use Powell's term, "vocational correspondents." "The average American reporter in Europe during 1914–1918 lacked both experience and the requisite background in education . . . then both secondary and higher education almost ignored contemporary history, both domestic and foreign. Most of us had to educate ourselves in the ways and structure of this new, strange world as we went along. The men who handled our copy at home were almost equally ignorant. That was the main reason why a few fakers got by."[21]

The quality of the writers in Europe can be assessed only through subjective means, but other factors may be considered in determining why there was a news lag during the summer months of 1914 and why interest was low. These include the diplomatic secrecy that prevailed in European capitals and British preoccupation with the Irish Question.

Why would it make any difference to American newspapers if a high degree of diplomatic secrecy existed or if the British press carried more news about the rebellion in Ireland than it did of the rising European crisis? Were not American correspondents at the capitals digging and arguing in an effort to learn the truth? An observation of *Chicago Daily News* owner Victor Lawson, while setting up the first midwestern newspaper syndicate in 1898, helps clarify the problem. Lawson discovered that while many American papers had been sending writers abroad, it had become a habit to place a permanent man in London and to rely on the cartel-organized news agencies for the bulk of the Continental news. He complained that the foreign agencies' job had been poorly executed and that European state officials had too much to say about what American readers read.[22] Since nothing had happened between 1898 and 1914 to arouse the American editors into sending a mass of correspondents, the situation was about the same up until the war broke out. In fact, Irwin said that the situation had deteriorated by that time. There was too much American dependence on Fleet Street for background information. The Associated Press was a member of the four-power cartel (Reuters, Havas, Wolff, and AP)[23] and it was the German service which had the obligation to supply news from Austria and the Balkans. Kent Cooper, senior AP executive, was bitter in his denunciation of the Wolff agency's propaganda efforts in collaboration with the German foreign office.[24] Secret diplomacy was an established practice and there was a strong effort on the part of foreign officers to imitate the manipulative Bismarck. All of these secret documents, agreements, pacts and conversations added to the newsman's problems. Today's practice would be for the diplomats to use the newspaper columns for propaganda purposes, to "leak" trial balloons or disinformation. Instead a lid was placed on the whole of Europe. The year 1914 was not a time of bombastic threats, grand speculation, or grave warnings, but one of tenseness and uneasiness. Will Irwin did say that foreign offices occasionally issued printed pamphlets to describe their vague policy positions, but "wobbled so ignorantly that their early pamphlets are now curiosities of journalism."[25]

The withholding of vital information from reporters was something the older hands already had experienced. Strict censorship became necessary, in the eyes of all European officials, after the Boer War, when military students and critics discovered that German intelligence agents had pieced together snatches of stories to form larger pictures that aided the Boers. The Japanese showed how effective censorship could be in 1904–05, being the first to employ universal restrictions in wartime. It also was established that German agents took advantage of a liberal press policy to assist their forces during the Franco-Prussian battles of 1870–71. Thus an extreme move was made by British and French officials, from a somewhat free and easy policy to one of acute censoring. This attitude, which developed out of a concern for military secrecy, spread to diplomacy, traditionally a closed-door procedure anyway. In some immeasurable way this contributed to the atmosphere in 1914 and led to a general lessening of information. The British historian Philip Knightley put the phenomonen of censorship into perspective in his

1975 work *The First Casualty,* where he looked at war correspondence from the Crimea to Vietnam. While he paid little atttention to the time period described here, he characterized the entire war as a lie, with the correspondents for the most part caught in the machinations of their home governments. The "first casualty," of course, is truth.[26]

C. P. Scott, editor of the powerful *Manchester Guardian,* explained why the British government was not more candid with its people from 1911 to 1914 when Herbert Asquith's cabinet possessed an accurate picture of European affairs. Scott said the true story was not told until the eve of the war because of two major difficulties in Great Britain which precluded the releasing of information of this serious nature. First of all, the disclosures would have destroyed the Liberal Party. "If [Sir Edward] Grey had gotten up in the House of Commons and stated that Germany's policy was so unfriendly and her designs so dangerous that we had attached ourselves to France and Russia and had discussed military measures with France, and that this was the governing fact in our foreign policy, the Asquith government could not have survived the storm which would have followed." "Europe was a great surface of exposed and sensitive nerves," Scott said, in adding a second reason why Grey, the foreign secretary, did not wish to open up the issue. British political thinking, according to this influential British observer, was that the balance of Europe might have been upset.[27]

Scott hit the Irish Question hard as another reason for public ignorance:

> We were now paying the penalty for the breach of the great tradition left by Wellington and Peel. A European crisis found a British government faced with rebellion. When Gladstone tried to settle the Irish Question we had no foreign trouble on our hands and Home Rule could have been established under the best conditions. The use of violence in resisting his policy has now put a British government in peril of two wars at the same time: one a foreign war, the other a civil war. Both to the ministers and their opponents the civil war obscured the other, the larger problem. If this had not been the case, they would have taken any risk at home rather than allow the Buckingham Palace Conference to collapse. Its collapse convinced the few Englishmen outside the inner circles who drempt of the danger in Europe that the danger had passed. Unhappily it convinced some important observers in Europe that a nation which could not compose its own quarrel was not in a position to take an active part in the quarrels of Europe.[28]

Thus, the Prussians in charge of German policy held to a rigid system, the British and French worked under self-imposed silence, and other diplomats provided little help. Europe was being lulled into a false sense of security.

One German paper indicated that its editors felt secure when Emperor William II went on another of his vacation trips on July 6. Instead of wondering why the erratic William was taking a pleasure cruise at this time, the paper commented, "Our patriotic Emperor is not the man to withdraw his hand from the helm of State if there was peril in the air."[29]

In addition to the Irish Question, other events were to gain public attention during the summer of 1914. The Mexican army and Pancho Villa were capturing most headlines, and veterans such as Jack London, Jimmy Hare, and James F. J. Archibald of *Collier's* were among the dozens of correspondents covering that action. Many would soon be in Europe, but the Mexican border raids created a big story in the United States. Theodore Roosevelt was defending "dollar diplomacy," and his Panamanian policies still were being disputed. President Woodrow Wilson was a powerful figure, in the center of progressive reforms. The International Workers of the World were accused of bombing incidents, American and British suffragettes paraded daily, and after July 4 Boston's "Miracle" Braves began their drive from last to first, the only team in history to accomplish that feat.

THE PROLIFIC FREDERIC WILLIAM WILE

The most active American correspondent in Europe during this period was Frederic William Wile, whose summer 1914 dispatches appeared in the *Chicago Tribune* and *Chicago Herald* as well as the *New York Times* and the *London Daily Mail*. Victor F. Lawson, owner of the *Chicago Daily News* and the *Chicago Record*, had sent the *Record*'s star reporter Edward Price Bell to London in 1900 to build a foreign service. During the next 22 years Bell became the most influential and prestigious American journalist in London.[30] When he needed an assistant later that first year, the 30-year-old Bell asked for someone like himself, the young and aggressive Wile. In April 1900, Wile sailed on the *St. Paul*, with John Philip Sousa, James J. Hill, Frank A. Munsey, Charles Schwab, Henry Adams, and other prominent Americans. In 1901 he was posted in Berlin. It was in 1906 that Lord Northcliffe saw a special dispatch Wile had written from Berlin and personally lured him from Lawson's service. From 1906 his allegiance was to the *Daily Mail* and the *New York Times*, although he continued to send specials to Chicago newspapers. Wile was consistent in his belief that Germany was making palpable and purposeful plans for a future war.[31] But he had trouble in conveying this impression, as he later recalled:

Between the years 1901 and 1914, I must have written for publication in American and British newspapers close to a million words from Germany. The overwhelming bulk of that Niagara of copy was dispatched over the government-owned telegraph wires and cables, at different periods, successively to Chicago, New York and London. Roughly, one-third of the contents of that correspondence consisted, year in and year out, of news of military, naval and air developments, and of other maneuvers, political, financial and economic, to make Germany ever more formidable ashore, afloat and aloft. Such information was of particular importance to the English-speaking countries, though, to their eternal regret and eventually tremendous cost, they scarcely realized it at the time.[32]

"The Chief," Lord Northcliffe, was, in Wile's opinion, "indefatigable in the tedious and thankless task of arousing a lethargic British people to the immediacy of the challenge looming across the North Sea."[33] As early as 1908 Northcliffe sent Wile to get an exclusive story on the birth of Germany's new fleet, the Kaiser's answer to British battleships. Wile and Admiral von Tirpitz watched the show together.

Following that experience Wile was alert to the special problems of German rearmament and noticed the general lack of reaction in American and British newspapers. Wile covered the annual Kiel Regatta in late June 1914, as he had for the previous decade. His first dispatch told of a humorous incident concerning the British Lord Brassey, who was arrested for rowing too close to the Kaiser's dockyard. The Kaiser was annoyed by the blunder, but the Regatta was a holiday and the story was light in tone.[34] The next Wile story told of a warship speeding to the Kaiser's yacht, the *Hohenzollern*, with the news of the Archduke's assassination. Calling off the race, the Kaiser "stood silent but acknowledged the salutes offered to him enroute. How deeply he was affected could plainly be seen by those on the British flagship *King George V*."[35] That dispatch was quickly sent and was run with the assassination story from Sarajevo. The next time a Wile story appeared in the *New York Times* was on July 22, the day before Austria gave Serbia an ultimatum that aroused the entire world to at least the possibility of war. That dispatch—a short piece buried by other news—saying the war spectre had been "revived" was placed on page four.

Wile had been on the *King George*. He later returned to his dockside hotel room when suddenly Otto von Gottberg, a distinguished Berlin correspondent, rushed in. Wile labeled him as a friend but also as a typically arrogant Prussian who had popularized "Dollarica" as a nickname for America. Gottberg exclaimed, "The Archduke Ferdinand and his wife were assassinated today at Sarajevo . . . It's a good thing." Wile decided that the Germans had found a pretext for forcing upon Europe the struggle for which they considered themselves more ready than any combinations of foes.[36]

"In the British Isles they saw what truly looked to most of the world like rebellion in Ireland," he said, "and across the Rhine they saw a France, of which a great senator had only a few days before confessed that her forts were defective, her guns short of ammunition . . . and they saw Paris, the nerve center of the republic, shaken to its foundations by the scandalous revelations of L'affaire Caillaux. They saw a Russia agitated by industrial strife . . ."[37]

On July 1 Wile recorded in his diary that "the shock of Sarajevo had spent its force."[38] On the 6th he noted that the Kaiser had sailed for the fjords of Norway, allowing Germany to be rocked asleep.[39] While watching the Kaiser cancel the boat races at Kiel, Wile had told another American, "It means war." Now he saw the storm clouds, and yet nothing he wrote to this effect received publication.

On July 15 Wile noticed the drop of German stocks and the emergence of what he called "real war rumors." But "England, we Americans and British in Berlin gathered, was thinking exclusively in terms of Ireland. Correspondents of great London dailies, vainly trying to impress their editors and the British public with the gravity of the situation, found their dispatches backpaged, if they were printed at all. Charles Tower, who represented the pacifist and liberal *Daily News*, and the *New York World*, had arranged to start his holidays at the end of July. He telegraphed his editor that he thought it advisable to remain in Berlin. 'See no occasion for any alteration of your plans,' was the complacent reply from Fleet Street."[40] The Berlin group continued to fight what it termed a game of diplomatic deception and camouflage. The Germans insisted that they viewed the Austro-Serb situation without anxiety and that they were leaving no stone unturned to preserve peace. And whenever a correspondent for a British or American paper felt compelled to file something to the contrary he had to buck the Irish Question— or indifference. It was from the London papers that American writers in London took many of their cues or even complete stories. Unfortunately Ireland was close to British hearts and to the hearts of all the Irish who had moved to New York, Boston, and other American cities. It was good copy and the conflict was outlined in black and white, while the European argument was hazy to those who had not studied the background. Some of Wile's best work, pieces in which he expressed his professional analysis, appeared in the *Chicago Tribune*. One of them, written June 15 and published on the day of the assassination, June 28, was almost prophetic:

> When European statesmen talk of Austria-Hungary in connection with the big international questions they talk of Germany at the same time, for the alliance between the two great German-speaking nations is re-

garded as the keystone of central European politics. Relations between the two countries, their governments and monarchs are, therefore, of the utmost importance in the tortuous and turbulent problem known as the European situation. They are once more in the limelight in consequence of the visit which Emperor William has just paid to the future Emperor of Austria, the Archduke Francis Ferdinand at the latter's Bohemian estate of Konopischt.[41]

Reporting on possible effects of the death of Emperor Francis Joseph on Central Europe—that Austria-Hungary would be overthrown from within and melted into different nations—Wile added that it was the old Emperor's intense desire to outlive his nephew, with whom he was on bad terms. On successive Sundays beginning July 12 the *Chicago Tribune* published Wile's accounts of the dramatic end of the Regatta, German Socialist Rosa Luxemburg's charges of brutality in the German army, U.S. citizens using German health spas and the early closing of Berlin nightspots once war loomed.[42] Perhaps even Wile was sidetracked by the apparent complacency of the European governments during the week he chose health spas for his topic. On the other hand, maybe using a feature angle was his way of getting some attention.

FROM CHICAGO TO PARIS: PAUL SCOTT MOWRER

Paul Scott Mowrer sat in a Chicago tavern with his friend Dick Hebb on a cold March afternoon in 1910. It had been another hard day at the *Daily News* and he was getting ready to take the "L" home. Only 22, Mowrer already was advancing within the staff, but it was rough work. The friend told Mowrer that the paper's Paris correspondent, Lamar Middleton, had died. When Hebb suggested that Mowrer apply, the young man scoffed. But that night he and his wife, Winifred, decided he should see publisher Victor Lawson the next day. After checking city-room recommendations, Lawson agreed, saying Mowrer would start at $50 per week.

The Mowrers sailed on a White Star liner, with the words of another friend in their minds: "Paul, you are making a terrible mistake . . . a fellow goes to Europe for a few months and he stays for years . . . what do we care about Europe . . . what's the matter with Chicago?"[43] Nineteen years later he was awarded the first Pulitzer Prize in the category of "correspondence."

Getting the Midwest out of his system actually was Mowrer's biggest problem. As a teenage cub reporter for the *Daily News* he had shunned reading Stanley Washburn's dispatches from the Russo-Japanese front. He remembered riding in the same elevator with Richard Henry Little, captured by the Japanese at Mukden and at that time writing a new series about the Russian army. Mowrer did not read that, either. He cared only about Minnesota and Michigan and especially Chicago.[44] But soon all he cared about was his office at the corner of the Place de l'Opéra, where he maintained a luxuriously fitted reading room for travelers. His orders from Bell in London and from the Chicago office were to avoid getting overly concerned with European politics and to provide "feature stories, quaint episodes illustrative of French life, human-interest stories, stories of Americans abroad." Privately he was disturbed when the possibility of a European war came up in discussions with new Parisian friends.[45]

By all odds Mowrer should have been in the right spot when the assassination and subsequent events occurred. During the previous four years he had taken on assignments in different capitals, including one in Berlin where he secured a job for Raymond Gram Swing, later well known as a journalist and radio commentator. But luck was not with Mowrer in the spring and summer of 1914. The Chicago office authorized two months' leave for him on about May 1. Back in the United States he noticed the excitement over the Mexican problem and the taking of Vera Cruz, and he heard some talk about growing American-Japanese differences. He noted that interest in European affairs was "again in eclipse." The *Daily News* took advantage of his being home and had him cover the ABC conference, the effort by Argentina, Brazil, and Chile to settle the Mexican-U.S. fight. Then followed a genuine Cape Cod vacation. His plan was to sail for Europe alone, with family to follow, because *Daily News* editors wanted him to accompany a group of Chicago aldermen and civic leaders on a tour of European railroad terminals, a trip considered vital by the Chicagoans and called a junket by Mowrer. This was when he saw the "extra" that alerted him to the possibility of war in Europe. His excitement had to be pushed aside, however, as he received more details of his babysitting assignment with the aldermen and realized that his time was accounted for.

After two days in London the tour moved to Paris for four more days of official greetings and sightseeing. Mowrer was in a daze, keeping track of international developments while informing tour members of the height of the Eiffel Tower.[46] The tour ended at Antwerp on July 31, the Chicagoans went back to Liverpool for the boat ride home, and Mowrer began to cover the mobilizations. Incredibly, the *Daily News* editors had not realized that Mowrer was in a position to supplement the Associated Press stories, and Mowrer apparently did not feel he could rebel and protest his assignment. Later he recalled his feelings as Austria delivered the ultimatum to Serbia which within a few days set off a series of war proclamations as Europeans took sides:

> So it had come at last, the catastrophe people had talked of, conjectured over, foreseen and denied, denounced and dreaded, ever since I had lived in Paris. I went out into the streets. Around every poster silent groups were reading Vienna's gravely worded text . . . here and there I saw a young man running, or some couple locked in a desperate embrace. The taxis were driving faster now. A haze of dust shimmered over the city. In the pale sunlight of this August day, all Paris, all of France, the whole of Europe, as it seemed to me, was rushing into war.[47]

PACKING FOR THE FRONT

Others were caught in the wrong place that summer, and the sum total of bad luck, ill timing and lack of judgment meant that the American reader was being deprived of the personal experience which might have helped explain the swift-moving, confusing European developments. Will Irwin, for example, had been in Europe but at this time was back in the United States. He was spending July in Connecticut, "writing enthusiastically of mornings and playing energetically of afternoons." He had never covered a war, and as the crisis grew in the last week of July he tried to line up a sponsor. Other freelancers had beaten him to it in Philadelphia, but *Collier's* and *American Magazine* signed him up. He sailed on the *St. Paul* with a host of others on August 6, 1914, for a six-month war that for him was to last six years. He didn't forget the six-month prediction, because one magazine editor had told him, "I'm going to play this war hard for six months—in case it lasts as long as that—and drop it. By then the American people will grow sick and tired of reading about it."[48]

E. Alexander Powell was in the High Sierra on June 28 but being a journalist possessed of unusual perception, he cut short his vacation and headed for New York—sure that this meant war. Actually Powell was a "professional onlooker" who had written magazine articles on world affairs but had not worked for a newspaper. He recalled:

> At that time only a handful of American writers, notably Richard Harding Davis, Stephen Bonsal, Frederick Palmer, could be considered vocational war correspondents and they were under contract to the big syndicates . . . Consequently major newspapers were cutting their staffs. Sporting editors, baseball reporters, dramatic critics, book reviewers, gossip columnists, even cartoonists were being provided with passports,

riding breeches, and American Express press checks and rushed across the Atlantic to cover the impending conflict. Of these only a handful had ever been in Europe, save as tourists, few spoke any language but English, most of them were abysmally ignorant of continental politics.[49]

Charles Lincoln, managing editor of the *New York World*, finally decided Powell would be a good risk, but a passport had to be obtained in Washington and when he and Joseph Medill Patterson, co-owner of the *Chicago Tribune*, finally arrived in Rotterdam the war was two days old. Powell later was to witness the first bombing of Antwerp by a zeppelin, the first air raid in history.[50] His earlier observations would have been important. Ned Buxton of the *Providence Journal* was in Europe at the time of the assassination, and he returned home to warn Americans about the need for military preparedness; he was headed in the wrong direction.[51]

H. V. Kaltenborn, whose contributions via radio later made his name a household word, played a part in the 1914 prewar coverage. In January of that year he sailed for Paris with his wife and small daughter. His keen journalistic senses told him that war was close—"You could feel it in the air." He blamed the press of the various European nations for inflaming nationalistic sentiments. In April Kaltenborn paid a visit to Germany, where he wrote, "I was astonished at the extent and thoroughness of the German war preparations. On a visit to the barracks of my cousin's regiment I found his unit in total readiness for instant action." By the spring of 1914 the French were beginning to boycott German goods and Kaltenborn mentioned these scenes in a "brief dispatch" to his paper, the *Brooklyn Eagle*. He said his stories on French fashions and various visiting Brooklynites received much more space in the newspaper. Then, in June just before the assassination, he returned home. He did prepare a large feature for the Sunday *Eagle*, "Big Powers of Europe Stand Ready for War," but by leaving he removed himself from a position of authority. He became war editor of the *Eagle* and, along with all other American telegraph editors and deskmen, awaited and sifted through the dispatches of those who were there.[52]

Willis J. Abbot, whose career began with the University of Michigan paper and moved through the *New York Tribune* and Chicago and Kansas City journalism, was with the *New York American* when he sailed for Europe on a pleasure trip in July 1914. He noted that although the Sarajevo crime had been committed, "New York journalism took it so lightly that no suggestion was made by my managing editor that I should seek any special news, or do any work for the paper on the other side." He arrived in Rotterdam, was in Paris at the declarations of war, and after two months returned home. Soon disgusted with the Hearst attitude on the war—neutral but accused of being pro-German at times—he took a place on Frank Munsey's *New York Sun* as editorial writer.[53]

Frederick Palmer and Richard Harding Davis were in Mexico, riding horses near Vera Cruz and wondering where their next story was going to break, when it became obvious that Europe would provide the excitement. They parted company, to meet again in New York. Both boarded the *Lusitania* in New York on August 4, the day Britain declared war. Palmer represented *Everybody's* magazine, not having been associated with a newspaper for years and being more interested in books than dispatches. That changed as he noted, "The statesmen and the masses of Europe had gone mad together, and they were to demonstrate what amateurs in destruction the Villaistas were."[54]

Davis represented the *New York Tribune* and several other papers, all signed up by his syndicate manager, Jack Wheeler. The salary would be $600 a week, far more than any other correspondent, and Davis put off thoughts of a summer vacation. He was 50, still boyishly handsome, and married to former musical comedy actress Bessie McCoy. She traveled with him, as his first wife did during the Boer War. He was carrying a letter from former President Roosevelt, introducing himself to President Poincaré as a friend of France.[55]

THE LUCK OF WYTHE WILLIAMS

One talented writer was not caught out of place. Paris had been home for Wythe Williams of the *New York Times* for one year, although he had been in London with the *New York World* staff from 1910 to 1913. Williams was one of the great correspondents of his time, his career paralleling those of Mowrer and Wile and his youth and brilliance matching theirs. Williams had worked on Minneapolis, Milwaukee, and Chicago papers before landing his first job with Joseph Pulitzer's *New York World*. Then he left the paper and made his first trip to Europe—also on the *St. Paul*—on his own. By chance he met the *World's* Charles Lincoln, the managing editor, who had been yachting with Pulitzer in the Mediterranean. The *World's* London office was in a turmoil trying to cover the funeral of King Edward VII, and his hotel room provided one of the best views in the city. Partly for that reason Lincoln gave him a position—and he stayed in Europe for 26 years.[56]

Historian Barbara M. Tuchman opened her *The Guns of August* with a description of that magnificent funeral procession:

So gorgeous was the spectacle on the May morning of 1910 when nine

kings rode in the funeral of Edward VII of England that the crowd, waiting in hushed and black-clad awe, could not keep back gasps of admiration. In scarlet and blue and green and purple, three by three the
sovereigns rode through the palace gates, with plumed helmets, gold
braid, crimson sashes and jeweled orders flashing in the sun. After them
came five heirs apparent, forty more imperial or royal highnesses, seven
queens—four dowager and three regnant—and a scattering of special
ambassadors from uncrowned countries. Together they represented sev-
enty nations in the greatest assemblage of royalty and rank ever gathered in one place and, of its kind, the last. The muffled tongue of Big
Ben tolled nine by the clock as the cortege left the palace, but on history's
clock it was sunset, and the sun of the old world was setting in a dying
blaze of splendor never to be seen again.[57]

Peering from his window that brilliant sunny morning was Wythe Williams. He was to be there when the dynasties fell, one by one, and he was to
be there in 1936 when five kings walked behind the casket of King George V
in the January gloom. He later noted that this period of his career was the
only calm one—"those few years before the World War came with a rush
that jolted every one, including foreign correspondents, out of his leisure and
made us suddenly realize the monumental task ahead."[58]

In 1910 Williams, Wile, Mowrer and Bell were among the few Americans
in Europe. Twenty years later Williams noted that he was the only *Times*
bureau chief in a continental capital with an American passport. The war
changed things only temporarily.[59] He got his break when Carlos F. Bertelli,
chief of the Paris bureau, quit to head Hearst's Paris office. Ernest Marshall,
an Englishman working for the *Times*, recommended Williams to Carr van
Anda, the *Times* managing editor, who cabled back the appointment. During the next few years Williams became well known in Paris. His assistant
was Walter Duranty, later the paper's controversial correspondent in Moscow. He built a friendship with James Gordon Bennett Jr., eccentric owner of
the New York and Paris *Heralds*, which lasted until Bennett died in 1918.
One of Bennett's last acts was to try to hire Williams because many of Bennett's
corps of writers, mainly British, had left and his Paris bureau was almost
deserted. Williams's talents were known to all.[60]

During July of 1914, however, Williams was involved with the Caillaux
trial, the greatest *cause célèbre* in years. There were two schools of thought
in France, one pushed by Caillaux and the other by his archenemy
Clemenceau. Clemenceau favored alliance with England and saw Germany
as the future enemy. Caillaux argued for cultivating German friendship because it was vital to French national interests. Calmette's hatred of Caillaux
was known, and personal love letters were involved in the trial, which held

public attention from mid-July until war was certain. Mme. Caillaux was acquitted, but her husband was arrested by Clemenceau during the war, to emphasize the "Tiger's" return to power. The murder of Calmette did more for European politics than many realized, and Williams went so far as to say it may have hastened the beginning of the war because it publicized the anti-German ideas of Caillaux's enemies.[61]

THE ULTIMATUM

When Austria delivered her severe note to Serbia, only a handful of persons knew that Germany had given Austria a free hand on July 5 and that Count Berchtold, the Austrian foreign minister, had secretly set out to frame such an ultimatum. Its terms were agreed upon at a secret Vienna council on July 19. The time of delivery to Serbia was set for 6:00 P.M., July 23, and for announcement to the world on the morning of July 24. Part of the reason for the delay in Austrian public reaction to the assassination was that French President Poincaré had left Paris on July 15 for a July 20–23 visit to the Czar, and Berchtold had wanted Poincaré to be started home before the news of the ultimatum broke—to avoid French cooperation with the Russians, which might not have been included in previous agreements.[62] These secret dealings prompted future historians to suggest that Berchtold was the most dangerous man in Europe because of the way he apparently also kept information from the Germans.

The Hearst papers gained a one-day edge with news of a "note." Finally picking up on the speculation that had appeared for several days in Vienna's press, the *New York American* ran a three-paragraph item that began:

> Vienna, July 22—Austria has sent an imperative note to Servia, it is reported, demanding within forty-eight hours satisfactory assurance regarding the Pan-Servian movement, to which is laid the assassination of Archduke Francis Ferdinand and his wife . . . the question of war with Servia is being freely discussed in the Viennese newspapers, some regarding it as inevitable.[63]

It would have taken an unusually perceptive reader to notice the significance of this short story in the *American's* foreign news section.

The *New York World* carried only one item before the ultimatum that mentioned the Sarajevo crime. Reporter Frances O. Fay earned a byline for her historical feature on the little town, which traced the ancient rivalries of the district.[64] The best news coverage of the Austrian ultimatum was given by the *New York Times*, mainly because Wile was its Berlin correspondent.

To illustrate the incompleteness of this initial coverage, an Associated Press story, carried by all morning papers, detailed the demands but did not imply that Austria would invade Serbia unless the demands were met. The *New York World* placed it on page three under the ominous headline, "Austria Sends Ultimatum to Little Servia,"[65] the *New York Herald* buried it on the foreign news page,[66] the *Chicago Tribune* gave it 18 lines at the bottom of the first page,[67] and the *Baltimore Sun* failed to carry the story. The *Times of London* used a dispatch from Reuter's that called the note "severe, not to say violent" and did not mention the threat of invasion.[68]

The *New York Times* used the AP story but ran Wile's above it, with the major headline reading, "Austria Ready to Invade Servia, Sends Ultimatum." The subheads read, "Servia May Not Comply," "7 Army Corps at Tenesvar," "Germany and Italy to Aid," "Prepared to Prevent at All Cost Interference on Behalf of the Little Kingdom."[69]

The Austrians had given the Serbs 48 hours to reply. Serbia was charged with "abetting propaganda against the Monarchy, with tolerating apology for crime, and with at least indirect responsibility for the assassination of the Archduke Francis Ferdinand and the Duchess of Hohenberg by Bosnian Serbs at Sarajevo on June 28 . . . the note further alleges that it results from the confessions of the perpetrators of the Sarajevo outrage that the assassinations were planned in Belgrade, that the arms and explosives with which the murderers [committed the crime] were provided by Serbian officers and officials belonging to an association called the Narodna Obrana, and that the passage into Bosnia by the criminals and of their arms was organized and effected by the Chiefs of the Servian Frontier Service."[70]

The ultimatum specified that before 6:00 P.M. on Saturday, July 25, the Serbs had to declare in the *Serbian Official Journal* and embody in an army order their intent to cooperate fully with Austria-Hungary in suppressing propagandist organizations. Serbia, of course, would have been humiliated in front of the world if she had given this formal assurance to Austria-Hungary. Wile's story, which sped to London before 7:00 P.M. Berlin time, some five to six hours ahead of the official announcement, gave extra facts and much-needed interpretation:

> Berlin, July 23—A note from Austria couched in the peremptory terms of an ultimatum and demanding a reply by 6 o'clock Saturday evening was delivered to the Servian Government at Belgrade this evening at 6 o'clock.
>
> It demands the punishment of all accomplices in the murder of the Archduke Ferdinand and the suppression of all societies which have fomented rebellion in Bosnia. The Servian government must publish on Sun-

day an official disavowal of its connection with the anti-Austrian pro-paganda.

It is understood here that Belgrade will refuse to comply with the de-mand for the suppression of the societies.

Grave importance is attached to the fact that Baron Hoetzendorf, Chief of the Austrian General Staff, yesterday visited Tenesvar, from where the Austrian Army would invade Servia. Seven corps have been ordered to be held in readiness and several monitors have proceeded to Semlin.

In case of Servia's non-compliance with the ultimatum the army will invade the kingdom without further parley.

Germany and Italy have expressed full approval of the Austrian programme and announced their readiness to go to extremes to "keep the ring" for their ally in case interference in support for Servia comes from any quarter.

German officers, it is learned from an authoritative quarter, have been able to obtain leave during the last few days only on condition that they will return instantly to their posts on telegraphic notice.[71]

If Americans were surprised at the upsetting news, so were most Europe-ans. French newspaper readers, for example, probably paid little attention to stories about Austria-Serbian press fights. The Caillaux trial, trouble in Albania, and disputes centering on French Socialists were more likely topics of conversation. The Austrian ambassador to France was a guest at a week-end party of novelist Elinor Glyn when he got the news on July 23. When someone suggested that his quick departure was a sign of impending war, "everyone searched in the newspapers to see what he could mean and with whom the war could be."[72]

Events moved fast from this point. The Austrian minister in Belgrade, Giesl, broke off diplomatic relations immediately upon receipt of the Serbian reply. Both nations mobilized, spreading more shock waves across Europe. The key day was July 27, when German Chancellor Bethmann-Hollweg sabo-taged British Foreign Secretary Sir Edward Grey's mediation proposal and Austrian Foreign Minister Berchtold obtained Francis Joseph's signature on a declaration of war against Serbia by reporting a fictitious border attack.[73]

One of the reasons Wile had enjoyed his years in Berlin was his belief that the German people, if not their leaders, were rooted in a fundamental devo-tion to peace. To him, Berlin had been "the phlegmatic capital of a stolid people." About 8:30 P.M. on July 25 this long-standing notion was shattered. Wile's dispatch in the *New York Times* told of a Berlin babbling in a war frenzy, thousands of persons roaring "*Serbien hat abgelehnt*" (Serbia has rejected) and "*Krieg! Krieg!*" (War! War!).

Berlin, July 25—The capital is afire tonight with war fever. It broke out spontaneously and dramatically at 8:30 o'clock when the news arrived that Servia had rejected Austria's demands and that hostilities were no longer to be avoided.

Only an hour or two earlier the statement gained general currency that Servia had unconditionally yielded. Then like a flash of lightning the bulletin boards of the newspaper office in Unter den Linden proclaimed the real facts. The crowds, which had been waiting since 6 o'clock, greeted the announcement with frenzied cheers. Hats were thrown into the air, and shouts of "War! War!" reverberated up and down the street . . . shouts of "War with Russia" could be heard above the cheers for Austria.

The *New York Times* correspondent happened to be driving through the Linden as the mob started across Pariser Platz.[74]

Wythe Williams, in Paris, told of a similar reaction:

Paris, July 25—The Austro-Servian crisis has caused a more panicky feeling here today than at any time since the outbreak of the Balkan War. Tonight crowds on the Boulevards are shouting, "On to Berlin."

On the street corners and in the cafes are heard many expressions of belief that Austria's break with Servia means the beginning of the big war so long prepared for by the powers.[75]

The Austro-Hungarians declared war against Serbia on July 28 and fired the first shells against Belgrade the next day. Germany broke with Russia on August 1. On August 2 German armies invaded Luxembourg, following the Schlieffen plan for the capture of the west whereby the "last man on the right should touch the Channel with his sleeve."[76] The Germans also signed an alliance with Turkey on August 2 and declared war on France on August 3. Britain returned the favor on August 4 after Germany failed to answer her demands that Belgian neutrality be honored. Italy (which would join the Allies in 1915) declared herself neutral on August 3, pulling out of an alliance with Germany and Austria [in 1915 Italy joined the Allies]. By August 12 the Austro-Hungarians' tight alliance with Germany was completed. The Emperor declared war on Russia and received declarations from Britain and France.

Despite the initial Austrian attack on Serbia there was momentary hope that the mobilizations would not lead to total war. This was dashed by the Kaiser when he let the world know where he stood with his famous "sword" speech 24 hours before he broke with his cousin the Czar. From this point there was no doubt. Wile cabled his story at 11:10 P.M. on Friday, July 31, sending it in German because of quickly imposed censorship rules. Germany was in a state of readiness for war:

> Berlin, July 31—Late this afternoon a crowd of 50,000 persons gathered before the Kaiser's palace and cheered again and again for the Emperor and the German Empire.
>
> At 6:15 the Kaiser appeared in a window. The enthusiasm of the crowd knew no bounds. Hats, caps and handkerchiefs were waved aloft. In a voice that rang out over the crowd the Kaiser said:
>
> "A fateful hour has fallen for Germany. Envious people on all sides are compelling us to our just defense. The sword is being forced into our hand. I hope that if at the last hour my efforts do not succeed in bringing our opponents to see eye to eye with us and in maintaining peace, that with God's help we shall so wield the sword that when it is over we shall again sheath it with honor."[77]

The *New York World* dispatch put the event into historical perspective:

> Berlin, July 31—At 6-o'clock tonight, before an immense throng which assembled before the Imperial Palace, the Emperor with his whole family appeared on the historical balcony where his grandfather, Emperor William I, appeared years ago under practically the same circumstances.
>
> A tremendous ovation greeted the Kaiser, and as he started to speak it was impossible to hear him. But Prince Edelbert, the "Marine Prince," lifted his hand and everybody knew that the German Emperor was about to say some momentous words. And so he began the most serious speech that perhaps was ever delivered by a mighty monarch to his people. He said . . .
>
> All eyes are toward Russia, for whose benefit Emperor William apparently spoke.[78]

In Paris that evening Williams, Mowrer, and Carlos F. Bertelli of the Hearst papers were shocked to learn of the assassination of Socialist leader Jean Jaures. At approximately the same time as the Kaiser's Berlin speech, Jaures was sitting in a small cafe near an open window. The Associated Press reported that "as if by prearrangement the curtain covering the window was lightly brushed aside and a hand holding a revolver was thrust through." Two bullets struck Jaures in the back of the head and he was killed instantly, before the eyes of several Socialist deputies and the editors of *L'Humanité*, a leading newspaper. "I did it because when M. Jaures fought the three years military law he fought France," was attributed to the 29-year-old accused assassin, Raoul Villain. Only hours before Jaures had delivered a speech against hostilities; for years he had spoken eloquently against French involvement in a war.[79]

By the evening of August 3 the European foreign correspondent corps was in the center of world attention. That afternoon Sir Edward Grey had made his first explanation of the crisis to Parliament, telling of a naval agreement made to protect the French coast from German bombardment and asking support to resist German domination of France and the Low Countries. Two hours later the Germans gave the French a declaration of war, although Germans and Frenchmen already had engaged in battle.[80]

Williams remembered:

> That first night in the *New York Times* office, writing and sending to the cable office every scrap of information available, Duranty worked with me.
>
> We sensed the censor soon would be on the job and toiled feverishly, crowding the wires until five that morning. We then went for a long walk that took us to the Champs de Mars. We started up at the great golden dome of the Invalides that shelters the tomb of Napoleon. The same thought was in both our minds—did France have a general comparable to the one sleeping there? We wandered back across the Seine, stared into its waters glinting in the early sunlight, and then went to a Turkish bath, in preparation for another hectic day and night. The complete stillness of that luxurious marble-lined room, except for a tinkling fountain and the soft padding of barefoot attendants, was unreal, apart from the new nightmare of life.
>
> The day was a repetition of the one before—the youth of the capital hurrying to the field of war—the majority never to return . . . that famous old newspaper *Gil Blas*, located near my office, had big posters in the tricolor of France over its entrance, stating, "Every employe on this paper is of military age and therefore is now in the service of France. *Gil Blas* necessarily suspends publication, perhaps forever." That afterthought proved true: *Gil Blas,* one of the most brilliantly edited papers of its day, died with the beginning of the war.[81]

So it was that Russia refused to allow Austria her cheap war against Serbia, Germany refused to allow Russian intervention in the Balkans, and Germany decided to invade the west first, hoping for a quick knockout before turning to face Russia in the east. The *Chicago Tribune* earlier had reported, "Whether a European war breaks out, those who doubted Germany's readiness will have received a lasting lesson."[82]

Paul Scott Mowrer's efforts of August 3–4 were reflected in his story:

> Paris, August 4—Crowds of youths and men carrying French, English, Russian and even Italian flags have paraded the "entrenched camp of Paris" day and night for the past 36 hours shouting "To Berlin" and "Spit

upon William!", singing the Marseillaise and "'Tis Alsace We Must Have!"[83]

THE PRESS CORPS MOBILIZES

Edward Price Bell organized his *Chicago Daily News* colleagues quickly once it became apparent that a major war was upon them. Harry Hansen—on August 2 writing the final story about the Chicago terminal commission— was sent to Belgium from London, where he had been assisting Bell.[84] As Mowrer scurried around looking for permission to head for the front, he broke in his brother Edgar, who thus began a long and distinguished career. After sneaking through enemy lines for an exclusive story, Edgar Mowrer was allowed to accompany mining engineer Herbert Hoover to Holland. He was granted a permit to travel into Belgium but finally was ejected by the Germans, who did not know that he carried documents from the Belgian underground out with him. He had proven his ability and in May 1915 was given the job as Rome correspondent.[85] Meanwhile, his brother contributed many outstanding pieces, some of the most important being about the horrors at Verdun.

The romantics among the early arrivals were Ellis Ashmead-Bartlett, who traveled in 11 countries during the first two weeks of the war for the *Daily Telegraph* without being able to file a word,[86] and Richard Harding Davis, who devoted the final two years of his life to this war. Later in 1914 the *New York World's* Herbert Bayard Swope gained a spectacular scoop from Berlin by reporting the sinking of three British warships by the German submarine U-9. In 1916 Swope returned to Germany to gather details about that nation's war effort for a series of articles that gained him the first Pulitzer Prize for reporting. Frederick Palmer was the only American correspondent accredited with the British Army when tight controls were imposed shortly after the German advance westward. The other correspondents had to hunt for news while risking capture. Temporarily covering for all American wire services, Palmer wrote graphically of the debut of tanks in war and had many adventures, but ended up as the chief censor, a major in the United States Army.[87]

American writers began getting into trouble with nervous young officers from the onset of the war. On the day England decided to defend Belgium and France, Wile of the *New York Times* and *London Daily Mail* was hounded and arrested, being held for several frantic hours. Others arrested in Berlin were S. Miles Bouton and Seymour Conger of the AP, Dudley Ward of the *Manchester Guardian*, and Henry W. Levinson and Charles Tower of the

London Daily News.[88] All were released. In Belgium three groups of Americans ran into trouble. Will Irwin of *Collier's,* John T. McCutcheon of the *Chicago Tribune,* Irvin S. Cobb of the *Saturday Evening Post* and *Philadelphia Public Ledger,* and Arnot Dosch-Fleurot of *International News Service* and the *New York World* were one venturesome quartet. They drove through the German lines in a taxi and were held four days before being allowed to head back.[89]

Harry Hansen of the *Chicago Daily News,* James O'Donnell Bennett of the *Chicago Tribune,* and Roger Lewis of the Associated Press (transferred from St. Petersburg) also tried to find the war in Belgium.[90] Richard Harding Davis, representing the *New York Tribune,* and Gerald Morgan, the American magazine writer who carried *London Daily Telegraph* credentials, were together.[91] Eventually Lewis, O'Donnell Bennett, Cobb, Hansen, and McCutcheon became the first American correspondents to see the German front after being captured again and deported into Germany.[92]

Meanwhile Morgan, Dosch-Fleurot, Irwin, Davis and Mary Boyle O'Reilly of Newspaper Enterprise Association (the only U.S. woman correspondent in Belgium) had been in Brussels, from where Davis was to be sent to Germany under accusation of being a British spy. The others decided to go with him because they would pass through Louvain, where they knew a historic atrocity was occurring. They saw it from their railroad car, the flames reaching into the summer night, the citizens carrying bundles of clothing down the dark roads. Their train finally reached Aix-la-Chapelle, where they were set free, re-arrested (except for Mary O'Reilly, who escaped into Belgium) and then sent by train back to Allied lines.[93] Once the action started a number of women were active overseas. Andrea Beaumont won bylines in the *New York American,* and Peggy Hull was known for her writing in the *Cleveland Plain Dealer.* The list of women included Sigrid Schultz of the *Chicago Tribune,* later important during the Munich Crisis of 1938 for her dispatches from Berlin, Rheta Dorr of the *New York Mail,* and Bessie Beatty of the *San Francisco Bulletin.*

Davis, who a few days earlier had written a classic story on the German entry into Brussels,[94] then wrote his account of the destruction of Louvain.[95] He was to have several more adventures, again being arrested by Germans along with Ellis Ashmead-Bartlett and Wythe Williams and crusading in the United States for American preparedness. He had ignored chest pains while in Europe and his heart failed on April 11, 1916, a few minutes after he had talked to his old Tokyo friend Martin Egan from his Mount Kisco, N.Y., home.[96] Davis covered six wars and saved some of his finest work until the very end.

The preface to Davis's *With the French* (Scribner's, 1916) is dated April

11, indicating that he finished it the day he died. His last lines were a plea for American support of the French. The final line read: "Every word and act of . . . the average American now that helps the Allies is a blow against frightfulness, against despotism, and in behalf of a broader civilization, a nobler freedom, and a much more pleasant world in which to live."

It is clear that once the fighting began the original reporters in Europe—Bell, Williams, Mowrer, Wile, and others— performed as well as the professional war correspondents who arrived in early August. It is unfortunate that secret diplomacy, the draw of other events, the shortsightedness of their home editors, and sometimes their own failure to interpret caused a void in the summer news flow just after the assassination of the archduke.

However, once the ultimatum was released, this hardy corps of American writers did a remarkable job of filing all bits of news to the United States and of manning their posts right up to the first shot. Before the war ended 50 U.S. writers had been with the British, 31 had been accredited by the American Army, and more than 400, including all of the roving freelancers, had been at the battle zone.[97] Their combined experiences allowed vast improvement in European news coverage, as larger American newspapers and magazines and the wire services learned after 1917 that America was tied to Europe. Admittedly, as the years passed these busy capital bureaus would again become lonely outposts as American attentions would be focused on domestic issues, but a handful of European experts would be ready the next time events warranted a gigantic news media effort.

Jack London and Richard Harding Davis were dead; great British reporters like Henry Nevinson, Frederic Villiers, and Bennet Burleigh, whose reports had been published in U.S. newspapers, had seen their last major war; Palmer would never be under fire again. The future was left to reporters like Paul Scott, Edgar Ansel Mowrer, Floyd Gibbons, Sigrid Schulz, and Webb Miller. A continuity of excellence was assured.

Chapter Two

The Rise of Stalin:

Winter of 1928-1929

Walter Duranty of the *New York Times* covered the Stalinist period and was recognized as a leading, if controversial, analyst of the period. UPI/Bettmann

INTRODUCTION

The Russian upheavals from 1905 to 1917 ruined the 1904 open-access agreement between Czar Nicholas and Melville Stone of the Associated Press. Russia was closing again, and the police terror was a sign of the subjugation that was to be the fate of the Russian press and foreign writers. Gradually the old censorships were reinstated, so that years later Eddy Gilmore, the famous AP Moscow correspondent, would say: "I wrote for the smallest audience in the world, that one censor whose blue pencil ripped my copy—and my heart."[1]

Introducing the emerging Russia to the world was to be quite a task for the correspondents who ventured from Europe's more exciting capitals, especially Paris, after World War I. The overthrow of the Czar, the temporary establishment of the Kerensky government in early 1917, and their betrayal by the Bolsheviks in November of that year caused great excitement in the West. But few American reporters were present to allow for adequate news coverage. The fighting along the Western front had been the natural story. In addition, heavy bias already had been built against Russia because of her signing the Brest-Litovsk treaty in 1918, allowing the Germans relief from the Eastern front and the freedom to make their near-successful drive against Paris. Walter Duranty of the *New York Times* remembered a high official of the French War Department shouting, "It's the Russians who did this to us. While we fought the Marne they lost the Battle of Tannenberg through treachery, when they should have driven through Berlin. Now they've made a separate peace and released a million Germans more to break our front."[2]

Americans took more interest in Russia when in early 1918 small contingents of Allied troops landed in northern Russia to protect the railway line running into the port of Murmansk, first against German attack and then against Bolshevik interference. Six hundred Americans landed in May and in July an Anglo-American force seized the port of Archangel from the Soviets. Now the enemy was the Red Soviet Army, and the action was direct intervention in Russia's internal affairs, mainly at the insistence of the British.[3]

Frazier Hunt of the *Chicago Tribune* rode a thousand miles by sled through these civil war areas and received credit for dispatches which—after having been read in the Senate—speeded the withdrawal of American troops.[4] American forces supporting the anti-Soviet White army in Siberia in 1919–20 also were withdrawn when it was revealed that the entire operation was a waste of resources and that there was little enthusiasm for the adventure at home. Junius B. Wood of the *Chicago Daily News* helped tell that story.[5]

Despite the hostility of the Soviet government, a few American writers did cross the border after the war ended in the west. Hunt was the first, on March 1, 1919, and he predicted the victory of the Reds in the civil war.[6] Later that year Duranty left his position as Wythe Williams's assistant in Paris and accompanied a new American commissioner to the Baltic States. Heading on his own to Abo, Finland, he got his "first glimpse of what the Russian Revolution meant," by hearing of the bitter fighting and executions.[7]

It has been said, though, that the only solid, continuous foreign correspondence received in the west from Russia before 1920 was that appearing in the *Manchester Guardian* written by Arthur Ransome.[8]

Meanwhile, in the United States, a major postwar reaction to the Russian Revolution and to the domestic "threats" of the International Workers of the World led to the "Red Scare." The display of red flags was forbidden in New York, Attorney General Mitchell Palmer chased "Communists" and herded them off to Ellis Island, and the offices of the socialist *New York Call* were wrecked. American newspapers "failed dismally to defend the civil liberties of those being questionably attacked," Russian Reds or American Socialists—to many they were alike—and one of the chief offenders in confusing them was the usually reliable *New York Times*.[9]

One reason the *Times* later was instrumental in trying to re-open the Russian door was the biting criticism it received on its 1917–20 Soviet coverage in the *New Republic* from Walter Lippmann and Charles Merz. The authors charged the *Times* with serious offenses, such as allowing editors' policy to influence news column presentation, not taking seriously enough the importance of the events, not taking steps to ensure accuracy, being misled by propaganda, and overlooking the mishandling of dispatches by deskmen.[10] American readers had gotten off to a poor start in learning about the new Russia.

The situation improved slightly in January 1919 when the United Press began to exchange news with the Russian Rosta Agency, to be followed by the Associated Press. Rosta was replaced in July 1925 by TASS, which was organized to supervise the news flow from local agencies and to distribute the foreign news, besides government information.[11] An attempt to have censorship lifted failed in 1923, however, when a group of writers argued with Maxim Litvinov, then the assistant foreign commissar, that their readers were not getting a true picture of Russia—that things were not so bad but that people could not believe this unless censorship were removed. Litvinov's reply was that censorship was necessary for the screening of rumors and biased stories, and because Russia still was in a state of "semi-war" surrounded by enemies.[12] This attitude, which demonstrated the isolation already felt by the Russian leadership, was somewhat justified because of the Allied intervention in the civil fighting and the scare tactics used by American and British newspapers.

Russian secrecy; the dominance of British, French, Italian and German affairs; the scarcity of regular correspondents in Russia or on her borders,[13] the "return to normalcy" in America during the 1920s; deep American and British prejudices against the Communists—these were obstacles the American foreign correspondent had to overcome in trying to present a clear picture of Russia. By the late summer and early fall of 1928 the world knew only that followers of Leon Trotsky had fallen from grace and had been thrown out of the party and that Russia was struggling to keep her balance, somewhat like the Weimar Republic in Germany. There had been no Red revolution in Germany, and Russia had been left to save herself from herself.

Stalin first wanted to build "socialism in one country" as a first step, while Trotsky had set world revolution as the chief goal.

In a sense the average American reader was as isolated from the facts as any Russian. Dwellers in the growing cities were exposed to dashes of sensationalism. Prohibition, crimes, sports, scandal, political personalities, and heroes of all types dominated the front pages. American life was influenced by the economic policies of the Harding, Coolidge, and Hoover administrations. There was a trend toward international cooperation, as the United States took part in humanitarian conferences sponsored by the League of Nations and in the various naval limitations conferences. But the average reader could not have realized that the nation's general policy of isolationism was to affect people as much as the rising tide of prosperity that obviously was changing daily life. Overall, the American reader was preoccupied with personal issues because of the times. If, as some editors still claim, American readers were not interested in foreign news, there were extra reasons for their not being especially interested in the 1920s, despite their exposure to the world during World War I.

As for Russian citizens, they were isolated from decisions of their government, and especially from crisis within it. During July of 1928 the powerful Bukharin turned to his opponent Kamenev for support against the increasing strength of Joseph Stalin. "He will strangle us," whispered the leader of the Rightists. Arguments were waged in vain behind the closed doors of the Politburo, but Stalin's opponents were careful not to drag their crucial grievances into the open because they shared responsibility for the purge that was beginning against the land-owning class, the kulaks.[14] The average Russian may have sensed deepening trouble and misery in the land, but there was no chance of knowing what pressures were causing it, and for which motives.

It was from this Russian atmosphere—in late 1928 and early 1929—that foreign correspondents attempted to reach their American readers in a totally different atmosphere. To what extent did they manage to tell of the great collectivization of Russian farms, of the removal of Stalin's final opponents in the wake of this massive social rearrangement, and of the near consolidation of power by the dictator? Did they focus on Stalin? Did they link collectivization with the growth of Stalin's influence, or was this a separate story? Did they include details of the struggle against religion and civil rights in general? And while telling of harshness in Russia, did they at the same time convey an understanding of the Russian citizen and of why all this was happening?

Facts were needed, but so was interpretation. This was a strange situation for the writers. Some came and liked Moscow, and others could not wait to get back to Paris, London, or Vienna—anyplace but that dark, cold, and suspicious city. Those who stayed because of their fascination with the Russian world and their appreciation of the importance of their dispatches really could not blame those who left. To write from Moscow in 1928–29 was one of the hardest jobs in the world. This chapter looks at how individual correspondents left their marks in Moscow.

WALTER DURANTY: DID HE DISTORT THE TRUTH?

Walter Duranty went to Russia in August 1921, after covering treaty negotiations at Riga, Latvia, where Herbert Hoover's American Relief Administration had begun to attack the famine sweeping the Soviet Union. One of Hoover's chief lieutenants, Walter Lyman Brown, signed for the Americans, and Maksim Litvinov was the Russian negotiator. The *Times* had instructed Duranty to be prepared to go into Russia once the treaty had been signed, and he and a dozen reporters did so.

Duranty, then 37, might not have been allowed entry because of previous anti-Bolshevik dispatches had it not been for an exclusive story he wrote telling of Lenin's New Economic Policy. Duranty's story was written August 12 after he had secured a translation of the original announcement as found in the August 9 *Pravda*. He later felt that the story had been received favorably in Moscow, despite the statement, "Lenin has thrown Communism overboard," because the Communists did not expect bourgeois reporters to be very accurate. Had he added "temporarily" he would have been prophetic.

During this initial period Floyd Gibbons, the indestructible *Chicago Tribune* correspondent, flew into Riga from Berlin on a chartered plane and maneuvered himself into special favors. Gibbons arrived in Moscow a full week before the others and his exclusive stories of the famine were published in 35 nations. Nevertheless, Duranty and the others were learning quickly, also filing stories that alerted the world to Russia's plight.[15]

Returning to Paris in January 1922, Duranty began to form definite opinions of Russia. During his five-month stay he had followed the *Times* rules explicitly, not quoting Soviet statesmen or newspapers in order to avoid repeating Communist propaganda. Duranty called his paper's attitude "fear of the 'Red Bogey,'" but he pleased his editors and received permission to quote as long as he withheld his own opinions.

Duranty headed back to Moscow in April 1922 and until 1934 was the resident correspondent. From 1934 to the German invasion of Russia in 1941, he was a special traveling writer, spending perhaps four to five months each year in the USSR. As he began this 19-year stint his own philosophy about the rough character of Communist rule began to evolve. At the outset he had feared and hated the Bolsheviks, but, as he told H. R. Knickerbocker of the International News Service in 1935, he learned to appreciate the Russian position:

> Of course I didn't go Bolshevik or think Bolshevism would work in Western countries or be good for them. I don't believe I even cared in those days whether it would be good for Russia, or work there in practice. But I did think the Bolsheviks would win in their own country and that the Soviet Union would become a great force in world affairs. If you want to know, Stalin himself expressed my attitude rather neatly the last time I saw him, on Christmas Day, 1933. He said, "You have done a good job in your reporting of the U.S.S.R. although you are not a Marxist, because you have tried to tell the truth about our country and to understand it and explain it to your readers. I might say that you bet on our horse to win when others thought it had no chance, and I am sure you have not lost by it . . ."
>
> The trouble with you and so many other people is that they won't admit that the Bolsheviks regard themselves as fighting a war in which it is their duty to be as ruthless and dispassionate in gaining their objectives as any leaders in any war. As far as I am concerned, I don't see that I have been any less accurate about Russia because I failed to stress casualties so hard as some of my colleagues . . . I am a reporter, not a humanitarian, and if a reporter can't see the wood for trees he can't describe the wood. You may call this special pleading or call me callous, and perhaps it is true, but you can't blame me for it; you must blame the War, because that was where my mental skin got thickened.[16]

Duranty also found that he had become free to interpret in the *New York Times* columns, and he felt this was his duty because of the lack of information available to the editorial writers who should have been explaining the significance of events. Duranty claimed that his copy was never cut or altered in the *New York Times*, "which every foreign correspondent knows is as rare a privilege as it is encouraging to the writer."[17] Since his copy often contained new information or startling statements and facts, this was unusual treatment. Heywood Broun once criticized Duranty, accusing him of "writing editorials from Moscow disguised as news dispatches."[18]

While many praised him as one of America's foremost correspondents of his era, others thought he was too sympathetic to the Soviet government. The criticisms continued long after his death. In 1990 his biographer, S. J. Taylor, charged Duranty with being a shill for Stalin, supporting earlier assertions that he overlooked Stalin's ruthlessness and the long-term Soviet goals of world power. She said that among his many sins was a dismissal of the 1932–33 Ukraine famine, which claimed millions of lives and was attributable to the Bolsheviks.[19] Brutal criticism also came from James William Crowl in his 1982 work *Angels in Stalin's Paradise*. Crowl analyzed the careers of Duranty and Louis Fischer, finding both guilty of grossly distorting events, basically by going beyond the accepted compliance with censorship and overlooking the police-state atmosphere and mass human-rights violations. Duranty used "half-truths and unwarranted comparisons" to ease his readers' fears about the Soviets, Crowl claimed.[20] Dipping into the two writers' psychological states, he passes along the contention that they suffered from inferiority complexes, particularly Duranty, and were in awe of power and being in the presence of strong people. Also cited were the comments of the UP's Eugene Lyons and the *New York Herald Tribune*'s Leland Stowe, both of whom suggested that the *Times* was more interested in having a reporter in Moscow than in making a determined effort to uncover the truth.[21]

Despite growing criticisms of his work, Duranty was awarded the 1932 Pulitzer Prize for his economic reporting from Russia. However, the domestic pressures and his own declining health hastened his switch, in 1934, to the roving reporter's job, which took him out of the limelight. In fairness to Duranty, an enormously complicated man, the hypocritical nature of some of these attacks on his work should be underscored. After all, some of the journalists and politicians who jumped at the chance to pin down Duranty—and who ignored the wealth of information that he provided about Russia—were typical of those always "slow to criticize the fascists of the 20th Century, from Mussolini and Hitler to the likes of Marcos, Pinocet, and Somoza, particularly those corrupt leaders supported by the American government."[22] Whatever his faults, it must be remembered that Duranty is only one in a long list of foreign correspondents condemned by one side or the other for allegedly biased coverage. The truth is that in many of these instances few other journalists were offering alternatives—and thus the hypocrisy.

One of the more charitable assessments of Duranty's work came from Lillian T. Mowrer, widow of Edgar Ansel Mowrer, who in 1977 recalled that her good friend had known more about the horror of the famine than he had revealed. Calling him a "damn good reporter" who was "immensely well-informed," she said that he was "somewhat cynical" about the 1930s famine in private and that his dispatches were "watered down." Both Eugene Lyons and British journalist Malcolm Muggeridge later recalled that Duranty had strong reactions to what he had seen in the countryside but defended the government. He once yelled to Muggeridge, "You can't make omelettes without cracking eggs," and on another occasion told Lyons and visiting *New*

York Times correspondent Anne O'Hare McCormick that the vast number of dead peasants were "only Russians."[23]

During his first years in Moscow, Duranty was able to report on Lenin's apparent illness at least a year before he died, the early emergence of Stalin, the significance for Russia of the Treaty of Rapallo, and the trend away from the New Economic Policy that Western leaders greeted as a permanent shift toward capitalism. He also knew and even entertained Big Bill Haywood, the exiled "Wobblie," and other personalities who were part of the early 1920s.

Duranty's observations of Stalin's development are most interesting. He first began to pay attention to the new party secretary in the spring of 1922, but there were many things he had no way of knowing. For example, on December 16, 1922, Lenin suffered a serious stroke, and the battle for his succession accelerated. It wasn't known until later that party leaders entrusted Stalin with Lenin's medical care and that Stalin's verbal abuse of Lenin's wife, Krupskaya, turned his mentor against him. Lenin preferred that Leon Trotsky emerge as his successor and prepared a recommendation that Stalin be removed as general secretary. But he was incapacitated by another stroke in March 1923 and died in January 1924 without the papers being opened.

To outsiders, however, Stalin was only one of many leaders among Trotsky, Zinoviev, Kamenev, Rykov, Djerzhinsky, and others. On January 15, 1923, Duranty filed a story to the *Times* wherein he analyzed all of Russia's leaders before adding:

> Finally there is the Georgian Stalin, little known abroad but one of the most remarkable men in Russia and perhaps the most influential figure here today . . .
>
> Of these five men Trotsky is a great executive, but his brain cannot compare with Lenin's in analytical power. Djerzhinsky goes straight to his appointed goal without fear or favor and gets there somehow, no matter what the obstacles, but he also is inferior to Lenin in analytical capacity. Rykov and Kamenev are first-class administrators and hardly more . . . During the last year Stalin has shown judgment and analytical power not unworthy of Lenin . . . suppose today Stalin outlines a policy that he thinks should be adopted; others criticize it—Stalin answers.[24]

Duranty was to meet Stalin twice in his career, in the fall of 1930 and at Christmas in 1933. On the first occasion he wrote that Stalin was "the inheritor of Lenin's mantle." Checking the copy upon prior agreement, Stalin corrected this to read, "Lenin's most faithful disciple and the prolonger of his work."[25] The exiled Trosky must have ranted when reading such phrases.

They knew full well that Lenin had tried to purge Stalin prior to his death and that Stalin was "influential in the creation of the Lenin cult" which the Bolsheviks used to solidify support for their regime.[26]

The only major interruption in Duranty's Moscow career came in November 1924 when, on a brief trip to France, he lost one foot in a train wreck between Paris and Le Havre. It was at this time that his devoted friend, *Manchester Guardian* reporter William Bolitho Ryall, tried to talk him into leaving newspaper work for magazine or book writing. Optimistic about his narrow escape, Duranty did not listen. The older reporter did not accompany him back to Moscow in August 1925, and one of Duranty's later regrets was that his keen-minded friend did not get a chance to crack the Russian riddle. Duranty claimed that of all his writer accomplices "Bolitho" would have had the best opportunity.[27]

Obviously, then, Duranty was quite familiar with the career of Joseph Stalin before Trotsky's decline in 1927–28. By actual count Duranty sent 41 dispatches from October to December 1928 and another 58 from January to March 1929. Inexplicably, none of Duranty's stories made page one. At this crucial time, when Stalin was making decisions that would decide the fate of Russia's millions, he was linked by name to his ideas and actions only six times in late 1928 and four more times in the first three months of 1929. While Duranty was describing Russia's turbulent political situation, analyzing the collective movement, and covering many other aspects of Soviet life, he was not giving a picture of the man in control. But Stalin was moving stealthily and skillfully, the censor was a barrier, and the Soviet press was not very informative when it came to reporting internal arguments. Official names were rarely mentioned. And then there was Duranty's own conviction that Stalin's leadership was vital to Russia's progress at this time.

Stalin made his first and last inspection tour of Siberia in January 1928, accompanied by Malenkov. The reason was to emphasize the need for more cooperation on the part of local grain farmers. Farmers had been speculating in grain prices, they were not delivering the grain at the prices government wanted to pay, and some even felt confident enough to form combinations. During this tour Stalin made speeches, argued with grain farmers, and began to threaten them with government action. His common target was the wealthy landholder, known as a kulak—someone from peasant stock who had worked his way up to a position of status. He probably never forgot the kulak who, after listening to him speak, said, "Let me see you dance, young fellow, and I will give you a bushel or two."[28]

Upon Stalin's return the government began to move against the kulaks, and Stalin's persecution of "rightists" was initiated against the background of this grave social crisis. In January government purchases of grain were two million tons short of the minimum requirement for the urban population. By June, Stalin was calling for stronger emergency measures against the kulaks, and in July he said the party should "strike hard" against them. Beginning in March all party functionaries opposing or obstructing the emergency acts of force against the rural population were dismissed. Throughout this entire period, as Stalin waged war against the kulaks as well as all those who dared argue against his actions, he realized that Trotsky's presence in Russia was the main threat to his eventual success. Trotsky was removed from the Politburo in 1926, expelled from the party in 1927, sent to Alma-Ata in Turkestan (Kazakhstan) in 1928, and exiled from the Soviet Union itself in 1929. By the end of 1928 Stalin had built enough strength to call for a merciless war against the kulaks. The First Five-Year Plan aiming at national industrialization was under way. A year later, on his fiftieth birthday, December 21, 1929, the party officially saluted him with the pomp required for Lenin's successor.[29]

Stalin was possessed with the idea that he could transform the whole of Russia through a single *tour de force*. Living in a "half-real and half-dreamy world of statistical figures and indices," he was in the midst of his "socialism in one country" scheme. As the power plays continued during the tense months of late 1928 and early 1929, the fate of Russia, and that of the worldwide Communist movement, hung in the balance.[30]

Duranty first met exiled kulaks in 1930 on a trip to Central Asia, where a group of correspondents had been promised a chance to see the linking of the Turkish-Siberian Railway.[31] But he had followed the pattern of government action for several years.

It was obvious to Moscow insiders why Stalin was not allowing his thoughts to be spread to the outside world through personal interviews during 1928–29. The risky business of collectivization was determining many careers. On October 21 Duranty told *Times* readers that a nationwide election was in progress in Russia and that "Kremlin spokesmen make no secret of their intentions to continue the policy of trying to socialize the villages by suppressing the richer peasants and uniting the poorer ones into communal farm groups."[32] Rarely did Duranty's interpretative dispatches receive prominent display. Often his efforts were placed on the Sunday "Roundup" page, along with those of Wythe Williams in Vienna, Paul Miller in Berlin, and Arnaldo Cortesi (son of famed AP Rome correspondent Salvatore Cortesi) in Rome or Allen Raymond in London. But more typical was the treatment given another October 21 story. It was fitted into a six-paragraph hole on page 15. This item described the dismissal of four executive officers of the Moscow Communist Party for participating in the new "petit bourgeois" heresy, which Duranty said was more serious than previously believed, but which *Pravda* said "fell short of the Trotsky opposition."

Duranty said in this significant story that the criticism of the agriculture policy was not limited to the Moscow organization. He predicted that the dismissals were the prelude to a greater internal struggle, and he also said that the discussion was open, as compared to the Trotsky fight of the previous year. At the same time, Duranty reported, the Central Committee was "trying to hold the rudder of the Soviet vehicle as far to the left as possible."[33]

In his stories Duranty often indirectly referred to earlier dispatches about general problems in Russia, erroneously assuming that the editors and readers had been avidly following his words. He was a sophisticated writer who did not spell out what he considered to be simple explanations. Another reason why it would have been impossible for the average person to keep track of earlier events was that Duranty and his colleagues covered all of Russia. During the October-December period, for example, he wrote three articles on party problems, but also reported on Moscow art, vodka, suicides, crime, and even a Siberian meteorite.

A central theme in many of the stories dealing with politics, party, economics, the provinces, city workers, food shortages, and rumors was the conflict between "right" and "left." This was not always explicitly mentioned, but it was present. Duranty once commented that the terms "right" and "left" were part of a "loud nonsense" that had not occurred under the practical Lenin. Perhaps he was referring to the overuse of the terms by Russians on all levels, which was similar to the overuse of "dove" and "hawk" in the United States during the Vietnam years. He was aware of the deep divisions and that the country would be pushed hard in one direction or the other, depending on who won the power struggle.

Duranty reported there were three alternative solutions to the economic crisis: private enterprise could be given more freedom; peasants could be given higher prices for grain and could be charged less for manufactured goods, encouraging the higher production of grain; or capital could be obtained from abroad.

The first idea was part of the "petit bourgeois" heresy and the second was called capitulation to the kulaks.[34] The third idea had been carefully considered for some time and this was attempted. But Stalin thrust at the peasants, despite statements by opponents such as Bukharin, who was quoted as saying in *Pravda* that Stalin's industrialization was wasteful.[35]

A few days later Duranty wrote:

> Arson, the old weapon of the Soviet peasant seeking revenge, is being turned against the Soviet government's attempts to socialize the countryside.[36]

He minimized reports from London of a full-scale peasant revolt, and apparently was correct. The first wave of government terror did not spread over the land until 1929–30. Between 1929 and 1934 peasants of all economic levels resisted the government by many means, often in pitched battle. Here the fight could better be described as a full-scale revolt, as hundreds of thousands of poor peasants were killed while the kulaks were eliminated as a "class."[37] It appears that Duranty did not understand the ominous nature of the government action he reported, because he offered his favorite suggestion—that the government would be better off by lowering prices on manufactured goods to encourage grain production—and said "signs are not lacking" that considerable moderation of agriculture policy was possible in the near future.

While he repeated that writers should not exaggerate the danger of a massive revolt against Soviet power, saying the Kremlin was "far from deaf" to the rumblings, he admitted having little forecasting ability on this issue. Huge gaps appear in the *Times* coverage of Russia, possibly because the paper was interested in what it considered the significant news and Duranty was not able to file major dispatches on a daily basis.

Readers got a glimpse of Stalin in December 1928 as part of colorful news dealing with the opening of the All-Union Soviet Congress (or Proletarian Congress; different names were given this gathering), a joint meeting of the Council of Nationalities and the Central Executive Committee, one thousand delegates in all. The men wore sheepskin coats from the provinces and rough blouses, and the women wore shawls. They sat "unabashed, these new masters of Russia." Duranty himself was caught up in the extraordinary scene:

> M. Kalinin . . . sat chatting with M. Stalin, who wore a khaki tunic buttoned up to his neck, and M. Kueusif, president of the Textile Workers Federation. M. Stalin seemed animated and looked strong and well. His full mustache now curves at the end in a real cavalry sweep.[38]

He continued to describe the golden columns, blaring trumpets, dazzling glare, and the meek raising of hands in assent by the delegates—who sat in the Czar's room and gave approval to new policies. The reader was supposed to understand that this was a smooth operation being run by the Bolsheviks; Duranty did not describe the lack of real participation, and probably the censor would not have permitted it. But he did explain how the Soviet system worked, theoretically. There were two houses. The Central Executive Council was elected at annual meetings of this All-Union Soviet Congress. The Council of Nationalities was selected from the Federated States Union, which met thrice yearly. The seated All-Union Soviet Congress was the nation's supreme authority, and to achieve a balance of representation it had been "decided" to have one delegate for every 2,500 urban citizens and one for every 125,000 rural citizens, since the nation was predominantly rural. If the urbanites received a few extra delegates somehow, no one complained.

In another story he did comment on the participation of the delegates, however. He wrote, "In reality, of course, the country is run by the Communist Party, as the docility with which Congressional delegates approve suggestions of the presiding committee shows clearly enough."[39] He said the elections were not completely "steam-rolled" through, that all over the age of 18 can vote, but he admitted that the government had been somewhat concerned over public opinion regarding the agriculture issue that year. "Communists," he wrote, "consciously and deliberately, are training in self-government and self-expression this gigantic nation which for centuries has been dumb."

A thorough reader keeping track of events in Russia might have noticed that Duranty occasionally painted Russia as moving forward in a dynamic way, capturing the wholesomeness and energy of the people, even if actually she was tottering. Those interested in foreign affairs might have seen reviews of Leon Trotsky's 1928 book, *The Real Situation in Russia*, which balanced overenthusiastic ideas reported by Duranty and others. Trotsky wrote in exile at Alma-Ata, on the border of Turkestan, and some 50,000 copies were smuggled into Russia after publication in Berlin.[40]

Trotsky's message, not repeated by Duranty, alleged the helplessness of workers under Stalin and Stalin's trickery at the time of Lenin's death—his refusing to release Lenin's last will and testament. Trotsky wanted it known that he had been maneuvered into the leadership of a radical minority opposition and, with his chief supporters, had been deprived of his posts in the Soviet government, the International, and finally the Communist Party itself.

Christmas 1928 brought Duranty's final major dispatch of the year.[41] While walking the streets, which were packed with 20 inches of snow, he noticed that the Soviet ban on Christmas trees and celebrations had not dimmed the season spirit, that the people were hurrying about, buying special foods, issuing greetings, just like New Yorkers or Londoners. This was another colorful, well-balanced story. There was no political bias present, just the facts. Duranty apparently hoped that various peoples could understand each other despite the activities of their governments.

Meanwhile, although Duranty had covered the major happenings in Russia and offered a reasonably clear picture of life in that nation, the American reader had not received one essential type of story, devoted entirely to Joseph Stalin, in whose hands the future of the nation lay. Nor was there one story about Soviet leadership in general, listing the different individuals and their positions. Biographical information may be elementary to a sophisticated writer, but occasional references to a public figure's background every few months is not enough for the average reader. This is the main weakness of Duranty's work in 1928 and 1929.

There always are exceptions to such general statements, of course, and Duranty's came on January 1 and 5, 1929, when he traced the Stalin-Trotsky competition as part of a look back at 1928. Among other things, he was able to say that Trotsky's exile displayed the Asiatic part of Stalin's mind. Duranty said Stalin was aptly named "Man of Steel" because he had used government forces, secret police, and Communist youth organizations to force grain collectivization.[42] That was strong language. No one explanation appears as to why the reader got so little of that, but it can be explained at least partially by Duranty's consciousness that such a story would be career-threatening and that the interests of the *Times* were served by having a correspondent there.

The New Year opened. Franklin D. Roosevelt was to take the oath of office as governor of New York. The U.S. business community was headed for its own rendezvous with destiny, while Europe already was in the throes of economic depression and political chaos. An article by Edwin L. James in Paris indicated the general American attitude toward Europe—one of deep isolation and alienation. He wrote:

> . . . that 1929 will contribute further towards establishing the impossibility of American foreign policy being based on the illusion that the richest and potentially the most powerful nation on earth can pursue a course of isolation from the rest of the world.[43]

In January 1929, a few days after Duranty had explained the background of the Soviet economic situation, a *Times* editorial writer replied that it was unlikely that the moderation in Soviet diplomacy (cited by Duranty) would bring about any changes in political relations between Russia and the Western world. The *Times* said Russia's aim was to hurt Europe through Asia (possibly referring to Communism in China).[44] This blunt, uncompromising statement, typical of those issued by other U.S. publications, was the only editorial comment on Russian problems found in the *Times* during a six-month period, indicating again that interests were elsewhere.

The Duranty dispatches continued to flow, however, and in early January he reported more violence in the countryside. Prosperous peasants had been terrorized through land confiscation and boycotts of their privately owned collection points. Duranty even reported cries of "chuck him in the Black

Sea" and "take his land away" on the part of poorer peasants. This may have been a bit of poetic license, but possibly not. The situation grew worse. Duranty reported that the December 1928 collections had been very unsatisfactory and that all methods were being used against the wealthy peasants. He described how parades of Communist youths and poor people, along with the government grain collector, would walk along, ready to buy "surplus" grain from any "converts" to the new system.[45]

Duranty's stories were often mild in that they included color besides the hard facts. He did not press at issues. In not mentioning Stalin as being behind the general policy, however, Duranty appeared naive in his understanding of how the system worked. This was unfortunate, because he obviously realized to a high degree, if not completely, the extent of Stalin's power.

At one point Duranty hinted at why he apparently felt he should not go far in criticizing or praising:

> The past eleven years have shown the futility of attempting to predict the future in such a vast country as the Soviet Union, with its 150,000,000 inhabitants and one-sixth of the total land of the globe harnessed by a relatively small minority to a novel experiment.[46]

The illustrious Paul Scheffer of the *Berliner Tageblatt*, who spent seven years in Russia, once told writer Dorothy Thompson, "Only two sorts of people can write about Russia . . . those who stay here for years and give up their lives to the study of this extraordinary country . . . and those who come in for a very short time and leave before their first vivid impression becomes confused . . . if you stay much longer but not long enough all that you see and feel so clearly becomes chaotic."[47] Walter Duranty certainly was of the first type, spending most of his time trying to analyze Russian behavior. His private apartment was important, not only because he was fortunate enough to have a fireplace, but also because he was able to entertain persons who knew the land. The names of other Moscow correspondents do not appear in his writings, indicating that he was not a close friend to any one of them. He spent some of his free time playing bridge with the Greek ambassador; that was his quiet style.

Duranty's contribution in the field of foreign correspondence was immense. His keen intellect and analytical ability made him invaluable to the *New York Times* and thus to thousands of readers. He was a strong reporter, confident enough to interpret the facts. He was opinionated, as he admitted, and it is the contention of some that these conceptions crept into his analyses. Hardened by his war experiences—he had seen the worst of deaths—he accepted the brutality of Russia as a basic point. From that he wrote his stories. Setting aside the issue of humanitarianism, it can be argued that he did brilliant work just keeping track of major events. Predictions accompanying his interpretations usually were correct. He did understand Russia—he had learned the language—and this knowledge was conveyed in precise, descriptive dispatches.

In later years Duranty held to the beliefs he developed in the early 1920s. In 1935—three years after he won a Pulitzer Prize—he looked back upon the last seven years and commented,

> This country has made an unprecedented investment in socialized industry and has simultaneously converted agriculture from narrow and obsolete individualism to modern Socialist methods. What is more, both of these operations have been carried out with success. Their cost in blood and tears and other terms of human suffering has been prodigious, but I am not prepared to say that it is unjustified. In a world where there is so much waste and muddle it may perhaps be true that any plan, however rigid, is better than no plan at all and that any altruistic end, however remote, may justify any means however cruel.[48]

But he finally also admitted that he may have missed something in not considering the final results of such a program:

> In 1928 there began for me a period which lasted nearly four years upon which I look back with mingled regret and pride. During much of that time I was in the position of seeing through the wood so well that I did not distinguish the trees well enough. What I mean is that I gauged the "Party Line" with too much accuracy and when my opinion and expectations were justified by events, as they frequently were, I was so pleased with my own judgment that I allowed my critical faculty to lapse and failed to pay proper attention to the cost and immediate consequences of the policies that I had foreseen. I had no intention of being an apologist for the Stalin administration; all that I was thinking was that I had "doped out" the line that the administration inevitably must follow, and when it did follow that line I naturally felt it must be right. In other words, I had tried to make myself think like a true-blue Stalinist in order to find out what true-blue Stalinists were thinking, and had succeeded only too well . . . instead of feeling sympathy for the N.E.P. men, [those supporting Stalin's New Economic Policy] or at least remembering that their fate would seem worthy of sympathy to ninety-nine per cent of my readers, I said to myself, "Well, they got what I knew was coming to them, so that's that." . . . My office in New York made no remarks on the subject, but I had a number of letters from friends which showed I had made a mistake.[49]

While that 1935 explanation did not mollify his critics, it showed an ability to evaluate his role as a foreign correspondent. He was concerned about the readers, and he did stimulate thinking about Soviet Russia even if he were not able or willing to put Joseph Stalin into better perspective.

NEGLEY FARSON: STOPOVER IN MOSCOW

Negley Farson experienced a lifetime of adventures before he applied for a job with the *Chicago Daily News* foreign service. He had written for the *New York Sun*, the *New York Herald*, and other publications, but more important, he had seen more history in the making than most men alive. In March 1917, Farson and an English friend were riding through St. Petersburg when the friend halted the sleigh. Within a few moments they were caught up in Alexander Kerensky's revolution, the upheaval that toppled the Czar and gave Lenin his opportunity.

Farson narrowly escaped death as mounted Russian troops galloped at full speed into the growing crowd, snow flying from the horses' pointed hoofs. He saw the first victim of the 1917 Revolution, a motorman beaten to death after he tried to drive his tram through the mob. "This is the Revolution," his friend shouted. "I was here in 1905—I know."

From the Crimea to Archangel, Farson saw it happen. John Reed, the American writer who chronicled the Bolshevik Revolution with his *Ten Days That Shook the World*, was an acquaintance during the three pre-Revolution years Farson spent in Russia. He also was active in Egypt, France, or wherever else there was excitement, even for a short time as a pilot for the Royal Air Force. Then, after returning to the United States, he sought another overseas job. Taking the advice of *Daily News* reporter John Bass, he visited Victor F. Lawson, who seemed to resent the idea that Farson thought himself capable of taking over a *Daily News* assignment. Lawson told Farson of Paul Scott Mowrer and his brother Edgar Ansel, of how each of the world's capitals boasted a top-ranking *Daily News* correspondent.

But the old man consented when Farson told him of his plan to sail across Europe, beginning at Rotterdam and ending up where the Danube poured into the Black Sea from Rumania. "It is a splendid idea," Lawson said. "Do it." That was 1924. Farson had been working for the Mack Truck Company and was making a sizeable salary. But he was an explorer first, and a journalist. Seven years later he held the coveted *Chicago Daily News* post in London.[50]

Farson and his wife, Eve, did sail their boat, the *Flame*, to the Black Sea, and during the next six years he was not in any one nation more than six months. He sat with Gandhi, hunted whale in Norway, and in September 1928 re-entered Russia. One of Farson's first impressions was that men like Walter Duranty, Paul Scheffer, and William Henry Chamberlin of the *Christian Science Monitor* often were in "violent disagreement" about how to interpret a certain event. This was in great contrast to conversations outside Russia, where people felt they knew what was happening in the Soviet state.

Once, Farson and Scheffer wrote what Farson claimed were the first two big dispatches about the collective farm movement. For two weeks they traveled together, pooled their notes, and finally wrote their stories together. The facts were identical but the conclusions were different. Years later in London Farson credited his colleague with seeing the difficulties that caused Stalin to admit in 1930 that the collectivizers were "dizzy with success."[51] Farson and Scheffer had other experiences before Farson departed for other lands, and Scheffer must have been a great source of information for Farson, who lacked recent experience with Russia's new leaders.

Farson and the traveling writer John Gunther, who spent three years in the paper's employ, gave Chicago readers solid accounts of Russia's basic problem in late 1928. The shortage of food now was hurting the cities. Farson traveled to Kiev, Odessa, Kharkov and other cities in the Ukraine in the last three weeks of November and reported no outright evidence of famine and, like Duranty, no widespread, organized opposition to the government. However, he did detect deep discontent—the same unhappiness demonstrated by President Kalinin at the December Moscow meetings:

> We must improve agriculture and raise production. If we do not solve this problem I do not know if the communist regime can exist or that even the soviet power can live.[52]

Farson reported that there seemed to be no answer to the question of how Russia would be able to balance her trade with foreign nations, raise enough grain to begin exporting again, feed the hungry in the cities and the Ukraine, provide the peasants with cheaper manufactured goods, and prevent the kulaks from either being taxed out of existence or becoming petty bourgeois. His interpretation was that the Soviets had to bring in cheaper imports to prevent the poorer peasants from aligning themselves with the rich kulaks. Stalin had his own answer for this problem, though, as events proved. In fact, Stalin had already been moving physically against the large landowners in the countryside before Farson arrived in Russia.

The *Daily News* reporter was confident that he had not been given "conducted" tours of different areas. He found that people were afraid to talk to him, sometimes because he was a foreigner and sometimes because of the presence of the G.P.U. (secret police).[53] The order to "produce more" was the subject of more Farson dispatches. He reported on a speech given by Rykov to Leningrad party officials where a strong plea was made for increasing the production of cast iron. Rykov cited the poor grain collection figures and Farson commented that many felt the government caused the low amounts because of pressure on the kulaks—who in retaliation sold only the minimum amount to the government. Of course other journalists had reported earlier that low grain collections were a problem. But Farson was able to show how some blamed the government and that there was a division of opinion within the party as to the wisdom of these moves. He also wrote that foreign observers believed the government wanted to speed industrialization because of the fear of war.[54] Either by fate or by long-range design, the tractor factories of the 1930s made great tank factories in the 1940s.

Like the other writers, Farson covered all of Russian life. One humorous article described the coming of Christmas 1928 and how *Pravda* announced an "antireligious campaign" to last from December 10 until mid-January. Meanwhile, he wrote, stores displayed Christmas trees and other decorations just as they did before the Revolution. "Moscow Upset by Santa Claus" was the headline.[55] Another story dwelt on arguments as to whether the drinking of vodka, "the colorless curse of mighty Russia," should be curtailed.[56] Plays and literature also were subjects.

The only mention in 1928 of the real power, Joseph Stalin, came when Gunther listed the nine members of the Politburo and offered background sketches. He placed Stalin first, pointing out his influence with Lenin and the fact that he was the only professional revolutionary among the group. But the word "dictator" or other terms signifying growing power were absent.[57]

Farson was present on December 11 with Duranty, Chamberlin and others when Litvinov made his "peace with the world" speech.[58] During the first week of January he reported on Russia's suggestion that she and Poland sign the Kellogg antiwar pact. Despite public cynicism as to Russia's motives—that she was trying to embarrass her enemy Poland or impress the United States—Farson quoted a high Soviet official who simply claimed that Russia, like all nations, wanted another barrier between nations and war. Farson's dispatch also described Litvinov's note to Poland as "amazing" for its obvious simplicity, and he continued to pay attention to this "diplomatic Shuttlecock."[59]

Farson displayed great versatility as he filed a stream of dispatches for the Chicago office. Whether it was a housing problem in Moscow, bread rationing, or an increase in timber exports, he had the facts. Being an aggressive reporter, when he wasn't planning a springtime expedition into the Caucasus, he was ready when an important story broke, such as when the details of the exiled Trotsky's influence inside Russia began to emerge in late January 1929:

> Within the last few weeks the government has been staging a roundup of Trotsky followers and some details of the movement are at last appearing in the newspapers. One hundred and fifty Trotsky sympathizers have been arrested in Moscow alone and most of them will be strictly isolated by a moderate form of exile in the outlying districts of the republics . . .
>
> Leon Trotsky, who has been supposed to be sitting out in Alma-Alta in middle Asia, peacefully writing violent books against the present regime, has been smuggling letters both inside and outside of Russia. One such letter, widely reprinted in European newspapers and reprinted in the organs of the white refugees, declared that the present soviet regime reminded him of the worst side of the Kerensky rule.
>
> It is said that many of Trotsky's strongest comrades and his former glory, the Red Army, looked upon him as a likely leader in a Bonapartist revolution.[60]

This story reveals the excitement Trotsky caused from exile and gives a clue, probably inadvertently, as to why Stalin shrank from imprisoning him and instead banished him. Stalin's hold was strong but not complete. Also, the phrase used by Farson, "present regime," might further explain the absence of references to Stalin in his and others' stories. The Communist state, in great confusion, had gone through several periods of leadership. There were nine men in the Politburo scheming for power. How could any reporter know for sure that one would consolidate his power over the other eight in the midst of the obvious instability?

Farson's story on the arrest of Trotskyists was among the first indications in American newspapers that something important was developing regarding Leon Trotsky's future role in Russian politics. The wire services carried the story only one day earlier. Another important dispatch dealt with the visit of Montana farmer Thomas D. Campbell, who told the Russians of the fleets of "combines" that swept across his many acres. Throughout this story Farson reported on the need for Russia to industrialize, but, as he had earlier, he neglected to comment on the difficulties caused by government-inspired bloodshed.[61]

Farson's continuous reporting of the movement against Trotsky supporters was comprehensive. He probed into the growth of Protestant evangelism and the efforts of religious people in a supposed godless state. He and John Gunther followed political developments as closely as possible, and Farson made good use of Moscow newspapers for gaining information. He was at a distinct disadvantage because of not having been there long, but perhaps he got out before that "first vivid image" got confused. Victor F. Lawson must have been pleased at his decision to send Negley Farson to Moscow.

Overall, the *Chicago Daily News* provided some of the finest reporting on Russia done during this period. Nevertheless, Joseph Stalin remained a man of mystery to Chicago readers and the trauma of the Ukraine largely went unreported.

WILLIAM HENRY CHAMBERLIN OF THE *MONITOR*

One of the most prolific writers covering Moscow in 1928–29 was William Henry Chamberlin, the former United Press and *Manchester Guardian* reporter then sending dispatches to the *Christian Science Monitor*. Between 1922 and 1934 he devoted himself to journalistic work and historical study of Russia. He, Walter Duranty, Louis Fischer, and Maurice Hindus were the mainstays who had lasted for more than a decade—the experts, if there were any experts, on the Soviets.[62] Chamberlin's coverage of Russia for the *Monitor* was similar to Duranty's stories for the *Times*. Duranty sent more stories and enjoyed more newspaper publication, but Chamberlin sent comprehensive, well-written items that demonstrated a high degree of understanding. He sometimes used an indirect question-and-answer technique that allowed the reader to judge the Russian official's response for himself. Perhaps this relieved him of the embarrassing task of criticizing, at the risk of being further embarrassed by the official censor. Incidentally, Chamberlin did not receive bylines, and for some unknown reason the *Monitor* did not include Moscow as one of its bureaus, listed as Berlin, Vienna, Paris, London, Geneva, Rome, and Melbourne.

On January 5, 1929, Chamberlin sent a story about a Soviet gesture that could have led to increased American interest in Russia. When one considers that Stalin's chief aim was to build "socialism in one country" before advancing toward the world revolution, in opposition to Trotsky, who wanted to advance at once, Chamberlin's stories take on added significance. A. Ksandrov, the head of the Main Concessions Committee, which passed on the applications of foreign capitalists for leases of various enterprises in the Soviet Union, apparently gave Chamberlin an exclusive interview. The Russians were saying American capital could "safely and profitably" work in Russia. The interview was held, "if rumor be correct," in Trotsky's former villa. When Chamberlin asked why the Soviet government thought relations could be expected to change, Ksandrov replied they had clarified the rules for the exchange of rubles and had simplified the tax system. The Russian said the Soviet trade unions were agitated only when foreigners paid up to

50 percent more wages, thinking they could afford this because of an antici-
pated "killing."

Chamberlin reported that only $900,000 of American money was invested
in Russian plants and businesses at that date. He listed many possible "prof-
itable deals," like "a tractor factory in Stalingrad with annual capacity of at
least 10,000 tractors. The estimated amount of required capital is $20 mil-
lion, or 30 million rubles." The story was favorable in tone toward the Soviet position. As usual, only the official Soviet position was mentioned, not
Stalin.[63]

The *Christian Science Monitor* occasionally carried items from other capitals about Russian relations; one dispatch from Bucharest relayed the information that "it's believed locally" that Russia acted to ratify the Kellogg
antiwar pact because of U.S. threats to withhold financial support.[64] If a
serious reader followed daily he could put the dispatches together to form a
comprehensive picture. But it should be pointed out that the *Christian Science Monitor*, although it boasted the services of Chamberlin, did not cover
Russia as consistently as it could have. Of course, the same criticism was
made of the *Times*, even though it had Duranty filing dispatches full-time.
Editors at home, deciding the placement if the story were to be used at all,
held much power. Interest in European discussion of the Kellogg-Briand pact,
the Hoover trip to Latin America, news about Franklin D. Roosevelt's taking the governor's office in New York, and financial developments kept the
pages full.

Chamberlin, Fischer, Hindus, and Duranty authored magazine and journal articles on all aspects of Soviet life during the period 1925–32. A comparison is revealing. Of these, Fischer contributed 45, almost all to *The Nation* magazine (21 in the 1925-27 period and 24 more between 1930 and
1932). Chamberlin wrote 28, 15 coming in 1925–28 and 13 in the 1929–32
years. Hindus's total was 13, nine of them being published before 1928 and
four others in 1930–32. Hindus, the Russian-born and American-educated
writer whose books offered extraordinary accounts of Eastern European life,
visited Russia almost annually beginning in 1923. While the general newspaper readership was deprived of his ideas, opinion makers were not. His
articles appeared in *Asia, Century*, and the *Round Table*. Few observers saw
as much as he did. Duranty had time for only four pieces, two in 1927 and
one each in 1928 and 1929. Another who had an interest in Russia was the
traveler-lecturer Sherwood Eddy, who published a half-dozen articles at this
time.[65]

But only Chamberlin, writing primarily for *Atlantic*, covered the crucial
gap. Six of his articles appeared in 1928–29 when Stalin was making the
final decision to go ahead with collectivization, an act which left the nation

in a state of imbalance until the kulaks were stilled. None of the other writers contributed a relevant article during this time, and Stalin was featured in only two articles written by these men before 1929, both 1926 pieces by Chamberlin. Nonjournalists provided the only other deep insights into Stalin's role. Jerome Davis, Yale University professor, wrote in *Current History* of his 1927 conversation with Stalin and of a letter received from Trotsky. The article left no doubt that Stalin easily was the most powerful man in Russia. Another by M. A. Aldanov in the *Contemporary Review* and a biography in *Living Age* came to the same conclusion.[66]

The articles submitted by Chamberlin over the years were a sizeable contribution. In 1925 he reported on the problems of the peasant—the man who fought in the World War and the Civil War, drove out the Czarist landowners, and now made demands on the government. Chamberlin sensed the natural resistance against the already formulating collectivist schemes and said that the Red propaganda had "hit hard" because many peasants had been exposed to new ideas during their army tours. "When one takes a long view of Russia's future," he predicted, "nothing stands out more clearly than the fact that Russia is a peasant country, by right of numbers, and that the peasants, in the end, will make of it, to a very large extent, the kind of country that they want."[67]

In August 1926, the *Literary Digest* borrowed heavily from an article Chamberlin had published in *Asia* magazine, and headlined the piece "Djugashvili, Alias Stalin, New Ruler of Russia." Chamberlin said that a "man of mystery, secrecy and reserve" had risen to supreme power in Russia. Tracing Stalin's life, he called him "very tall and dark," demonstrating that he had not ever seen him in person, since Stalin was short and unimpressive physically. Astounding as this error may seem to today's reader/viewer, it calls attention to the difficulty of covering Stalin's police state. Chamberlin said Stalin's chief contribution to Soviet policy had been his "keen appreciation" of the necessity of conciliating the peasants. Then he added two statements that were not borne out within the next few years. Chamberlin said Stalin did not seem to believe that foreign capital would play an especially significant role in the nation's transformation. And he said that since Stalin came from a "very old country [Georgia] in the shadow of the gigantic Caucasus range," he had an "Asiatic capacity for patient waiting."[68] It was true that he had waited to gain total power and it may have been correct that at that time he was not in favor of outsiders becoming involved with investments and trade, but once Stalin—the practical man—made up his mind to industrialize and to equalize the political and economic strengths of the cities and country by moving against the wealthy peasants, he was a very impatient person. He was a tough man to analyze and one can appreciate why some of the writers did not even bother to try. Everything they said could have been wrong, as it turned out.

Chamberlin, like Duranty, was a hard realist, but unlike the *Times* reporter he did not seem to get lost in rationalizations for harsh government programs. In his reminiscences he stated flatly, "Stalin is indebted to both these rulers [Ivan the Terrible and Peter the Great] for many models of policy, especially in such matters as carrying out a thorough liquidation of undesired or suspected individuals and classes."[69]

THE INSIDE REPORTING OF LOUIS FISCHER

Louis Fischer was considered one of the Moscow veterans in 1929 when, at age 33, he was writing a two-volume history of Soviet foreign policy. He had understood Stalin's position since 1925 and on September 9, 1927 had been privileged to attend one of the few interviews granted by Stalin. "Abler and stronger than Zinoviev is Stalin," he wrote. "From the little he says much dynamic energy oozes. His office, where he sits most of the day and night, is a gigantic power house; from it issues the current which electrifies the entire party into unremitting activity. He is its secretary and therefore its manager-in-chief. Lenin trusted Stalin. Stalin trusts no one. That is the way they speak of Stalin in Russia."[70] Fischer recorded that and other observations primarily for *The Nation* magazine.[71] The account of his interview with Stalin is worth detailed mention because of its rarity.[72]

Present that day, only a few weeks before Trotsky made a severe error in judgment and completely lost out in his quest for power, were Anne O'Hare McCormick of the *New York Times*; future U.S. Senator Paul H. Douglas; author Stuart Chase; Rexford Tugwell; trade union leaders John Brophy and James Maurer; Jerome Davis, faculty member of the Yale University Divinity School; and a few unknown nonjournalists. The group entered Stalin's office at 1:00 P.M. and left at 7:15 P.M. Here is Fischer's account of that day:

> During those six and a quarter hours Stalin never left the room, never received a message. There was no telephone in the office. He had arranged his work so that he could give undivided attention to the American visitors. This concentration is characteristic of Stalin's method as an organizer . . .
>
> Stalin looks ordinary. Neither his face nor figure is distinguished. If he were not Stalin he would pass unnoticed in any Soviet street . . .
>
> Stalin seated himself at the head of the table. I sat next to him on the left making pencil sketches of his face and notes on how he looked and

what he said. I have kept the notes . . . it is the face of a man who schemes and traps, not the face of a sportsman or painter or poet . . .

My notes say that Stalin's eyes are "crafty." His eyes are grey-brown. They seldom open fully. Thick brows, heavy lids, and a moist film over the eyeballs seem designed to protect his eyes from inspection while he studies the person facing him. When he listens he does not look. When he speaks he stares at the visitor. He wants to know the impression he is making. He wants to know what the other person is thinking. "What is this fellow up to?" Stalin's eyes ask.

"It isn't easy to fool Comrade Stalin," Stalin wrote on July 9, 1929 in a personal letter not to be published until 1949. That is the warning conveyed by Stalin's eyes: "Don't try to fool Stalin."[73]

During that interview Stalin spent four straight hours answering questions that Fischer said reflected neither a desire to embarrass Stalin nor an intimate knowledge of Russian conditions. Stalin held his pipe throughout the session, occasionally puffing on it. One series of quick questions caught him by surprise and Dictator Stalin had the good sense to "surrender." The argument revolved around the question: "Suppose a non-Communist group, which was pro-Soviet, advocated the scrapping of the Soviet monopoly of foreign trade; could it present candidates in an election and campaign for them?" When Stalin finally offered a "spirited and logical defense of Communist policy," by saying it would be wrong to return the rights of the bourgeoisie, an American sharply rephrased the question. "How can the opinions of the workers and peasants, as distinguished from the opinion of the Communist party, find legal expression?" "Very good," conceded Stalin. "In other words the question is not the restoration of the political rights of the bourgeoisie but a conflict of opinions within the working class and the peasantry." He escaped by saying there were different opinions but since no one advocated an overthrow of the government but rather all wanted improvement of the regime, there was no problem. He had been caught confusing the issue and the Americans had pressed the point. The next question followed logically, about Stalin's differences with Trotsky. Of course, some thought, here would be a good chance for a second party within Russia. Stalin said he would not discuss internal political problems with foreigners, and then he quizzed the delegation for two hours, asking such things as, "How do you explain that on the question of recognizing the U.S.S.R. the leaders of the American Federation of Labor are more reactionary than many bourgeois?"

Fischer's analysis of Stalin's behavior was graphic:

He was neither brilliant nor magnetic. He cannot wave the magic wand of personality to captivate or charm. He does not establish a personal relationship; he makes an impression. He made his impression in the interview the same way he built his political power: methodically, brick by brick. The impression is one of cold strength, iron will and unsentimentality. His statements were sensible, solid, simple and pedestrian. He lacks the capacity for witty epigram or terse phrase which lights up a whole field of thought. He plows long and deep. He wins by siege rather than by blitz. His weapon is the club, not the rapier. What he lacks in brilliance, grace, inspiration, and personal electricity he makes up by hard work, persistent plodding, shrewdness, weight and time. He is like a glacier, icy, slow-moving, massive and irresistible.[74]

Shortly after that experience Fischer wrote on "The Passing of Trotsky." In that piece he criticized Trotsky for "numerous political errors" and said Stalin's plan for industrialization would be less at the expense of the villages than the Trotskyists' plan would have been. He also said that "it is safe to prophesy that there will always be an opposition."[75]

A few weeks later Fischer saw the end of Trotsky. It was November 7, 1927, the tenth anniversary of the Bolshevik Revolution. Those in opposition to Stalin circulated rumors that the military would revolt during the parade after a shout, "Down with Stalin!" This did not happen. Fischer wrote that a group of Chinese Communist students did shout "Death to Stalin" and were arrested by GPU men. Trotsky himself made what was to be his last public appearance in Russia at 2:00 P.M. that day when he attempted to speak to a crowd near the Red Square. After a few minutes his picture was torn down and he was forced to stop because of booing. He was through. At 6:00 P.M. Fischer saw Trotsky and his brother-in-law Kamenev driving away from the Red Square area, and nine weeks later Trotsky was arrested. Banishment to Alma-Ata followed.[76]

As noted earlier, Fischer was singled out for severe criticism on the grounds that he was pro-Soviet to the point of ignoring Stalin's brutal excesses and the effects of the devastating famine of the early 1930s. He remained enthusiastic about the chances for democracy in Russia until the purges of the late 1930s, when his deep disillusionment began to settle in.

REPORTING FROM THE FRINGES

Writer Sherwood Eddy traveled to Russia in 1911, 1912, 1923, 1926, 1929, and 1930. His observations about those who covered the Soviets showed the importance of the Moscow correspondent. Eddy was convinced that Russia was a challenge to the United States, but he was concerned about misinformation and false propaganda being distributed on both sides. "Whether as a menace, or as a challenge to set our house in order, or as a vast experiment which may in time work out some values that may be of use to the rest of humanity, we ought to know what is going on in that part of the world," he wrote.[77]

Through his Russian friends and the freedom allowed him on his visits, Eddy felt he could correctly assess Soviet claims regarding production as well as the political situation. He used the books of Hindus and Chamberlin, which he said, "probably give the truest pictures of life in Russia today in the English language."[78] Alarmed at the high state of emotion aroused during discussions of Soviet Russia, Eddy said it was extremely unfortunate that more readers could not learn to trust reporters like Chamberlin, Hindus, Duranty, and Fischer. Instead, he said, many depended on unreliable sources in Berlin and Riga, Latvia.[79]

Nevertheless, without exception during the six months of October 1928 to March 1929—the period when Stalin decided to plunge ahead against leftists and rightists alike—these talented writers failed to clearly "identify" Stalin, particularly as the prime force behind the collective farm movement. The reasons for this have been listed: the censor, the mysterious habits of Stalin himself, the vast distances in Russia, and the secretiveness of the official newspapers.

Much has been implied in these preceding pages about the power of the censor, in practice or through intimidation. In fairness, however, the testimony of the United Press correspondent Eugene Lyons should be taken into account. He said that between 1928 and 1931 the government interfered with major stories only a half-dozen times.[80] The censor's real or imagined role was part of another debate that affected coverage. The question: How badly is a paper's coverage hurt by stationing reporters on a nation's borders instead of assigning them directly to the action? Neither the *Times of London* nor the *Chicago Tribune* had correspondents in Moscow, but instead preferred Riga. While some observers said this was better because Riga was free from censorship and the writers could develop their own reliable sources of information, other critics said these cities often were filled with rumors and were centers of intrigue. The most important news comes from Moscow, they said.

Others unhappy with Russian coverage charged that publications with writers in Moscow tolerated biased and incomplete coverage in order to have the prestige, whereas other papers stationed their reporters in the Baltic area where there was plenty of anti-Soviet news to report. If one's goal was to report anti-Soviet news, then Riga obviously was the place to be.

These arguments aside, Donald Day supplied his *Chicago Tribune* readers with important news from Riga. For example, he produced one of the best stories on the arrest of Trotsky's followers. The story had been held up; Day chose to write in a "second day" style. It appeared in the *Chicago Tribune* the same day as Negley Farson's *Chicago Daily News* dispatch, several days before other major papers carried the news. Day felt free to be blunt:

> Riga, January 24—Exclusion of the Trotsky opposition from the ranks of the Communist Party, and the exile and imprisonment of adherents of the former war commissioner, will have an important effect on the future inner policies of the Soviet government.
>
> It is reported that mass meetings of workers called to discuss the counter-revolutionary activities of Trotsky voted solidly to support the Russian dictator Joseph V. Stalin, who is steering a middle course between the extreme left group of Trotsky followers and the avaricious right group led by the less important Communists.
>
> The newspaper *Isvestia* hints that . . . the Communist Party, under M. Stalin's leadership, is more concerned with the immediate economic future of Russia than the prospects of starting a world revolution with Soviet government funds.[81]

If the handful of U.S. reporters in Moscow and Riga could not cover enough by themselves, U.S. bureau chiefs in Europe could always supplement the coverage by picking up stories from such sophisticated papers as the *Manchester Guardian Weekly* or the *London Times Weekly Edition (Illustrated)* as well as the leading daily editions (such as the Paris *Le Temps*, which featured good exchanges of Russian news). An interesting one would have been the bulletin of the opposition, *Biulleten Oppozitsii*, published in Paris from 1929 to 1941. Informative as the newspaper stories were, they followed the pattern of not giving much specific attention to Stalin.

Perhaps the most valuable for foreign observers was the *Times Weekly Edition*, which reflected Great Britain's deep interest in the world from floods in Alabama to problems in Turkey. Whatever the problem, the *Times* was there. Regarding Russian coverage, F. A. McKenzie was the man on the spot. In early 1928, after Trotsky's exile, McKenzie, author of *Russia Before Dawn*, gave *Times* readers a close look at how Stalin had stood patiently in the background, growing ever stronger:[82]

> Strong, virile, still under fifty, Joseph Stalin is more and more for assuming Lenin's mantle . . . molding the new Russia to his will.

As might be suspected, Henry Luce's *Time* dubbed Stalin "the dictator" early and periodically provided strongly worded and vivid descriptions of the general situation in Russia. Sometimes *Time* reverted to a mocking tone.

But to its credit, *Time* was capable of hard straight reporting, such as when Trotsky, with his wife and son, headed back to the civilized world from exile. *Time* said:

> The trickster, if any, was Soviet Dictator Josef Stalin, who banished Trotsky a year ago for the crime of organizing a political opposition. Stalin brooks no opposition. Last week he muzzled correspondents in Moscow with a censorship so drastic that the only thing really known about Trotsky was that he had left Alma-Ata.[83]

So there were some exceptions to the findings that Stalin lived in the shadows of press coverage. Nevertheless, it was not until the early 1930s that the world became more aware of his murderous policies that ravaged Russia's countryside. Stalin used police terror, purges, and eventually "show trials" to terrorize his own people into total submission, becoming one of the most brutal dictators in history.

While the small group of correspondents gave their readers a glimmer of the maneuvers that Stalin used on his road to power, it was left to historians to interpret much of what happened. That is understandable. Nikita Khrushchev's "secret speech," denouncing Stalin and giving information about his police-state methods, was delivered in 1956. More disclosures about the Stalin era only emerged in the early 1990s following the end of Soviet Communism. Ironically, it was determined that the greatest failure in post-Soviet Russia continued to be that of farm production. The question emerges: Is it fair to single out this group of journalists for critical scrutiny when foreign correspondents often have access to an incomplete picture? Yes, because of the importance of U.S.-Soviet foreign relations and the long-term effects of the Soviets on U.S. domestic life—and because the case study exposes all of the problems of covering such a complex person and story.

Chapter Three

The Eve of World War II:

The Radio Reporters and the Munich Crisis

Edward R. Murrow (center), CBS's European news chief, and William L. Shirer (right), famed correspondent and author of *Berlin Diary,* at a Paris sidewalk café with an unidentified friend. UPI/Bettmann

INTRODUCTION

Adolf Hitler's annexation of Austria, on March 12, 1938—the *Anschluss*—struck fear in the heart of neighboring Czechoslovakia, the next apparent target of the German dictator. Within a week Nazi agents renewed their campaign to stir pro-German emotions in the Sudetenland, the mountainous chunk bequeathed to Czechoslovakia's founder-president, Thomas Masaryk, at the Paris Peace Conference of 1919. Masaryk and his eventual successor, Edvard Benes, had demanded defensive terrain for their new state and it was given them along with three million German inhabitants. Now,

19 years later, Hitler was crying for freedom for the "exiled" Germans and was pledging nonviolence after Germany had expanded to her natural linguistic boundaries.

It was clear to German leaders that expansion into Central Europe had to precede the long-planned drive eastward into Poland and the Ukraine—this meant taking both Austria and Czechoslovakia, by force if necessary. By November 1937 Hitler was convinced that Britain and France had "silently written off" the two countries. He was aware that British Prime Minister Neville Chamberlain pursued an appeasement policy based on the hope that Germans would be satisfied with the reunification of German-speaking persons. German military commanders knew the British had allowed their military strength to be depleted and were confident that France would not be able to solicit British support to defend other nations.[1]

It was ironic that the rim of territory on the Bohemian and Moravian borders would be the source of the next crisis of the late 1930s. The German-speaking inhabitants had fitted nicely into the Czech mixture, and the country itself had enjoyed a higher degree of prosperity than had her neighbors, including Germany to the northwest.[2] The Czechs were tied to France by a military treaty and to Great Britain by England's perpetual interest in maintaining balance on the Continent. But now, after the seizure of historic Vienna, Hitler controlled the lifelines of southeastern Europe, and Czechoslovakia was in effect isolated. However, her small but sturdy army held the mountainous Sudetenland and, as Winston Churchill's investigations were to prove later, Hitler greatly dreaded the thought of sending his regulars into combat so soon.

Without a doubt the Germans would have been smothered by the French in 1936 had the large French army challenged Hitler's brazen move into the Rhineland. And his sorry entrance into Vienna was further ammunition for his enemies in Germany, both political and military, who said Hitler was going too far, too fast. Some of his tanks had to be towed into the city. Hitler knew his limited capabilities because, as Churchill wrote later, the Fuehrer figured it would take thirty-five divisions to crack the Czech lines.[3] There would be other ways to gain German "living space."

Two days after the travesty in Austria, Churchill told the House of Commons that Hitler's move was only the beginning and begged for British action. "Where are we going to be in two years," he said, "when the German army will certainly be much larger than the French army?" Churchill was frighteningly right. The German General Staff Plan of 1937 called for the liquidation of Czechoslovakia in order to eliminate potential Russian air bases and to negate any chances the Western-minded Czechs had of attacking from the rear in the event of a general war. On May 28, 1938, Hitler ordered preparations for possible military action against the Czechs and the expansion of the defensive front in the West. He remained supremely confident that Britain and France would not risk an all-out conflict over his tiny neighbor. Only a week earlier a nervous Czech government had begun partial mobilization, as "incidents" between Nazis and Czechs increased in frequency. Russia called for negotiations aimed at stopping any German movements eastward. Through its treaty with France the Russians hoped to stall Nazi Germany's apparent plans. Stalin, like Hitler, needed time to prepare for the inevitable conflict between Nazism and Communism which only the dictators could foresee at this time.

Throughout the summer of 1938 tension mounted in Czechoslovakia, while France's Edouard Daladier, the new premier who had promised stern measures against aggressors, gradually slumped and followed the lead offered by the British Prime Minister, the sincere and gentlemanly Chamberlain. The only persons determined to resist Hitler's obvious plans were the Czechs. Benes and his associates had arched their backs as Hitler's harangues became more violent in midsummer. Since May there had been rumors of troop movements toward the southeast. When the Czechs declared martial law in Sudeten German towns in September, the stage was set for the outbreak of a conflict foreseeably involving Europe as a whole, willing or unwilling.

America had lifted an eyebrow at the fall of Austria but it would take more than that to swing her interests from pleasant living. In September 1938, Joe DiMaggio's third year in the major leagues was going to be another World Series year for his team, the New York Yankees. Congressional elections were approaching, and Franklin D. Roosevelt was preparing the country for more of his New Deal. And while these were hard economic times for most Americans, it was an exciting period because of new entertainment, not only in the world of sports but on stage, screen, and radio. The effects of the 1920s, the reversion from thoughts of war, and the Depression greatly affected American attitudes. In September 1938 more and more was heard from Adolf Hitler, but Americans were solidly against any international commitments and participation in any future wars, and the Roosevelt administration, ever sensitive to popular desires, was silent.

"Revisionists" argued that America had been tricked into helping the Allies in the World War, that the Versailles Treaty was a fraud and that Europe in general was perverted.[4] The committee headed by Senator Gerald Nye of North Dakota, an extreme isolationist Republican, cemented ideas that American businessmen and bankers had influenced America's entry into war in 1917 for their personal profit. Americans were told this mistake should not be repeated. A Gallup Poll of April 1937 showed two-thirds of Americans felt American participation had been a mistake.[5]

Overall, Roosevelt was prevented from offering material assistance to

France and Britain because of the Neutrality Acts, legislation which prohibited America from selling arms to belligerent nations. In addition, these nations would have to conduct nonmilitary business under "cash and carry" agreements, whereby they would be required to pay cash for these goods and carry them home in their own vessels. In October of 1937 the President's speech in Chicago on the need to "quarantine the aggressors" was greeted with overwhelming disapproval. From that time on, FDR moved cautiously in foreign affairs, with the nation moving even more slowly behind him. Thoughtful Americans slowly began to change their minds, however, in 1938, as evidenced by passage of the Vinson Naval Expansion Act, which authorized the expenditure of one billion dollars over 10 years. While most Americans still wanted no part of militarism, a few realized that the Western hemisphere had to be protected as a minimum gesture of defense.

Just as Americans, particularly congressional leaders, were shortsighted with respect to the rising dangers of Nazism, broadcasting industry leaders failed to realize the potential of their own business. Despite the encouraging growth of the national networks and the development of programming variety, there was little sponsorship of news. Foreign broadcasts were still a novelty prior to 1938, although executives like Paul White of CBS, Abe Schecter of NBC, and G. W. "Johnny" Johnstone of Mutual fought to develop overseas news organizations.[6] A major reason for the lack of news shows, and especially those concentrating on foreign events, was public apathy. Sponsors determined that trying to counteract provincial ideas would prove to be financially disastrous. The Columbia and National broadcasting systems dominated the network competition in the 1930s, despite the entrance of the Mutual system in 1934, while the Associated Press and United Press were the principal suppliers of news to newspapers. Later these huge organizations would be able to see how they could join hands for mutual profit. United Press and International News Service set up radio wires in 1935 and the Associated Press followed suit in 1940.

Entertainment! That was radio in 1937–38. More than 26,666,500 families were attracted to 626 broadcast stations. Of urban families, 91 per cent owned at least one radio. And 69 percent of their country neighbors tuned in. Overall, 82 percent of America had access to the news via the airwaves.[7] Here is what America listened to in the last year of relative peace. Voted the best program by radio editors was the Charlie McCarthy Show. Jack Benny was the top comedian; Guy Lombardo's orchestra was tops in that field; Kate Smith was the number one female singer. The *Radio Theatre* and *One Man's Family* captured most votes for the best dramatic programs and Ted Husing and Clem McCarthy were judged the best sports announcers. Don Wilson was the favorite announcer and Boake Carter, Lowell Thomas, and Edwin Hill were the regular news commentators most appreciated. Others not forgotten were Burns and Allen, Nelson Eddy, Eddie Cantor, Don Ameche, and Bing Crosby.

Then everything changed. Between September 10, the date of President Benes's speech in which he outlined his nation's desires to resist Hitler, and the final Four-Power Agreement in Munich of September 29, Americans heard network broadcasts from London, Paris, Berlin, Munich, Godesburg, Cologne, Nuremberg, Budapest, Prague, Padua, Trieste, Rome, Udine, and Geneva. Hitler, Chamberlain, Benes, Goebbels, Hodza, Mussolini, Litvinov, Pope Pius XI . . . they were all heard in America, while Franklin Roosevelt's plea for peace was beamed to Europe.

Adolf Hitler's threatening and insulting speech to 100,000 Nazi Party leaders at Nuremberg on September 12 brought Europe to the choking point. "The air is so tense one can't breathe," was one comment.[8] The story of how radio handled the threat posed by Hitler and his eventual success must be broken into separate tales—of challenges to the individual journalists and to the giant networks. There was the continuous chasing of news by the Continental correspondents, William L. Shirer of CBS and Max Jordan of NBC, part of the frantic competition for "scoops" by all three major networks. H. V. Kaltenborn's *Studio Nine* performance in New York deserves special attention, as does the broadcasting work of young Edward R. Murrow in London.

For those three weeks America was subjected to a pressure unequaled in the previous 20 years. Europe was on the brink of total war. Either the Allies backed the Czechs and called Hitler's bluff, the Czechs stood up to Hitler alone, or some agreement was to be reached. Otherwise the motorized divisions would roll to "liberate" the 3,318,445 German-speaking inhabitants of the Sudetenland and bombs would fall on Czechoslovakian cities. Germany's first military air bases were only 21 minutes from Prague. This was the picture, clotted with several alternatives, as the American radio teams began sending home the vital facts in September 1938. The *Anschluss* had been covered by the networks, and by a few of the same reporters, but the Czechoslovakian situation called for superior talent on far more levels than ever before.

The *New York Times*, *New York Herald Tribune*, *Chicago Tribune*, *Chicago Daily News*, and other papers, plus the three wire services, had maintained their European bureaus after the end of the First World War. They were prepared to handle a breaking situation and the print journalists contributed often to the radio broadcasts, but overall the Munich Crisis was radio's chance to show its capabilities in time of crisis, and the measurement of this effort is an important part of the history of foreign correspondence.

RADIO AWAKENS AMERICA TO HITLER'S THREATS

The networks snapped to full attention on September 10 and carried the Edvard Benes speech. NBC and CBS both broadcast the emotional words tracing the democratic origins of his nation. But it was Hitler who started the earphones and cables buzzing on the 12th when he challenged the world. Again both NBC and CBS broadcast the Nuremberg speech with the aid of interpreters, who gave running translations. Max Jordan gave an eyewitness account of the enthusiastic reaction in Berlin over NBC's two networks, called NBC Red and NBC Blue, while M. W. Fodor of the *Chicago Daily News* Service added to the NBC coverage with a report from Prague. (NBC had two chains of stations until 1943, when the Federal Communications Commission ordered the Blue network sold; it became ABC.)

CBS followed a long commentary by H. V. Kaltenborn in his New York studio with reports from Edward R. Murrow in London, William L. Shirer in Prague, Melvin Whiteleather of the Associated Press in Berlin, and John T. Whitaker of the *Chicago Daily News*, speaking from Paris. Murrow's major comment that night: "There is little optimism in London tonight." Shirer, Jordan's counterpart on the Continent, commented, "Don't think the Czech people are gloomy or depressed or frightened. Not a bit of it." Said Whiteleather in a report similar to Jordan's, "Nazi interpreters of Hitler's thoughts say a plebiscite in the Sudeten region might be acceptable." And Whitaker added, "If he were going to make war within the next few weeks, Frenchmen reason, why would he tell the Germans their forts would not be ready until next winter?"[9] Americans would come to recognize this technique of CBS—*The European News Roundup*—which consisted of continuous spontaneous conversation usually lasting 30 minutes. September 12 ended with rumors flying worldwide and with Shirer writing in his diary, "The Great Man has spoken . . . everyone in Prague seems to have listened to the speech . . . what poison in his voice.[10]

Frederick T. Birchall of the *New York Times*, Sigrid Schultz of the *Chicago Tribune*, Wallace R. Deuel of the *Chicago Daily News*, Frederick Oechsner of *United Press*, Louis Lochner of the *Associated Press*, and Ralph Barnes of the *New York Herald Tribune* were among the American foreign correspondents in Nuremberg covering the speech. Leland Stowe was the *Herald Tribune*'s roving correspondent during this period. Birchall wrote:

> Nuremberg, Germany, Sept. 12—Chancellor Hitler fulfilled all expectations by speaking out in his final utterance in Nuremberg tonight. Without going into details he demanded, amid the frenzied enthusiasm of the crowd in Congress Hall, that the "oppression of Sudeten Germans must end and the right of self-determination must be given to them."[11]

Ten minutes after Hitler finished, U.S. print and broadcast clients of the United Press wire service had received a 2,000-word summary of the speech. The full verbatim text followed. More than 5,000 words of "reaction" material was then filed. The Associated Press offices also reported one of the busiest nights in years, as several thousand words were channeled through the London bureau and across the Atlantic to newspaper clients (AP did not supply broadcast news until 1940). And in Great Britain and Scotland crowds waited for extra editions of newspapers, after hearing a BBC summary of the talk. The crowds had not been so large since the night of the Abdication in 1936.[12]

From the outset there was a recognizable pattern to the network broadcasting. While most of the original scripts are unavailable, it was possible to piece together the following picture through the journalists' reminiscences, network publicity materials, and articles that appeared in professional publications, newspapers, and magazines. CBS operated around its New York headquarters, extensively using the "roundup" style. NBC relied on a scattering of broadcasts, attempting to divide them between its Red and Blue chains if it were not possible to carry the programs simultaneously. Mutual's reporters, John Steele in London and Louis Huot in Paris, occasionally were heard in person but cabled their news during most of the period. Mutual noted that the foreign governments regularly broadcast news programs in English via powerful shortwave stations and gave their own interpretations to English and American listeners. MBS transcribed these shortwave broadcasts and rebroadcast them in America. The shortwave pickups included speeches by Hitler, Mussolini, and other European political figures, and they kept MBS reasonably in step with the two larger networks.

Variety was the pattern on September 13 when the Sudeten Germans, tremendously excited by Hitler's speech, gave the Czechs an ultimatum demanding a form of self-government in the disputed territory. It was rejected. The Press-Radio bulletins and United Press kept the American stations informed on the Sudeten flare-up. Shirer's broadcast from Prague late at night was ruined by poor atmospheric conditions, and CBS listeners instead heard Murrow describe how "pictures of Hitler were received in complete silence at London newsreel theatres."[13] Alistair Cooke, the British journalist and commentator who many years later hosted PBS's *Masterpiece Theatre*, described the British reaction to the rising threat of war over NBC Blue. Early the next day Harold Ettlinger of United Press in Paris was on the Blue system describing the reaction in the French capital.

NBC also scored later on the 13th when Fodor's broadcast from Prague, unlike Shirer's, got through with a description of the Czech crackdown in the Sudetenland and the declaration of martial law. The networks flashed the news later in the day that Chamberlain would fly to Berchtesgaden the next morning—to see Hitler. There were no broadcasts from Central Europe that night because of sun spots and static, although Shirer tried to send an account of Czech reaction to Chamberlain's announcement. By this time actual fighting had broken out in the Sudetenland and only the action of the British Prime Minister prevented major blood-letting. Murrow came through from London with a static-interrupted interview with Lord Strabolgi, who gave the impression that Britons were relieved at the news of Chamberlain's flight. Said Kaltenborn in New York, listening through earphones, "There is grave doubt as to whether or not the visit will bring peace."[14]

Between September 15 and 30 frequent electric storms over the Atlantic forced the networks to rely on the same overcrowded telephone lines and cables used by the wire services and newspapers. NBC's ingenious staff set up a relay system that enabled it to stump CBS for several days. Broadcasts from Europe were sent to Cape Town, then to Buenos Aires, and on to New York, all by shortwave broadcast. CBS caught on to the transmission trick a few days later and quickly recouped, pushed on by Murrow and Shirer.[15]

Murrow had arrived in Europe in 1937 at age 29 as a one-man staff to begin a nine-year stint, the first stage of the most remarkable career in broadcast news. For an assistant he hired Shirer, who had worked for the recently expired Universal Service. They switched from the broadcasting of cultural programs to news at the time of the *Anschluss* in early 1938. To everyone's relief their coverage was exciting and creditable. Murrow hustled from Warsaw at the last minute when CBS news chief Paul White sensed that a closed radio station might be opened by authorities. It was, and that night, March 12, 1938, the first multiple pickup news broadcast in history went on the air. Shirer spoke from London, Murrow told the story in Vienna, and newspaper reporters Pierre Huss in Berlin, Edgar Ansel Mowrer in Paris, and Frank Gervasi in Rome gave their impressions.[16] Murrow, the chief European correspondent for CBS, then began lining up the core of what became an excellent news staff as Europe hurtled off toward war. NBC and Mutual did likewise. This took time, however.[17] During the Munich Crisis Murrow coordinated 116 broadcasts that were heard from 18 different points and also made 35 broadcasts himself. "Calling Edward Murrow, come in Ed Murrow," was the cue thrown out by Kaltenborn, with the familiar Murrow voice replying, "Hello, America, this is London calling."[18]

KALTENBORN: ANCHOR IN A STORM OF NEWS

Prime Minister Chamberlain and Hitler met at the Chancellor's summer home on September 15; it was the Prime Minister's second-ever airplane trip. The meeting was the first of three scheduled to be held between the British and French leaders and Hitler during this period. German censors cut the news flashes to a minimum, and American stations were forced to depend primarily on news bulletins instead of direct reports. NBC Red carried two reports from Prague with Karl Von Wiegand of International News Service at the microphone. In the morning Von Wiegand commented on past events in the crisis and gave insights into the personalities of the persons chiefly involved. That night he was back on the air with reports that 29 Germans and Czechs had been killed in Sudetenland border incidents.[19]

As the blizzard of news bulletins continued, Kaltenborn bore the brunt for CBS as he did so many times during the crisis, offering a long analysis of Neville Chamberlain's visit. His conclusion was that if the meeting did not produce evidence of some accord the Prime Minister's "pro-dictator" policy might be curtailed. In general the atmosphere was more relaxed than at any time in the previous five days, as reporters prepared for Chamberlain's trip back to London.

September 16 was the networks' busiest day since Hitler's speech. Both NBC systems were able to carry an exclusive interview with Chamberlain from the Munich airport when the tired Prime Minister paused on his way home. Then at the London airport a BBC correspondent drew the comment that Chamberlain was going to visit with Hitler again, this time at a half-way point. Both CBS and NBC carried this interview in the United States, while NBC gained another exclusive interview with Chamberlain at the London airport. He reiterated his intention of returning to Germany and advised the vast audience not to accept prematurely any unauthorized account of what took place at Berchtesgaden. Adding to the NBC report was the journalist Cooke, who said the Prime Minister had met with King George and later with the cabinet.

Then CBS put some reality into the discussions. Shirer broadcast from Prague that night, hooking up with Kaltenborn to warn CBS listeners that the Czechs were determined never to accept dismemberment and were beginning to fear a "sellout" on the part of the British and French. A few hours later Kaltenborn played host to Murrow and British journalist Sir Frederic Whyte, who translated the British feeling as follows: "People say, well, if the Czechs don't want a plebiscite, Czechoslovakia is perhaps really not worth fighting for. That if the Czechs have got to swallow something they don't like, maybe that's the necessary price to pay for preserving peace." Kaltenborn ad-libbed after both broadcasts, agreeing that the Czechs realized what was in the wind.[20] Appeasement! There was a bright note on this dreary and confusing day. Shirer was elated that his broadcast got through, the first direct program in four days, and wrote "Hoorah" in his famous diary.

Kaltenborn began to gain enormous attention for his commentaries. While Murrow undoubtedly was the brains of the CBS overseas organization and Shirer was the star reporter, it was Kaltenborn in his *Studio Nine* who gave continuity to the varied overseas broadcasts. The dean of radio commentators, he had joined CBS as a full-time commentator in 1930 after a long newspaper career with the popular *Brooklyn Eagle* that had included foreign reporting. He had gained fame in 1936 by broadcasting from the French-Spanish frontier for five weeks, with gunfire in the background, interviewing participants in the Spanish Civil War. Listeners of 1938 easily recognized his voice, with its high-pitched, precisely accentuated tones. A dignified man, he was trying to maintain order in a world gone crazy.

During these three weeks he was on the air 85 times. His translations of German and French broadcasts were invaluable. At age 59 he displayed amazing stamina, sneaking naps in the studio between broadcasts and research. *Broadcasting* magazine, which followed the coverage closely, saved its highest praise for Kaltenborn, the son of a former Hessian officer who had moved his family to America.

> Americans were listening to interpretations of the news by expert commentators who drew upon their intimate knowledge of European history to give their listeners a clear picture of each crucial event . . . its significance and probable result. In the rank of these interpreters stands H. V. Kaltenborn . . . although he had a German accent he showed nothing but a fair disposition. He has never been accused of being partisan by his vast and loyal audience. From six to ten times a day his clear, crisp voice has been going out over the network, perhaps in a trans-Atlantic interview with some front-page figure from whom Kaltenborn had skillfully drawn the essential facts on the situation . . . he had the command of four languages and his desk was piled high with paper from the wire machines.[21]

Reporters used September 17 to regroup forces and to speculate, just as Americans continued to guess what would happen next. One thing was certain. In America there was no division on foreign policy. Americans were of one mind—in contrast, the English were split—as to what course this government should take. There was no sympathy for the Czechs that would force Americans into aiding her in any material way.[22] Hitler had made four major demands to Chamberlain. The Czechs would have to cede the Sudetenland, bring Czech foreign policy into line with that of Germany as opposed to Russia, surrender to the Germans economically, and begin producing munitions that Germany, rather than France, specified.

CBS announced early that morning: "Prime Minister Chamberlain and his cabinet are at this moment gathered around the polished table at No. 10 Downing Street, deciding whether to surrender to Hitler's demands or send Europe to war . . . Hitler is waiting impatiently in Germany for a decision and there are intimations that it must come soon if hostilities are to be avoided."[23] Walter Kerr, *New York Herald Tribune* correspondent, broadcast from Prague over the NBC Red network. Kerr commented on the terms of the proposed cession of the Sudeten area to Germany and said it appeared that the Czechs would fight.[24]

The day grew more ominous as it progressed. The British cabinet held its second emergency meeting around noon and Kaltenborn announced from New York: "As before there has been no announcement of any kind, except for the news of an hour ago that French Premier Edouard Daladier and M. Bonnet, the Foreign Minister, have been summoned to London."[25] Then came the news that Konrad Henlein, the Sudeten Party leader, had announced the formation of an armed "Free Corps" along both sides of the border. There were rumors that Hitler was not going to wait for a decision and that an attack was imminent. The Czechs declared the entire nation (instead of just the Sudetenland) in a state of emergency. Philip Jordan, correspondent for the *London News Chronicle*, told America of the Czech decision and commented, "London isn't as cheerful today as it was yesterday. I saw Mr. Chamberlain return to Downing Street yesterday and the silence in which he was received was a formidable silence."[26] While Kerr's broadcast was the only major NBC production on this eventful day, in addition to the news bulletins, CBS carried Murrow from London and used Murrow's broadcast to transmit some information from Shirer in Prague—all woven around the commentary of Kaltenborn. The day ended with the British and French preparing for gas attacks and digging trenches.

The two major networks were in direct competition between 5:00 and 6:15 A.M. on Sunday, September 18. The Columbia network opened its stations early and carried the arrival of Daladier and Bonnet at the London airport. Murrow stated at that time, "Few people here believe that any real release from tension has been achieved." Then both CBS and NBC switched to Trieste, Italy, where Premier Benito Mussolini told an enthusiastic audience his solution to the Czechoslovakian problem. The networks carried a running translation of Il Duce's suggestion that all minorities in Czechoslovakia have a plebiscite. Less than an hour later, between 7:04 and 7:10 A.M. on NBC (Red and Blue) and 7:01 and 7:35 A.M. on CBS, Milan Hodza, Premier of Czechoslovakia, was declaring that a plebiscite on the Sudeten-German proposals would be unacceptable. NBC had cut off the conclusion of Hodza's address to offer a complete English translation of Mussolini's speech. Then a few minutes later both Red and Blue networks finished up the Hodza declaration.

It was a satisfying day for everyone connected with the new concept of radio news. NBC's man in Prague, M. W. Fodor, followed at 8:00 A.M. with comments on the speech by Mussolini, in light of Mussolini's following Hitler's line that the Sudetens had the right of a plebiscite. At 8:08 A.M., Ralph Heinzen of UP related a few more facts from Paris on Daladier's flight. And at 8:15 A.M., Victor Gordon Lennox of the *London Daily Telegraph* told Americans of the latest British opinion.

An hour later both Red and Blue systems carried a complete translation of Hodza's speech, all on NBC.[27] Shirer and Kaltenborn linked up in the early afternoon to give CBS listeners a firsthand report of fighting in the Sudetenland. Shirer said, "All the American correspondents who have seen fighting in the Sudetenland this week agree on two things: first, that the fighting in each case was started by the Sudetens who were well armed with German guns; second, that the Czech police and troops acted with remarkable reserve under the circumstances. They used the arms only when fired upon and made very few arrests." Mr. Houghton of the *Toronto Star* wandered by at this moment and was dragged into the conversation:

> "You've just come from the Sudeten territory, I take it," said Shirer. "Do you find any tension or excitement there?" "Yes," Houghton answered, "I have just this moment returned from there . . . we found men, women and children living in the suspense on top of a volcano."[28]

Cooke, the British journalist, was heard on the NBC Blue system from London, again bringing the "man in the street" into the picture. CBS wrapped up its broadcasting of foreign events with a roundup. First Kaltenborn called into his microphone for Ed Murrow and then for Pierre Huss, chief of the International News Service bureau in Berlin. Murrow said that Jan Masaryk, Czech minister in London and son of the founder of the little republic, informed the British and French that his government would have no part of any deals with Hitler. He said Mussolini's speech caused no great surprise in London and that he was warned by an observer in Italy (via telephone) not to be misled into believing the two fascist powers were in disagreement.

The scene then switched to Berlin and Pierre Huss. "Konrad Henlein issued a new appeal tonight to the Sudetens in which he says 'The hour of liberation is near, therefore show resistance everywhere.' Thousands of Sudetens are now streaming into the ranks of the Free Corps, ready to stake life and blood for liberation of the homeland from the Czech yoke." It was said that night that the legionnaires already numbered 40,000 men.

Kaltenborn ended the evening—or had planned to end the evening—with a commentary. But first came the bulletins that the French and British were in agreement on a policy for a peaceful solution to the European problem, meaning they would in all probability submit to Hitler's demands and press them against the Czechs.

Kaltenborn then gave his commentary, in which he said:

In effect Premier Hodza and Il Duce engaged in a radio debate today with half the world listening in. What a change in relations among statesmen when they fly to appointments and when they stage their debates for the world.[29]

Shirer heard the news of the Anglo-French agreement at midnight when Murrow called from London and ordered him to Berlin. "I protested to Ed that the Czechs wouldn't accept any such plan and would fight," Shirer said. But it also had been announced that Chamberlain and Hitler would meet at Godesberg on the 22nd, and Shirer headed for Germany, leaving Maurice Hindus to cover Prague for CBS.[30] It was Hindus, a noted author and international observer, who would provide CBS with one of the biggest scoops of the crisis two days later.

The morning of September 19 was no brighter in Europe. At 6:00 A.M. both Red and Blue systems carried the comments of Vernon Bartlett, diplomatic correspondent for the *London News Chronicle,* who emphasized the importance of the Franco-British agreement to divide Czechoslovakia. The rest of the day NBC hopscotched about Europe getting the latest reaction to Hitler's demands. Programs were broadcast from Paris, Berlin, and Prague. The Berlin report was handled by Wallace Deuel, *Chicago Daily News* correspondent. He told of Hitler's impatience to take the Sudetenland and of German preparations for general war. A few hours later Walter Kerr spoke from Prague on the Czech determination to fight alone if necessary, rather than cede any territory to Germany.[31]

On CBS Kaltenborn was making his own survey of the different European countries. He predicted French Socialists would object to the dismemberment and that there would be parliamentary disapproval in Britain (there were riots in London when the policy was announced). Later in the day all networks carried the news that the Czechs, who had been given the decision of the British and French officially, had appealed to the Russians for help. That evening Kenneth Downs, INS chief in Paris, told CBS followers about the arrival of Osusky, Czech minister to France, in Paris after a quick visit to Prague. "He was visibly shaken. There were tears in his eyes. He said 'Our country has been condemned without being heard.'" From Berlin Shirer added that the German capital was as tense as Paris, waiting for the word from Prague—had the Czechs given in or not?

From Prague Hindus told Kaltenborn over the telephone that in his opinion a change in the editorial policy of the leading newspapers meant that the Czech government was trying to prepare the people for surrender. He said the cabinet was nine to one in favor of accepting the French-British-German proposals. This apparently was only an educated guess on Hindus's part. The final bulletin of the evening came from the wires of the United Press. It read: "Military experts reveal tonight that Soviet Russia has six and one half million soldiers on the Ukraine and White Russian frontiers; Russia said to be ready to deal with any situation which may arise out of the Czech crisis."[32]

Tuesday, September 20, was a day of exclusives for both networks. The Czech cabinet met early in the morning to discuss the Franco-British proposals. Morning papers in London had predicted the British would not have to worry, the Czechs would give in. Kaltenborn reported these facts and told his listeners that at 2:45 P.M. Maurice Hindus in Prague might have some news. In the meantime, Mussolini spoke in Udine, Italy, and NBC was on the scene, broadcasting from 12:52 to 1:53 P.M. from Udine. Later Mussolini's call for a partition of the entire Czech nation was summarized. The Blue system carried the actual speech and the summary and the Red did not.[33] Then it was 2:45 P.M. and Kaltenborn and Hindus made contact. Hindus began a 15-minute account of how the editorials in the morning newspapers had changed their tone, making it appear that the Czech cabinet would resist the proposal. Hindus went on:

> Late last night or rather early this morning I dropped in at a number of wine cellars. Music was playing; young people were singing or dancing . . . we have just received an official announcement of the government as to the decision of the cabinet! The communique reads: "The Czechoslovak government has handed to the British and French foreign ministers in Prague a note in which the government expresses its point of view with regard to the proposal which has been interpreted to it by Great Britain and France. This point of view makes further negotiations possible in the spirit of conciliation which the Czech government has always shown."[34]

The Czechs were playing for time. Hindus beat all opposition by 11 minutes in reading this news to Americans.

At 5:00 P.M. Shirer collared several colleagues as they boarded a train at Berlin, heading for Godesberg. Pierre Huss of INS sauntered up to the microphone and said, "The Czechs have been sold down the river but the Czechs have not yet given up." Following Huss with comments were Cedric Patten of the *London Daily Express*, Webb Miller, UP's European Manager, who was looking desperately for his baggage, and Ralph Barnes of the *New York Herald Tribune*. Americans then heard the sound of the train pulling out—a most unusual broadcast and one set up by Ed Murrow in London in a quick change from the ordinary roundup.[35]

Then it was NBC's turn to benefit from the experiences of the writers. G. Ward Price of the *London Daily Mail* had conducted an exclusive interview with Hitler at Cologne and broadcast the substance of the talk over the Blue system, saying that Hitler would give the Czechs until October 1 to cede the Sudetenland. Hitler said that he would order the invasion of that territory to liberate the Germans living there if the Czechs did not agree. "Herr Gott! What couldn't I do in Germany and for Germany if it were not for the infernal Czech tyranny over a few million Germans," Hitler had screamed at Price. "But it must stop. Stop it shall." The interview was one of the scoops of the crisis. Hitler continued:

> It was the existence of Czechoslovakia as an ally of Soviet Russia, thrust forward into the very heart of Germany, that forced me to create a great German air force. That in turn led to France and Britain increasing their own air fleets.
>
> I have doubled the German air fleet once already because of the situation now prevailing in Czechoslovakia. If we fail to settle the crisis now, Field Marshall Goring would be asking me to order it doubled again and the British and French would redouble and so the mad race would go on.
>
> Do you think I like being obliged to stop with my great building and development schemes all over the country in order to send 500,000 German workmen to construct at top speed a huge system of defense works along our western frontier? . . .
>
> All this is madness, for no one in Germany dreams of attacking France. We harbor no resentment against France; on the contrary, there is a strong feeling of sympathy in Germany toward her. Nor does any German want war with Britain either.[36]

Walter Kerr later broadcast from Prague the reasons why the Czechs thought it impossible to comply with all of Hitler's wishes.[37] Murrow came back with a late evening report that the Czechs had asked that their 1926 arbitration treaty with the Germans be invoked. This treaty had been reaffirmed by Germany in 1936 when she retook the Rhineland. Murrow also reported anti-British opinions of Americans who had been very pro-British, and news that the Labour Party of Clement Attlee was trying to force Parliament to rally the nation against Chamberlain.[38]

Then came a double shock. First the Czechs surrendered conditionally to a second Franco-British ultimatum on the morning of September 21. Then they changed their minds. The networks carried a news bulletin that said: "Czechoslovakia has accepted Adolf Hitler's terms and will surrender her Sudeten territory to Germany, assured by Britain and France . . . German newspapers are lashing the public temper to a high pitch with stories about Czech atrocities . . . Chamberlain will leave for Godesberg tomorrow for his second conference with Hitler."[39] So it appeared at 9:25 A.M. that Europe had escaped major troubles. Earlier that morning both NBC systems had been able to carry an address before the League of Nations by Maxim Litvinov, commissar of Foreign Affairs for the USSR. The speech from Geneva, condemning the British and French, was translated for Americans by Paul Elbel of the French Chamber of Deputies.

CBS then beat NBC by a full hour with the news that Mussolini, speaking in Rome, had praised Chamberlain. An about-face. At 12:15 P.M. when NBC was giving its listeners a summary of Mussolini's speech, CBS was announcing that Chamberlain was to leave for Godesberg at 10:00 A.M. the following day. In mid-afternoon came more startling news. The Czechs now said in a message read by Premier Hodza that they had not yet specified how or what sections of the Sudetenland would be ceded. Chamberlain would be facing an angry Hitler, and Europe, especially England and France, was not yet out of trouble. Americans too must have been confused at the rising of the Czech spirit. Walter Kerr on NBC and Maurice Hindus on CBS both described crowds in Prague shouting and singing for the army of General Jan Syrovy to make war on the Germans. Later in the evening Kaltenborn and Hindus talked for a second time over the CBS "phone"— another airing of a two-way conversation with Kaltenborn pumping his distant colleague for facts and insight.[40]

On this busy day CBS was fortunate to broadcast for the first time the opinions of Anthony Eden, the former foreign minister, who joined with Winston Churchill and Lloyd George in protesting against the "betrayal of the Czechs." Without attacking the government, Eden told Americans that it was time Britain made a stand for what he considered a good cause.[41] Webb Miller of UP was heard over NBC Blue from Cologne with a summary of the events leading up to the crisis as the networks began to prepare for the Godesberg conference, only a few hours away.

COUNTDOWN TO A SECOND WORLD WAR

Germans wept in the street on the morning of September 22 when Adolf Hitler arrived to prepare for his meeting with the British Prime Minister. In Prague the wild marching stopped. The Hodza cabinet had resigned and

Hindus phoned Kaltenborn that General Syrovy was to head the new group. Hindus said the situation in Prague was so unstable that things could change in the next five minutes. NBC carried only one major broadcast from Europe that day, while CBS had two roundups from several capitals, visiting London, Prague, Paris, Rome, and Godesberg. Murrow reported from London that the city was in a state of "collective insecurity." The same might have been said of the journalists. Downs, the UP man in Paris, told of the disgust of Parisians over their country's bow before Hitler. Frank Gervasi in Rome told of Italian amazement that Mussolini would call for a "totalitarian solution to the Czechoslovakian problem"—in his own words. Il Duce previously had said he wanted peace. Murrow noted that Churchill had canceled a tour of the United States to fight the Chamberlain government. Hindus said the new Premier and War Minister, General Syrovy, was a hero and had been responsible for stopping the Sudetens from grabbing territory. The actual meeting was set for September 23, so the networks continued to gather speculation from the four corners of Europe. Ed Beattie of UP was in Godesberg and spoke to NBC Red listeners on what could happen when Chamberlain and Hitler met.

The second CBS roundup wrapped up the news day from Europe. The highlight was when Murrow interviewed a taxi driver named Hodges who had been gathering opinion about the crisis. Hodges said people were beginning to wonder if the Chamberlain government was pro-Fascist, were beginning to approve of Eden a little more, and were disappointed in the United States, which had suggested the League of Nations in the first place but which had not joined.[42]

The following day NBC increased its efforts and broadcast seven times, while CBS and Kaltenborn maintained the usual steady pace. The correspondents were puzzled when in the morning the negotiations between Hitler and Chamberlain failed to materialize. Tension heightened and the networks carried the bulletin that Germany had 22 army divisions on war footing in the immediate neighborhood of the Czech frontier—units totaling a half-million men. Max Jordan was in Godesberg for NBC, reappearing at the crucial moment. He went on the air three times that afternoon and evening but had little to report.[43] Walter Kerr and his rival, Hindus, gave eyewitness accounts from Prague on the massing of Czech troops along the German border. Still the world waited. In the early evening the United Press reported that the talks would resume that night.

Shirer's account of further developments is the best:

It seems that Hitler has given Chamberlain the double-cross. And the old owl is hurt. All day long he sulked in his room at the Petershof on the Petersburg on the other side of the Rhine, refusing to come over and talk with the dictator. At 5 p.m. he sent Sir Horace Wilson, his "confidential adviser," and Sir Nevile Henderson, the British Ambassador in Berlin (both of whom we feel would sell-out the Czechs for five cents), over the river to see Ribbentrop. Result: Hitler, agreeable, and Chamberlain met at 10:30 p.m. This meeting, which is the last, broke up at 1:30 a.m. without agreement and now it looks like war, although from my studio in the porter's lounge I could not see any strain or discern any particular displeasure in Chamberlain's birdy face as he said farewell to Hitler, who was also smiling and gracious. Still the Germans are plunged deep into gloom tonight. They are really afraid . . . just as I was about to go on the air with the day's story at 2 a.m., Goebbels and Hadamovsky, the latter boss of Nazi radio, came rushing in and forbade Jordan and me to say anything over the air except the words of the official communiqué . . . it says merely that Chamberlain has undertaken to deliver to Prague a German memorandum containing the German's final attitude concerning the Sudeten question.[44]

Ralph Barnes of the *Herald Tribune*, one of the outstanding reporters of the decade and fated to die two years later in a British bomber crash in Yugoslavia, sat out the long evening. He wrote:

> Godesberg, Germany, Sept. 24—After a dramatic three-hour interview with Chancellor Adolf Hitler at the Rhein-Hotel Dreesen, which ended at 1:40 a.m. today (8:40 p.m. Friday New York time), Prime Minister Neville Chamberlain said in reply to a query, "I do not consider the situation hopeless. I am going home this morning to present new proposals to the Czechs. It is up to them."[45]

The Czechs' first answer to Hitler was a mobilization of their troops. The Russians warned the Poles that an attack on the Czechs would mean an end to the nonaggression pact between the two nations and the spectre of a wider war loomed. From London Murrow and Jan Masaryk talked of the tiny republic's last days. Masaryk ended a tearful speech to Americans with the words, "Truth must triumph and will triumph. I salute you brother democrats."[46] Unofficial communication between Czechoslovakia and the rest of the world was halted during part of the 23rd and 24th while the task of mobilization was under way.

John T. Whitaker of the *Chicago Daily News* used unusual ingenuity to get his story home. He used a shortwave station and asked any listeners to take down his words and to relay them to the *Daily News*. Station WOR of Newark, New Jersey, picked up his voice and complied. The story was printed in its entirety in the Monday edition, September 26. His lead read:

By shortwave radio—

Unafraid before the military might of Greater Germany and ready if need be to defend its independence with these arms, Prague, the capital city, is blacked out. It has already been emptied of military reserves under 40 years of age, and many a home, with the husband and father gone, waits tremulously for the air raid siren.

Across the frontier in Nazi Germany is Hitler, the man who can send the airplanes. The peace, not merely of this little democracy but of all Europe, rests in the hands of that dictator. Czechoslovakia has done all that it could. Hitler asked that this country should cede to him the area which is inhabited by German-speaking Sudetens. France and Great Britain, fearful of war, abandoned Czechoslovakia and urged such concessions as have never been demanded of any undefeated country in history.[47]

Hitler had given the Czechs until Saturday, October 1, to cede the Sudetenland. Chamberlain flew home with a six-day interval to work within. William Stoneman of the *Chicago Daily News* reported from London that events had finally gotten ahead of the politicians and that British public opinion might not allow the "peace at any price" members of the cabinet to force Hitler's demands upon the Czechs.[48] Radio news bulletins that day told of Great Britain preparing to mobilize her forces (the entire Navy was mobilized on September 27) and of Frenchmen in a frenzy. NBC adopted the CBS "roundup" format and between 7:29 and 7:48 A.M. jumped from London to Paris to Prague. The centrally coordinated reports showed farmers, laborers, housewives, and generally everyone still felt a peaceful solution was possible—with the exception of the citizens of Prague, who continued their mobilization. Neville Chamberlain expressed this same optimism when he arrived at the London airport at 8:11 P.M. NBC time. The rest of NBC's broadcast day on September 24 was devoted to speculation and reports of possible happenings in the coming week, although Jack Stark of the London AP office told Americans that it was impossible to prophesy what would take place.[49]

Murrow had the news that Daladier and Bonnet were on their way to London (for the second time), and Shirer said in Berlin that the German people expected peace because Chamberlain had taken it upon himself to communicate Herr Hitler's demands to the Czechs. Then later in the evening the networks carried the news bulletin that the Czech legation in Moscow had said there was no chance the proposals would be accepted in the form suggested. Kaltenborn and Sir Frederic Whyte followed with a trans-Atlantic conversation in which Whyte said England had a moral but not a legal obligation to join with the French (the French were linked to the Czechs by treaty). Hindus finished the CBS report with a description of the Czech mobilization. The city was in darkness, he said, and he had jotted down the notes for his broadcast under the dim light in his hotel room.[50] Communication lines were open again and the entire mobilization had been completed.

Both the French and the Czechs rejected Hitler's proposals on September 25. Jan Masaryk declared in Prague that his nation considered the Nazi plans entirely unacceptable and in Paris the French cabinet agreed unanimously. Hitler had severely changed the terms and American newspapers hurried to remake page one of their final editions when this was clarified. "New Terms Would Leave Czechs Helpless," said the *New York Herald Tribune*. The original demands accepted by the British and French called for the transfer without plebiscite of areas with more than 50 percent German inhabitants and adjustment of the Czech-German frontier by an international commission. Now Hitler submitted a map where all areas shaded in red would be "surrendered" without alteration of fortifications, all areas in green would be subject to a plebiscite, and Prague virtually would be cut off from the "rump" section that remained. Sudeten Germans would be immediately released from the Czech army, greatly weakening it. Joseph Driscoll in London wrote that Hitler's demands were more strict than those of the Versailles Treaty to which he refused to subscribe.[51]

The situation was so grave that Franklin Roosevelt decided to make a plea for peace. Newspaper editors remade page one once more, with the *Herald Tribune* now shouting: "Roosevelt Appeals Directly to Hitler and Czechs; Nazi Ultimatum Is Rejected by Paris and Prague; Hitler to Deliver Surprise Pronouncement Today."[52] CBS gained a scoop on the President's talk. Network technicians were alerted at 1:58 A.M., two minutes before the signoff time for European coverage. They aimed the directional antennae of the network's powerful shortwave station W2XE at Europe and at 3:00 A.M. broadcast the message that had been sent to Adolf Hitler and Edvard Benes.[53] Anxiety was growing in America, and some persons were beginning to take sides. The previous day William Randolph Hearst's *Chicago Herald Examiner* had editorialized on the front page:

> Furthermore there are only two periods in Europe's existence. One is the period of war—and the other is the period of preparing for the next war. Americans should keep out of both.[54]

The tension increased. CBS had reported that from one-and-a-half to two million men were armed in Europe and that troop trains continued to roll toward the frontiers. The President of Ireland, Eamon de Valera, had delivered a plea for peace, and Kaltenborn had commented that it was ironical that the names of towns mentioned in a report on French mobilization were very familiar to Americans: Metz, Verdun, Strasbourg.

Thus on September 26, 1938, CBS had one scoop behind it as Shirer and Max Jordan of NBC prepared for Hitler's speech from Berlin. The networks killed time by flashing around Europe for a quick check. Murrow reported "London is waiting to hear what Herr Hitler has to say tonight . . . everyone is clutching at a straw . . . the British pound sterling fell to the lowest level in three and one-half years . . . Daladier left for Paris."

Then came the big moment. In New York the CBS announcer said: "At this time, just five minutes before the speech by Adolf Hitler, the Columbia Broadcasting System takes you to the Berlin *Sportspalast* where William Shirer, CBS Central European representative, is stationed at a microphone." Both Shirer and Max Jordan gave thrilling descriptions of the colorful setting inside the building, the enthusiasm predominating among the throng of 15,000, and the thunderous bursts of applause. In his fiery speech Hitler traced Germany's position from 1918 (not unlike the Benes speech of the 10th) and warned the world that Germany was a mighty power prepared to brook no interference. Hitler's speech was translated by members of NBC's International Division and by Kaltenborn of CBS. Shirer noted that after Hitler had finished, Goebbels sprang to his feet and yelled, "One thing is for sure, 1918 will not be repeated."

Hitler looked at him with an eager expression, as if those words were the ones he had been searching for all during his talk. He jumped up and with a grand sweep, pounded a table with his fist, yelling "Ja" with all the power in his lungs, before slumping into a chair exhausted.[55] During the Hitler speech the British Foreign Office announced that England would join France and Russia in a common front if Hitler decided to attack the Czechs. This was not reaction to Hitler's talk, Kaltenborn told CBS listeners. The reaction was soon to come, however.

In New York, Votya Benes, brother of the Czech president, was interviewed for CBS. He said war would come only at Hitler's wishes, and in no other way. Hindus in Prague tried to break in with some general reaction but was stopped by static, and the interview with Benes continued.[56] A few minutes later the networks announced that King George had signed the general mobilization order and that hundreds of workmen were busy in London and other British cities digging trenches and building more bomb shelters. William Hillman, INS correspondent in London, told NBC Red listeners of these preparations in detail. He sent a chill down many an American's neck with his descriptions of the huge searchlights scanning the British skies, the government's warning to purchase gas masks, and the mounting of antiaircraft guns on public buildings. Kenneth Downs of INS and Henry Cassidy of AP told Blue and Red listeners, respectively, of reaction in Paris to Hitler's speech and of "blackout tests." Edgar Mowrer, the *Chicago Daily News* man in Paris, summed up the feeling of Europe when he broadcast for CBS:

> Europe tonight is still tottering on the edge of a horrible abyss. Hitler has spoken . . . Hitler can still avert a war . . . by realizing there is room in Europe for a great and prosperous Germany, but . . . there is no room for a country that keeps no promises, observes no forms of law . . . and publicly educates its children in the cult of war.[57]

In Prague G. E. R. Gedye of the *New York Times* waited all day for the speech. Many Czechs felt that Hitler would announce that German armies had been ordered to attack Czechoslovakia, and Gedye reported a slight release of tension when this did not happen. But he wrote, "The relaxation did not go very far because it is universally felt that the speech of Herr Hitler now makes war by Saturday inevitable."[58]

Early-morning listeners heard an ominous news bulletin on Tuesday, September 27. The CBS announcer in New York was saying, "The world wakes this morning with three fateful words ringing in its ears . . . four days more." King George had declared his nation to be in a state of emergency. Queen Elizabeth, at Clydebank, Scotland, christened a new liner named for her and wished for peace. And at 2:00 P.M. both NBC systems and CBS went to 10 Downing Street to pick up the speech of Prime Minister Chamberlain. Here are the words carried by the networks that day:

> I am myself a man of peace to the depths of my soul. Armed conflict among nations is a nightmare to me. But if I were convinced that any nation had made up its mind to dominate the world by fear of its force I should feel that it must be resisted . . . for the present I ask you to wait as calmly as you can for the events of the next few days. As long as war has not begun it is always hoped that it may be prevented. And you know that I am going to work for peace till the last moment.[59]

Millions of Germans, including Nazi leaders, listened to Chamberlain's talk. Poor reception caused some confusion and the German Foreign Office had to ask for a copy of the speech from the German Embassy in London. Hitler was eating dinner and was given a summary later. But a German official told the Associated Press that no comment would be made because, after all, "Chamberlain and Hitler told each other all there was to be told in their conference last week and the radio address gave no new facts."[60]

In the moments following the speech, the CBS announcer read AP and

UP bulletins reporting that the British foreign office expected Germany to reach full mobilization on the 28th and that Italy had begun to call several classes of reserves to the colors. Then NBC broadcast news from Edouard Traus, the AP correspondent in Brussels, who said Belgium had called 275,000 men to protect her neutrality. Kerr of the *Herald Tribune* cabled details of the Czech resistance, his dispatch displaying his own emotion:

> Prague, Sept. 27—Determined Czechs and Slovaks were waiting tonight like the defenders of Bunker Hill, expecting to see the whites of the German invaders' eyes on Saturday at the latest. They realized that their fate was likely to be that of those American revolutionists who resisted the British soldiers in 1775 and got death, but their will and determination were unshaken.
>
> Frontier guards were on a twenty-four hour vigil, and troops were digging in along every inch of Czechoslovakia's border. The people themselves were preparing to withstand the shock of the enemy assault, all convinced that the die already had been cast for both sides.[61]

With Europe in a turmoil, the time was ripe for another appeal for peace by FDR. The President's second message again was carried quickly by CBS, but this time NBC gained the admiration of the industry for scooping the opposition by 14 minutes, a decisive whipping. Both CBS and NBC beamed the plea to Europe via the powerful shortwave stations, and NBC translated the address into French, Spanish, German, Italian, and Portuguese and sent it to Latin America in addition.[62] The FDR speech dropped full responsibility for war into Hitler's lap—Hitler, the man who that night was deciding the world's fate. The President had said, "Allow me to state my unqualified conviction that history and the souls of every man, woman and child whose lives will be lost in a war will hold us, and all of us, accountable should we omit any appeal for its prevention."[63] Again the world spent a wretched night, full of speculation on tomorrow and Chamberlain's speech in the House of Commons.

Because no microphones were permitted in Parliament, the networks were stuck with a problem on the morning of the 28th, when Neville Chamberlain was to explain to the British people and the world why he thought it best to allow the Sudetenland to be chopped from Czechoslovakia. It was apparent the networks joined hands to overcome the handicap by enlisting the help of two British insiders. Both NBC and CBS listeners tuning in about 8:45 A.M. heard Sir Frederic Whyte (a former member of Parliament as well as a newsman) and Howard Marshall, a commentator. Marshall set the stage by describing the extraordinary sights of "wartime London." The streets were cluttered with light tanks and army trucks, and soldiers were work-

ing on parapets; trenches were being dug in Hyde Park. Whyte then followed with a colorful description of the opening of this momentous session of Parliament:

> My mind goes back to 1914 when Sir Edward Grey told the House
> at 3 o'clock August the 4th that the die was cast. The House meets to-
> day with a tragic sense that history is about to repeat itself . . . the mem-
> bers are grave and solemn rather than excited. There is an air of tension
> about the House. And here comes Mr. Lloyd George, short, stocky, walk-
> ing to his seat with a jaunty air of a youngster . . . In spite of the shaggy
> white hair that reminds us all that he has sat here in this House for nearly
> 50 years. On his heels comes Winston Churchill with a sort of air of his-
> toric tragedy about him. He goes to his seat below the gangway on the
> Government side with his square cut jewel, which seems to glint defi-
> ance to all comers . . . the Prime Minister slipped in almost unnoticed
> and took his place on the front bench . . . that long slow crescendo, the
> chorus of "hear, hear, hear" which some of you who have attended House
> sessions in the past will remember, with which the House always greets
> a national leader. And the scene is set.[64]

Whyte and Marshall read stenographic reports of the Prime Minister's
address as it was brought to them page by page. Chamberlain finished his
speech and then, as if the whole thing were planned, he was handed a small
sheet. The networks flashed the contents of the penciled note a minute later.
The Prime Minister had announced that he had been invited to meet the
next day in Munich with Hitler, Daladier, and Mussolini! Immediate war
had been averted and there was a final choice for peace; this was the thought
of all Americans who understood the importance of the invitation.

Webb Miller of United Press, the dynamic European news manager killed
in May 1940 when thrown from a train on a curve outside of London,
gained bylines in American newspapers, among them the *New York World-
Telegram* and *Chicago Daily News*, with his graphic account of
Chamberlain's announcement. Miller explained that Chamberlain had been
discussing his proposal for a four-power conference but did not know that
it had become a reality (later it was learned that pressure from Mussolini
forced Hitler to accept).

> I sat in the gallery immediately behind Viscount Halifax, foreign min-
> ister, Stanley Baldwin and the Archbishop of Canterbury and had a clear
> view of what happened. Halifax read the message, showed it to Baldwin,
> jumped up and departed.
>
> In a moment he appeared on the floor of the Chamber and went to the

government bench. The message with its momentous potential was passed hand to hand. The government members stirred with excitement.

Just as Chamberlain neared the end of his speech the message was handed to him. He immediately announced it to the House.[65]

William Stoneman of the *Chicago Daily News* learned that Chamberlain was not ready to allow the Czechs an "observer" at the conference. He wrote, "Chamberlain's answer to the request of Czechoslovakia submitted by its minister to London, Jan Masaryk, was highly vague and the indication was that no interference would be welcome."[66] Louis Lochner, the AP's Berlin bureau chief from 1924 to 1941, was there from start to finish, correctly analyzing the meaning of the document—immediate war was to be avoided for a price. This was the message that flashed across America, and observant readers and listeners were being given a clear, accurate assessment of this event. But anyone thinking seriously was left with a question: Would the Germans stop here? Ironically, Munich only temporarily delayed the formal opening of the Second World War.[67]

Kaltenborn told Americans: "The four-power conference probably will work out some way of settling the Sudeten problem with a cession of considerable territory to Germany." He pointed to the Roosevelt message and the appearance of Mussolini as having been big factors in the Fuehrer's change of heart. Shirer and Karl Von Wiegand, the INS man reporting for NBC, told of the great relief which spread through Berlin at the news of the conference. Shirer noted that a great mass meeting which Nazis had planned to use as propaganda was turned into a peace meeting. Fred Bate in London gave NBC Blue listeners an eyewitness account of the manner in which the British people awakened from a war nightmare. Then Maurice Hindus reported from the country everyone had forgotten, poor Czechoslovakia, a country the great nations had decided was not worth fighting over.

Hindus broadcast two Czech reactions. One was of gloom, "Another sellout." The other was a little more optimistic because, Hindus said, the Czechs figured the Sudetens were getting panicky. Indeed, "The Sudetens might in the event of war be subjects of the greatest havoc a people ever knew . . . they might be annihilated."[68] The Mutual system carried a shortwave broadcast appeal from Czechs asking for support.[69] In Geneva, CBS reported, the Czechoslovakian delegation to the League of Nations said it was satisfied with the decision. Kaltenborn and the veterans seemed to be guarded in their statements and predicted the cession of land, but others sensed an air of British determination. One of these hard-line Britishers called into the broadcasting service was Stephen King-Hall, who wound up the CBS report with these words: "What makes an Englishman mad, you know, is to have to dig a trench seven feet deep in a garden that he's been spending a whole summer getting into order. When an Englishman gets to that stage, he means business."[70]

Sigrid Schultz of the *Chicago Tribune* provided one of the most vivid dispatches—one that demonstrated the irony of the British and French position. In bitter, tough words she told Chicagoans:

> Berlin, Sept. 28—The premiers of Great Britain, France and Italy, who were allied against Germany in the World War and who believed they had vanquished her, will rush to Munich tomorrow. The statesmen will beg the new master of Germany to safeguard the peace of Europe and furthermore will help him obtain the territories he demands in the name of his people.[71]

Pierre J. Huss, already in Munich, added for International News Service clients:

> Munich, Sept. 28—By fast train and airplane—for speed is the eleventh-hour watchword of peace—Europe's four greatest leaders started rushing tonight toward this 880-year-old Bavarian capital.[72]

MAX JORDAN'S MAGNIFICENT SCOOP

Thursday, September 29. Max Jordan and William Shirer were in Munich for the climax of the crisis. Shirer, at age 34, was the mainstay in the field for CBS. His first European job was in 1925 with the Paris edition of the *Chicago Tribune*. Jordan, a few years his senior, had served as NBC's European representative since 1931. Raised in Europe, Jordan attended schools in three nations and earned a Ph.D. from Jena University before heading into journalism. At 6:00 A.M. Jordan gave a description of the conference leaders' arrival. Prime Minister Chamberlain and Premier Daladier arrived at the Munich airport about an hour apart and were greeted by Herr von Ribbentrop. Hitler and Mussolini had met at the Brenner Pass and traveled to Munich together. As the morning passed, Shirer and Jordan told America of gaily decorated streets and gave further details of the conference as it began. Americans were just arriving at work on the East Coast and were still asleep in the Midwest and on the West Coast.

Philip Booth, NBC commentator in London, read editorials from newspapers warning readers not to be overconfident and saying that the Munich conference merely offered a respite from immediate armed conflict. The networks skipped about Europe during lulls in the conference day. A highlight of their efforts was a plea for peace early in the afternoon from Rome, from Pope Pius XI. The voice of His Holiness was stronger and more steady than in previous radio talks, NBC reported.[73] He spoke in Latin and an English translation followed immediately.

By mid-afternoon both Jordan and Shirer were able to announce that the Allied side had been able to make Hitler agree to a slow occupation of the Sudetenland—at least slower than he had demanded previously. Rumors were that there would be a "careful settlement" of the rights of the Czechs in the doubtful territories. But a huge uncertainty accompanied these official events up to the last moment. Everyone waited for the official signing of the document that would end the long, tense period. And Max Jordan was in the right place at the right time to scoop Shirer and the others.

Determined to use German radio facilities that he had discovered housed in the attic of the Brown House, the conference site, Jordan got through to a German broadcast executive in Berlin on the night of the final session and was given permission. Foreign broadcasters were scheduled to use another German studio about two miles away.

At about 1:00 A.M., Jordan overheard some Italian officers in the lobby saying the meeting was about to close. He ran back up to the attic and called New York, alerting the network to stand by for a bulletin.

Racing back down the stairs, he gained the attention of Sir William Strang of the British delegation, who promised to get an English-language translation of the final communiqué. In his eagerness to alert New York again, he almost missed his scoop, returning to the lobby just in time to chase after Strang and Sir Horace Wilson. Copy in hand, he tore up the stairs. His voice hoarse with emotion, he read the text of the official communiqué 17 minutes after its issuance and 46 minutes before it was given over any other American network.[74]

A frustrated Shirer, the mainstay for CBS at this point, apparently assumed Jordan had been granted the favor for political reasons. This was his version:

> Incidentally, I've been badly scooped this night. Max Jordan of NBC got on the air a full hour (roughly) ahead of me with the text of the agreement—one of the worst beatings I've ever had. Because of his company's favored position in Germany he was allowed exclusive use of Hitler's radio station in the Fuehrerhaus where the conference was taking place. Wiegand was also in the house and he tells me how Max cornered Sir Horace Wilson of the British delegation as he stepped from one of the conference rooms, procured an English text from him, rushed to the

Fuehrer's studios and in a few moments was on the air
. . . New York kindly phoned me about 2:30 a.m. to tell me not to mind—
decent of them . . . fortunately for CBS Ed Murrow in London was the
first to flash the official news to America that an agreement had been
signed. He picked it up from a Munich radio station."[75]

In America, Thomas E. Dewey was standing before an NBC microphone
about 7:30 P.M. on the 29th. He was about to make a major political address in which he would accept the State Republican Convention's nomi-
nation for governor of New York. At 7:44 P.M. he was cut off, one of the
few times a major speech has been canceled. The reason: NBC wanted to
broadcast the text of the communiqué, captured by Jordan.[76]

America's newspapers carried the blow-by-blow description and the world
reaction to the signing. Most featured reports from the Associated Press directed by Kent Cooper or the United Press headed by Hugh Baillie. These
competitors were highly skilled in improving news-communication methods. Wallace R. Deuel of the *Chicago Daily News* called Hitler's feat "one
of the most amazing political and diplomatic victories in human history,
won on what seemed to be the very brink of disaster." The *Daily News*
headlined his story, "Rout for Democracies."[77] Frederick T. Birchall of the
New York Times wrote dispassionately of the conference, commenting, "It
may be said at once that the decisions give Germany just about all she has
demanded except the total extinction of Czechoslovakia itself, which has
never been in fact among her formulated demands."[78] Jan Masaryk and another Czech official were at the conference and were not consulted once,
but were merely told by the French and British that they had to accept the
proposals.

Ralph Barnes of the *Herald Tribune* filed a factual summary lead to the
effect that the agreement was designed to "effect a settlement by peaceful
methods, without the war which Europe and the world had feared."[79] The
Chicago Tribune headlined it an "Overwhelming Victory for Germany" and
Berlin correspondent Sigrid Schultz wrote, "If the Czechoslovaks refuse to
accept, France would not come to their assistance in case of invasion, and
Britain, which is pledged only to support France, would not be drawn into
the conflict."[80]

Edmond Taylor of the *Tribune* said, "A tone of joyous relief was felt
throughout France yesterday."[81] M. W. Fodor of the *Chicago Daily News*
cabled from Bucharest that the Rumanians now feared German aggression,
and he added with precision that Poland, with designs on part of Czechoslovakia, "does not realize that with the Czech question on the way to settlement, her turn will come next as far as German ambitions are concerned."[82]

Demaree Bess of the *Christian Science Monitor* took a different approach in his dispatch. His lead read:

Munich, Germany, Sept. 30—When the Third Reich reoccupied the Rhineland in 1936 many observers predicted that it would obtain what it wanted—namely dominance in Central and Eastern Europe—without fighting for it.

That prediction appears to have been confirmed by the agreement signed in the early hours of this morning at Munich.[83]

From Prague came the news that the soldier-premier Jan Syrovy, "in an appeal broadcast to the nation tonight declared 'superior force compelled us to accept' the four-power Munich agreement for dismemberment of the country."[84] There would be no resistance and thus no invasion.

The rest is history: the wild reception when Chamberlain arrived home; his statement, "I believe it is peace for our time"; the gloating of the German press; and the lone prophetic words of Winston Churchill, "We have suffered a total, unmitigated defeat . . . it seems to me all the countries of Mittel Europa will be drawn into the vast system of Nazi politics."[85] Murrow, Shirer, Jordan, and the bulk of their colleagues were depressed. In their words of commentary, after the factual presentations, they showed their concern for Europe's future. On October 1 the Germans rolled into the Sudetenland and the Czechs reluctantly withdrew. President Benes retired and left the country, and in March of 1939 the rump Czechoslovak state became a "protectorate" of Germany. With its mountainous fortress gone and its will and confidence in old friends shattered, the tiny nation was finished.

The days had been momentous, both for the world and for radio. NBC and CBS had both enjoyed scoops of substantial nature while providing consistent coverage. Overall CBS had the stronger team because of Murrow and Kaltenborn. The important thing for radio journalists was that they were cognizant of their potential and were ready to continue broadcasting in-depth foreign news, no matter where it occurred. In the following months Americans were to hear often from Kaltenborn, Murrow, Jordan and the many other wire-service and newspaper reporters who offered their expert commentary during the Munich crisis. America, still in the grips of its traditional isolationism, responded to their descriptions of the European scene with a vast and growing interest. This was radio's contribution to the nation's awareness of the coming war.

It is left to the historian to decide what part radio played in the immediate events. One survey showed that 19 percent of network listeners heard news shows in September 1938. The previous figure was in the neighborhood of 10 percent or lower. A more startling survey claimed that in 1937 fewer than half the population preferred radio to newspapers as a news medium but that the figure jumped to 66-2/3 percent in October 1938.[86] A 1939 Fortune survey indicated 70 percent of Americans relied on the radio for news and that 58 percent thought it more accurate than that supplied by the press.[87]

The sentiments of the European reporters were summarized by Murrow during the middle of the period, when public opinion in Europe was divided and Americans were beginning to grasp the seriousness of the Nazi threat.

> I would like to say just one final word, that broadcasting by virtue of its speed and its intimacy is playing a tremendous role in the formation of public opinion over here. If you could just hear, as we do in London, nations hurling invectives at nations through the air, you would understand what I mean. I just want to tell you that those of us here who talk to you are fully conscious of our responsibility and propose to give you an undistorted picture of the history being made in Europe during these long days and nights. We are trying to find you material on which your opinion can be based. We are not trying to tell you what your opinion should be. [88]

Chapter Four

Holding the Line Again:

Korea, 1950

Marguerite Higgins of the *New York Herald Tribune* and Walter Simmons of the *Chicago Tribune* (center) with Alan Winnington of the *London Daily Worker* in Korea. UPI/Bettmann

INTRODUCTION

Marguerite Higgins of the *New York Herald Tribune* reported from Tokyo on June 21, 1950 that Gen. Douglas MacArthur felt there would be no war in Asia for at least 10 years and that a Communist attack upon Japan herself would not merit a major commitment of American troops. He believed the main purpose of American safeguards to Japan was to deter Soviet aggression.[1] That same day John Foster Dulles, State Department special representative, returned from a four-day visit to the 38th Parallel and Seoul, Korea, where he had predicted that the Communists eventually would lose their grip on Korea.[2] In Tokyo Dulles said the Communist world was too weak to seek war with the free world.[3] That week the Central Intelligence Agency completed a study which concluded that North Korean forces "have a capacity for attaining limited objectives in short-term military operations against southern Korea."[4]

The United States government, as early as May 1947, had publicized its disinterest in including Korea within the circle of vital Pacific bases, and a Joint Chiefs of Staff memorandum signed by World War II heroes Eisenhower, Nimitz, and Spaatz verified that Korea was considered nonessential to American military security.[5] The plan was for a United States–Japanese peace treaty and for MacArthur to come home. Defense Secretary Louis Johnson and Gen. Omar N. Bradley, chairman of the Joint Chiefs of Staff, discussed the future of Asia with both MacArthur and Dulles. Keyes Beech of the *Chicago Daily News* wrote that "Pentagon reluctance to part with Japan as a base against Russian aggression has reportedly held up agreement," but that Johnson and Secretary of State Dean Acheson hoped the treaty could be pushed along. Americans would maintain air and naval bases in Japan for an indefinite period, but only garrison troops would be stationed there.[6]

The American newspaper reader was being told that the target of Communist aggression would be Formosa, the new home of Chiang Kai-shek. Despite the fact that President Harry S. Truman and the State Department "wrote off the island" in January 1950, by limiting aid and proclaiming that it was Chinese territory whatever the regime, Senator William Knowland of California and others felt Formosa was the key to Pacific defense.[7] Admiral Radford, U.S. Navy Pacific commander, met with MacArthur early in June and warned that Russia would threaten all American Pacific bases if her ally Red China captured Formosa. An attack was expected. But Radford added that the U.S. Navy did not need Japanese bases to offset a Russian thrust if war began.[8]

Attention was on Formosa, where Chiang had fled only seven months previously, and not on Korea. But actually most interest was in Eastern Europe, where Acheson was urging the United States to continue its leading role as long as Russia maintained powerful armed forces. Homer Bigart of the *Herald Tribune*'s Washington bureau described Acheson's speech before a joint meeting of Congress where the much-criticized secretary reviewed the results of a recent Big Three Foreign Ministers Conference.[9]

Nevertheless, Korea had been an important pawn in postwar negotiations between the United States and the Soviet Union. The July 26, 1945, Potsdam Declaration reaffirmed the December 1, 1943, Cairo Declaration that the powers were committed to Korean independence "in due course."[10]

A provisional Korean government for the whole country was to have been set up by occupying Russian and American forces. The Russians entered northern Korea in August 1945, accompanied by one or two divisions of Koreans already trained in Russia, but MacArthur felt able to spare only one regiment of American troops in September and sent them over from Japan. Eventually two divisions, 45,000 men, were stationed there.

Between 1946 and 1948 several efforts were made to set up a unified government, the last by the United Nations. The Communists refused to allow free elections, and the South Koreans demanded immediate independence. Led by Dr. Syngman Rhee, who had established a Korean government in exile in 1919, South Koreans forged the Republic of Korea on August 15, 1948. In the north, Kim Il Sung assumed office as premier of the Democratic People's Democratic Assembly on September 3, 1948.[11] All Russian troops had left by December 1948 and by June 1949 all Americans except a small advisory force had departed.[12] Forty years of Japanese rule were over, but the nation was hopelessly divided.

The fall of China to the People's Army of Communist Mao Tse-tung in late 1949 had been a blow to the Truman-Acheson Administration and had held its Far Eastern policy up to partisan criticism. But military policy was clear. The term "limited war" was not yet in the "American military lexicon." Instead the contingency planners followed the advice of Gen. George Marshall, who in 1945 had said, "We can be certain that the next war, if there is one, will be more total than this one." Long-range air power with nuclear weapons would be the key, they felt, and that is why MacArthur and others decided that the American line of defense started in the Philippines, continued through the Ryukyu Archipelago, then bent back through Japan and the Aleutian Island chain to Alaska.[13]

One thing remained outside of defense plans and political decisions, and that was America's moral obligation to protect the new government she had helped to form. And at the moment of truth, June 25, 1950, military leaders realized that Korea did play a role in the defense of Japan despite everything said previously. U.S. planners had not been completely oblivious to the possibility of action in Korea, though. They had decided years before that two major ports would be required to sustain American forces and therefore suggested that the line be drawn north of Seoul to include Inchon. General Marshall approved the plan, and Inchon as well as Pusan were to become famous names in American military history.[14]

Prior to the invasion there were few signs of impending trouble. Guerrilla attacks within South Korea were part of life, and the North Korean radio offered the expected propaganda messages calling for the freeing of South Korea from its oppressive government. A few stories appeared in early

1950, however, which in retrospect demonstrated the anxiety of some Koreans over the intentions of their northern neighbors. In February a U.N. commission visited guerrilla-struck areas and discovered wide-scale executions of persons suspected of aiding the infiltrators. The commission chairman, Kasim Gulek of Turkey, saw banners held by peasants asking for U.N. support but told the *New York Times* reporter that the United Nations did not have troops at its disposal.[15] In May a *Times* editor gave a short item from Seoul one paragraph on page 19. It read:

> Seoul, Korea, May 10 (AP)—Defense Minister Sihn Sung Mo warned South Korea today that invasion by North Korea was imminent. Mr. Sihn said intelligence reports indicated the North Koreans were moving in force toward the border.[16]

The *New York World-Telegram and Sun* carried this account also, but added "this latest 'scare' was calculated to influence the May 10 election" according to some sources.[17] Usually reports from Korea were optimistic. In April it was reported that all of 700 Communist guerrillas who had crossed the border in March had been tracked and killed.[18] And in Washington testimony before the House Appropriations Committee disclosed the confidence of Americans in South Korea's 100,000-man U.S.-trained force to resist any future invasion. The testimony was in support of President Truman's request for an additional $60 million in nonmilitary aid.[19] Burton Crane of the *New York Times* reported this feeling on May 30 after the Communists failed to disrupt elections by mortaring Kaesong on the 38th Parallel and assaulting two hills near Angjin. He quoted the American commander, Brig. Gen. William L. Roberts, on how the threat of attack from the north had been virtually eliminated because of the efficiency of the South Koreans. Roberts headed a U.S. group numbering 200 officers and 300 enlisted men.[20]

The election outbreaks were the last of any consequence before the invasion of June 25. During the intervening three weeks the handful of Tokyo-based correspondents, most of them veterans of World War II, reported on the possibility of the peace treaty being planned, MacArthur's talks with military leaders, and the Dulles trip. There was no indication that they and many American-based correspondents would be involved in some of the most bitter and confusing fighting ever reported.

Between the first shock of invasion and the thrill of MacArthur's success at Inchon, the American public was kept informed by official communiqués and by reporters. Joseph Stalin was making a bold attempt to gain an Asian satellite and the Red Chinese were ready to back up the North Koreans;

the specter of world Communism was great. American boys were giving their lives to stop its spread into South Korea.

But beneath the obvious were other considerations. General MacArthur's relationship with his government, the use of American land forces in Asia, the "discouraging" of stories describing low morale and poor equipment, the concept of a "police action"—the public became aware of these questions and its main source of satisfaction was to be the reporter in the foxhole. Often the truth was unpleasant and gained at the risk of the correspondent's life. In the excitement and confusion of June and July 1950, the early dark days of the Korean War, the public took these efforts for granted. They are recounted here because the correspondents were forgotten along with the war, except by the South Koreans—who dedicated a war memorial near the truce line to all correspondents who died covering the 1950–53 fighting.

FROM NIGHTCLUBS TO FOXHOLES

Jack James was disappointed when he awoke at 7:00 A.M., Sunday, June 25, 1950. It was raining in Seoul, and the United Press bureau chief had planned on a picnic. Heading for the office to finish a story, he discovered his raincoat missing. Now he had to stop and look for it at the United States Embassy. At that moment 150 Russian-built T-34 tanks moved south on a 150-mile front from the Yellow Sea to the Sea of Japan, supporting North Korean infantrymen who had moved across the 38th Parallel at 4:00 A.M. following a coordinated artillery and mortar barrage. The total Communist force numbered 90,000 men and included seven infantry divisions, an armored brigade, and other independent units, as well as uncounted guerrillas.[21]

As he ran up the embassy steps, James was startled when an Army intelligence officer asked him, "What have you heard from the border?" Murmuring something in reply, James asked the officer what he knew, which turned out to be the skimpy but shocking news that North Koreans had crossed the 38th Parallel. By 9:30 A.M., about the time Kaesong had been captured, James had put together enough details to substantiate his story, and by 11:00 A.M. the exclusive dispatch had circled the world and was being broadcast from Manila to South Korean newspapers.[22] James's story was the only one filed in time to make the Sunday deadline in the eastern United States, and the United Press claimed a two-hour world beat over its opposition.[23] This was a follow-up lead:

Seoul, Korea, Sunday, June 25—The Russian-sponsored North Korean

Communists invaded the American-supported Republic of South Korea today and their radio followed it up by broadcasting a declaration of war.

The attacks started at dawn. The Northern Pyongyang Radio broadcast a declaration of war at 11 a.m. (9 p.m. Eastern Daylight Time Saturday).

North Korean forces attacked generally along the border, but chiefly in the eastern and western areas, in heavy rain after mortar and artillery bombardments which started at 4 a.m. (2 p.m. Eastern Daylight Time Saturday). They were reported two and a half miles inside South Korea at some points.[24]

Radio broke the news to the American people on Saturday evening, just as it had told first of Pearl Harbor. All networks stopped regular programing to carry the war bulletins. Robert P. Martin, stringing for CBS, was heard shortly after the first news of the attack, and he broadcast several more times during the first week. (A "stringer" is a journalist who works part-time for one or more organizations on a fee-per-story basis.) George Thomas Folster was there for NBC; Mutual was represented by a stringer; and John Rich of International News Service was the ABC stringer in Tokyo.[25] But because of the scarcity of personnel and the lack of a transmitter in Korea, much of the early broadcast work had to be done from Tokyo. Radio was unable to provide the full story, leaving that to the nation's newspapers. The emphasis here is on print journalism, where a handful of correspondents were permanently stationed in the battle zone and provided continuous coverage.

During those first hours the wire service chiefs went into action. The "palace guard" (as Marguerite Higgins called the men who were allowed to travel with General MacArthur)—Tokyo bureau chiefs Earnest Hoberecht of the United Press, Russ Brines of the Associated Press, Howard Handleman of International News Service, and Roy McCartney of Reuter's—dispatched reporters to the front and called for reinforcements. Jack James of UP in Seoul already had sent one of his Korean staffers, George Suh, to the forward battle area, and Rutherford Poats flew to the Itazuke (Japan) air base, seeking a free ride. In a few days Peter Kalischer, a seasoned reporter at age 35, would arrive in Korea with the first contingent of American troops, and manager Hoberecht flew in and out with MacArthur. Bob Miller was called from Formosa to assist. Hoberecht was the first applicant for radio-teletype facilities at the Japanese Ministry of Communications. Soon the Tokyo UP office was hooked up with its wireless receiving station at Moraga, California, near San Francisco, which relayed news to New York.[26]

O. H. P. King became the AP's representative at the front during the first days, along with Tom Lambert and Charles P. Gorry, who was a photographer as well as a writer. William Jordan assisted Russ Brines in Tokyo, and William Moore of the Hong Kong bureau was one of those summoned to Korea. Y. H. Lee was the INS resident correspondent in Seoul and Ray Richards joined the action during the first week.[27] Reuters reporters in Tokyo were Roy McCartney and J. E. Wilson. A stringer handled everything until McCartney could fly in with MacArthur. Lionel Hudson then took over the Tokyo office.[28]

Walter Simmons of the *Chicago Tribune* was the only regular newspaper correspondent in Korea when the attack occurred. The others, including the only woman correspondent, Marguerite Higgins of the *New York Herald Tribune*, Lindesay Parrott and Burton Crane of the *New York Times*, Keyes Beech of the *Chicago Daily News*, and Gordon Walker of the *Christian Science Monitor* were elsewhere, most of them in Tokyo. Some American correspondents tried to fly into Korea later on June 25 after U.S. military observers had flown across, but their transport was called back when enemy planes strafed Kimpo airfield in Seoul.[29]

Simmons had gone to Seoul for the opening of the South Korean national assembly, was present when John Foster Dulles spoke, and had stayed there for a few extra days. His account in the *Tribune* on June 26 was the first from someone other than a wire-service reporter. In his story he called the fighting a "civil war."

Uijongbu, South Korea, June 26 (Monday)—This is how the Korean civil war looks in the muddy rice fields and the slippery mountains where it is being fought:

Two divisions of khaki-clad infantry are pushing north this morning to regain the ground they lost yesterday. Every kind of transport is being used, from modern American trucks to ancient Japanese buses and taxicabs.

The road from Seoul, 12 miles to the south, is choked with a motley array of vehicles, some broken down. A trainload of troops has just pulled in.

Two Russian built North Korean tanks clanked 25 miles yesterday and almost overran this grimy village on the main invasion route. Twenty more Red tanks are approaching today, but the enemy has not moved up his infantry.

More than 60,000 refugees spent the night plodding thru the rain toward Seoul . . . a handful of American military advisers is unshaven and exhausted after a sleepless night. Each of them had at least one close brush with death yesterday.

Lt. John Airsman of Peoria, Ill., was trapped at Pochon, nine miles south of the border, when tanks overran the defense positions. He slammed his jeep into a flooded rice paddy and managed to escape, covered with mud, by a side road . . .

The confused fighting had scenes of both bravery and cowardice. One company stood off an enemy regiment for 5-1/2 hours. Other troops ran in the face of the tanks. Capt. Lowry chased one anti-tank crew a mile and a half, turned it around and put it back into the battle.[30]

The Communists smashed the Uijongpu defense line early on June 27 and moved toward Seoul. Correspondents in Tokyo fumed at being denied transportation to the front, complained of a "virtual press blackout," and relied on telephone calls to Seoul instead of the Tokyo headquarters for basic information.[31] At the front George Suh of United Press had a front-row seat. He wrote of the South Korean counterattack that temporarily gave hope that the drive toward Seoul could be halted,[32] but a few hours later Walter Simmons sent a message that the Rhee government and the assembly had fled to Suwon, 20 miles to the south.[33]

Marguerite Higgins, Keyes Beech, Burton Crane, and Frank Gibney of *Time* flew into the heart of the fighting zone under jet fighter cover on the 27th. Landing at Kimpo field in an evacuation plane (there had been approximately 2,000 Americans in Korea, most of them civilians), they saw two planes in flames and abandoned Buicks, Dodges, and jeeps. They headed for Seoul, moving against the heavy refugee traffic going south. Locating Col. Sterling Wright, the head of the American advisory force, they learned that he had been vacationing in Japan during the first attack and that the old commander, Brig. Gen. Roberts, had been on his way to the United States. It had been a total surprise.

During the night of June 27 the Communists broke through South Korean lines and plunged into Seoul. Awakened by Col. Wright's aide, Marguerite Higgins joined a quickly assembled convoy of 60 jeeps, trucks, and weapons carriers headed for Suwon. The Americans were forced to abandon their equipment when jittery South Koreans prematurely blew up the only bridge across the Han River but were ferried across while being harassed by "steady but inaccurate rifle fire."[34] Crane, Beech, and Gibney escaped death only by the closest of margins. Their jeep was 25 yards from the blast that demolished the bridge filled with bumper-to-bumper traffic. They were protected by a large truck filled with South Korean soldiers, all of whom died, but the windshield was blown into Crane's face and the jeep was rolled backward. Gibney also was cut about the head, but Keyes was unhurt and led them away from the wreckage. In all, several hundred Koreans were killed because of a tragic mistake.[35] Keyes Beech, 36 and in his third year in Asia, told it best for Chicago readers:

Suwon, Korea—I have a feeling that I have just witnessed the beginning of World War III.

As I write this from the edge of a friendly airstrip, an American fighter plane is burning on the field, a victim of the strafing Russian Yaks presumably flown by North Koreans.

Yaks and American twin-fuselaged F-82 Mustangs were dog-fighting overhead less than a half-hour ago. Six American B-26's just passed overhead bound for targets in the vicinity of Seoul, 20 miles north of here.

A Korean wept and kissed my hand as they passed.

Forty to fifty Americans planes will be in action before the day is over. Our pilots say the Yaks are getting faster and better all the time.

If I need any reminder that we are at war, I have only to look at the bandaged heads of two of my colleagues, Burton Crane of the *New York Times* and Frank Gibney of *Time* magazine.

A bridge blew up in our faces at 2:30 this morning Korean time. We were attempting to escape by jeep from Seoul as it was falling to Communist forces that were spearheaded by tanks . . . Crane was bleeding so badly that I went back to the jeep to get a pack so we could fashion a tourniquet.[36]

Praising the fighting of the South Koreans, Beech said three factors led to their retreat: the total surprise, which he laid at the feet of intelligence officers; the Communist tanks; and the Communist air power. It later was demonstrated that the South Koreans had not been given tanks and jet aircraft because of a fear that the belligerent old Syngman Rhee would carry out an often-voiced threat to invade the north.[37]

Crane, Beech, and Higgins flew to Itazuke Air Force Base in Japan, the forward headquarters for the Korean operation, to file their stories. Maurice Chanteloup, the Agence France-Presse reporter, wrote on June 28 that he was the only Caucasian reporter in Seoul. Soon afterwards all communication with the capital ceased.

Meanwhile, on the same day Walter Simmons of the *Tribune*, Peter Kalischer of UP, and U.S. Ambassador John J. Muccio narrowly escaped when Red planes strafed the Suwon airstrip. Simmons wrote that Muccio was riding alone in a jeep when the jets came in for their run. Bystanders yelled at him to stop but he did so only after bullets splattered in front of him. Muccio hid in a rice paddy with Simmons and Kalischer while the Communist planes roared over the field for 20 minutes. A fully loaded B-26 bomber parked 100 yards from the trio was not hit.[38]

It had been apparent on Tuesday, the 27th, that the South Koreans would not be able to stop the invaders, and in Washington President Truman was faced with a decision some said was as eventful as his order to drop the A-Bomb on Japan. He ordered American air and naval units to fight the North Koreans, opening the way for total U.S. support and United Nations action. Drew Pearson got the major beat on this announcement, broadcasting the news 66 minutes before it was official. His story was read over ABC by Gordon Fraser. At 12:06 P.M. the networks carried the official announcement.[39]

The decision broadened the concept of presidential authority and was referred to in future crises. Truman's decision earned him the grudging respect of his bitter Republican opponents and gave Gen. Douglas MacArthur the green light to plan the inevitable counterattack. Later in the day the U.N. Security Council backed the U.S. decision and voted to fight. MacArthur first thought of the Inchon landing on June 29, when he flew into Korea for quick inspection. The enemy supply lines were being lengthened daily and could easily be cut, and the added attraction was the psychological lift the recapture of Seoul would provide.[40] Marguerite Higgins knelt by the *Bataan*, the general's famous plane, and typed a story the day he first visited the front. And to her surprise she was given a free ride back to Tokyo and an exclusive interview, which enraged the "palace guard," who she said considered MacArthur their personal property on trips.[41] Sassy and bright, Higgins, then 29, was controversial throughout her career, because she often was the only woman there but also because she could be as abrasive and opinionated as her male competitors. Both Higgins and Beech reported that MacArthur's visit ended the panic and boosted the morale of the Korean troops and U.S. military advisers. "It is plain we are not abandoning South Korea,"[42] Beech wrote, and Higgins added, "News of MacArthur's presence spread like wild-fire among the South Korean troops and more than any other event furnished proof that America is backing South Korea to the hilt."[43]

Walter Simmons of the *Chicago Tribune* sat on that dusty airstrip also but he emphasized MacArthur's action in "wiping out the 38th Parallel," which Simmons said would give the South Koreans a chance to win all of the north and would give the Russians their first setback in Asia.[44] For the first time newspaper accounts from Korea contained some optimism, but that lasted only a few hours. Suwon, with its tiny airstrip, was the next objective of the enemy force moving toward Taejon, the key communications city on the road to Pusan, the southern supply port at the tip of Korea.

Marguerite Higgins, Keyes Beech, Tom Lambert of the Associated Press, and Gordon Walker of the *Christian Science Monitor* were forced together there on June 30. Beech and Lambert became heroes early in the day by rescuing a jet fighter pilot whose plane had crashed near the airport. They drove their jeep across several fields to pick up Lt. Edwin T. Johnson of Seattle after seeing his plane go down in flames.[45] But that was forgotten later in the evening when the word spread that the Reds had made another breakthrough and surrounded the camp. The correspondents and about 50 others armed themselves with carbines. When the panic had subsided it was discovered that a road was open to Taejon and the Americans hurried in that direction, but it was three more days before the enemy actually took the Suwon airstrip. Not only were mistakes made in judgment, but physical errors hurt as well. Peter Kalischer of UP came across a South Korean convoy which had been strafed by American planes and then saw an ammunition train "in full eruption."[46] Beech said the disorganized retreat from Suwon was "unnecessary and undignified" and that he would always remember it "with distaste."[47]

THE FIRST AMERICAN TROOPS FLY INTO KOREA

The first American troops were flown to Pusan on July 1, 1950. The two rifle companies of the Twenty-first Infantry Regiment, Twenty-fourth Division, were commanded by Lt. Col. Charles B. Smith of the regiment's First Battalion. The men arrived in Taejon by train on July 2, and two days later Maj. Gen. William F. Dean set up his command headquarters.[48] The United Press reported from the front that the Americans had taken up defensive positions about 25 miles north of Taejon and that South Koreans were digging in along the Kum River line.[49] For the next dozen days the fighting would be scattered across that area north of Taejon.

Roy McCartney of Reuters, Carl Mydans, the famed *Time-Life* photographer, and Marguerite Higgins were on the front line on July 5, the first day Americans went into battle. Enemy tanks roared across the distant fields and the green U.S. bazooka teams were told to attack. The first tank opened up and enemy soldiers leaped off it into action. Then in her binoculars Marguerite Higgins saw the first American death of the Korean War. A head poked up from the grass—Pvt. Kenneth Shadrick of Skin Fork, West Virginia, had fired at the lead tank and looked up to see if he had scored a hit. A machine-gun bullet from the tank struck him in the chest. Reflecting the confusion on the home front, Kenneth Shadrick's father said, "He was fighting against some kind of government." Shadrick was 19 years old.[50] As the tanks moved forward, shocked American officers and correspondents began to move out. "My God," said Mydans as he saw the bazooka teams retreating toward him, "They look as if the ballgame was over and it's time to go home." Later, after Pvt. Shadrick's body was carried to a small shack, a medical officer glanced down and said, "What a place to die."[51] Before the fighting ended in July 1953 with a truce, 33,629 Americans had died in Korea, along with at least 1,263 U.N. troops. Republic of Korea casualties (dead, wounded, missing, prisoners) totaled about 1,300,000, with a million of these being civilians. The United Nations estimated North Korean civilian casualties at about one million, North Korean combat casualties near 520,000, and Chinese Communist losses at 900,000.[52] It all began on the retreat from Seoul.

Keyes Beech, who had been in Tokyo temporarily, rejoined the others at this point and the five, including Higgins, McCartney, Mydans, and Lambert, traveled together. Oddly enough, Higgins also was covering for the *London News Chronicle* and Beech for the *London Evening Standard*— and Roy McCartney was receiving regular bylines in the *London Star*. The practice of American readers learning from British correspondents had been reversed. Even so, a flock of experienced British correspondents traveled in Korea, some with WWII experience.[53]

The main difficulty faced by any reporter was filing the dispatch. One telephone connected the correspondents and their Tokyo offices after the retreat from Suwon. It was in the United States Information Service office in Taejon, and Marguerite Higgins and Tom Lambert were directed to it by Ambassador Muccio. Because of the crush of writers demanding to use it, their stories were hastily conceived and dashed off often without being typed out.[54] During the rest of July the only direct outlet was the single Army radio-telephone circuit shared by the Army, the U.N. Commission, and the correspondents, with the writers taking turns and sometimes being limited to three minutes per call. Since the military and the United Nations had priority, it was not unusual for a vivid front-line dispatch to be delayed up to 24 hours.[55] In addition, because of the different deadlines back in the United States, it was hard for some correspondents to break away from the action and make it back to the communications headquarters.

Keyes Beech, who wrote for the afternoon *Daily News*, could wait for hours to update a story, but Marguerite Higgins and the other morning-newspaper writers had to file early, as of course did the wire-service reporters. There was a 14-hour difference between Korea and New York. In addition a communications-room rule of "no substitutions" hampered all filers. This meant that once copy was placed in the basket it could not be removed for insertions or updating. If it were taken out, it had to be placed on the bottom.[56]

Marguerite Higgins spoke for all the correspondents later when she wrote that "never once during the Korean war have I been satisfied with the writing and organization of a single story. I know all of us in the beginning kept thinking, 'Well, next time maybe there will be more of a chance to think it through,' or 'Next time I won't be so tired.'"[57] In expressing her frustration, Higgins spoke not only for her Korean era colleagues but for every correspondent of merit mentioned in this book. The reading public has little knowlege and thus no appreciation of the degree of perfectionism to which many carry their stories, photographs, or video packages. Journalists can be arrogant, demanding, and absolutely unreasonable, but some of this is due to the pressure—a good deal of it self-imposed—to turn in that "A" story every time.

TENSIONS BETWEEN MACARTHUR AND THE PRESS

The constant arguing with military officers over the rights of correspondents hampered effective coverage almost as much as the lack of facilities. MacArthur had held himself aloof from the writers throughout his stay in Tokyo; there had been frequent misunderstandings. Now in Korea his policy, as announced by his controversial press officer Col. M. P. Echols, was that there would be no censorship. All correspondents merely were asked to prevent the North Koreans from gaining "strategic or helpful information."[58] This censorship was voluntary. The *Chicago Sun-Times* gained praise from MacArthur for an editorial supporting such a policy, the general calling military censorship "unrealistic" and "ineffective."[59] But while there was no censorship imposed on material written or broadcast by correspondents, there was strict control at the news source. A memorandum sent by Secretary of Defense Louis Johnson outlined these regulations on July 13. Nonreleasable items included such obvious things as "status of equipment," "strength of unit," etc.[60] It was the interpretation of these regulations that prompted many arguments between tired, anxious correspondents and tough press officers. Some correspondents claimed that the daily official communiqués had been "both meager and inaccurate," and Col. Echols rebuked part of the press corps for "lack of decency, honesty and regard for procedure." Fifteen regular correspondents filed from Taejon in the first week of the war.[61]

To assist the media the Armed Services information offices combined in the United States. The Radio Division provided broadcasts for radio and television stations and the Pictorial Division supplied photos and maps (the Army Signal Corps transmitted photos from Tokyo to San Francisco for the war photographers). The Press Division handled hundreds of inquiries and two daily briefings were held for some 80 reporters in Secretary

Johnson's office. But all of this was irrelevant to the reporter in front of the press officer's desk in Taejon, asking questions about a particular retreat, poor morale, or lack of equipment. Homer Bigart of the *Herald Tribune*, who to Marguerite Higgins's displeasure was to arrive at the front shortly, reported one serious argument in Tokyo on July 3. MacArthur threatened to enforce regular censorship unless correspondents held to the voluntary guidelines. Apparently several stories had referred to specific units, bases, and departure times.[62]

Later Tom Lambert of the AP and Peter Kalischer of UP were barred from the front on the grounds that they had given "aid and comfort to the enemy" in writing about an Army battalion dubbed "the lost battalion" because of confusion about its status and its high casualty count. Many U.S. papers used the phrase. The writers were reinstated by MacArthur after protests from Russ Brines and Earnest Hoberecht. MacArthur claimed the psychological factor was highly important and that these stories reflected great disillusionment among U.S. troops.[63] The stories were true, of course, and truth won this battle. Eighth Army Comdr. Gen. Walton H. Walker sent Marguerite Higgins to Tokyo, for being a woman, but MacArthur sent her right back. This sidelight drew nationwide attention and won "Maggie" praise from all quarters, except from Homer Bigart, her colleague, with whom she feuded throughout their joint coverage for the *Herald Tribune*.

Beech claimed that except for one memorable occasion Bigart and Higgins spoke to one another only once during the war. They were near the front lines with Beech and other reporters when suddenly a *New York Times* reporter left to file his story. It was unclear whether Higgins or Bigart should return with their competitor. Finally, Beech offered to ask Bigart to speak with Higgins. They did so, briefly, in the middle of a road. "I always felt that a plaque should be erected on the spot suitably inscribed: 'Homer and Maggie spoke here.'"[64] Antoinette May, Higgins's biographer, later wrote, "Homer may have been a great correspondent and a fine writer but he was not a very good judge of character, at least where Maggie was concerned. A sweet approach could work wonders, but attempted intimidation merely set off that fierce competitive instinct. Homer's prestige added to the challenge. She wasn't about to let him get ahead of her."[65]

Years later Whitelaw Reid, son of the former *Herald Tribune* publishers Ogden Reid and Helen Rogers Reid, commented about Higgins's personality traits:

> My recollection is that Marquerite did a very competent job in Berlin. She covered the news with a kind of single mindedness and determination. These were the characteristics . . . that I think contributed to her success . . . In the case of the Far East she became increasingly aggres-

sive, and the kind of competition she gave her contemporaries was exceedingly tough. Homer Bigart, who had been our star correspondent on almost every front, was placed in a cruel dilemma. He had been sticking his neck out . . . for several years. All of a sudden a woman appeared on the scene ready to finagle and maneuver and stick her neck out even a little further. I am afraid he was driven up the wall by her. Her willingness to sleep on the docks with the troops and seek no privileges as a woman was impressive. She had grit and courage and an ability to get her way.[66]

Bigart was there when the first two correspondents were killed on July 10. He, Ray Richards of International News Service, and Cpl. Ernie Peeler of *Pacific Stars and Stripes* were with a small American force overrun by North Koreans. Richards and Peeler were cut down trying to run from the area. That day other Americans were dragged from their jeeps and murdered.[67] Ironically, Richards's last story in the Hearst newspapers described how the "lost battalion" had faced ten-to-one odds in rejoining its regiment near Chonan.[68] Richards, 56, had gotten his first big assignment covering Gen. John Pershing's expedition against Pancho Villa, while Corporal Peeler had alternated for 20 years between the Army and a San Bernardino, California, newspaper. Within a month four others would be dead, several wounded, two missing, and one captured, and by September the death toll of correspondents would be 11.[69]

By far the most important photographs, the most striking portrayals of the opening of war, were taken by *Life* photographer David Douglas Duncan, who was there from the beginning. Duncan's full-page shot of leather-jacketed Douglas MacArthur, standing by his plane on the lonely Suwon airstrip, along with other photos of retreating South Koreans, burning airplanes, and victorious young U.S. jet pilots, were featured in the July 10 issue. He told millions of readers:

> We roared into a full-throttle landing at the airfield in southwestern Japan, where the U.S. was operating its shuttle service of rescue planes and jet fighters across the straits to Korea. Two F-80 jet pilots screamed in behind us with minutes to go before their fuel would be gone.
>
> As we stepped off the plane, two more F-80s whistled down from nowhere, then flashed over in double rolls—a symbol of combat victory. I couldn't believe it. Either these pilots were hot-rod jockeys with jets, or else we Americans were again directly involved in a killing war and these had just killed.[70]

The following week Duncan became the first war photographer to carry his camera along on a jet-fighter strike and take pictures at 600 miles per hour, offering a memorable account of "the earth and sky, life and death" and photos of the destruction of an ammunition truck.[71]

During the first two weeks of the fighting the American reader had received a clear picture of the confusion and shock that complicated efforts to halt the invaders before they rolled all the way to Pusan. Without exception the frontline dispatches underlined the bitterness of the fighting. The ambushes, desperate jeep rides along side roads to escape enemy tanks, the overrunning of U.S. and South Korean outposts, and the seizure of vital airstrips all were described in vivid detail. While writing of acts of unparalleled heroism, the correspondents had not neglected to point at the gross mental and physical unpreparedness of American troops. This became more apparent during the next several weeks as the retreat continued. Marguerite Higgins described the confusion on July 9:

> During the fighting yesterday American observers in the frontline had a first-hand experience of the dangers of this infiltration. At least twice a group of white-clad Koreans was seen disappearing into buildings within American lines. Minutes later they emerged either in the mustard-colored uniform of North Korean soldiers or with weapons in their hands. They joined in sniper attacks on the American troops who were lined up along a road.[72]

And Keyes Beech interviewed two young soldiers who had played a game many were forced to play in order to survive:

> When the order came to retreat we started down the reverse side of the hill. We were under fire all the time. Sometimes we lay in the rice paddies and played dead until they stopped firing. When we stood up to run they opened up on us again. We ran, crawled and played dead some more.[73]

REPORTING FROM HELL: THE DEFENSE OF TAEJON

"We desperately needed the six days between July 12 and 18 and General Dean and his men won them for us."[74] That was General MacArthur's tribute to Maj. Gen. William F. Dean, commander of the Twenty-fourth Infantry Division, who stood between the Communists and a march to the southeastern coast. The main American forces fell back across the Kum River line north of Taejon on June 12. The "wide stream" was the last natural barrier faced by the North Koreans, but MacArthur's forces moved southward to avoid further envelopment by the enemy. Hanson Baldwin, military writer of the *New York Times*, said simply that heavy sacrifices were being made by the few because the bulk of the American forces had to be held in defense of the Pusan area. United Press frontline dispatches pictured the front as a "slaughterhouse." One company, which boasted 148 men when it left Japan, numbered 30 when it straggled to temporary safety.[75]

"You don't fight two tank-equipped divisions with .30-caliber carbines. I never saw such a damned useless war in my life," a weary GI told an Associated Press writer.[76] The strain of fighting a delaying action was proving too great for some U.S. troops. Many were dispirited, and the word that elements of the First Cavalry Division and the Twenty-fifth Infantry would soon be in Korea barely cheered them. Nevertheless the example of American field-grade officers, who daily risked their lives in close combat action, kept the American forces in order.

The Communists crossed the Kum River early on July 15 after being hurled back in spots on the previous two days and being pounded by U.S. aircraft. Marguerite Higgins wrote:

> With American forces in Korea, Saturday July 15—North Korean Communist infantry disguised in captured American fatigue uniforms crossed the Kum River toward dawn today and made a lodgment in the center of the American defense positions on the south side of the river.[77]

Charles Rosecrans Jr., the International News Service writer-photographer, wrote the evening before of South Koreans pulling out of Taejon. A Communist rumor campaign that the city was about to be captured spurred the mass exodus, Rosecrans reported, and the constant roar of artillery into Communist lines did little to pacify the civilians.[78] John Rich of INS noted the success of U.S. pilots in harassing the Communist river crossing. One pilot bragged, "When I gave them a burst they started to run. That was the worst thing they could have done. When they ran my buddies came in behind me and shot them down like rabbits."[79]

The pilots were having the only real success, though, and two days later the Communist breakthrough was complete, as reported by UP's Robert Miller from the very front positions:

> With the U.S. Forces in Korea (UP)—The Communists came by the thousands in fanatical, screaming waves. Right into American foxholes and beyond.
>
> American artillery was fired at point-blank range as fast as it could be loaded, but it couldn't stop them for long.
>
> Neither could U.S. machine gunners who piled up Communist bodies like cordwood in front of their guns.

For every one killed, 10 took his place. And still they came.

An aid station was enveloped. The North Koreans killed all the wounded—and the Chaplain who stayed behind to comfort the men.[80]

The sheer horror of the war was coming home with the story of Communist suicide charges. Later in the war, after the Chinese Communists entered, these stories would be commonplace and expected by Americans.[81] But not in mid-July. Later, also, the murdering of prisoners would be written about frequently, but this bitter news was especially hard to report at the beginning. Marguerite Higgins told the home front of the Catholic chaplain who insisted that a Protestant colleague and a Medical Service Corps chaplain escape while there was still time: "The Communist guerrillas went after the patients with their rifles, shooting them in the side," Captain Buttery said. "As I escaped over the hill I saw the chaplain shot."[82]

Father Hermann Feldhoelter was kneeling by one of the stretchers and made no sound as he fell. The massacre occurred after the litter patients had been carried across rough terrain under sniper fire. When the firing got too heavy the three chaplains told the able-bodied to escape, and then Father Feldhoelter persuaded his friends to leave also. The ruthlessness of the North Koreans only served to stiffen American determination to retaliate, however, and the correspondents aided this effort through their dispatches, which often were written after they themselves had left a contested area.

Enemy tanks rushing the Taejon defenses got a surprise on July 20, when Americans used their new 3.5-inch rocket launchers against them, destroying eight of the Russian-built vehicles. Again the success was short-lived, because the Communist frontal attack broke down U.S. defenses and an enveloping force raised havoc in the American rear area. Quentin Pope, who had joined Walter Simmons to cover for the *Chicago Tribune*, learned what it was like from a lucky man:

> Around a curve two miles down the road I ran into a road block and we began to receive fire. Soon one sergeant got hit and I got a bullet in the knee. . . he reached up from the ground and started the jeep running, then we both hopped aboard and raced down the road under fire from a hillside . . . the Reds hit the jeep tires and we had to give up . . . started out with another jeep and this time got way behind the road block when our engine was knocked out. Again we made it back and tried in an ambulance, which also was smashed by North Korean fire.[83]

The young soldier's experience was multiplied in Lionel Hudson's dispatch for Reuters:

> American troops, withdrawing from burning Taejon at dusk after a

bloody day-long street battle, ran a murderous gauntlet of flame and bullets as they fought their way to the east.

When the Americans, remnants of the 34th Infantry Regiment, which had fought almost continuously for two weeks—found their lines untenable and tried to withdraw, the Communists lighted searing fires along their escape road and concentrated heavy sniper and automatic fire.

Houses were set ablaze on both sides so that the vehicles would have to pass thru a wall of flames fanned by a strong wind.[84]

In the flaming ruins of Taejon was INS reporter Philip Deane (whose real name was Mike Gigantis), who also was covering the war for the *London Observer* and Radio Athens. A native-born Greek, he had been hired by INS when hostilities broke out. Deane saw Gen. William F. Dean, immaculate in battle dress, directing bazooka fire against tanks not fifty yards away.[85] General Dean, wounded in the street fighting and one of the last to leave the city, wandered in the countryside for several days before being captured. Philip Deane suffered the same fate, being shot while trying to rescue several wounded Americans from a small hut under enemy fire. Both spent the rest of the war in prison camps. Not so lucky was Wilson Fielder Jr., 33-year-old *Time* and *Life* reporter with the Twenty-fourth Infantry, who was killed by a burst of machine-gun fire as he tried to escape Taejon. His friend Carl Mydans relayed word of his death. Fielder had been chief of *Time*'s Hong Kong bureau but was shifted to Korea a week after the war began.[86]

Homer Bigart and Keyes Beech told the horrifying story of how Communist tanks rumbled through an American convoy parked along both sides of a road near Taejon. The dozing Americans had nothing but carbines and scattered, while the tanks headed into the city. "What we need here is some armor with 90 mm guns," said a veteran of Iwo Jima. "We can lick these guys easy if we just get the equipment."[87] The equipment was coming, if Pusan could be kept open.

Beech called Taejon's capture the Americans' worst defeat. In a gloomy dispatch he said:

> The U.S. Army suffered its worst defeat of the Korean war Thursday.
> Taejon fell to the Reds from North Korea in a thunderous climax to the 15-day-old campaign.
> As trapped American forces attempted to fight their way out of the city explosive flashes could be seen . . .
> Lt. Ralph Vargason of Newark Valley, N.Y. said he saw Dean running the bazooka team before the roof fell in.
> He was doing a good job of it too. I saw him holding a bazooka shell in

each hand. After our guys knocked out that tank I saw him walk up and measure the bore while it was still on fire. He said it was a 75. [88]

It was indeed the worst defeat, something the U.S. public was not used to. General Dean later was awarded the Medal of Honor for trying to hold Taejon with his 4,000 men. But the U.S. troops won the frantic race against time and prevented the fall of Pusan, which would have led to a total withdrawal from Korea. One Communist force almost turned the tide. The North Korean Sixth Division turned west and began to flank the Americans about the time Taejon fell. Moving south, it faced little opposition in taking Kunsan, Chonju, Namwon, and the southeastern cities of Mokpo (where Jack London had begun his Korean journey a half-century before), Posong, Chinju, Yosu, and Kosong, where the drive stopped. Gen. Walton Walker later admitted that if the Communists had headed straight for Pusan he probably could not have stopped them; he said that poor leadership had cost the North Koreans a total victory.[89]

THE FIRST CAVALRY TO THE RESCUE

At this darkest moment for U.S. forces since the early days of World War II, General MacArthur launched his strike at Pohang on Korea's eastern coast, in an effort to cut into the Communist advance. The first amphibious landing since the Pacific campaign of WWII, it won honors for the First Cavalry Division. Twenty-two American newspaper and radio correspondents prepared in Tokyo for this story, among them Homer Bigart, Walter Simmons, Keyes Beech, Gordon Walker, Carl Mydans, and Lindesay Parrott. The landing was 70 miles north of Pusan, on July 18, and the writers were able to cover the recapture of Taejon two days later. The First Cavalry force was sent to blocking positions south and east of Taejon, while the South Korean Third Division managed to hold off the North Korean Fifth Division, which was only 90 miles north of Pusan.[90]

Murray Moler of the United Press came to war with the First Cavalry, and this was his lead:

> Pohang, Korea (UP)—First Cavalry Division troops bounced over rutted, dusty roads on their way to the fighting front Wednesday after the first Allied amphibious landing of the Korean War . . .
>
> The division is headed into the thick of the fighting and the men are eager to get there and to get the job done. The 1st Cavalry liberated Manila and was the first unit to enter Tokyo in World War II.[91]

Bigart wrote from the beachhead:

> In the first amphibious assault landing since World War II, reinforcements came safely ashore this morning at Pohang, a port in southeast Korea, to bring relief to hard-pressed American forces . . .
>
> It was the first cheering news since the Americans began their long retreat down the Korean peninsula two weeks ago.

But he added:

> It was a shoestring operation . . . normally such an operation would require three months' planning. This show was thrown together in ten days. Plans were necessarily haphazard. Only two of the ships assembled by Admiral Doyle were adequately prepared for amphibious landings . . . the landing was unopposed . . . this was fortunate.[92]

Bigart got into trouble with his colleagues, not from his criticism, but because he received an unexpected beat when a carbon of his original story was sent to the telegraph office and filed by the U.S. Public Information Office in Tokyo. The original was held along with the others. When home offices began firing queries, the other writers broke their voluntary censorship and rushed out their stories. The official announcement, a few hours later, did not mention the amphibious landing, but just said the 1st Cavalry was in Korea.

A week prior to this the *New York Times* had published several stories relating to the Chinese Communists, apparently the first dispatches to mention the future enemy. The *Times* said a Chinese Communist division had been landed below American lines on the eastern coast (about where the 1st Cavalry landed) and had been identified by an American intelligence officer with experience in the Chinese civil war. This was discounted by the Pentagon, whose briefing officer conceded that small groups of Chinese might have moved into the area. However, the Hong Kong bureau reported on the same day that three Chinese army groups totaling 200,000 men were reported moving into Manchuria, "according to the best Hong Kong intelligence sources." Quite possibly these were some of the troops who crossed into Korea in mid-October. One other story contained ominous news. Burton Crane, who had been transferred to Formosa, predicted that the Communists would intensify their activities in Vietnam.[93]

Radio teams increased their coverage during this period. Ed Murrow left his CBS evening news show for several weeks in July and August to shuttle between Korea and Japan, along with staffers Bill Downs and Bill Costello. Mutual finally got a regular man there, Robert Stewart, and was taking reports from Walter Simmons and his wife, Edith, and Pat Michaels and Jack

Reed of INS. William Dunn, a World War II veteran, joined George Thomas Folster at NBC. And ABC, still without a regular correspondent, was helped by Jimmy Cannon of the *New York Evening Post*, and John Rich and Ray Falk of INS.[94]

The first television news cameraman in Korea was Charles J. DeSoria of KTTV-TV, Hollywood, who offered coverage on a syndicated basis. Stations signed to use his motion pictures included WPIX, New York; WGN, Chicago; KRON, San Francisco; WWJ, Detroit; and WCON, Atlanta.[95] Television had made a mark when President Truman—the first president to have this opportunity—used the medium to tell of military matters, but for the most part Korea was a print reporter's war, the last of its kind.

A good deal of radio material was provided by the military. Two officers were sent to the front to make radio recordings for the four major networks. They were Army Maj. Wes McPherson and Navy Ens. Jack Siegal, and the offerings included both "hot" and feature material. These were played over voice circuits to San Francisco and then relayed to the East Coast. Some of it later was heard on the popular Defense Department shows, *Time of Defense* (ABC) and *Air Force Hour* (MBS).[96]

News photos were used by television stations to supplement voice broadcasts. "Put vivid realism in your tv news shows" said an advertisement run by Acme Telephoto, whose photos were flashed by wireless to the West Coast.[97] But television was in its infancy (only 16 percent of homes had sets, compared with 95 percent for radio) and documentaries and other films were not part of the media picture until later in the war, 1952 and 1953. The Defense Department did cooperate by setting up a pool for newsreels for all stations willing to share expenses, and the networks began to send their own newsreel cameramen.[98] The networks supplemented the coverage by occasionally flying in correspondents and camera teams—Murrow made two such trips. It should be emphasized, however, that television played a minor role in the U.S. public's debate over the handling of the Korean fighting. In contrast to how such an event would be handled today, when television influences most major governmental decisions, President-elect Dwight Eisenhower fullfilled his 1952 campaign pledge ("If elected I shall go to Korea") without the benefit of cameras. His December visit and return was announced on NBC's *Today* show.

Radio enjoyed a boost because of the war, however, as evidenced by a Hooper poll of July 5–11. Average ratings for news programs went up 63 percent and listening to all programs increased 24 percent over the previous July. NBC offered the most news shows at this time, and that network's increase was 73 percent.[99] This included coverage of the United Nations sessions in New York. One NBC special was its daily *Report from Korea*.[100]

The radio crews were facing the same hardships and voicing the same criticisms as the newspaper and wire service correspondents. They said that background briefings were inadequate and that the military was slow in helping to construct mobile radio units in Korea.[101] Since all news had to be broadcast from Tokyo, and much of it was learned from the general headquarters there, the radio reporters were at a severe disadvantage.

In addition, network officials were hesitant to allow broadcasts critical of the U.S. Command. CBS suppressed a Murrow recording made only seven weeks into the fighting which predicted a long war and questioned whether U.S. reoccupation of South Korea would lessen or increase the attraction of Communism. Cutting against the grain, Murrow was one of the few journalists seemingly concerned about the horrible loss of civilian life and property—in the 1990s dubbed "collateral damage" by the military.

THE FIGHT FOR THE PUSAN PERIMETER

The fight for the deep-water port of Pusan intensified during the final week of July. North Korean Sixth Division troops were moving toward Mansane, 30 miles from Pusan, at the average speed of two miles per hour night and day. They would have been even closer had they not taken a wide circular path around the southwestern tip. The Twenty-fourth Infantry Division was in tough shape, having taken the brunt of the Communist drive down the center through Taejon. These were the facts facing General Walker. But beginning on July 24 other reinforcements began to arrive, until by August 4 American ground combat troops numbered 47,000. There were about 45,000 South Korean troops and about 70,000 enemy troops, although at the time the numerical discrepancy was not known. Later it was discovered that the enemy suffered roughly 58,000 casualties on the drive south, while MacArthur's headquarters was estimating 31,000.[102]

Nevertheless, MacArthur knew that he had at least equal strength and that Americans were guaranteed some mobility in checking the invaders. In addition to the rapidly building reserve forces in Pusun, General Walker was indebted to the Fifth Air Force, whose daily pounding of enemy fortifications stilled many an assault. In fact, Walker later said that, had it not been for this air support, the American forces might have been driven out of Korea, despite the enemy's errors in tactics.[103]

Marguerite Higgins was the only daily "newspaperman" (her term) on the scene when the Twenty-fifth Infantry Division responded to General Walker's "stand or die" order. Walker had visited the front and told his officers, "I am tired of hearing about lines being straightened. There will be no more retreating. Reinforcements are coming, but our soldiers have to be impressed that they must stand or die. If they fall back they will be responsible for the lives of hundreds of Americans. A Dunkerque in Korea would be a terrible blow from which it would be hard to recover."[104] Higgins drove her jeep from Mansan down the valley to Chindongni, where she found the popular regimental commander, Col. John ("Mike") Michaelis, a one-time aide to Gen. Dwight Eisenhower. Harold Martin of the *Saturday Evening Post* was there, but the other regulars, including Higgins's rival Bigart, were in Pusan covering the landing of the first Marine group.

Bigart had tried to get Higgins to leave Korea after his arrival and great jealousy flashed between the two WWII veterans. Higgins, who was a young college student working on the University of California, Berkeley's *Daily Californian* at the war's start, finished it in charge of the *Herald Tribune*'s coverage in Berlin. Hired off the street in 1942, she begged Helen Rogers Reid, the wife of publisher Ogden Reid, for a chance to go overseas. Her coverage of the famed Hartford circus fire in July 1944 gave her a boost, and in August 1944 she was off to see "the big show."[105] She was one of the first reporters to see the horrors of the Dachau concentration camp. Bigart, one of the first to report on the effects of the atomic bomb destruction in Japan, was slightly older but was unable to outfox Higgins. They both took incredible chances. Bigart once wrote: "This correspondent was one of three reporters who saw the action and the only one to get out alive." Not to be outdone, Higgins wrote:

> A reinforced American patrol, accompanied by this correspondent, this afternoon barrelled eight miles deep through enemy territory . . . snipers picked at the road, but the jeep flew faster than the bullets which nicked just in back of the right rear tire.[106]

The night Higgins arrived from Mansan was the first time she became uncontrollably afraid. Communists surrounded the regimental headquarters and bullets cut through the building where the two correspondents hugged the floor. Yet in a few minutes she was administering plasma to a wounded GI and Col. Michaelis was turning defeat into a stiff resistance. That battle was the first of many at Chindongni. The Marines came in, and later the Fifth Regimental Combat Team fresh from Hawaii. One of the key routes to Mansan and Pusan was held.[107]

The correspondent corps continued to receive bad news regarding some of their colleagues. Often finding themselves in danger, many carried weapons—after all, as Fred Sparks of the *Chicago Daily News* once commented, picturing an enemy soldier leaping into his foxhole, "What do I do then? Say to him, '*Chicago Daily News*'?"[108] William R. Moore, a 40-year-old

Associated Press writer who had gained many bylines in U.S. papers with his graphic descriptions of battle, was listed as missing in action after disappearing July 30 near Chinju. And all hope was abandoned for four writers lost at sea when their C-47 transport plane crashed July 27 off Japan's Oshima Island. They were James O. Supple, *Chicago Sun Times*; Maximilien Philonenko, *Agence France-Presse*; Stephen Simmons, *Hilton Press* and *London Picture Post*; and Albert Hinton, *Norfolk* (Va.) *Journal and Guide*. Hinton, 46, associate editor of his paper, was the first black war correspondent casualty in the two world wars or the Korean War.[109]

Nevertheless, other writers continued to be assigned to the front. Among the "stars" were H. D. (Doc) Quigg of UP, who had covered MacArthur's Pacific campaign; Bob Considine of INS, who continued his column "On the Line" and wrote special features, while also broadcasting weekly for NBC; and Frank Conniff of INS, whose language echoed the racism that began for Americans in the days of the Philippine Insurrection:

> The little brown brothers who squander their bullets firing at correspondents are merely one item on the list of occupational hazards. They are only slightly ahead of (one) the insects (two) the dust (three) the primitive sleeping, eating and sanitation arrangements (four) the roads.
>
> It is sheer terror to ride along with a jeep jockey who mistakes a trip to the front for qualifying trials at the Indianapolis 500-mile race. One slip over the road shoulder and the vehicle careens 20 to 30 feet into a ditch while its occupants fly through the air with the greatest of unease.[110]

Homer Bigart could testify to Conniff's description. He escaped serious injury on July 25 when the truck in which he was riding slid down a 30-foot embankment and overturned in a rice paddy. He also reported how a guide shot a Communist soldier who was drawing a short-range bead on a British newsman.[111] But it was Reuters man Roy McCartney, one of the few who had been there since the first shots, who provided the best spot-news description of how it really was:

> The Korean campaign is one of the toughest, most frustrating and mentally worrying that any correspondent was ever called upon to cover . . .
>
> In addition to the physical difficulties of covering the campaign and the filth and disease abounding in the country, there is a responsibility resting almost entirely on the correspondents alone to see that nothing is published which might cost American soldiers their lives.
>
> Ninety per cent of the correspondents in Korea have indicated they would prefer open censorship to General Douglas MacArthur's "unique

experiment" of fighting a war without it . . . correspondents asked a senior officer to impose censorship after he threatened to order one correspondent to Tokyo for "re-orientation" and "warned" two others for alleged breeches of security . . .

They hitchhiked possibly 100 miles daily to the front and back to headquarters, over incredibly rough, dusty roads searching for stories . . .

In the crowded press hut correspondents slept on flea-ridden tables. There was always somebody shouting a story over the weak radio link to Japan . . . stories had to be read by the correspondents themselves in the order which they were submitted to an information officer. This frequently entailed a night-long wait to clear stories gathered during the day . . .

Each man was averaging three or four hours sleep nightly, living on a diet of canned food and heavily chlorinated water.[112]

Rutherford Poats of UP added, "The American beachhead in Korea is today the most completely reported and, for correspondents, the most dangerous battleground in journalistic history.[113] Poats was not exaggerating when he said "most completely reported." By the first week of August MacArthur's headquarters had accredited 280 correspondents, more than 200 of whom were in Korea. Of these 156 were American and 28 were British. Before the war only 27 correspondents were accredited with the Far East Command. Assisting the flow of copy were two radio-teletype machines operated by the Army Signal Corps. Average elapsed time between filing in Korea and delivery in Tokyo was cut to one or two hours, a vast improvement over the 12-to-24-hour waits at Suwon and Taejon.[114] Yet there would be many more bitter complaints against the military.

An embittered Keyes Beech sent a story—with commentary in the style of Jack London—in which he told how "miserably unprepared—spiritually, physically and materially—we were for the Korean war." He described how Americans did not know how to plant mines, park trucks, or maintain communications. Continuing, he said:

> It may be said with some truth that a dispatch like this gives aid and comfort to the enemy.
>
> Certainly it won't give aid and comfort to folks back home.
>
> But this is not the time for Americans to be comfortable. If our experience with World War II means anything, it is better we know now so we can do something about it.
>
> Our one consolation should be that we discovered our inadequacies while we were up against a second-class enemy. Maybe it's a good thing.
>
> Maj. Gen. Bill Dean, commanding general of the 24th Division, was a brave man. Now he's missing and may be dead or captured.

If I know anything about Dean he'd prefer to be dead.

The day before Taejon fell he took one correspondent aside and said worriedly:

"My men won't fight. I know the odds are against us and all that, but they still won't fight. I can't understand it."

One reason they wouldn't fight was that they had poor officers.

There were brilliant exceptions to this generalization. I saw one first lieutenant running a battalion when his commanding officer, a lieutenant colonel, didn't know what to do.

There were brave company commanders and platoon leaders. But they were the exception rather than the rule.

Often as not, when the enemy came close, officers were the first to run. They, like the enlisted men, were unprepared.[115]

MARGUERITE HIGGINS: ALWAYS IN THE LINE OF FIRE

Jumping out of an amphibious craft with a typewriter is quite a maneuver and Marguerite Higgins did it well, into three feet of water along a sea wall in the Inchon harbor. It was September 15, 1950, and Operation CHROMITE, the envelopment of the North Korean divisions, was under way.[116] Seoul would be recaptured in seven days and only 30,000 North Koreans would ever make it back to the north.[117] The prediction of a harassed information officer at Pusan nearly came true, also. He had said, "By the time we start getting some ground back, there'll be a reporter in every rifle squad."[118]

But again tragedy struck the correspondent corps, this time only a week before the invasion. Frank Emery, Charles Rosecrans Jr., and Ken Inouye of INS were among 11 persons killed when a C-54 transport crashed in Japan. Emery, only 23, had been wounded earlier and had spent two weeks recuperating at the home of his boss, Howard Handleman. Rosecrans's stories and pictures of front-line action won him widespread praise. His photos of a U.S. tank crew under fire outside a Communist village were featured in *Life* magazine a month before the crash.[119] Rosecrans, a greatgrandson of the Civil War general, was a World War II correspondent and a favorite of Mrs. MacArthur, who always wanted "Rosy" to take the picture. Phillip Potter of the *Baltimore Sun* arrived and was wounded September when a jeep was ambushed by guerrillas. Bigart also was in the jeep but again escaped injury. Tom Lambert of the AP broke his foot and numerous other incidents were reported. WWII Marine correspondent Jim Lucas, now with the Scripps-Howard papers, was in gear, and the Associated Press was keeping its WWII star Hal Boyle in cigars.[120]

The invasion of Inchon, MacArthur's last great victory, gave everyone a lift. General Walker's forces broke through the perimeter and the rout was on. But the bitterness of those first days would not be forgotten—the flaming bridge over the Han River, the crank-phone to Tokyo, the airstrip at Suwon, the arguments with Colonel Echols. *New York Times* reporter Richard Johnston could not erase the memory of an interview with a young soldier who saw 10 friends murdered by North Koreans: "An 18-year-old farm boy from Walla Walla, Wash. told today how he has passed from boyhood to manhood in three hours," was his lead.[121] Bigart had many escapes but he never forgot the outpost where Ray Richards of INS and Cpl. Ernie Peeler of *Stars and Stripes* died. Keyes Beech and Marguerite Higgins had been shocked severely by the unpreparedness of the first American troops and worried about the nation's ability to fight Communism in Asia—specifically Indochina.

The correspondents had memories of each other, too. There was Walter Simmons muttering about "women correspondents," and Jack Percival, an Australian, telling the others how he pushed a sleeping correspondent and found out he was between Marguerite Higgins and Charolette Knight of *Collier's*. Carl Mydans consoled an unhappy Higgins and encouraged her to stay in Korea after she had been pressured to leave. Beech was remembered as the champion jeep driver for his team of colleagues.

When Jack Burby of UP arrived in Korea he laid down his rules for war coverage, learned the hard way: (1) be scared, (2) be mobile, and (3) play hunches. He was able to tell the story only because he played a hunch one day, crawling away from a mortar observation post overlooking the Naktong River. He got 50 feet away, heard the whine of a shell, and saw the O.P. suffer a direct hit.[122] The "Jones boys" photographic team, Eugene of the *Washington Post* and Charles of the *Washington Times-Herald* (25-year-old twins who also served together in the Marines during World War II), had a difficult time carrying newsreel cameras for NBC television. Always up ahead of the others, they gained a fast reputation but also shrapnel wounds. After three months in Korea they returned to Washington reporting.[123]

Communication problems did not diminish. The Army began moving a mobile transmitting unit of Press Wireless, Inc., from Long Island, New York, to Korea. Correspondents were promised that when installed it would deliver 120 words per minute to San Francisco. In the meantime the United Press had discovered that it was easier to call New York than Tokyo, and a direct call was made to the main bureau desk.[124] Then it was learned that the Pentagon had tied the Press Wireless machine in red tape, and its delivery was held up. As winter approached the Army Signal Corps still controlled the news lines.[125] But one man was able to boast that he conquered the problem, at least once. That was Bob Bennyhoff of UP, who had made friends with the Signal Corps staff. While lying on a hill overlooking the Naktong River on the Pusan perimeter, a Signal Corps man fixed him a special line connected directly with Tokyo. From that remote battle front he gave one of the quickest play-by-play accounts in history. After the fall of Seoul, Bennyhoff stuck with little-publicized Korean units and was rewarded by U.S. advisors by being given permission to use a radio-teletype in a special communications van. It was several days before Bennyhoff raised the suspicions of another correspondent who followed him into the woods and to the vehicle. By that time the other writers were receiving queries from their home editors.[126]

In general the correspondents were unhappy with General MacArthur, and the feeling of distrust was shared by the general. A few months later, in the wake of the disastrous Yalu campaign, the tension caused by press criticisms increased to the point where MacArthur finally, in January 1951, resorted to actual censorship. This changed back to "voluntary" only after President Truman replaced MacArthur with Gen. Matthew Ridgway.

Higgins, Beech, Duncan, Bigart, and the others were to distinguish themselves throughout the rest of the war. Winners of the next Pulitzer Prizes for international reporting were Beech and Sparks of the *Chicago Daily News*; Higgins and Bigart of the *New York Herald Tribune*; and Relman Morin and Don Whitehead of the Associated Press. Higgins was the first woman so honored. Many of his colleagues thought Bigart, known for his tremendous stamina and fair-mindedness, was the best war correspondent of his generation. Duncan would be remembered for his magificent photos of the Marines' Christmas 1950 retreat from North Korea.

The outstanding field coverage for the first months of the campaign had been that of the *New York Herald Tribune*. The one-two punch of Higgins and Bigart, strengthened by their fierce rivalry, gave their readers in the nation's largest city more about the real nature of the Korean War. Beech of the *Daily News* was the tough reporter. Daring, realistic and ingenious, he minced no words in telling the truth about any situation. It was his story from North Korea saying that General MacArthur had ordered an immediate withdrawal that angered MacArthur into considering full censorship. Tireless in the search for interviews, Beech relied on hometown angles more than most of the others—a style appreciated in Chicago. Jimmy Cannon of the *New York Evening* Post also tried this modified Ernie Pyle style.

The most comprehensive coverage was in the *New York Times*. The reports of William H. Lawrence beefed up its Korean reporting. For word-by-word rundowns of Washington decisions and speeches, the *Times* was the leader, but for front-line reporting, the foxhole stories, it often lagged behind.

Of all the reporters of the Korean War, the most controversial was Higgins, the winsome blonde who wrote her first Korean battle story from a jeep, while dressed in a navy-blue skirt and flowered blouse.[127] The next time anyone saw her she was wearing fatigues, including the soft fatigue cap. Her cute smile did not get her the bylines, but many thought so. Keyes Beech spoke out years later about bitter allegations that Higgins had slept her way to fame. "Maggie liked men," he said, "[but] she didn't deliberately sleep with men to get stories. That's a lot of crap."[128] She got them because she could be as tough as the men, if not tougher than most of them, without losing her basic femininity. Later in the war she walked with frozen Americans down a mountain pass under Chinese Communist fire—just to be with the Marines as they made it to safety.[129] Higgins's luck finally ran out in Vietnam. She contracted a rare Asian disease in 1965 and came home to America, where she died in 1966.

ENTER THE CHINESE COMMUNIST ARMY

The war intensified on November 26, 1950, when the Chinese Communist forces launched a full-scale attack on U.N. forces that had pushed far into North Korea. After a disastrous retreat, Seoul fell to the Chinese and North Koreans in January 1951. The capital was retaken a few months later after heavy fighting, truce talks began, and the battle lines stiffened around the 38th Parallel, where it had all begun. Meanwhile the American public was greatly dissatisfied with the progress of the fighting and the thousands of American casualties. This was America's introduction to the concept of "limited war."

Beginning with Vietnam it became fashionable to blame the correspondents when the foreign military adventure did not live up to expectations—when the agony and frustrations produced a backlash. The Korean-era reporters, however, deserved praise for including answers to the "whys" they inserted in many dispatches. Throughout the period they told why Americans had to retreat, why the Army was unprepared, why morale was low, and why this war would be shocking to read about at home. They contrasted the early defeats with the still-remembered victories of 1945 and they demonstrated the need for home support of the troops in the field.

There is no question that when reporting this kind of "damaging" information, the press corps felt an obligation and fought for its rights. The reporters saw themselves as being "on the same team" as the military, as they had in WWII, but this did not prevent honest criticism. Irritated commanders may have questioned reporters' judgments, but they did not impugn their patriotism as officials later did in Vietnam, Central America, and the Middle East.

In addition to this applause for the general field coverage, however, major questions remain about the willingness of U.S. reporters and editors to accept without question the decision to cross the 38th Parallel in 1950 and to risk engagement with the Chinese by approaching their Yalu River territory. One important critic, the legendary I. F. Stone, analyzed this aspect of coverage in detail and concluded that lack of press scrutiny actually lengthened the war and raised the wall around China.[130] The dart here, as usual, should be aimed more at the hometown editors and their Washington bureaus rather than the field reporters, but they should not escape unscathed.

Without a doubt the repressive anti-Communist political atmosphere in the United States precluded the building of any sort of antiwar arguments in the press. The initial invasion by North Korea had created a black-and-white situation. But as the war continued with the Chinese Communist presence—and as casualties mounted at an alarming rate—there were legitimate questions about the worth and validity of the effort. Revisionist historians have put the Korean fighting into the larger context of the Cold War, blaming Western interests for creating conditions for the Korean, Vietnamese, and other conflicts. That discussion, duly noted, is outside the purview of this chapter. Some facts cannot be dismissed, however. It was well known that the South Korean government of Syngman Rhee was horribly corrupt and that his soldiers routinely executed his political opponents. These mass killings continued throughout the war. Yet there were few reports about this in the U.S. press, just as there was little examination of the effects of massive U.S. firepower on the civilian populations on both sides, such as during the recapture of Seoul or the bombing of North Korean cities. MacArthur's imposition of regular censorship was an additional barrier to criticism.

Stone, in Paris on assignment for the *New York Daily Compass*, noted that field reports in French and British newspapers differed from the American versions, in terms of critically analyzing overall strategy and possible future consequences. The British and French journalists felt free to criticize the U.S.-led effort with their traditional skepticism, whereas their U.S. counterparts were bound up in a more rigid system dictated by domestic politics. Stone's experience in trying to find a publisher for his dissident *Hidden History of the Korean War* is an example. Turned down in Great Britain because of growing British support for the war, he went through 26 U.S. publishing turndowns before landing a publishing contract.[131]

There was sharp criticism of the American press corps' overall quality as well. British journalist Reginald Thompson, whose own book *Cry Korea* (1951) described the war as a "political, military and strategic blunder," said of the Yanks: "With American correspondents the quality is so uneven. At the top you get the very best. Below that you get illiterates."[132] In citing Thompson's opinions, British historian Philip Knightley underscored "the racist character of the war, the contemptuous attitude the Americans [speaking here of the military] adopted towards the Koreans, North and South." "'They never spoke of the enemy as though they were people, but as one might speak of apes . . . I don't think it ever occurred to them that these Koreans were men, women and children with homes, loves, hates, aspirations and often very great courage.'"[133] It is not surprising that Knightley said the more detached British correspondents offered better overall coverage than their U.S. colleagues. However, it should be noted that racist attitudes about Asians were not solely an American characteristic—the Yanks had good teachers in the Brits.

For some of these reporters, Korea was the last war they were to cover. Others, like Lucas, Higgins, and Beech, witnessed the buildup to the Vietnam War. In a sense the Korean fighting was an extension of World War II for the reporters. There was a new enemy but the military used the same tactics, and a familiar dogged, do-or-die spirit was prevalent in the dispatches sent home. It cannot be avoided that reporters in the field and the commentators at home failed to report the war as truthfully and accurately as possible—basically not questioning whether the entrance of the Chinese Communists could have been avoided and the war ended much sooner. This obviously is a major criticism of press and government worthy of extended discussion. On a lower, practical and important level, however, journalists in Korea managed to enlarge upon the basic right to report and to demand access, no matter if the news damaged a reputation as great as General MacArthur's or caused disillusionment at home. For that alone they deserve great credit.

David Halberstam succinctly summed up the journalists' experiences in his mammoth history *The Fifties*:

> Unlike Vietnam in the next decade, it [Korean War] did not come back to America live and in color on television. The nation was not yet wired, and Korea, so distant, the names of its towns so alien, did not lend itself to radio coverage, as did the great war that had preceded it. The best reporting in Korea was done by daily journalists, who caught its remarkable drama, heroism and pathos for a nation that largely didn't care and was not at all sure it wanted to pay attention to such grim news. America

tolerated the Korean War when it was on but could not wait to forget it once the war was over. In contrast to World War II and Vietnam, it did not inspire a rich body of novels, plays and even movies. Fittingly enough, the most recent history of the war was entitled *The Forgotten War*, a phrase used originally by General Matthew Ridgway. Some forty years after it had begun, there was no monument to it in Washington.[134]

Chapter Five

Vietnam: The Far-off War We Decided

to Win, 1962–1963

The Associated Press's Pulitzer Prize–winning photographer Horst Faas in the Vietnam jungle, around 1963. AP/Wide World Photos

INTRODUCTION

Prior to the classic battle of Dienbienphu in 1954, few Americans could identify French Indochina. During World War II the area was on the periphery of interest; it was occupied by Japanese, who at war's end surrendered to the British in the south and Chinese Nationalists in the north. No one paid much attention when, on September 2, 1945, the Viet Minh—a combination of Communists and nationalists led by Ho Chi Minh and supported by the United States during the war—declared an independent republic with Hanoi as its capital. That should have been the climax to years of struggle by anti–French Vietnamese—and the end of that particular story. Instead it was the beginning.

The occupying Chinese left the Hanoi region, but conspiring British officials, including Lord Louis Mountbatten, allowed French forces back into the south. The French wanted the new independent state of Vietnam to be part of a French Indochina federation (including Laos and Cambodia) and the French Union. Thwarted in this attempt to control all of Vietnam, they created a separate state in the south, a decision that made inevitable the war which began in November 1946, when French warships shelled Haiphong, killing 6,000 Vietnamese civilians. Determined to maintain a colonial presence dating from the seizure of Saigon in 1859, the French relied on U.S. aid in what was described by conservatives during this period of McCarthyism as a fight to curtail Communist expansion. Outnumbered progressives saw the conflict as a last-ditch effort to preserve parochial French interests. The 1949 Communist victory in China and the Korean War of 1950–53 accelerated fears that, if the Communists won in Vietnam, all of Southeast Asia would fall. President Eisenhower effectively dubbed this possibility the "domino effect."

The Eisenhower administration considered using nuclear weapons and sending U.S. troops to save the French from defeat at the time of Dienbienphu—Vice President Nixon was one strong proponent—but backed off in the face of British reluctance to assist. By this point U.S. taxpayers were covering 80 percent of the war's costs. The French capitulation and withdrawal from the region gave the Vietnamese another chance for unification. An agreement at the 1954 Geneva Conference, signed by the French and the Viet Minh, called for a temporary division at the 17th Parallel and general elections in July 1956. The South Vietnamese refused to go along with the elections; the United States created the SEATO (Southeast Asia Treaty Organization) alliance and placed South Vietnam within its protection. This led to two more decades of war that lasted until April 30, 1975, when North Vietnamese forces captured Saigon and the U.S. ambassador was evacuated by helicopter.

An early turning point for direct U.S. involvement came in 1961, when the new Kennedy administration signed a military and economic treaty with the beleaguered South Vietnamese government of President Ngo Dinh Diem. Diem's government was helpless against an increasing number of assassinations and other terrorist acts aimed at rural officials. Guerrillas in the south established the National Liberation Front (NLF) in 1960. There were only 686 U.S. advisers there that year; President Kennedy raised the number to 3,200. The U.S. Military Assistance Command was formed in 1962, and its strength was 16,300 at the time of Diem's assassination in 1963. U.S. involvement hit its peak in 1969, with 550,000 personnel listed in the Vietnam war zone.

This chapter deals with the crucial period of 1962–63 when a small group of foreign correspondents tried to explain the deteriorating political and military situation, shortly before U.S officials made the decision to plunge into the conflict headfirst. The reporters faced the wrath of U.S. officials in Saigon and Washington, risked danger from South Vietnamese police thugs in Saigon and guerrillas in the Mekong Delta, and suffered from the narrow-mindedness of colleagues at home who saw Vietnam as another Korea or Iwo Jima. It was an entirely different experience, as the nation was to discover during the Lyndon Johnson years. The following examination shows that, whatever their faults, the Americans in Saigon in the early 1960s were eager to report what they perceived to be the truth and were dismayed to discover that not everyone agreed to this practice.

FRANÇOIS SULLY PIERCES THE STRATEGIC HAMLET PROGRAM

Scott Leavitt of *Life* returned to the United States in early 1962 after spending five years as Far Eastern correspondent. During that period he had become acquainted with the leaders and people of South Vietnam. His frank assessment appeared in the March 16, 1962, issue: "The United States is now committed to win a far-off war, to prevent Vietnam from being overrun by the Communist guerrillas of the Viet Cong. Eventual victory over the Communists, the Kennedy administration has made clear, will take skill, stubbornness and, perhaps, 10 years."[1]

At the moment Leavitt was telling of the constant jungle search for Viet Cong hideouts, of a missing American sergeant, and of a little girl found in the ruins of a hut destroyed in an attack on a village. The early figures on U.S. battle deaths were hazy, but Leavitt said that 13 U.S. servicemen had died there already and "inevitably more will die."[2] At this very early stage, when Vietnam was only one of a dozen foreign terms thrown at the American audience by the news media, Leavitt wrote: "But in the end it is the Vietnamese themselves who must beat the Viet Cong. The important element in the U.S. commitment is to see that this is what happens. The stake is high and the undertaking is one of the most delicate and difficult in all American history."[3]

Diem was a problem, Leavitt said, with the possibility of a coup very much alive. He referred to the spectacular 1960 attempt of two South Vietnamese pilots to kill Diem by bombing his palace, an event that very briefly focused attention on Vietnam.[4]

Overall, *Life* was carrying the opinion that would become a common theme: The obstinate Diem must be persuaded to stay out of the tactical war situations and to adopt some ways of restoring public confidence in him so that total victory over the Communists could become a reality. The guerrillas were attacking in force at isolated outposts and melting into the jungle; set battles did not happen in the sodden paddy fields or in the high grass of the plateaus. Meanwhile the NLF continued its murderous campaign against government officials, teachers, and anyone else working for the Diem government.[5] Leavitt's insightful reporting echoed the concerns of colleagues left behind.

One of those was François Sully of *Newsweek*, a witness to the first firefights. Sully was a veteran of harrowing experiences, including being wounded as a teenage member of the underground movement in Paris. Discharged from the French Army in Saigon in 1947, he remained in Indochina to cover that long conflict and the fall of Dienbienphu. When *Newsweek* secured his services in early 1961, he began to dispatch detailed accounts of the growing U.S. commitment. By April of 1962 Sully had developed a theme that would eventually cause him to be driven temporarily from Vietnam by hostile authorities. It was that the Communists had such a head start in the villages that the newly installed "strategic hamlet" concept was doomed to fail. The idea was to physically separate the villagers from the guerrillas by having them live in fortified areas. Sully said it would lead only to frustration for Diem and the U.S. officials pushing it.

One of Sully's dispatches told of My Thuan, a village that for hundreds of years had elected its own group of leaders. But government policy was to ignore the wishes of the peasants, Sully wrote. To his dismay he discovered that the Diem regime considered village leaders "sleepy elders" who could not be counted upon. But the government also could not trust the younger men, so all officials were appointed by the central government, from a building never seen by any of the villagers, some of whom had never traveled more than 10 miles from their huts. As for government protection, in his story Sully said "hundreds of local officials have been killed by the Viet Cong in the past five years."[6]

In My Thuan a 69-year-old chief had been fired by the government once it discovered his son was a NLF officer. Sully found that the villagers, angry with the government's move against the chief, gave more support to the guerrillas in subsequent days. Indeed, the question of how the government could expect to defend the tiny, bamboo-ringed villages was a massive one. More significantly, it was becoming clear to Sully and other reporters at this early date that the people themselves would never be educated to respond favorably to what one Vietnamese farmer called "the whim of a remote government."[7]

In early 1962 Sully was one of the few journalists probing the hamlet program. Later in the year, by which time more than 3,000 hamlets had been constructed, Peter Arnett, of the Associated Press, wrote a major piece describing how a quarter of the population spent each night behind locked gates while Communist guerrillas roamed outside at will, consolidating their power.[8] A few years later a critic looked back at 1962:

> At least two important questions arise as the result of the lavish praise heaped upon the strategic hamlet program by foreign official observers. Most importantly it must be asked whether foreign, and particularly United States, officials were in fact aware of the weaknesses and difficulties which the program faced by the end of 1962. If the officials were not aware of the difficulties . . . it points either to a lack of objective reporting at some level in Vietnam or to an unwillingness by senior officials to face and admit the facts as they were. If, indeed, the officials were aware . . . their wisdom in giving encouraging reports must be questioned now [1965] that the weaknesses of the hamlet program have been revealed, not only by newspaper correspondents but by the South Vietnamese themselves.[9]

While U.S. ambassador to Saigon Frederick E. Nolting Jr., and Gen. Paul D. Harkins worried about the military situation, lower-ranking advisers were becoming more upset with the political side of the war. *Newsweek's* Sully helped answer the question: Why is the Diem government losing the crucial battle of the countryside?

In a dispatch that told of 90 government troops being gunned down from ambush while eating—killed by guerrillas hidden by villagers until after a larger government force had left the area—Sully said:

> The best answer at the moment seems to be that in its efforts to beautify the major towns and provincial capitals with neon lights, kindergartens, Roman Catholic churches, and Confucian memorials, Diem's officials have often overlooked the needs and sensitivies of the villages. One Vietnamese officer recently moved his troops into the village of Long Ngai Thuan, west of Saigon, and found that the wretchedly poor farmers had not seen any government authority in three years. In Thanh Dien, 55 miles northeast of the capital, there is no administration, just a deserted information hall and an office of Diem's National Revolutionary Party with flapping doors and faded government posters peeling off the

walls. In Trung Lap, a town just 3 miles off the main road to Saigon, the only sign of the outside world is an empty, rusty, Nestle condensed milk can on the side of the road. Government officials do not dare to go to Trung Lap but Viet Cong leaflets are pinned to every tree.[10]

Sully wandered through those villages and around Saigon, becoming more disillusioned with the spectacle of farmers being subject to draft labor for the government and being forced to listen to worshipful lectures on the Diem family, when each day that farmer's own physical existence was at stake. Maintaining the pressure, Sully joined with other *Newsweek* writers later in April in cabling information to New York that editors incorporated into a four-page analysis under the headline: "Americans in Vietnam: What Price Victory in the Jungle?"[11]

> There are few more dedicated anti-Communists in the world. Yet, by common consent, Diem is a dictator under whose one-man rule the equally anti-Communist but far more democratic Vietnamese opposition has been intimidated into silence, thrown into "re-education" camps or forced into exile . . . "I am putting loyalty above competence," says Diem when Americans ask why he does not pick the best men to serve Vietnam . . . Many U.S. officials especially military men, are convinced that it can and will [win]. Unable to see any realistic alternative to Diem, they take the public position, don't knock our man . . . he can win.[12]

So fighting moved into the drifting stage and it became obvious to an increasing number of observers, within both the U.S. government and the press ranks, that all of the Special Forces advisers in Fort Bragg, N.C., could not beat the Communists if some reforms were not produced by the central authorities. It was not obvious to those planning policy in Washington. Written into the *Newsweek* account was one of many quotations that in retrospect illustrate why the Saigon press corps became so bitter and unhappy as the Diem regime continued the fruitless hamlet program and the U.S. commitment grew. Roger Hillsman, from his State Department desk, blurted: "I thought it likely before that Diem would beat the Viet Cong, but now, with the new program, I think it will be easy."[13]

As the year dragged on, the news magazines and major newspapers occasionally published brief glimpses of the horrible realities of the situation. The reader needs to know that at this early point television played a minimal role. There were no full-time television correspondents in Saigon, and it would be unfair to criticize the superficiality of the occasional overview reports from roving reporters. Given the limitations, television had little chance to put the situation into perspective. It was almost as difficult for the print reporters. Sully and a few others may have pierced the official lies, but their stories had little if any effect. They were vindicated later when it became apparent that from this very beginning the combination of Communist terror and propaganda and the psychological remoteness of the Diem government reduced the hamlet program's chances for success to close to zero. It was abundantly clear that American policy and grassroot feelings coincided when it came to the desire to stop Communism: Russian, Chinese, or Vietnamese. But while scanning these short reports, anyone truly concerned with the state of the world because of problems in Europe, the Congo, and Latin America should have worried about the next steps to be taken in Vietnam.

There had been many government-originated dodges and denials published prior to 1962 about the U.S. role in Vietnam, but more contradictions began to appear. Sully was involved with one of these happenings in May 1962, when two U.S. Army sergeants were released by the Viet Cong after having been held prisoner 22 days. The men were told by superior officers not to admit they had been given Viet Cong propaganda to bring back and their denial caused the *New York Times* reporter, Homer Bigart, to cable that the men had lied. Sully finally reported that the men had been well cared for and probably had been released for propaganda purposes. They told of being with large groups of guerrillas marching silently through the mountain area and of discussions about U.S. unemployment and missile defenses with the surprisingly well-informed troops.[14]

President Kennedy ordered the Seventh Fleet to land U.S. Marines in Thailand in May 1962, when the Thais became alarmed at the prospect of a Communist invasion from Laos. While the action served only as a temporary show of force, it was one more bit of evidence that U.S. policy aimed at maintaining the security of the entire area. The illusion it created was that fighting had spread across all of Southeast Asia. Headlines in the nation's press were large for a while, but then attention went elsewhere and the only genuine war, the one in Vietnam, continued without fanfare.

Sully wrote of Vietnamese claiming a massive victory, 300 Viet Cong killed, when the next day it was determined only about 20 Viet Cong had been killed and other guerrillas had ambushed and killed 27 government civil guards aboard a train. Three GIs had been wounded by a grenade, guerrillas had raised a flag at former Emperor Bao Dai's old "love nest," and other scattered incidents were reported by the handful of reporters in the country.[15]

THE *NEW YORK TIMES* STANDS ALONE

The only U.S. daily newspaper represented in Vietnam in the early period of American involvement was the *New York Times*. Homer Bigart had switched from the *Herald Tribune* and in late 1960 was sent to Saigon. He was intimately familiar with Vietnam, having first visited there in September of 1945 when Ho Chi Minh declared his land independent of France. He made occasional trips there in the 1950s for the *Herald Tribune* and witnesssed the steady growth of U.S. involvement with the Diem regime. He took the younger members of the Saigon press corps under his protective wing, and they looked to him as a hero. "Everyone looked up to Bigart," the Associated Press's Malcolm Browne recalled. "He was the beau ideal of younger correspondents like myself and Sheehan. He was our only link with World War II and the Korean war. He hated Vietnam, hated the war, hated the bureaucracy and hated the American cant."[16] Bigart left in early July 1962, fed up with the wars that he had been covering since 1943 and particularly the hypocrisy in Vietnam. Jacques Nevard filled in admirably until David Halberstam arrived in September. Many of the *Times* stories and those coming from the wire service and newsmagazine reporters were of bulletin-board nature. But they allowed the perceptive reader a chance to assess the continuing U.S. commitment. Unfortunately, the headlines assigned these items showed the Cold War language that accompanied the majority of the war's activities ("Vietnamese Slay 85 Reds in Attack," *New York Times*, July 21, 1962; "Reds Drive Deeper into South Vietnam," *Los Angeles Times*, April 3, 1972).

Nevard wrote of the helicopter war, which caught the fancy of not only the television cameramen who recorded colorful scenes from high over the Delta, but also the American public, which saw it as an extension of the American frontier days. The tactic was to get a quick response from an isolated outpost under attack, fly to the rescue, then use the helicopters as the main military power because the government troops were not effective or quick enough to catch the enemy in the open. "The operation, described as one of the most successful in recent weeks in this country's grinding war against Communist insurgency, was supported by thirty United States Army and Marine Corps helicopters."[17] A four-column picture showed servicemen guarding five caskets. The U.S. contribution, it was clear, was in blood as well as money and machines.

The most significant story to appear in the *New York Times* during these early days was Homer Bigart's final contribution, written after his departure. It was one of the few stories to be published anywhere, including the newsmagazines, which completely spelled out the increasing misfortunes.

His warnings should have been given strict attention. Instead, as always was the case in Washington, they brought mutterings about the disservice being rendered by the press:

> The United States, by its massive and unqualified support of the regime of President Ngo Dinh Diem, has helped arrest the spread of Communist insurgency in South Vietnam. But victory is remote. The issue remains in doubt because the Vietnamese president seems incapable of winning the loyalty of his people.
>
> From the strict military point of view, the situation has improved. "We are doing a little better than holding our own," was the cautious assessment made a few weeks ago by Maj. Gen. Charles J. Timmes, Chief of the United States Army element of the Military Assistance and Advisory Group . . .
>
> For in 1963 the Republic of South Vietnam will put well-equipped forces totalling more than 350,000 men against 25,000 guerrillas who have no artillery, no anti-aircraft guns, no air power, no jeeps, no prime movers, and only basic infantry weapons . . . they will have more helicopters, armored personnel carriers and other gadgets to enhance mobility, more sentry dogs to sniff out guerrillas, more plastic boats for the Delta region, more American advisers with fresh, new tactical doctrine.[18]

And, as Bigart's story rolled off page one and filled an entire page two, it became clear that the *Times* was offering both a history of the Vietnam conflict and an up-to-date briefing on the slim chances that existed for the success of U.S. policy. He emphasized the failure of President Diem to authorize his troops to chase guerrillas who had ambushed a convoy 40 miles north of Saigon. Two American officers had been killed, but it was hours before U.S. helicopters were able to put the South Vietnamese on the trail of the Communists. Bigart used this as an illustration of how "American officers are frustrated and irritated by the constant whimsical meddling of the President and his brother, Ngo Dinh Nhu, in the military chain of command." Regarding the political situation, he continued:

> There is no accurate gauge of sentiment in Vietnam. The press is rigidly controlled and there is no freedom of assembly. Even the election scheduled for this year was canceled when the rubber-stamp National Assembly altered the Constitution to give itself another year of tenure.
>
> In some areas the signs of disaffection are clear enough. Observers of sweeps by the Vietnamese army through the Mekong Delta provinces are often struck by the phenomenon of deserted villages. As troops approach,

all flee, except for a few old men and children. No one offers information; no one hurries to put out flags. Most of the rural area is controlled by Viet Cong, whose agents will move back as soon as the troops have departed.[19]

President Diem, well aware of the importance of securing the countryside, moved to build 8,000 of the "strategic hamlets" by the end of 1962. Bigart reported that the American aid mission, while "appalled by the dreary regimentation of life in these fortified villages," nevertheless believed the hamlet plan was part of the answer to "pacification." However, the Diem regime nullified their confidence by building village defenses with forced labor, even making the peasants supply their own food on those long, hot days. Unfortunately, all of this was tolerated far too long:

> But Washington decided it was risky to prod Ngo Dinh Diem publicly. Efforts to obtain major political and social reforms were quietly dropped after a few major concessions had been obtained: higher pay, fringe benefits and merit promotions for the armed forces; creation of a National Economic Council, quite impotent but useful as a forum; the establishment of provincial advisory councils and, at the top, the equivalent of a National Security Council . . . these improvements failed to touch the main problem.[20]

Bigart stated that "gadgets will not win this war, and neither will war dogs." He described how hundreds of sentry dogs were arriving in Vietnam, only to become sick. They were fed frozen horse meat at $1.20 per day, while the average Vietnamese soldier was receiving 19 cents' worth of rice daily. In the effort to be creative, one American wanted to surround each hamlet with poisonous shrubs. Malcolm Browne (AP) agreed with Bigart. Reflecting on all of these ideas, he said, "Our gadgets are superb, but they are not enough."[21]

The Bigart story ended with a clear warning about the future:

> On the political front the Americans are less inventive. Washington insists there is no alternative to President Ngo Dinh Diem. United States official policy is tied to the status quo. This policy is doomed in the long run, some feel, because the Vietnamese President cannot give his country the inspired leadership needed to defeat the Viet Cong.
>
> In the last seven years, the United States has spent $2,000,000,000 to prevent a Communist takeover in South Vietnam. Holding the line in Southeast Asia was a major premise of the strategy for containing a communism formulated by John Foster Dulles, President Eisenhower's Secretary of State, who felt the whole of Southeast Asia would go down the drain unless South Vietnam were saved . . .

By last year the Communists controlled most of the countryside . . .
Should the situation disintegrate further, Washington may face the alternative of ditching Ngo Dinh Diem for a military junta or sending combat
troops to bolster the regime.[22]

When Bigart, one of the finest reporters of his era, was gone,[23] Nevard
continued the drumbeat, writing on July 29 from Saigon:

The consensus here is that political apathy and even hostility on the
part of large segments of the population to the Saigon regime continues
to be the Communists' biggest asset.[24]

He also told of the growing frustration of U.S. officers training the Vietnamese. The object of criticism was the government's policy of dotting the
countryside with tiny triangular forts manned by six to ten members of South
Vietnam's Self Defense Corps, the home guard or local militia. There were
more than 2,500 of these in the South Vietnam lowlands, Nevard reported,
and U.S. advisers wanted to consolidate the local men into larger patrols
for nighttime action. "We are preaching that the only way to beat the Viet
Cong is to get out and patrol the countryside, find out where the Viet Cong
are and then go in and kill them," said one adviser.[25] Later in the war such
tactics, when used on a large scale, were called "search and destroy" missions, the futile contribution of Gen. William C. Westmoreland to America's
war effort.

THE PUSH FOR "NATION-BUILDING"

One highly regarded observer who quickly realized that the endless Communist raids would cause the strategic hamlet concept to fail was the French
writer and historian Bernard Fall, who chronicled the tragedy of the French-
Indochina War and the early U.S. involvement in his books and numerous
articles. Those familiar with his *Street without Joy* (1961), referring to the
famous Highway 1 running from north to south, knew that the United States
was only following the folly of the French. Ironically, President Kennedy,
privately skeptical about chances for success, reportedly read the book. Fall
told of the Communist trickery which circumvented the elaborate defense
measures instituted by the U.S. and Vietnamese governments. It took only
a few bursts from automatic rifles to cause the inhabitants of several villages to call for help on the expensive two-way radios supplied as part of
the program. The one village left alone during the wild scramble of local
troops then was easily overrun by the guerrillas, who disappeared into the

jungles or paddies with equipment and prisoners. During 1962 and 1963 the Communists often took mortars, machine guns, and new rifles after destroying the bamboo pikes and running past the earth bunkers supposed to keep them out of the hamlets. Diversionary attacks on outposts forced district troops outside of strategic areas, whereupon the Communists would cut the approach roads, block canals by sinking sampans in them, and then attack the weakened garrison guarding the area.[26]

For the home audience, however, the Vietnam story remained obscure and relatively simple. From the *New York Times* to the smallest weekly, this was a war that had to be won. There was little dissent. We were helping some friends fight Communism and the outcome was not clear. Most U.S. papers carried short press-association stories that simply told of another small battle. There were few broadcast news reports. Other news dominated. In 1962 the civil rights struggle in the South led by the Rev. Martin Luther King gained much attention. Berlin was a crisis point in Europe, and Cuba in the Western hemisphere. Late 1962 was dominated by the Cuban Missile Crisis. There were major problems in Africa. In the middle of this major foreign news came the story on July 2 from Algeria, whose independence from France was now achieved.

The French experience in Algeria provided another chance for military experts to learn of the new terminology, "revolutionary warfare." Bernard Fall wrote of Charles DeGaulle's awakening to the political realities of such fighting tactics and of how both French and American experts failed to grasp the lesson of Indochina and Algeria. In fact, as the United States rushed toward war in Vietnam by initiating guerrilla training at the U.S. Army Special Warfare School at Fort Bragg, N.C., what Fall termed "an almost fatal blind spot" was apparent to only a few persons. This is best illustrated by a statement of Dr. Walt W. Rostow, a key aide to President Kennedy and later President Lyndon Johnson's chief war adviser, that it was not necessary to have popular support or a popular cause to win a revolutionary war. What was the definition of "revolutionary warfare" that the generals and politicians should have learned? Two French colonels wrote that it was "the overthrowing of the government established in a given country and its replacement by another regime . . . thanks to the active participation of the population, conquered physically and morally by simultaneously destructive processes, according to precisely developed techniques."[27] Quite different was the American concept introduced in Vietnam, which utilized "guerrilla techniques"—the same tactics as the enemy—in an effort to defeat the foe militarily. It is true that the psychological warfare phrase "to win the hearts and minds of the people" later became the American slogan, but the various programs from "strategic hamlet" to "pacification" to

"Vietnamization" all ended up pockmarked with failure because of the Communists' superior ability to use resources of the population.

In May 1962, John Mecklin began a 21-month stint as United States Information Service (USIS) press chief in Saigon. He described his feelings about American antiguerrilla tactics after he resigned to join *Time*. In a most aptly named book, *Mission in Torment* (1965), Mecklin said the Pentagon described "insurgency" as being in between "subversion" and "conventional warfare," something to be dealt with on both the military and political levels. He was among those unwilling to admit that the Communist success had been inevitable, given the corrupt nature of the South Vietnamese system. He claimed that a major U.S. error was failure in the 1950s to prepare the Vietnamese people for guerrilla fighting, so that when Ho Chi Minh gave the go-ahead for a renewed Vietnam war, the people of the South would be at least mentally ready. Mecklin candidly admitted, "There was a disturbing lack of coherent Pentagon doctrine and organization for effective counterinsurgency programs in the early sixties. Vietnam in fact had become a laboratory. The United States, unlike the French in their war, tried to learn from the challenge [ignoring the French experience]."[28]

While it became fashionable in high circles to quote China's Mao Tsetung—"the people are the water and the army is the fish"—and to declare that the United States should learn from Vo Nguyen Giap's book, *People's War, People's Army*, policy makers found it difficult to abandon conventional thinking. In 1962 the United States and its South Vietnamese allies were split on objectives. Americans were interested in "nation-building," restructuring Vietnam along Western lines to fight Communism. The Vietnamese opposed this concept and were labeled as obstructionists. Above all, their leadership wanted large-scale U.S. support in order to remain in power. To do so they had to reverse Communist successes in the countryside, an almost hopeless task. The Americans were split also: some favored the pure military approach, while others wanted more social and economic changes.[29] Despite their differences, U.S. officials on the scene and the Kennedy planners all felt "time had to be bought" so that the South Vietnamese could learn to defend themselves. The same concept was being adhered to a decade later, in the same rice paddies, on the same highland plateaus, where some of the same little hamlets were being overrun by some of the same guerrillas. Vice President Spiro Agnew explained Nixon Administration strategy to returning troops on April 6, 1972, when he proclaimed the use of U.S. military power to allow the South Vietnamese extra time was "perhaps the most moral act the United States has performed as a world citizen."[30]

François Sully of *Newsweek* again put his finger on the problem in late

August when interviewing Fall, who had just returned from several weeks in Hanoi, repeating his oft-stated conviction that political considerations were being neglected and that "To win the military battle but lose the political war could well become the U.S. fate in Vietnam." A top South Vietnamese officer, whose identity was protected, made similar complaints, charging that the central government had no plan for the countryside even if all guerrillas were removed. He said, "We must admit that enthusiasm and drive seem to be on the enemy's side."[31]

The piece included this observation, with which *Newsweek* editors obviously agreed:

> The uncomfortable truth is that despite certain tactical strides forward in the past year, notably the increased use of helicopters, the war in South Vietnam seems in some ways affected by a kind of military Gresham's Law at the strategic level: Bad policies and directions are driving out good ones . . . Good Soldier (Paul D.) Harkins is rigidly proscribed from commenting on political considerations. And it is here, in the view of many qualified observers, that the war in South Vietnam at the present time is a losing proposition. [32]

There was immediate reaction to the two-page spread. The *Times of Vietnam*, the Diem-controlled newspaper, began a vitriolic campaign against Sully, demanding his expulsion. Despite the efforts of U.S. officials, the Vietnamese government finally sent Sully a letter in early September informing him he had to leave immediately because he had failed to apply for an extension of his residence permit. The letter included a harsh warning to Sully and the other Saigon writers about "the ill-considered campaign of intimidation," which the government charged had been waged on Sully's behalf by writers trying to "dictate their own law." Don Hutch of the Associated Press said Sully was expelled because he had pierced "the veil of secrecy which shrouds news coverage of the bitter war in Vietnam." Sully had visited forbidden battle scenes, walked into Viet Cong territory (one time talking his way out of a trap by showing he was unarmed), and in general had been brutally frank about the unhappy aspects of the fighting. As one angry newsman complained, "the good guys don't always beat the bad guys."[33]

Sully fired off a final salvo for an article entitled "Vietnam: Two Views, Official and Unofficial." A U.S. official in Saigon—one of those vague sources that popped up in nearly every Vietnam story—was quoted as predicting, "We're going to win this war, with this [Diem] government, and as it is. It is in our interest to deny this area [Vietnam] to the Communists. If we insist on reforms now, the whole thing is liable to fall apart. Perhaps we'd be able to hold up our heads as defenders of democracy, but 16 million more people would fall to the Communists."[34]

Noticeably absent in this and other critical dispatches was an indication of whether any government, Diem's or any other, could ever institute the massive reforms necessary to offset the Communists' natural advantage in the countryside. If the answer were negative, then the next question would have related to the need for U.S. presence. But the correspondents gave every appearance of being highly sympathetic to the need for some U.S. aid in fighting Communists in Asia. They were trying to differentiate between the official and unofficial truths; they were intolerant of the harshness of the Diem regime; many wanted to see reforms begun. Not one suggested withdrawal of U.S. forces; not one suggested that the Communist way of life was preferable to the style in Saigon; no one wrote of American colonialism or imperialism; no one questioned the assumption that China was the force behind Vietnamese Communism. Despite efforts to be honest about a sad situation, writers like Sully received much criticism from conservative editors and columnists in the United States and from officials on all levels in Washington and Vietnam.

When the official sources attempted to pad statistics, brush off Vietnamese defeats, and in general gloss over the fact that 10,000 U.S. servicemen were helping to spend more than $1 million per day in a soggy land a half-world distant, correspondents had little choice but to pound away. As the AP's Browne once said, "The world is divided into two classes: journalists and fact suppressors." Sully's last dispatch, from Hong Kong, was a long analysis of the Diem family's role. Although it would be an entire year before Diem's regime would be ended with his assassination, it already was apparent that his aloofness was costing him dearly. Sully described the secret police of Ngo Dinh Nhu, Madame Nhu ("grasping, conceited and obsessed with a drive for power that far surpasses that of even her husband"), and the various religious elements of the nation that would be involved in the 1963 protests.

> The whole effect seems to suggest that Diem regards himself as ruling with the mandate of heaven . . . there is a crying need for action and reform; if President Diem can galvanize himself and his personal clique into recognizing the need for action, they may yet win through; if not, then they will lose the mandate from heaven and fall.[35]

In the wake of Sully's expulsion, the Saigon correspondents fretted but could do nothing except protest to President Kennedy and anchor their collective determination not to be taken advantage of. This did not help much; NBC's Jim Robinson was expelled later in the year, simply for commenting in the presence of Vietnamese officials that President Diem's speeches were boring. Journalists and media critics in the United States, warming up for the internal media fight over the quality of coverage that exploded in late 1963, took sides in the Sully matter. By late 1962 there was enough concern and controversy within the media for *Newsweek* to send Contributing Editor Kenneth Crawford to see for himself what the situation was. Short three-to-five paragraph items continued to appear in the news magazines during the fall, mainly objective in nature. Crawford's December article finished 1962 on a confusing note. He discounted Ho Chi Minh's prediction that the Communists would win a 10-year war, found great praise for the "strategic hamlet" concept, claimed Diem was "starting a social revolution for the benefit of villagers," said government troops were killing the enemy at a 5:1 ratio, and, after nine hours of talking with Diem and Nhu ended up with a subtly expressed admiration for the regime. The four-page piece, which leaned against all of Sully's efforts, ended:

> The most general complaint against Diem is that he doesn't inspire the peasants he is trying to help—that he isn't enough of a demagogue for his country's good. The most serious complaint against him is that he isn't establishing rule of law as fast as he might, even in a country at war. Whatever his shortcomings, confidence in his ability to hold out against Hanoi is growing. His wellwishers, whatever their feeling about the President and his family, see no preferable alternative.[36]

AN ASSERTIVE SAIGON PRESS CORPS FORMS

As 1962 ended, the Saigon resident press corps was at its peak in terms of raw talent. The coming year was to be decisive for the war effort, and the young regular correspondents, most in their late twenties and thirties, would face numerous group and personal challenges. David Halberstam, 29—Harvard class of '55—arrived for the *New York Times* in time for Sully's farewell party. The bulk of his time dating back to September 1961 had been in the Congo where, despite the excitement and recognition he enjoyed there, he dreamed of being sent to Vietnam. Peter Arnett, the wiry New Zealander, then 24, first worked in Asia in 1958, for the English-language *Bangkok World*. There he first met "old Asia hands" like Edgar Snow, Keyes Beech, and others from whom he began to learn what was beneath the surface of life in the Far East. He began stringing for the Associated Press in 1960 while working for another English-language paper in Laos and became a full-time AP reporter in Jakarta, Indonesia, the next year. Immediately displaying his aggressiveness, he quickly became a target of officials within the government of President Sukarno, a murderous dictator with close ties to the CIA. After a flurry of conflicts with the government, Arnett was expelled in May 1962. The AP knew they had a winner and assigned him to Vietnam. He joined Malcolm Browne there on June 26, 1962. Browne, the bureau chief, had been reassigned from the AP's Baltimore bureau in 1961, quickly establishing a reputation for well-detailed stories. Coming to Vietnam about that time, after stints in Frankfurt, Algeria, and the Congo (where he and Halberstam became friends), was the German photographer Horst Faas.

Neil Sheehan, only 26—Harvard, class of '58—joined the Tokyo bureau of United Press International in 1962 and was assigned to Saigon. Ray Hendron was with UPI also, while Nicholas Turner was there for Reuters and Pierre Chauvet was the Agence France-Presse correspondent. Charles Mohr was *Time*'s regular correspondent and Mert Perry was his capable freelance partner. Lee Briggs and Murray Gart came later. Larry Burrows was *Life*'s chief photographer. After Sully's departure *Newsweek* hired Beverly Deepe, at that time the only woman reporter living in Saigon, and Robert McCabe. Deepe had been a stringer for the *New York Herald Tribune* and later joined the *Christian Science Monitor* staff. Dennis Warner, a well-known Australian journalist, was a familiar figure. Jim Robinson was NBC's regular until he was expelled; the veteran Peter Kalischer was in and out for CBS, as were Bernard Kalb, John Lawrence, and Morley Safer. Other early arrivals were Garrick Utley of NBC and Lou Cioffi of ABC.

Among the rovers were Robert Martin of *U.S. News & World Report*, Takashi Oka of the *Christian Science Monitor*, Stan Karnow, who wrote for the *Saturday Evening Post*, Charles Arnot of ABC, Keyes Beech of the *Chicago Daily News*, and Marguerite Higgins, on periodic assignments for the *New York Herald Tribune*. Another female correspondent, freelancer Dickey Chapelle, made the first of several trips in 1961; she died in 1965 when a land mine exploded. Columnist Joseph Alsop flew in for a look-see, and Jim Lucas of Scripps-Howard began a five-month stay in the early days of 1964, the first of many for him. Robert Shaplen, the *New Yorker*'s Asian correspondent based in Hong Kong, was one of the few to cover the entire war. He published several volumes of collected writings.

The news media pattern for covering foreign events with a handful of reporters was being followed religiously. Despite the growing significance of the war and obvious major consequences for the United States, the quantity of coverage was low and the quality was hotly debated. In 1963 only the wire services, the *New York Times, Time, Newsweek* and *Life* gave regular coverage—the big names were Halberstam, Sheehan, Arnett, Browne, Faas, and Burrows. The nation was on the verge of the most divisive and costly commitment in its history, but news organizations were content to rely on this small group. Luckily for the public, it was the right combination of reporters. It should be underscored, however, that none of the regular correspondents had an ideological bias against war or this war in particular. They were there for the hot story, and they were turned off by the lies and manipulation of the U.S. establishment. Over the years their opponents and fans alike created a myth that this handful of reporters was "antiwar," fighting the military in every dispatch. This is false.

While Browne was known for his negative analyses of the deteriorating situation, he was among those filing stories containing praise for the strategic hamlet program; Halberstam and Arnett, critical of the U.S. command, nevertheless shared the idealism of the young Americans in the field. Many of their stories were in the "noncritical" category. It is true that Browne and Halberstam quickly became very bitter about the war. Arnett, however, said, "Only after time did I come to agree with David Halberstam, that it was the wrong war, in the wrong place, at the wrong time."[37] It also took Sheehan years to become an open critic, rooted as he was in right-wing Republican conservative politics. He summed up the reporters' collective mindset while they battled to get their stories out:

> We tried to write the truth and were denounced for it by [General] Harkins and those on high who shared his mirage. None of us wanted the United States to get out of Vietnam. We didn't know then that there was no way to win the war. We thought if we wrote of impending defeat, the Joint Chiefs of Staff, the president—someone up there who mattered—would take action to change our policy and win. We didn't understand yet that arrogance had rendered the American system witless, that the men in charge had made up their minds in advance and listened only to themselves.[38]

THE TELLTALE BATTLE OF AP BAC

It was mid-afternoon, January 2, 1963, when Halberstam, Arnett, and Perry heard about the disaster at Ap Bac, a Mekong Delta village 40 miles southwest of Saigon. The guerrillas had ripped apart units of a South Vietnamese division and shot down at least five helicopters, killing some American crew members. Sheehan and Turner already were on their way in a hired car. An early AP report that eight helicopters were lost enraged President Kennedy, who had trouble accepting the bad news.[39] Arnett and Halberstam put together short accounts, while Sheehan, bothered by the confusion he had seen on the battlefield, added details to what he considered to be the significant aspects of the defeat. No one at home was paying attention.

From the very beginning American reporters heard the same lament. "If we only could make them stand and fight, we'd beat them every time." One of the true believers was Lt. Col. John Paul Vann, U.S. adviser to the Vietnamese troops in action at Ap Bac. Vann, a favorite information source, was highly critical of the overall war strategy and predicted an eventual Communist victory. The South Vietnamese command had seen Ap Bac as the opportunity to demonstrate how helicopter-borne troops could sweep into an enemy-held area and spring a giant trap. "Instead, it was a battle which demonstrated on a grand and dramatic scale all of the tiny failings of the system, all the false techniques, evasions and frauds which had marked the war in Vietnam. It was also typical of the atmosphere existing at that time in Vietnam; having suffered a stunning defeat, the American military headquarters referred to it as a victory."[40]

The most ridiculous example of such false hopes and statements came on January 3, when the correspondents went to Ap Bac in a helicopter. Dead Vietnamese still were sprawled across the fields and friendly artillery fire killed five more troops who were helping clean up the area. Once on the ground, Sheehan and Turner had to hit the ground to avoid being struck. Returning to Saigon after this first-hand look, Arnett and Halberstam located General Harkins and asked him what was happening. "We've got them in a trap. We are going to spring it in an hour."[41] The writers had just seen government troops so dazed they were unwilling or unable to load their own dead on helicopters. And the province chief had shelled his own troops. But General Harkins, the top military man in Vietnam, was able to tell the correspondents that a trap was going to be sprung! The truth was that the Communists had escaped during the night and were far out of range, boasting about a victory from which they would gain much propaganda mileage.

While it was obvious to the writers and to subordinate military advisers that AP Bac had been a magnification of smaller disasters that had occurred throughout 1962, U.S. officials in Saigon maintained the fiction that a victory had occurred. Two days later Harkins and Admiral Harry Felt, overall commanders in the Pacific, held an airport press conference during which Felt claimed a victory because "We took the objective." He did not mention that the so-called objective had been taken five hours late, after the enemy had snuck away, Halberstam noted. Felt was known for the classic remark, "Why don't you get on the team?" made in response to a question of Malcolm Browne at a late 1962 press conference—a snap comment that writers said "eloquently" summed up the general attitude about the role of the media.[42] Harkins also issued a statement accusing the press of criticizing the "valor and courage of the Vietnamese soldier," which actually never was the issue. Instead the writers had been concentrating for months on the relationship between U.S. advisers and their Vietnamese counterparts and on the overall strategy.

There was more to the Ap Bac story, as it later emerged. Ap Bac was another case of a hand-picked local commander loyal to Diem ignoring the orders of superiors and the strong advice of the U.S. adviser, in this case Vann. Instead of moving against the smaller guerrilla unit that was in effect trapped, the South Vietnamese quit. Veteran Asian correspondent Stanley Karnow later wrote in his *Vietnam: A History* (1983) that Ap Bac represented "less a military disaster than a reflection of [Diem's] convoluted priorities."[43] For Arnett and his colleagues Ap Bac "exposed the glaring weaknesses that were to haunt American military planners seeking to shape their ally into a fighting force . . . the battle convinced the Saigon press corps that either the authorities were unaware of the full dimensions of the insurgency, or these dimensions were being concealed from us. This discrepancy, which later became known as the credibility gap, grew wider."[44]

Despite the accuracy of the Ap Bac reports, the Saigon press corps continued to draw heavy criticism. In return, Halberstam, Sheehan, and their colleagues were strongly defended by journalists of the stature of Harrison Salisbury and James Reston.[45] Throughout the period the Associated Press team received vigorous protection from General Manager Wes Gallagher in New York, who time and again supported the young reporters in the field.[46] In all of this Vann's role was crucial, as Sheehan so movingly wrote in his *A Bright Shining Lie*, the story of this tormented, brave, and misguided man. In another reminiscence, *After the War Was Over*, Sheehan explained his attitude and those of colleagues this way, as he struggled with Vann's image and influence:

> The most fearless and brilliant of the advisors was an articulate Lieutenant Colonel with a Virginia twang named John Paul Vann. I met him on my first helicopter assault in the Mekong delta a couple of months after arriving in 1962. He was destined to become America's Lawrence of Arabia in Vietnam. He helped me most during those first two years because, natural leader of men that he was, he could best explain what we youngsters were seeing for ourselves.[47]

A few months later the independent journalist I. F. Stone issued a warning that in fact was an accurate prediction. He said in his weekly publication, "The desperate attempt to hide the truth about this hopeless but savage war is pulling our government . . . toward the rewriting of history in an attempt to impose a party line myth on the press and public. Unless there is a counter campaign of pressure to bring home the truth, the war will drag on, poisoning the air of freedom at home, imposing misery on the bewildered people of South Vietnam and risking a wider conflagration."[48]

The Ap Bac story became the first of a series of hot encounters between the embassy staff and the press corps. John Mecklin was ordered by Ambassador Nolting to write a "white paper" on the press coverage, and when his first draft did not prove strong enough, he had to write a second.[49] It was the intent of the embassy to ignore suggestions that the Americans should protest to Diem about the failure at Ap Bac; instead officials pretended that a victory had taken place, so that the American people would not become worried about the war efforts. Correspondents picked up heavy criticism from U.S. majors and captains in the field who were serving as combat advisers, but policy came before evaluation. The Diem regime was not to be harassed for fear that it would come apart at the seams.

Marguerite Higgins and other writers not covering Vietnam regularly or at all (Higgins made a trip in the summer of 1963) saw an opposite picture. In their judgment the news of Ap Bac and other government failures overshadowed that of perceived victories. Actually both wire services and the newsmagazines filed many items attributing claims of victory to government spokesmen, just as disappointments about performance often were attributed to advisers or other sources. But Higgins was correct in that the general news was getting worse. When Higgins came to Vietnam in mid-July, she found evidence that in April Vietnamese troops had won a four-day fight at Quang Ngai in the North which had received no headlines proclaiming "victory." She found other advisers who felt bitter about what they called neglect on the part of the press corps in covering successful government operations. They made a direct comparison with coverage of the "defeat" at Ap Bac.[50] Her Korean War partner, Keyes Beech, shared her anger over criticism of the Saigon regime and the U.S. effort. He called Diem "the one true Vietnamese nationalist of stature in South Vietnam"[51] and defended the U.S. position this way: "We were not the French. The French were fighting a stupid colonial war they were doomed to lose. We were fighting an anticolonial war to prevent a new form of imperialism, Asian Communism, from picking up where the French left off. The French fought to stay. We were fighting to get out."[52] Beech was in Saigon at the end in 1975 and remained upset for years afterward over the coverage of some of his colleagues.

There is no satisfactory answer for these criticisms. Stories containing reports of government victories also often included qualifying comments about the overall situation. And it was these qualifying phrases that caused charges of "bias, loading stories," "going out of their way to find negativism." One short *Time* article of several months earlier appears typical. Government estimates of enemy casualties were accepted without question, but an estimate of continuing guerrilla strength took the edge off an otherwise "optimistic" story:

> A small South Vietnamese observer plane circled over a marshy checkerboard of wild rice fields 60 miles southwest of Saigon. Below, two companies of Communist Viet Cong guerrillas, flushed into the open after sporadic fire fights, were trying to escape across the fields in shallow-draft sampans. Alerted by the observation plane, ten huge grey U.S. supplied amphibious personnel carriers raced to the scene, ran head-on into the Reds. Churning through the sampan fleet, the amphibious ducks ground whole boatloads of Communist guerrillas under steel treads. Shielded behind armor plating, army troops machine-gunned the survivors. The toll: 154 Viet Cong troops killed and 38 captured to twelve government troops wounded.
>
> One of the biggest government victories of the year, the battle once again proved how much U.S. equipment and training have improved the Vietnamese army. Since January, government forces in the provincial area southwest of Saigon known as the 32nd Tactical Command have killed 5,000 Viet Cong troops. But the government has been unable to consolidate its military successes into a political victory. Under the nose of government officials, the Viet Cong have continued their recruiting campaign among the peasantry. Despite the heavy losses, Viet Cong strength in the area is the same as last January: 6,000 men.[53]

The pressure was building in January but the Washington pundits were worried about other things, indicating that Vietnam remained on the periphery of events. Walter Lippmann analyzed John Kennedy at "mid-term" for *Newsweek*'s January 21, 1963 issue, after agreeing to write a column for the magazine. This major story, which filled four pages, did not mention Vietnam once. Lippmann was preoccupied with the "revival in Europe," Kennedy's courage during the Cuban Missile Crisis, and in general with what Lippmann saw as a cooling of tensions between East and West. Lippmann's look into the future saw Kennedy holding "good cards" but "not all trumps." He also said the game could be lost by "recklessness, bad judgment, failure to master special interests at home."[54] Why didn't the Lippmanns of Washington's inner circle see the Vietnam disaster coming?

John Mecklin knew the answer. Mecklin was part of the "shadow government" set up to save Vietnam from the Communists. One Pentagon VIP summed up the feeling of many regarding this budding bureaucracy with a brisk, "We have a fifty billion dollar budget and this is our only war. Don't worry about spending money."[55] They didn't worry. At the top of the "military pyramid" was the Military Assistance Command Vietnam (MACV), headed by General Harkins. Until 1964 another organization was retained, Military Assistance Advisory Group (MAAG), headed by General Charles J. Timmes. MACV had command authority over U.S. units in the field and was responsible for operations advice to the Vietnamese, while MAAG dealt with supply and training programs.

But there was overlap. On the civilian side, John H. Richardson headed the Central Intelligence Agency operations, which was heavily into training paramilitary groups and creating a modern intelligence agency. Joseph L. Brent was in charge of the U.S. Operations Mission (the AID office), handing out anything from radio transmitters to fertilizer. Mecklin headed the United States Information Service office, working closely with the Vietnamese in propaganda efforts. And in charge of the Country Team, the grouping of agency heads and other experts including, technically, the military people, was Ambassador Frederick E. (Fritz) Nolting, a husky 50-year-old career foreign service officer with plenty of NATO experience but with no Asian background. Nolting was in overall command because legally there was no war, but in actuality he shared command decisions with Harkins because of the pressure on the military side.[56]

The Vietnamese had their own bureaucracy, the inner workings of which took the Americans a long time to understand. Mecklin was shocked after dealing with the Diems:

> In some ways Diem was a pathetic man. His marathon dissertations, delivered in a tone that was almost plaintive, gave a superficial impression of vast knowledge of his people and his country. He knew the names and something of the personal history of an astonishing number of officials, often down to such lowly levels as battalion commanders and district chiefs.

> But his information was filtered through such a morass of selfishly motivated bureaucrats that it was often inaccurate, sometimes seriously so. Events were to prove, for example, that neither he nor Nhu was aware of the degree to which the Viet Cong had infiltrated the strategic hamlets, which was the main reason the U.S. Mission was also fooled . . . it was remarkable that anything got done at all.[57]

THE BUDDHISTS' REVOLT

Buddha's 2527th birthday was celebrated throughout South Vietnam on

May 8, 1963, but in Hue, the provincial capital at the northern tip of the nation, an event occurred that proved to be the unseating of the Diems. Just as Madame Nhu had forbidden all dancing in Saigon, the government had banned the flying of religious flags. However, a few weeks earlier Roman Catholic flags were flown to mark the 25th anniversary of Diem's brother as Archbishop of Hue. Thus on May 8 several thousand angry Buddhists gathered to protest and were met by force. Troops equipped with armored cars broke up the crowd, shots rang out, and nine Buddhists died. The government repeatedly claimed that a Viet Cong terrorist took advantage of the situation and threw a hand grenade into the protesters. But later a court sided with the Buddhists and blamed the authorities for overreacting. Buddhists demanded on May 13 that the ban of flags be lifted; that Buddhists be treated equally with Catholics; that Buddhists be allowed to openly preach their religion; and that the victims of May 8 be compensated (including 14 injured) and those responsible be punished. Mass protests were held in Hue and Saigon on May 30–31, and finally there were riots in Hue in the beginning of June.

Diem, frightened by the political consequences of the nationwide protests, fired three officials at Hue and set up a commission headed by a Buddhist to try to settle the dispute. But it was too late. Capitalizing on widespread disillusionment with the Diems, the Buddhists had set up regional headquarters throughout the country and were concentrating in Saigon itself.[58]

The May 8 killings and the events of the next few weeks received poor "handout" coverage because the action was in the North; when on duty, reporters were obligated to stay close to their Saigon bureaus with the exception of occasional trips into the near countryside. In Washington, Arthur Sylvester, the assistant secretary of defense, told reporters of a "high level" Honolulu conference from which he had just returned. The Associated Press reported, as it and the other media outlets would so many times in the future: "A Pentagon spokesman said today 'the corner definitely had been turned' toward victory in South Vietnam and Defense Department officials are hopeful that the 2,000 man United States force can be reduced in one to three years."[59]

It was in June when the stories of Buddhist unrest made the front sections of the *New York Times* and other major papers. But making page one was rough—that would have to wait until the crisis reached the hopeless stage. Pope John XXIII was dying, JFK had committed himself to civil rights legislation to the dismay of Southerners, Sukarno was insulting the leaders of Malaysia, and there was severe fighting in Laos. A small AP story made page 9 on June 3, telling of the arrest of eight Buddhists in Saigon as Nhu's police continued their roundups of dissidents.[60] Finally, on June 5, Halberstam was on page one with a noninterpretive story that stated the gravity of the Buddhists' revolt. "The situation around the country, which is fighting a guerrilla war against Communist insurgency, is reported to be extremely tense."[61]

Halberstam gave both the government and Buddhist sides, saying that Diem had moved to meet some of the Buddhist demands but that the two sides were far apart. The key to this story was Halberstam's observation that "what started as a religious protest has become predominately political, it is believed, and the Buddhists are providing a spearhead for other discontented elements."[62] Halberstam wrote other stories within the next weeks, describing the Buddhist revolt as being basically political in nature.

Marguerite Higgins later was to complain in her book *Our Vietnam Nightmare* that Halberstam and others had sent dispatches giving the impression that religious persecution was being committed by Diem. Avoiding the reality that the Buddhists were trying to overthrow the Diem government, Higgins repeatedly condemned the Saigon press corps for taking "anything scurrilous said about the Diem regime as fact and any contrary information as fiction."[63] A check of those news dispatches, however, leaves the reader with the clear impression that the Buddhists were acting in a highly organized, political manner and that the downfall of the Diem regime would be welcomed. Higgins also went to great lengths to blame the monk Thich Tri Quang for the entire Hue disorder of May 8, claiming that the flag order had not applied on that day but had been misrepresented by the Buddhist leader. As for the deaths, Higgins said all of the victims were killed by a massive explosion and that they were not shot, according to medical examinations. Her documentation is impressive, as she spends pages of her book to show the media accepted a phony story.[64]

Mecklin, in whom Higgins placed some trust, as evidenced by other statements, dismissed the government charges that a plastic bomb or a grenade had been used. Mecklin said the entire incident was a misunderstanding, that Diem probably felt no one but the government should fly flags in wartime, that his brother's celebration with flags had been an oversight, and that Diem was slow at accepting advice on how to head off the demonstrations.[65]

Because no reporters were on the scene and the story had to be reconstructed days after it happened, the press never received the full truth. Browne said some grenades were thrown into the crowd, by "trigger-happy [government] soldiers."[66] The fact remained that Diem was unable to handle a political revolt in his country and the Communists were the only ones who would gain in the long run, as the press corps reported to the unhappiness of Higgins and others giving full support to the anticommunist Diem family.

The one scene remembered by most Americans from early summer 1963 is that of Thich Quang Duc burning to death in a Saigon street, with silent, prayerful crowds standing around him in stunned horror. One who would never forget was Browne, whose picture of the suicide made front pages worldwide. By the admission of even pro-Diem, anti-Buddhist observers, the suicides which began that day, June 11, put the salvation of Diem's regime out of reach. Members of the press corps had been tipped by friendly Buddhists that desperate measures would be used in an effort to bring down Diem, and Browne was told in late May that suicide would be included. On the evening of June 10, Browne was told by the Buddhists' official press spokesmen to be at an 8:00 A.M. meeting, because "something very important may happen." That morning, as Browne and Bill Ha Van Tran were watching Buddhist marchers form a circle in the middle of a street, Halberstam was being awakened by Nguyen Ngoc Rao, a Vietnamese reporter for UPI. "Get to Le Van Duyet and Phan Dinh Phung streets fast," was the message. When he got there, Halberstam was "too shocked to cry, too confused to take notice or ask questions, too bewildered to even think."[67] First mention of the monk's suicide in the *New York Times* and other papers came through Browne's report. Oddly, the *Times*, which often carried AP pictures from Saigon, did not use Browne's historic shot and put his story on page six. The story read:

> An elderly Buddhist monk surrounded by 300 other monks calmly put a match to his gasoline-drenched yellow robes at a main street intersection here today and burned to death before thousands of watching Vietnamese.
>
> The victim, Quang Duc, was protesting against alleged persecution of Buddhists by President Ngo Dinh Diem's Government. Nuns and monks around him carried banners reading: "A Buddhist burns himself for five requests."
>
> The demonstration was the latest in a wave of Buddhist protests against the Government. The Buddhists demand guarantees of religious freedom and social justice.[68]

Browne's story was the first of hundreds to come out of Saigon between then and November telling the world of the Buddhists' revolt. The next blowoff of major headlines came in August, when the Diem regime resorted to force in an attempt to stop the Buddhists. Halberstam's lead story in New York read:

President Ngo Dinh Diem ordered nationwide martial law today after Vietnamese troops and policemen had attacked Buddhist pagodas through-out the country.

Hundreds of Buddhist priests were arrested and many were beaten in the military and police action . . . screams and gunfire were heard and then troops began carrying Buddhists out of the pagodas . . . bore the stamp of planning by his brother and closest adviser, Ngo Dinh Nhu.[69]

Despite close friendships, the competition was keen. The only major problem was between Halberstam and Browne, which emerged when Halberstam shared a house with his old Congo friend Faas and worked out of the AP office. During the Ap Bac coverage in January 1963, Arnett and Halberstam stuck together. But Halberstam later argued with Browne over story content and switched to Sheehan's UPI office, often going on assignment with him and Reuters man Nick Turner.[70] This group cooperation ceased, however, when there was a chance for a scoop on a major story. For example, when news broke in August about violence against the Buddhists, Sheehan outmaneuvered the Vietnamese censors and gained a world beat with a 150-word story sent through an Army communications system.

Pressure now was on President Kennedy. The U.S. State Department issued an immediate protest to President Diem, charging him with breaking an agreement whereby he was not to have interfered with the Buddhists. There also was anger because the attacks were carried out when the new ambassador, Henry Cabot Lodge, was on his way to his Saigon job. The first reaction of other officials, both in Saigon and Washington, was to put a different face on the story. Stories from Tad Szulc in Washington and Halberstam in Saigon were so radically different that the *Times* was forced to publish "Two Versions of the Crisis in Vietnam: One Lays Plot to Nhu, Other to Army."[71] Readers were told in a page one statement that because of the wide discrepancies the paper felt the obligation to run the two interpretations.

Halberstam's story again fixed blame on Diem and Nhu, saying the military was surprised by the act but went along in order to have a united front for the government. Szulc's detailed account said top military leaders forced Diem to act, citing past crises when firm action by the central government prevented chaos. One point in Szulc's story was prophetic. "High administration sources . . . said this was probably only the opening chapter in a major power struggle."

During these days the *Times* filled entire pages with Vietnam-related material, from its own writers and from the wire services. It was at this point that the Kennedy Administration could no longer look elsewhere but had to face the reality that Diem was not going to defeat the Communists, the aim of U.S. policy. Details of the pagoda raids kept coming for days and each successive report was more grim. Descriptions of monks being hurled down stairs and over railings and being fired upon were common.[72] And within a few days the official U.S. position became clear: Diem and Nhu, not the military, were to be blamed.[73] That was the cleanest way out. But the administration never coupled an ultimatum to reform with a threat to remove advisers. Perhaps that was because they knew reform was impossible and they were not able to abandon Vietnam.

That left only one option for dealing with Diem: a coup. It was on the drawing boards. Mecklin later predicted that it would be a decade before anyone knew the details of the cables that went back and forth between Ambassador Lodge and Washington regarding what to do with the Diem family. He was close. Those transcripts became public in 1971 when Neil Sheehan, by then the *New York Times* Pentagon reporter, emerged with the Pentagon Papers, courtesy of former Pentagon aide Daniel Ellsberg. The cables showed how the United States felt it had to, in the words of Mecklin, Higgins, and other observers, "play God" in order to maintain the war effort.[74] Regarding the early time period examined here, they also revealed how the Kennedy administration deceived the public and the press by conducting bombings in Laos, landing raiding parties on the North Vietnamese coast, and putting Special Forces and other personnel into action well ahead of any public notice. Without question the Pentagon Papers showed that JFK considerably expanded the U.S. role in South Vietnam—even if he eschewed the use of ground forces—and that Lyndon Johnson inherited an almost impossible situation. (JFK did have doubts to the very end about how far he should go. On November 21, 1963, as he left for Dallas, he told White House assistant Michael Forrestal that Vietnam's history and origins required some hard thinking.)

Overshadowed by the political and diplomatic furor in Saigon, the war continued in the Delta and the country around Saigon. In fact, what was described as "the biggest government victory in months" occurred in early September 45 miles south of Saigon at Gocung. It was another of those battles in which the armored personnel carriers saved the day, this time by ferrying a government relief column right into the swamps to crush the enemy in their rice paddy dugouts. Aided by dive-bombing planes, the Vietnamese troops chased the Communists out, after 81 had been killed. But while this was heartening to U.S. advisers, the victory glow lasted only a few days. Typical of the stalemate nature of the entire war, the next news was bad. Feinting a half-dozen ways before attacking, the guerrillas overran a village, occupied it for 17 hours, and left behind the mutilated bodies of its male defenders and of its women and children. Perhaps 75 persons died. The bloodbath in one area had been matched by another many miles away.[75] Whether the Saigon problems actually affected the performance of the South Vietnamese was debatable. It was noted by some observers, after a successful August operation in the southern Delta region, that field commanders were in full control, "without the usual interference from President Ngo Dinh Diem's palace in Saigon."[76]

THE SAIGON PRESS CORPS UNDER SIEGE

There was only one group to blame for the Buddhists' success in embarrassing the Diems, the resident press corps. The Washington agenda-setters continued their all-out assault on information that ran contrary to their strategy: keeping the escalating U.S. involvement from the public. In doing so they deceived some progressive Washington commentators and numerous journalists across the land who tended to discount or at least downplay negative reports from Saigon. The most obvious target was Halberstam, whose stories had received the most attention in Washington and who had distinguished himself at many a Saigon news conference with his no-nonsense questioning. Along with Higgins's comments, Halberstam had to contend with Joseph Alsop, who visited Vietnam briefly in September 1962 and returned home to write of an "egregious crusade."

While admitting that all or most of what had been reported was true, Alsop said the press corps had "also helped to transform Diem . . . into a man afflicted with galloping persecution mania . . . all those reports of resentment have come true."[77] Pierre Salinger, by his own admission, was convinced that Halberstam, Sheehan, and Browne had purposely aimed at bringing down the Saigon government. He praised their military reporting but targeted their political efforts when he said, "Whether they intended it or not, their articles reflected the bitter hatred they had for the Diem government and their avowed purpose (stated to a number of reporters in Saigon) to bring down the Diem government."[78]

Like Walter Duranty before him and numerous correspondents in Central America and the Middle East who followed—including Arnett himself during the Gulf War—there wasn't much Halberstam could do at the time about the bashing of his reputation. But in 1964 he wrote *The Making of a Quagmire*, in which he responded to this and other charges against the press corps. He said Salinger had compounded the problem by telling Washington writers that the Saigon group was filing inaccurate and emotional stories.[79]

The Kennedy Administration, in full knowledge of the problems being caused by the overall war effort by Diem's slowness and aloofness, nevertheless maintained a stony attitude toward the Saigon reporters. Sometimes Washington was forced to help, however. On July 7 Halberstam, Browne, Kalischer, and Sheehan signed a protest letter to President Kennedy after Browne and Arnett were roughed up by Vietnamese plainclothes police while watching a peaceful Buddhist procession. Kennedy sent State Department official Robert Manning to Saigon to check into the press relations situation. Manning's final report called for the relaxation of some but not all of the restrictions of press coverage, observing with candor, "The problem is complicated by the long-standing desire of the United States government to see the American involvement in Vietnam minimized, even represented, as something less than in reality it is." He called this an "'Alice in Wonderland' miasma that surrounds the Vietnamese press situation." He felt that the early history of the handling of the situation was marked by attitudes, directives, and actions in Washington and in the field that reflected this desire of the United States.[80]

It was difficult for President Kennedy to understand the Saigon press corps reports. On April 29, 1963, Mecklin personally told Kennedy that the administration needed a new press policy, including taking reporters into confidence and realizing that the reporters were serious professionals trying to do a difficult job. The President was skeptical that anything would ease the bitterness he had learned of, but nevertheless a secret memorandum was sent that Mecklin said encouraged top embassy people to cooperate more. In October Kennedy was still bothered enough by some of the coverage, especially Halberstam's, to ask *New York Times* publisher Arthur Ochs Sulzberger if Halberstam might be given a "vacation." Of course Sulzberger politely defended his reporter and the matter was quickly dropped but not forgotten by those who learned of it.[81] It is at moments like these that weak-kneed executives supported by newsroom sycophants fall in line with Washington's conventional wisdom and ruin the efforts of the overseas correspondent. In this case Halberstam had the strong support of his boss.

The correspondents managed to withstand the attacks of the *Times of Vietnam* and the Diem government, including Madame Nhu's almost daily tirades against the writers. But they were not able to completely fight off their own colleagues. There are many political and financial contraints within large news organizations—the major one is fear of demotion or dismissal—that inhibit internal discussions about the merits of controversial stories. In the case of Vietnam coverage, Charles Mohr and Mert Perry were the first to suffer. That Mohr was one of Henry Luce's favorite reporters made the whole situation difficult for editors in New York who were irritated by the pessimistic reports. They failed to realize that Mohr, a White House correspondent at 27, chief of the New Delhi bureau, and then chief of the Southeast Asia coverage, was a true professional. Normally based in Hong Kong, he had spent most of 1963 in Vietnam. Perry was sent to Saigon by UPI but had resigned to take the *Time* job and was in his second year of providing excellent legwork and coverage (Halberstam said Perry was perhaps the best liked by military officers, who often visited him at his apartment for meals).

Although correspondents traditionally complain about copy changes, Mohr and Perry began to have serious problems in August. Mohr filed material for a cover story on Madame Nhu that Halberstam read and judged to be "one of the most brilliant I've ever read."[82] But the heavily edited published product, while giving every aspect of her personality, played down Madame Nhu's negative effects in Vietnam, and an upset Mohr exchanged some letters with his editors. Then in mid-August Mohr was asked to prepare an analysis of the Saigon press corps itself. He spent a great deal of time preparing it, but it was not printed. Under pressure because of other deadlines, he did not worry or wonder why. However, it is important to note that it was flattering to his colleagues. Finally, in early September, Mohr was asked to do a roundup on the war. He and Perry filed 25 pages in three days, running themselves into near exhaustion. "The war in Vietnam is being lost," Mohr began, as he quoted the men in the field who felt the American mission had failed, the Diem regime was corrupt, and there had been lies fed by military men trying to hide the truth.[83] When the story reached New York, it was immediately rewritten with an optimistic angle, describing the battle at Gocung ("biggest government victory in months"). "If last week's battles were any criteria, the government soldiers are fighting better than ever against a Communist foe that is exacting a hideous price in blood in the flooded paddies of the South," the *Time* writer said.[84] But since the *Time* story differed from the *New York Times*, UPI, CBS and NBC reports, *Time* managing editor Otto Fuerbringer decided the "Press" section should contain an explanation.[85] The September 20, 1963 *Time* therefore carried an account that in effect accused Mohr and Perry of joining with others to help confuse an already horribly complex story. The lead went:

> For all the light it shed, the news that U.S. newspaper readers got from Saigon might just as well have been printed in Vietnamese. Was the war being won or lost? Was the Buddhist uprising religiously inspired or Communist-inspired? Would the government fall? Only last month, the *New York Times* threw up its hands helplessly and, beneath an editorial apology, printed two widely divergent accounts of events: one presented the picture as viewed from Washington, the other as viewed from Saigon.[86]

After having distorted the *New York Times* double analysis of who started the raids against the Buddhists, *Time* continued its incredible attack against the journalists by implying they had formed a "club" that ensured unanimous agreement on all important subjects. Admitting the problems posed by Diem, lying military officials, and language barriers, *Time* nevertheless used an argument similar to that used in the 1970s by Vice President Agnew—that the newsmen had banded together for companionship and had begun to write for each other. "When there is defeat, the color is rich and flowing; trend stories are quickly cranked up." "The Saigon press corps is so confident of its own convictions that any other version of the Vietnam story is quickly dismissed as the fancy of a bemused observer."[87] Richard Clurman, *Time*'s chief of correspondents, tried to block publication of the press analysis. He had visited Saigon in April 1963 and gained some insight into the press problems. But Luce could not be reached in time, so the criticism was published. Mohr flew to Paris to discuss the piece with Clurman, who desperately wanted to keep one of his and Luce's favorites on the *Time* team. Mohr demanded the right to reply to Fuerbringer under his own byline, but Luce tried to avoid company embarrassment by having Clurman fly on to Saigon to write a follow-up, which appeared on October 11. While in Saigon Clurman became convinced that the first piece had been handled in an outrageous manner. He and Fuerbringer began arguing about his own piece, which eventually also was watered down. Mohr had decided to resign before Clurman came to Saigon but accompanied him around the city. The winner in the fight was *Newsweek*, which crowed in its October 7 issue that Mohr and Perry had shown up their bosses. The overall losers were members of the press, because this minor war caused a further credibility gap that allowed public officials to assume an "I told you so" attitude about the remaining members of the resident Saigon corps.

The "club members" were furious when Mohr was forced into resigning. Halberstam said later, "Probably the most malicious of all was the insinuation that those few Americans who knew the country better than others, who had friends there and who cared the most about the war, were deliberately or capriciously writing pessimistic stories."[88] Joining the controversy, other observers came to Saigon to check for themselves, including Igor Oganesoff and Norm Sklarewitz of the *Wall Street Journal*, Robert Hewett of the *Minneapolis Tribune*, and Frank Conniff's Hearst task force.[89] Conniff's initial reaction was to label Halberstam another Herbert L. Matthews, saying that the *New York Times* had misled the public during Castro's rise to power and that Halberstam was doing the same thing in Vietnam. However, Halberstam later gave Conniff credit for fairer comments once the veteran writer had gained a feeling for the country.[90]

COUP D'ETAT

In October 1963 Secretary of Defense Robert McNamara and General Maxwell D. Taylor, Chairman of the Joint Chiefs of Staff, finished a seven-day tour of Vietnam. Their report was extremely optimistic regarding the progress being made on the battlefield. They suggested that a thousand advisers could be withdrawn by the end of 1963 and the U.S. involvement could be largely completed by the end of 1965. But they urged Kennedy to withhold certain aid monies unless Diem cleared the political atmosphere.[91] *Newsweek* wondered aloud how McNamara and Taylor could have learned anything of significance during a whirlwind "guided" journey filled with briefings from those whose careers were involved. One officer who overhead what McNamara was being told admitted to a *Newsweek* reporter, "We were in tears."[92] McNamara met with U.S. journalists, but his guidelines for the session precluded his asking any questions of their opinions, meaning he could head home ignorant of information contradictory to that learned in official briefings.

As November approached the news was of the McNamara-Taylor mission, a trip by Madame Nhu to the United States, Senator Mike Mansfield's lonely speech suggesting that the war was going poorly, and arguments about the hamlet strategy. Then out of nowhere came the coup. Sheehan and Halberstam had been tipped off early that a coup was imminent. By bad luck Sheehan had been ordered to Tokyo for a brief vacation, despite his pleading to be allowed to stay in Saigon. But Halberstam was ready when, on the morning of October 31, 1963, a messenger gave him a scrap of paper with a prearranged code phrase. The coup was to take place the next day. The CIA, the embassy, and some military people had the word also. Admiral Felt was leaving that morning, and Halberstam covered his airport exit, all the time watching a Vietnamese officer who in turn kept glancing nervously at his watch. Murray Gart, Mohr's replacement, and Mert Perry, who was still there, had been clued in. When troops were seen moving into the streets, Halberstam, Ray Hendron of UPI, and others began running. Vo Huynh was filming incoming troops for NBC. Larry Burrows was shooting for *Life*, Le Phuoc was taking pictures for UPI, and several persons were photographing for AP.

Halberstam scurried around all day and night in the midst of chaos and rumors. Diem and his brother were dead, murdered by their own troops while being escorted in an armored car. His dispatch was buried the next day by the tonnage of words from Washington. Sheehan showed up on the next plane from Tokyo to begin wrapping up how it all happened, and the AP writers did the same. There would be speculation for years about the

CIA's role. The conventional wisdom was that JFK authorized CIA assistance for the coup but not for the assassination, and that he was genuinely shocked by the turn of events. The killings dominated U.S. media for weeks. Burrows's color photo of a Vietnamese soldier emptying his canteen in President Diem's front yard filled *Life*'s cover. Madame Nhu was in Los Angeles angrily accusing the U.S. government of her husband's death. The next in a chain of South Vietnamese governments was installed, each one needing more assistance that its predecessor. Within three weeks President Kennedy would be dead and from that point there would be no looking back.

CHANGING OF THE PRESS GUARD

Halberstam and Browne won Pulitzer Prizes for their 1963 reporting and new faces began to appear in Vietnam. Halberstam left for other assignments on December 9 after making a final trip to the Delta; Browne was to stay for another two years to fill out a five-year stay. Sheehan left in 1964 to join the *New York Times* and returned for another fling in 1965. Browne quit the AP in 1965, disillusioned with the war and the journalists' failure to affect policy. He stayed in Saigon with ABC television and later joined the *New York Times*. Faas won the 1965 Pulitzer Prize in photography and Arnett made it three in a row for the Saigon bureau in 1966, assuming leadership of the press corps as the war dragged on into the 1970s. Halberstam later called Arnett "the best reporter of the war."[93] Arnett hailed Browne for his consistent, tenacious reporting, calling him and Halberstam "the most influential correspondents" in those early days.[94] François Sully returned upon the death of Diem and again began sending *Newsweek* stories about how badly the war was going, until he was killed in a helicopter crash in Laos in May 1971. Daring and resourceful to the end, Sully had ignored a U.S. Command news blackout of President Nixon's Laotian invasion and had hitched a ride on a Vietnamese helicopter, which rammed into a hillside. Professor Bernard Fall was not destined to survive the war, either, and neither was Marguerite Higgins. Fall, who authored so many analyses and reviews of the war situation, stepped on a land mine in early 1967. Higgins contracted a rare virus disease in Vietnam and died at the age of 45 in January of 1966.

Jim Lucas of Scripps-Howard newspapers would be showing up in 1964, a World War II and Korean War veteran ready for action. Like Higgins, Keyes Beech, and other older reporters, he accepted war as a hard fact of life and was not one of the "activists probing into the humaneness of the military tactics."[95] For five months during that year he lived in the Mekong

Delta, eventually winning the Ernie Pyle award for his writing of the boys in the field. *His Dateline: Vietnam* is filled with anecdotes about that experience. He became a favorite of those at home who wanted to hear that the war wasn't going all that badly. But despite their differences in background and viewpoint, Jim Lucas and David Halberstam had one perspective in common—they both thought the American press in the main had done a miserable job staffing the war zone. Lucas, who had won a Pulitzer Prize in Korea and was on hand in Hanoi when the French were defeated in 1954, was greatly disappointed that in early 1964 he was the only correspondent for an American daily newspaper assigned to stay with troops in the field. Indeed, in mid-1964 there were only two dozen foreign correspondents from all nations covering the war and they all were bunched in Saigon reporting the succession of political crises that overshadowed the Communists' growing control of the countryside.

Halberstam, in a fit of anger after being attacked by two governments and some of his own fellow journalists, expressed the same feelings. During his 1962–63 tour, he had been the only regular daily newspaper correspondent in all of Vietnam. "I feel the *Washington Post*, the *New York Herald Tribune*, the *Baltimore Sun* and other papers which have great influence in the United States failed to meet their obligations," he stated. "If some of us had more journalistic power than was merited, it had been granted us purely by default."[96] But the question remains: How much power and influence did the press corps really have? While the thin-skinned Kennedy team reacted strongly to stories critical of the military and political efforts—and events took their course—the stories from Saigon did not change many minds in U.S. newsrooms. Salisbury's inside position at the *New York Times* yielded this discouraging assessment and gives merit to the argument that it was not until the casualties mounted in 1966–67 and the bloody pictures were brought home—mainly by television—that the U.S. public (including editors and broadcast executives) began to pay attention:

> If the *Times* editorial writers were paying any heed to the splendidly realistic correspondence which *Times* and other American correspondents had been transmitting since the end of World War II—the informed dispatches of Robert Trumbull, the *déjà vu* reports of Tillman Durdin, the hard-eyed realism of Homer Bigart—there was no evidence that it had affected the stream of editorials, each one as like the latest government pronouncement as one sausage resembles another.[97]

One of the Vietnam myths perpetuated by revisionists and believed by many in the U.S. military is that the news media lost the war. In short, liberal reporters consistently sent home negative reports that inflamed the antiwar movement. Nothing could be further from the truth, as Halberstam, Harrison Salisbury, CBS's Morley Safer, Arnett, and others argued at a 1983 "retrospective" conference on the war and its effects. Instead, Halberstam and Salisbury said they wished the Saigon reporters had been more critical of U.S. policies in the early days. One of their critics was Beech, who said that the 1962–63 reporting had been "lopsided." While the intramural debate continued to rage 20 years after it originally flared in Saigon's bars, the author privately asked Salisbury, the dean of the sessions, to evaluate the reporters with whom he had served over his nearly 60-year career. A specific question was: "If a major foreign story broke right now and you could take two reporters with you, who would they be?" Caught off guard for a moment, his mind flashed over the years. Then his eyes fell on Halberstam a few feet away and he said quietly, "Well, David," and after a pause he added, "and Sheehan."[98] The Vietnam-era journalists had earned their stripes.

Chapter Six

Central America: The "Good Neighbor"

Unmasked in Nicaragua and El Salvador

Penny Lernoux, a freelance writer, and the *New York Times*'s (second from right) Alan Riding, receive a distinguished journalism award from Columbia University President Michael Sovern in 1980 for their work from Central America. UPI/Bettmann

INTRODUCTION: NICARAGUA

Whether they knew it or not, reporters covering Nicaragua in the 1970s and 1980s walked in the footsteps of Carleton Beals, the *Nation* reporter who was the first U.S. correspondent to interview General Augusto César Sandino during his guerrilla war against occupying U.S. Marines in 1928. Those familiar with the region's history knew that Beals's classic nine-part series had been buried quickly in libraries and that U.S. policies in Central America had not changed much since the days of Presidents Coolidge, Hoover, and Roosevelt. It was during FDR's tenure (1933–45) that interest in maintaining the stability necessary for continued corporate profits evolved into this nation's self-serving "Good Neighbor Policy."

The legacies of Beals and Sandino are important factors in understanding recent coverage. Beals was one of the few journalists in Central America who reported the truth about U.S. barbarity and hypocrisy. His stories, like those of many other twentieth-century journalists, were ignored by the so-called opinion makers. Instead, the hysterical rantings in mainstream newspapers from New York to North Dakota raked up more fear of the Bolsheviks, who bankers, industrial leaders and politicians said were gaining power South of the Border by using "bandits" like Sandino.

The most telling quote on this matter was in Beals's February 11, 1928, cable to *The Nation*. Contradicting the terrible image of Sandino being manufactured in Washington, he wrote:

> "Do you still think of us as bandits?" was his last query as I bade him goodby.
> "You are as much as bandit as Mr. Coolidge is a bolshevik," was my reply.
> "Tell your people," he returned, "there may be bandits in Nicaragua, but they are not necessarily Nicaraguans."[1]

Tales of U.S. Marine atrocities became part of Nicaraguan lore. Beals wrote of his attempts to separate exaggeration from fact and then confirmed an endless number of murders and rapes of civilians and the burning of homes to the ground. Writing in the first person with great description, he told of his horseback rides over the mountains and along mud-filled roads, sick in the freezing rain, to find Sandino.

Sandino stuck with his successful hit-and-run tactics after suffering one major defeat, at Ocotal in northern Nicaragua on July 16, 1927, when U.S. planes conducted the first organized dive-bombing raid in aviation history. More than 100 of Sandino's men died in his assault on Ocotal and the air raid, including some killed by machine-gun fire from the planes while running for cover. Not long afterward President Coolidge made headlines by decorating the pilots at the White House with the same smugness later demonstrated by President Reagan when he brought Contra leaders and CIA agents into his office.

Just as U.S. politicians of the 1980s debated the strength and popularity of Daniel Ortega's government, Washington of 1928 was engaged in a similar dialogue. For those who doubted the legitimacy of Sandino's leadership, Beals had an answer, and a warning for the future:

Whatever the rest of Nicaragua may think of us [the North Americans] this little corner knows only bitterness and hatred. We have taken a place in the minds of these people with the hated Spanish conquerors of other days. The password runs among the people and it echoes in their songs: "We must win our second independence, this time from the Americans, from the Machos, the Yankees, the hated Gringos." Names enough they have for us.

My personal opinion is that if Sandino had arms he could raise an army of ten thousand men by snappng his fingers; that if he marched into Managua, the capital, tomorrow, he would receive the greatest ovation in Nicaraguan history. America's friends in Nicaragua are the politicians who have bled the country for so many decades; they are the politicians who wish to stay in power or to get into power with our help. I would not advise any American marine to walk lonely roads at night in Nicaragua.[2]

As for Sandino's place in history, the *Nation* of Oswald Garrison Villard made this prediction in an editorial:

Some time he will probably be slain on his own territory by United States marines and his little army will be dispersed. Then he will become a legendary hero to Latin Americans of all lands, and the Gringo will be hated with even more bitter hate. But meanwhile the war goes on. Towns are bombed and destroyed by the new Huns, and occasionally a few marines go to their death on soil that is not theirs for a cause that they can be hardly expected to understand.[3]

The exasperated U.S. forces did leave in 1933, at 5:00 P.M. on January 2 to be exact, but not before installing Gen. Anastasio Somoza Garcia as head of a newly created National Guard. On February 21, 1934, Sandino was assassinated by guardsmen, and two years later Somoza rigged an election that made him president. His reign turned into a dictatorship in 1944; finally in 1956 he himself was assassinated.[4] His son Luis took over until 1963, then turning the country over to a younger brother, Anastasio Somoza Debayle, who continued the systematic looting of the nation's wealth. Meanwhile in 1960 and 1961 a group of young revolutionaries, including Carlos Fonseca and Tomas Borge, organized to plot Somoza's downfall. By 1963 they were calling themselves the Sandinistas and used Sandino's old red-and-black flag.

In addition to the Somozas of Nicaragua, who ruled from 1933 to 1979, the U.S. supported the ruthless dictators Rafael Trujillo in the Dominican Republic from 1930 to 1961, and Fulgencio Batista in Cuba from 1934 to

1959. The 1932 Matanza in El Salvador, the extermination of about 30,000 Indian workers by forces of Gen. Maximiliano Hernandez Martinez, was sanctioned by the U.S. government. This makes understandable the CIA's overthrow of the democratically elected Guatemalan government in 1954, the Bay of Pigs invasion of Cuba in 1961, the sending of U.S. forces to the Dominican Republic in 1965, threats to invade Nicaragua in the 1980s, sanctioning of right-wing oppression in El Salvador, the 1989 invasion of Panama, and complicity in the continued suppression of dissent throughout the region.

The imperialistic urges felt first in the Mexican War period of the 1840s—Manifest Destiny—and revived in the Spanish-American War period of the 1890s really never went away. Nor did the ignorance of the U.S. public, which continually supported such a selfish foreign policy over the years, if only by not caring about what went on in the region. Of all of these Central American events, the Nicaraguan experience is the most revealing because of the lack of limits in the U.S. drive for power and money at the expense of its poor neighbors, from Mexico to the Panama Canal.

During the Contra War of the 1980s few North Americans had any idea about this nation's previous experiences in Central America and in Nicaragua in particular: that a North American mercenary named William Walker declared himself president of Nicaragua in 1856 after his small force seized the capital; that U.S. Marines came to Nicaragua in 1909 to intervene in politics and again from 1912 to 1925 and from 1926 to 1933; that the U.S. set up the repressive Nicaraguan National Guard, from which was spawned the Contra leadership of the 1980s.[5]

This chapter concentrates on the coverage of the Sandinista Revolution and the Contra War. The lion's share of attention is given the *New York Times*'s Stephen Kinzer, arguably for several years the most important correspondent there. While some of his exploits were atypical, for the most part his Nicaraguan experiences matched those of his colleagues—we can learn what it was like there through his eyes. The lessons learned by the Managua press corps are spelled out here. In addition there is a separate section, with its own brief introduction, on El Salvador. The focus there is on government efforts to intimidate and manipulate the press corps. As for the future, while Nicaraguan and Salvadoran news coverage dropped off sharply after the 1990 election of Nicaraguan President Violeta Chamorro and the 1992 Salvadoran truce between guerrillas and the government, there was every indication that the U.S. would be involved in regional politics for years to come.

KINZER OF THE *TIMES*: THE MAN IN THE MIDDLE

Stephen Kinzer sat in the bright late afternoon sunshine at a table outside of Antojitos restaurant, a favorite gathering place for reporters across from Managua's Intercontinental Hotel. It was July 1986 and President Ronald Reagan's Contra War was in full swing, generating widespread political controversy. In less than three months the biggest story of the war would pop into the open—the shooting down in Nicaragua of a C-123 cargo plane secretly carrying arms to Contra forces. The illegal supply network was the Central American end of covert operations which the news media dubbed the Iran-Contra scandal. Inexplicably, at this moment Kinzer was the only full-time U.S. newspaper correspondent stationed permanently in Nicaragua. Only 35, he had spent much of the past decade in Central America and had become the object of curiosity and some envy among his foreign press corps colleagues.

Sipping lemonade and hiding behind the dark glasses that were his personal trademark, the New York Times reporter was in a pensive mood. If anyone appreciated the historic importance of the vicious U.S.-sponsored war against the Nicaraguans, it was Kinzer, a Boston University history major and former press secretary for Massachusetts Governor Michael Dukakis, whose fascination with the people and their history first led him there in November of 1976.[6]

During our meeting Kinzer candidly discussed something that he could not escape: the opportunities and perils accrued by being the New York Times correspondent, the writer on the spot more than any other, reporting in the tradition of past Times foreign correspondents who found themselves uncomfortably in the spotlight—Tad Szulc disclosing the Bay of Pigs planning in 1961, David Halberstam describing the looming Vietnam quagmire in 1963, Harrison Salisbury unmasking lies in 1966 about U.S. bombing raids in North Vietnam, or perhaps Raymond Bonner, drummed out of El Salvador in 1982 after exposing a massacre of civilians.[7]

Kinzer fully realized that his errors stuck out like a sore thumb. His Managua critics, many of them housed within an outspoken European contingent that enjoyed considerably more editorial leeway with interpretations, considered his tit-for-tat style to be an extension of U.S. State Department bulletins. The fact that for most of his Central American tenure he lived and traveled apart from the company of other journalists added to his unpopularity.

He really was in a no-win situation, and his dilemma underscored the correspondents' problems in reporting the complexities of this conflict. During this conversation he explained how, only a few days earlier, he had driven to San José de Bocay in Northern Nicaragua to follow up on the deaths of 32 Nicaraguans who died when a mine blew up under their truck on a muddy dirt road, one of the biggest single incidents of the war. He had been on vacation at the time of the July 2 incident and upon returning had chosen to file a report based primarily on diplomatic sources instead of joining other journalists on a Sandinista-organized press tour to the area. His summary of conflicting opinions had the effect of throwing cold water on the Sandinista version. Balancing off the different possibilities, Kinzer indicated that the mine could have been planted by either side and that it was unlikely anyone would determine the truth.

Asked bluntly how he could have written such an unlikely story, given the Contras' record for terrorism in that region, Kinzer said simply, "I made a mistake." He had relied on "Embassy sources," not the first time a Managua regular had been the victim of either deliberate disinformation or bureaucratic ignorance, from one side or the other. "After that [first story], however, I still was not satisfied. I didn't feel that the magnitude of the event had been reflected in essentially a survey of diplomats . . . now [in the second story which had appeared on page one shortly before this interview] I am able to say apparently Contras are planting mines, that they are blowing up trucks and killing civilians. I *know* that civilians have been killed in truck explosions up there from my own reporting and observations *now*. This is something I didn't know at the time. That story is a much better candidate for front page presentation or a heavy amount of attention."[8]

Kinzer had driven into the Nicaraguan countryside hundreds of times, alone or with his trusted driver and friend Guillermo Marcia. His Land Cruiser was a familiar sight in distant villages where he endured primitive sleeping and eating conditions, often falling sick in his efforts to get personal accounts. There was no question about his personal courage; he demonstrated it numerous times, beginning with the prelude to the Sandinista triumph of 1979 when he ventured into guerrilla strongholds, and later when he drove into the Contra war zones.

What galled his critics on the left—from MIT's Noam Chomsky to members of Witness for Peace who had seen firsthand the destruction caused by Contra forces—was what they called Kinzer's practice of going out of his way to balance the anti-Contra elements of his war correspondence with tough criticism of Sandinista leaders. They saw him as the most important member of a group offering generally uncritical reporting of the Reagan administration's litany of lies about a Sandinista threat to the region. His more severe critics skewered Kinzer in their reviews for failing to use his position to pinpoint Washington's hyprocrisy in masking a colonial-era foreign policy under the guise of fighting Communism with Ronald Reagan's "Freedom Fighters." The criticism of Kinzer—some of it unfair—was symbolic of that aimed at numerous correspondents.

A relatively balanced position on all of this was taken by Darryl Hunt, a former Maryknoll priest who assisted the Sandinistas with press relations, someone who knew Kinzer and his colleagues. He said that while Kinzer, an aggressive reporter, certainly was not a toady of the State Department, he and others did "bend over backwards too far in an effort to be fair to the official U.S. position and thus at times were unfair to the Sandinistas."[9] The intimidating refrain charging bias was an old one, heard from both sides of a story by correspondents throughout the century.

GETTING THE SANDINISTA HISTORY STRAIGHT:
THE SOMOZA YEARS

Like so much of Latin American history, the events that led up to the 1979 Sandinista victory were not clear to the public during the subsequent showdown with the Reagan administration in the 1980s. Many references to the past were twisted by U.S. government officials. Reporters often failed to insert the key background paragraph that could provide a bit of perspective. Therefore, a retracing is vital to understanding the points of contention encountered by reporters like Kinzer. One path is to follow along with his career. Kinzer's goal was to write about Nicaragua's distinctive features and to put the anti-Somoza revolution and the Contra War into context with the nation's turbulent twentieth-century history. He also wanted to work in some stories about baseball, poets, and volcanoes along the way.[10] Genuinely enthusiastic about this, he was scholarly in his approach, fluent in Spanish and steeped in Latin American history. In his case an early turning point had been his purchase of E.G. Squier's 1860 book, *Nicaragua: Its People, Scenery, Monuments, Resources, Condition, and Proposed Canal; with One Hundred Original Maps and Illustrations.* Squier had been Chargé d'Affaires of the United States to the Republics of Central America.

Armed with this historical knowledge, he first ventured to Nicaragua in November 1976 as an inquiring freelancer eager to learn about the dictator Anastasio Somoza and his mysterious Sandinista foes. One of the highlights of that first trip was meeting Pedro Joaquín Chamorro, editor of *La Prensa* and Somoza's main opponent. His research led to some work for the Pacific News Service, a progressive San Francisco–based syndicate and a 1977 *New Republic* article titled "Nicaragua: A Wholly Owned Subsidiary."

He made one more trip for PNS in late 1977, when he met Somoza for the first time and became hooked more than ever on reporting the unfolding drama. Chamorro's assassination on January 10, 1978, by men thought to be associated with Somoza, led to widespread demonstrations and increased repression by the brutal National Guard.

Kinzer was ready for the challenge, and in February his bag was packed, this time in the name of the *Boston Globe*, which he was proud to represent first as a freelancer and finally as a regular correspondent between then and the fall of 1982. During this general period, while a freelancer washing his own clothes at night, he also did some work in the region for the *Washington Post*.

Somoza's world turned upside down on August 22 when a Sandinista commando unit headed by the shrewd and emotional Eden (Commander Zero) Pastora captured the entire Nicaraguan Congress and about a thousand National Palace employees after disguising themselves as one of Somoza's élite units. *Time*'s Bernard Diederich claimed that he would have "scooped" his newsmagazine rivals on this story had a plane carrying him from Panama to Managua landed in the right city. "I was up in the cockpit, pleading with the pilot to land," he said. But because of the "political situation on the ground" he had to go to another country and come back the next day. "By then everyone was there outside of the National Palace including my rival Stryker McGuire of *Newsweek*."[11]

Withstanding immense pressure to attack the building, Somoza feared the deaths of a relative and friends. Given no choice, and with the news media watching for his reaction, he agreed to the broadcasting of a nearly two-hour Sandinista communiqué which urged people to prepare for the "final offensive." A triumphant Pastora and his men rode nine miles through cheering crowds to the Managua airport, winners of an incredibly tense standoff unprecedented in Latin American history.

After spending a considerable amount of time with reporters and photographers at the unguarded airport, the rebels flew off with 59 political prisoners, including Borge, and $500,000 of Somoza's money.

In only two days, after 17 years of off-and-on skirmishing, the Sandinista

National Liberation Front (FSLN) emerged with the image as an organization with firm leadership. Soon to be supported by a broad coalition of business and church leaders, the guerrillas now had a chance to remove Somoza. Pastora's raid went into the storybooks, alongside the December 27, 1974, hostage-taking raid on a Managua cocktail party that resulted in the release three days later of 14 political prisoners, including Daniel Ortega. The Commander Zero of that daring encounter with Somoza was Sandinista hero Eduardo Contreras Escobar, destined to be shot to death in Managua by Somoza's anti-terror squad on November 7, 1976, the day before Fonseca, the FSLN's secretary-general, was killed up in the mountains. Fonseca's head was delivered to Somoza by helicopter.

The Nicaragua of 1978 leaped into America's headlines, with Alan Riding of the *New York Times*, Karen DeYoung of the *Washington Post*, Bernard Diederich of *Time*, and Silio Boccanera of *Jornal do Brasil* sharing a house. Kinzer was invited to live and work with them. It should be noted that DeYoung was the first of many women correspondents who would distinguish themselves in Central America in both the full-time and freelance ranks.

Riding, a British citizen born in Rio de Janeiro, worked for Reuters in London before moving to Mexico in 1971 to begin seven years of freelancing for the *New York Times*, the *Financial Times*, and the *Economist*. Then in February 1978 he became Mexico City bureau chief, with responsibility for the region. Known for his generally liberal attitudes and his disgust for the dictators of the right, he ended up on the death list of the Salvadoran death squads in the early 1980s.

One veteran journalist fondly recalled Riding's response to criticism of one of his stories from Max Kelly, a Nicaraguan graduate of West Point who was Somoza's frequent spokesman. Approaching a group of journalists waiting outside of Somoza's bunker, Kelly said, "Riding, the boss doesn't think much of your story." Without hesitation, Riding shot back, "You can tell your boss I don't think much of him, either." In 1984 he went back to Rio de Janeiro to become bureau chief there, but not before playing a major role in what became known as "the early days."[12]

Throughout 1978 and into 1979 the Sandinista guerrillas gained momentum in their popular struggle and the various opposition groups began their temporary merger into one unbeatable unit. All of this was reported in great detail by the growing number of journalists sent to cover this flashpoint, while elements within the Carter administration, including the CIA, began to warn about the consequences of a complete Sandinista victory. Carter prayed that "moderates" would assume control, not self-styled guerrillas who spouted Marxist slogans.[13]

Some unrealistic U.S. planners wanted to broker a settlement between Somoza and his opponents, but all such notions of compromise were shattered on June 20, 1979, when ABC correspondent Bill Stewart was murdered by a national guardsman. The scene, filmed by his cameraman and broadcast worldwide, brought a surge of anger from the United States. Diederich, who covered Mexico and Central America for *Time* in 1965, was at the Intercontinental Hotel in Managua that day when the distraught ABC crew came running in with the tape of their colleague's death. The 37-year-old Stewart's body lay in the back of their small van.

Diederich, the senior member of the 90-member foreign press corps, handed the group's official protest to Somoza at a news conference that evening, and ABC producer Ken Lucoff read it aloud. Diederich, whose duties were expanded to report for the *Washington Star* following its 1978 purchase by Time, Inc., organized a "safe house" for himself and other journalists as the danger level rose. The Intercontinental Hotel ceased to function as a center for activities. Journalists rarely went out alone.

Following Stewart's death several dozen journalists, including most of the television crews, fled to Panama for safety reasons. Diederich recalled later how, during the weeks surrounding Stewart's death, DeYoung, Mark Starr of the *Chicago Tribune*, himself, CBS's George Nathenson, Gilbert Lewthwaite of the *Baltimore Sun*, and others barely escaped injury or death in various shooting incidents.[14] "There was a lot of collaboration among journalists," he told this writer in late 1992. "It was a risky war."

Tempers were short, too. DeYoung reported an emotional exchange in Managua between Rep. Larry MacDonald, a Georgia Democrat supportive of Somoza, and an ABC correspondent. After MacDonald said there was "no question of the distortion of news [of Nicaragua] in the United States," the journalist asked MacDonald "to walk down here on the beach at the Lake and look at the bodies with their hands tied that the [National Guard] is burning in the morning. And you come down here and accuse us of distorting? Where the hell have you been, sir?"[15]

Despite pressure from the right-wing sector of U.S. politics during these final days, the Carter administration denied Somoza access to a huge shipment of arms from Israel, a longtime participant in Central American intrigue.[16]

Inspired by the front-page stories breaking around them, and by the heroics of the people revolting against the despised National Guard, a number of journalists earned their stripes during these days. While the true nature of *Sandinismo* was not clear to them, there was a black-and-white story there, almost a romantic tale of brave men and women overthrowing a U.S.-supported tyrant whose torture chambers included a room in his own home.

Those who were there fondly remember chronicling Somoza's resignation and departure on July 17, the seizure of Managua on July 19, and the great victory celebration on July 20 in what became known as the Plaza of the Revolution. The *Miami Herald*'s Guy Gugliotta, a former UPI correspondent in Brazil, covered the main events of the final offensive. As the end neared he was joined by Don Bohling, the *Herald*'s Latin American editor since 1968, who made frequent trips throughout the region until the early 1980s.[17]

Stanley Meisler was there temporarily for the *Los Angeles Times*, adding depth to the coverage as he had during six years as the Nairobi correspondent. Sizing up the past U.S.-Somoza relationship and the likelihood of meddling by the Carter administration, Meisler wrote on July 17: "To a Nicaraguan it is almost in the natural order of things for the United States to rule in this country's political future." This excellent and rare piece of work traced Nicaraguan history back to William Walker and put Sandino's life in perspective.[18]

On July 19 Meisler reported to the *Times*:

> Managua—The Sandinista rebel army, brandishing red and black flags and shooting more in celebration than in battle, overran Managua on Thursday, bringing the Nicaraguan civil war to an end.[19]

The *Chicago Tribune*, for the most part opposed to any form of socialism rearing its head south of the Mexican border, gave the U.S. government a surprising tip for the future in a July 18 editorial headlined, "Exit Anastasio." Noting Sandino's resistance to U.S. Marines, the *Tribune* said the earlier U.S. involvement and the current support for Somoza was one cause of the present conflict. Advice for the future: there might be temptation to use U.S. force in Nicaragua but this should be avoided.[20] Tim McNulty was in Miami covering Somoza's arrival into exile; Starr was in Managua, reporting on the din of honking auto horns and the spectacle of Daniel Ortega and other junta members speaking from the steps of the National Palace.[21]

DeYoung gave *Washington Post* readers a preview of complexities to come. The Carter administration, badly out of step and preoccupied with a cabinet shakeup, major Middle East developments, and the fabled energy crisis, asked for more moderates to appear within the anti-Somoza leadership. Fearing future "Sandinista radicalism," one week before the Sandinista takeover, U.S. officials actually requested that a settlement include a provision whereby elements of Somoza's National Guard would stay in power as a balancing force. The momentum was in the opposite direction, however, as the *Post's* Terri Shaw reported from San José, Costa Rica, where the junta leadership was preparing to return to Nicaragua.

DeYoung was among the mob of journalists outside of Somoza's bunker in the early hours of July 17 when the dictator left for Miami. Two days later she again was up early to write:

> Managua—The Nicaraguan civil war ended early this morning as Sandinista National Liberation Front guerrillas took control of the capital and called for a cease-fire jointly with remaining members of the National Guard.[22]

The huge Sandinista victory parade was on July 20, when Borge, Pastora, the Ortega brothers, Jaime Wheelock, and others carried rifles at the head of the procession and junta members rode on the top of a fire truck. Lurking beneath the celebratory rhetoric was another story, revolving around the shaky alliance between the Sandinista fighting force and businessmen. DeYoung's dispassionate analyses included all of the characters in the coming struggle for control.[23] Freelance photographer Susan Meiselas won the cherished Robert Capa prize for her photos of those days.[24]

Alan Riding described the victory day this way:

> Managua (July 20)—Escorted by hundreds of heavily armed Sandinista rebels, Nicaragua's Government drove into Managua today to a thunderous reception and was immediately sworn in as the successor to the long-ruling Somoza regime.[25]

The *New York Times's* Warren Hoge flew from San José to Managua with members of the junta and the new cabinet, including Foreign Minister Miguel D'Escoto, who gazed from the window as the plane approached Managua and worried about how much the people below had suffered to reach this moment. There would be much more suffering to come, as Riding pointed out in a Sunday analysis piece the following day. "The political struggle for democracy has just begun," he said. "The leftists who for so long fought the regime are not about to surrender the country to businessmen who squabbled with the dictatorship over 'unfair competition.'"[26] Although Riding and his colleagues did not know it at the time, many of those businessmen would end up supporting the Contra war and finally Violeta Chamorro's 1990 campaign against Ortega.

Stephen Kinzer, filing to the *Globe* and assisting DeYoung, was in and out of Central America during this period, but he was one of those who grew up as a journalist during the risky and exciting days of 1978–79. Even so, he probably had no idea how his fortunes would become intertwined with the Sandinistas and Central American politics. In addition to his basic newspaper reporting, he demonstrated his awareness of root causes of violence—corporate-inspired injustices—in his 1982 book, *Bitter Fruit*, in which he and Stephen Schlesinger documented the CIA's role in the 1954 coup in Guatemala and the failure of the U.S. press to put the story in a critical perspective.

After his numerous activities on behalf of the *Globe*—including an assignment to cover the Falklands War between Great Britain and Argentina—he was recruited by the *New York Times* in late 1982, starting his work on January 1, 1983. In April he was named Managua bureau manager. The *Times* was the first major paper to recognize the importance of having a full-time representative in Nicaragua, taking the lead as it had in Saigon with Halberstam.

THE EVOLUTION OF THE MANAGUA PRESS CORPS

The Managua scene was continuously surrealistic. The journalist's mind flashes back and images from a half-dozen trips merge. There is Daniel Ortega, driving alone to work, sitting in his Jeep at a traffic signal. The Sandinista newspaper *Barricada* again predicts a CIA-led invasion. The White House scoffs at any such possibility. Mexico, the original Colossus of the North for Central Americans, appears as imaginary hills on the northern horizon; in proportion the United States is a ring of huge dark mountains that dwarfs everything in the region. Pressure from Reagan's Washington can be felt everywhere, heard in every other conversation. But what is the reality?

Outside the offices of the opposition paper *La Prensa*, citizens openly check a bulletin board for stories cut from that day's edition by a Sandinista censor. A few miles away a large woman shouts anti-Ortega slogans in the middle of a black-market shopping area. "To hell with the Sandinistas, let's bring in the Americans," she screams in her private free-speech area, complaining of government harassment. Visiting diplomats, journalists, U.S. activists, and intelligence agents gorge themselves at the Intercontinental Hotel's noontime buffet, while three blocks away a young mother sells plastic bags of soda pop to scraggly young activists.

The city is a stop-off place for politicians and movie stars. Former President Jimmy Carter enjoys a quiet dinner at the end of a whirlwind day checking polling stations, interrupted by only one autograph hound; Bianca Jagger is deeply engrossed in conversation, almost unnoticed; Ed Asner is angry, talking to everyone; Kris Kristopherson is over at Managua's most sacred spot, the Plaza of the Revolution, dedicated to FSLN cofounder Carlos Fonseca, which is filled with tanks and vehicles being used in an antiwar movie.

Dust blows through the dirty streets as storm clouds come across the lake, bringing rain and some relief from the stifling heat. The sun bounces off the hollow shells of the few downtown buildings remaining from the 1972 earthquake, a disaster that enriched dictator Somoza with stolen earthquake relief funds. A man selling newspapers stands on the spot where *La Prensa* editor Pedro Joaquín Chamorro Sr. was assassinated in 1978, most likely by Somoza agents who thereby unwittingly hastened the Revolution. A torn FSLN banner hangs from the wall of Somoza's former bunker at the El Chipote prison; huge concrete lettering spells out "FSLN" on a hill overlooking the city, to the chagrin of all in opposition.

During the height of the Nicaraguan fighting in the middle 1980s, Managua was swarming with outsiders eager to share their skills to help the Sandinista government.[27] In addition to the Cuban doctors and nurses who volunteered in the hospitals and health clinics, several thousand North Americans, Europeans, and others from as far away as Australia built houses, taught in schools, and otherwise roamed the countryside. Competing for sleeping spaces were dozens of freelance journalists, including a number of Europeans who were less bothered about the socialistic nature of the Sandinista government than were the bulk of their U.S. colleagues. Their reports emphasized the constant U.S. pressure on the Nicaraguan people and how the Contras blew up health clinics and schools in the name of fighting Communism. They gave attention to sympathetic interpretations of the Sandinista viewpoint, often missing from mainstream U.S. accounts and particularly from those dominated by quotes from the U.S. Embassy.

The people of Managua, a city of contradictions, found themselves caught in the middle of a long-running news story. The slow pace of life clashed with the sight of television camera teams coming into their barrios to record their politics and their poverty. In the middle of all of this was a rotating crew of U.S. journalists who tried to make sense of charges that Nicaragua was a threat to regional peace and thus U.S. security.

A handful of U.S. newspaper and press association correspondents became frequent visitors to Sandino International Airport. Press association coverage was skimpy until the early 1980s. Up until about 1984 the general practice was to live in Mexico City, Miami, or El Salvador and to cover Nicaragua on a hit-and-run basis. Then Tracy Wilkinson of UPI and Bryna Brennan of AP became familiar faces, working under incredible pressure to get the news and then please U.S. editors being pounded by the Washington version. They were part of the "second wave" of journalists who arrived in the 1985–86 period when the Reagan Administration intensified its aid to the Contras. Some of those who had covered the last years of Somoza and the opening of the Sandinista era moved on.

With the added numbers in the mid-1980s the press associations and major papers stationed two or more correspondents in the region and switched the majority of attention to Nicaragua. Broadcast news made less of a commitment to full-time regional coverage, often flying correspondents in from Miami, Dallas, or other southern cities to pick up the next phase of this running story. Camera crews were maintained in Managua and San Salvador to provide tape, however, even if a correspondent was not on the scene, and several experienced freelance television cameramen living in the region were able to fill in. In the radio field, a number of freelance radio journalists provided the bulk of network coverage, with regular correspondents showing up for major events. The National Public Radio, Latin American News Service, and Pacifica systems routinely were ahead with Contra-related stories. Spanish-language feeds were handled by the LANS, based in Austin, Texas. A major contribution was made by Noticiero Univision, Spanish-language television. Univision news shows provided a true Latin perspective for its viewers, including U.S. journalists covering the region from Miami. In the late 1980s correspondent Monica Seoane and producer Rosanna Guevara regularly covered six nations for Univision.

From their Managua and San Salvador bases the print journalists and their broadcast news colleagues made quick trips to San José, Costa Rica, especially in the late 1980s when President Oscar Arias was earning his Nobel Prize by taking the lead for peace in the region, and to Tegucigalpa, Honduras, for sidetrips into Contra-camp country along the Nicaraguan border.[28] Some spent time in Guatemala investigating the government-sponsored atrocities against the Indian population, but for the most part Guatemala escaped scrutiny.

One prominent personality in the early years was Christopher Dickey, then with the *Washington Post*. Dickey gained fame with his 1986 book *With the Contras*,[29] detailing the other side of the Nicaraguan fighting and giving considerable information about the depth of CIA coordination and control. Two years earlier Dickey had introduced *Rolling Stone* readers to the legacy of Sandino in an introduction to a photograph collection from the period, penning a scorching denunciation of U.S. policy.[30] He also made a name for himself in El Salvador for his tough reporting about the government-assisted death squads. By 1987 Dickey was working for *Newsweek* in the Middle East, one of a number of journalists who made the leap from a complicated situation to a nearly incomprehensible one. In July 1994 he was one of the journalists in Gaza witnessing Yasir Arafat's return to form a Palestinian government.

The *New York Times* team included James LeMoyne, who spent considerable time in both Nicaragua and Honduras even though his home base was El Salvador. He is remembered more for his adventures there. With Kinzer and LeMoyne in the field, the *Times* was assured of a steady flow of long interpretative stories.

The *Miami Herald* carried the strongest reputation for Latin America coverage into the Nicaraguan and El Salvador conflicts. Juan Tamayo, then a UPI news editor in Mexico City, joined the *Herald* in 1981 and covered Central America out of Miami until 1987, when he moved to the Jerusalem bureau. In the early 1982–85 period he was joined by Guy Gugliotta. Gugliotta, the UPI bureau chief in Rio in the late 1970s, covered the last days of Somoza for the *Herald*. Latin American editor Don Bohling, who roamed the region for nearly 20 years, joined him for the final offensive. Alfonso Chardy, a freelancer covering Somoza's downfall, made occasional trips over the years, but his major contribution was being the first to cover Latin America from Washington.

Shirley Christian, the AP's bureau chief in Santiago, Chile, opened the *Herald*'s first Central American bureau, in San Salvador, in 1979. She remained until 1984, when she left to join the *New York Times*. Sam Dillon replaced her as chief and was a popular figure in San Salvador and later Rio until he resigned in 1992, also to join the *Times*. Dillon covered some of the most controversial events in the Salvadoran fighting in the 1983–85 period. He in turn was replaced by Tim Golden. Andres Oppenheimer was another familiar face in the late 1980s, and Tim Johnson was in the region in the early 1990s. The *Miami Herald* and the *New York Times* were the two newspapers available at major hotels, giving their reporters a high profile but also exposing them to instant criticism from colleagues, the same problem experienced today by CNN reporters.

As expected, the *Los Angeles Times* and the *Washington Post* both competed strongly in the region, with the Los Angeles paper pouring in additional resources to ensure double coverage. The *Times* paid dearly, however, on June 21, 1983, when its Mexico City bureau chief Dial Torgerson, a highly respected reporter who earlier had served in Jerusalem, was killed on the Honduran-Nicaraguan border. Edgar Chamorro said in 1986, "To this day I have my doubts about how exactly those reporters died [the other victim was Richard Cross, freelance photographer for *U.S. News & World Report*]." Chamorro, who had warned the journalists about the dangers the night before they died, demonstrated how a number of news organizations originally reported the U.S. Embassy and Honduran version—that the pair had died when a rocket grenade fired from the Nicaraguan side hit their car. The deaths had strong "propaganda value" and were shamelessly exploited. Later investigations proved that a mine commonly used by Contras had exploded under the vehicle. Were the journalists murdered by Contras and their CIA handlers to provoke an incident? Chamorro's uneasiness causes the question to remain.[31] The question is legitimate because in 1985 there was considerable talk in the region about how the deaths of North Americans, preferably journalists, at the hands of Sandinistas would add great fuel to the pro-Contra cause, justifying military action.

The author can substantiate this. My first trip to Nicaragua was in July 1985. At that time there was considerable concern about the possibility of a U.S. invasion or, more likely, some kind of provocation that would justify air strikes on Sandinista air bases and storage depots. The 1983 mining incidents and the 1984 Contra attempt to take Ocotal in the north (to establish a provisional capital) were fresh in everyone's minds. On a visit to a Nicaraguan army hospital a few miles from a regular battle zone, a nurse pointed to a field and told me that after a recent firefight they had "buried two gringos right over there." Gringos, U.S. mercenaries, Special Forces advisers, CIA agents—who were they? We never found out, but the U.S. presence was in the air. It was still there a year later when I met Stephen Kinzer, who noted how vulnerable the Sandinistas were to hit-and-run sabotage raids.

A host of *Los Angeles Times* reporters went south. The talented, multilingual Daniel Williams, a former *Miami Herald* correspondent in China and the Middle East, replaced Torgerson, becoming San Salvador chief in 1983. After being in the middle of the Salvadoran civil war he moved on to Mexico City in 1985 and Marjorie Miller moved into San Salvador, where she became known for her strong interpretative reports. She also spent considerable time in Nicaragua and Honduras. Miller became Mexico City bureau chief in 1988 when Williams headed for Jerusalem. Richard Boudreaux opened the paper's first Managua office in late 1986 as the *Los Angeles Times* rivaled the *New York Times* for the most overseas bureaus (about two dozen each). Boudreaux stayed there until late 1992, when he went to

Moscow. Ken Freed was another *Times* staffer who toured Central America for a number of years.

Julia Preston, who earlier earned a reputation for solid reporting for Pacific News Service, and Edward Cody gained attention for their *Washington Post* work, getting their fair share of kudos and darts. So did Joanne Omang, William Branigin, and stringer John Lantigua, who also worked for UPI. Among the television journalists, Peter Collins was a mainstay for ABC throughout the 1980s, traveling out of Miami. Known for his outspoken negative comments about the Sandinistas, Collins was not a favorite of those critical of U.S. policy. But he was liked at ABC's New York headquarters and stayed on despite his attitude. Mike O'Connor of CBS was considered one of the best and most fair-minded journalists in the region before he was let go in March 1986 during one of the many budget crises that robbed the home audience of solid journalism. Of the CNN crew, Leigh Green briefly prowled the countryside, and later Lucia Newman and Ronnie Loveler became familiar figures. NBC had no regular coverage, but Jamie Gangel made a number of trips, as did Dennis Murphy and others.[32]

The most realistic newsmagazine account of what it was like in the field—and perhaps the single best overall reporting effort of the entire war—came from *Newsweek*'s Rod Nordland and freelance photographer Bill Gentile, who was on assignment with Nordland in the spring of 1987 when the pair performed an amazing feat. They first linked up for a month's patrol with a Contra band that moved down into Nicaragua, crossing the Rio Coco, and slowly maneuvered in the mountain rain forests. The journalists observed the deteriorating behavior of the frustrated and hungry Contras as they attempted to persuade peasants to join their cause. At one point the unit was attacked by a Sandinista force. Then discipline broke down and Contra soldiers began stealing from the very people they were trying to recruit. Nordland and Gentile slipped away and eventually encountered a Sandinista unit. A few weeks later they were in the company of a Sandinista strike force that attacked the very group of Contras with whom they had traveled. There in a field lay the body of a Contra who had befriended them on numerous occasions. While the story generally differentiated between the brutality of the Contras and the more benevolent nature of the Sandinista forces—in contrast to accounts written by other reporters who lived with the "freedom fighters"—it also revealed the human element of journalism: how journalists are attracted by the good nature of people on both sides of an issue and feel emotional tugs when misfortune hits someone known from personal contact.[33]

Throughout the 1980s the annual media highlight was the July 19 celebration of the victory over Somoza. Everyone showed up for this occasion, from Bulgarian diplomats to Hollywood celebrities. Up on the stage with their television crews would be the hard-edged Peter Collins and his grim-faced competitors, grabbing onlookers for interviews.[34] The local CBS bureau manager, Cookie Hood—a "character" with a million contacts—would be assisting the hustling Mike O'Connor while Jamie Gangel or someone else from NBC would be claiming their spot for filming. Out on the fringes, looking on with a practiced eye, would be the workhorse freelancer Bill Gasperini, or perhaps it would be the cheerful Marjorie Miller of the *Los Angeles Times*, interviewing persons in the crowd before the speech, or Tim Golden of the *Miami Herald*, talking with Foreign Minister Miguel D'Escoto before he took his place. Swedish newspaper reporter Nitza Kakossaios was another with a nose for buried news. If Gentile was up on the stage with Ortega getting photos for *Newsweek*, Maria Morrison was nearby in the crowd shooting for Agence France-Presse and other outlets. Only Kinzer would have been hard to find. Like others under deadline pressure, Kinzer would watch Ortega's speech on television and call the U.S. Embassy and European sources for reaction. Managua, with all of its riddles and bizarreness, was home to everyone, even those who said they hated the place.[35]

Two of the best-known Managua journalists with their ears to the ground and their motorcycles ready to zoom were Dirk Vandersypen and Jan Van Bilsen, Belgians ready to head for the countryside to cover Contra activity for their television, radio, and print clients. During the last week of 1984 they ran into a story worth retelling. It made the rounds of the Managua press corps in those days and illustrates the frustrations experienced by freelancers who were trying to get recognition for their enterprising work.

They had traveled up to Wiwili, a border town on the Coco River, to do a television feature about life in war country. It was Saturday night and they saw a wedding party in progress. It was too dark to film, but they greeted the bride and attended the party. On the following Monday the groom, who was a local policeman, asked a local man to drive them and five family members to Jinotega, away from the battle area. When their red pickup reached Zompopera, in a hilly area near the Cua River, a Contra unit commanded by "Jimmy Leo" shot it full of holes, killing five of the seven. The Belgians were finishing their work at Wiwili when they were told to rush to a local hospital. There they saw the bride's body. Her husband had survived and consented to an interview on film. After filming the horrible scene they boarded a local bus filled with young people, including schoolteachers, headed for Jinotega. They wanted to retrace the truck's route.

The bus stopped at the truck and, while they filmed the dozens of bullet holes, the widow of the driver appeared and was interviewed.

The bus trip resumed for a few miles, until armed men appeared on the side of the road. As it turned out, these were the murderers of the wedding party. As the young passengers filed out one by one, the journalists debated whether to try to hide their camera. Instead they decided to be bold. Striding off the bus, they asked to interview the commander. After a long torturous wait, with rifles pointed at their stomachs, their wish was granted. But first the commander asked them to interview all of the young people who the journalists knew were Sandinista supporters. Playing the game well, the passengers all testified to their support of the Contras. "Jimmy Leo" was on camera for about 10 minutes telling how his cause was one with God's. Within a few minutes they all were freed, taking with them their unopened notebooks with incriminating pro-Sandinista materials. Had these been discovered they might have been shot, but the Contras were distracted by the journalists.

Hustling back to Managua, the two rather "green" freelancers went to the NBC room at the Continental and after some talk sold the film for $4,000, a low fee even for those days. It was acknowledged that this was the first filming of the results of a Contra ambush and the first filming of Contras in the field. But when the pair saw the edited version that had been sent off to NBC in New York, they were horrified. Vandersypen said the film had been hacked up to portray the murders as another action in a war where both sides do bad things. When seen by a U.S. audience it did not show how a gang of criminals—a group getting rave reviews in Washington—had killed innocent people in a noncombat situation.

Determined to get their version out, they sent the long version to Europe where it was shown on Belgian television and in Sweden, Holland, and Denmark. Later it was on Australian television and was used in the film *William Walker* and the documentary *Destination Nicaragua*. The crowning moment came in early 1985, before a vote on Contra aid, when they were asked to appear on the Phil Donahue show. Vandersypen recalled that the audience was shocked by the short clip, about 45 seconds, and by their explanations. About the same time the "official" view of the episode was mocked in a *Doonesbury* cartoon.

Why did the NBC crew butcher the original story? Vandersypen was not sure. Everyone in those early days knew of brutal Contra attacks—the story was still in the black-and-white stage. By the late 1980s there was more gray in the overall story, as mentioned earlier. The Contras were more of a diverse group then, for one thing, and they had more rural support. But in this 1984 case of wanton murder, in a zone known for Contra activity, there was little reason to try to find a middle ground. Hasty, poor, and insensitive journalism—hopefully that and not political bias—is the answer. In 1994 the Belgians were still working out of Managua as well as Mexico City, outlasting their mainstream competitors, most of whom had retreated to Mexico City or San Salvador.[36]

WASHINGTON SETS THE AGENDA

The theory that journalists in Managua and Washington were guilty of "bending over backwards" to be fair to U.S. policy was supported by Time-Life's Bernard Diederich, who told this writer in late 1992, "There were a hell of a lot of things that newsmen knew [particularly about Contra activities] that they didn't report . . . This was a Washington directed war." He explained how Washington's agenda-setting caused such "deep doubts about the Sandinistas" that in the early 1980s when reporters got trapped in a Contra ambush their first thought was that it was "a Sandinista setup."[37]

Diederich, who covered the Caribbean and Central America full-time for *Time* from 1965 to 1981, said that with Reagan and Secretary of State Alexander Haig in power at the start of the Contra war, the magazine went "right wing" in its Central American coverage. He credited it with improvement later in the 1980s. Regarding pressures on journalists, he said some who managed to get into the Contra camps and traveled with Contra units knew more than they reported about the dark side of their CIA-supported operations. He was convinced that all journalists "were put on notice in 1981 when Haig drew that geopolitical line that included Central America." The "Who Lost Nicaragua?" anti-press question was floated by an administration concerned about "losing" El Salvador.

Diederich agreed with the contention of others that Shirley Christian's March 1982 *Washington Journalism Review* attack on fellow journalists for being soft on the Sandinistas affected the press corps. He said this intramural warfare—including the 1982 controversy over the *New York Times*'s poor treatment of El Salvador correspondent Raymond Bonner (see the section of this chapter dealing with El Salvador), the intense Washington pressure, and the meddling of home-desk editors—made life difficult for those trying to get at the "other side." "There was pressure to ingratiate yourself," he said, ". . . but the Contras and Sandinistas knew where people stood . . . they saw Shirley (*Miami Herald*) as a rightwinger and

Alan (Riding of the *New York Times*) as liberal . . . the key was to keep a low profile and not carry your ideology on your sleeve."[38]

It is clear that Kinzer and his colleagues at their skeptical best only dented the administration's cover for its illegal actions. But the crucial point is that the major news organizations' heavy use of official statements from Washington sources and other pro-Contra groups diminished the impact of critical reports filed from the distant field. Simply put, anti-Sandinista statements by Washington officials too often were believed by the Washington reporters and their editors without properly checking with the Managua correspondent.

This coloration of news was substantiated by former press association reporters and other journalists familiar with internal pressures and politics in the 1985–91 period. It is clear that unskeptical Washington journalists, including some working for the Associated Press and United Press International, allowed the Reagan administration to dominate the news flow. "Washington [journalists] considered this a policy story," one recalled. "Washington sees everything in black and white . . . when I went to Central America I was more aware of the need for balance than ever before . . . I tried not to overplay the U.S. side but I knew not to play up the anti-U.S. side . . . the people of Nicaragua and El Salvador were in the gray area, in the middle.[39]

Regarding the flow of news, it should be noted that Mexico City was a gatekeeping spot for both AP and UPI. Bias in the Mexico City office could stop a story from moving on or cause it to be rewritten. Bias in New York or Washington could cause "rockets" (hot messages) to be sent back to the particular Central American bureau, asking why a certain pro-Washington angle was not being developed. One tactic for applying political pressure was to make comments about a journalist in the field, knowing that the word would get back. One journalist was called "Sandalista," meaning he was perceived as giving too much credence to the Ortega government in his wire service reports. While the press association staffers built a strong reputation among their colleagues for sticking to observable facts, they felt that extra pressure from the home front.

If major blame is to be assessed against news organizations for failure to reveal more of the Reagan-Bush administration's ugly underside, the bulk of it should be handed to print and broadcast executives and their U.S. desks, particularly in New York (including newsmagazines and network television) and Washington. If anything, home desks often failed to suggest or support tough anti-U.S. policy stories from the field, neglecting this side of the "balance" question. Nor did they care much about the "people" story. Instead, they sought confirmation for stories broken in Washington, such as the three Sandinista "invasions" of Honduras in the 1986–88 period.

Such announcements usually were tied to a vote on Contra aid and were designed to influence Congress. One press association reporter recalled being told by the Washington office that since the State Department said Sandinista troops had "invaded" Honduras, "it's true." U.S. helicopters ferried Honduran troops to the border and a crisis flared. As it turned out, Nicaragua never "invaded" Honduras, but Sandinista troops routinely chased Contras back across the border in a game well known to the U.S. government and more or less accepted by it.

While not absolving the field correspondents from their share of criticism, this observation about Washington manipulation and media acquiesence rings true for anyone who kept track of the avalanche of pro-administration editorials, op-ed pieces, and political columns that flowed through the system throughout the 1980s alongside neatly balanced news-analysis articles authored in the Washington bureaus. Perhaps the best look at the inside of this system is found in former AP reporter Robert Parry's 1992 book *Fooling America: How Washington Insiders Twist the Truth and Manufacture the Conventional Wisdom*.[40] The *Los Angeles Times* was one major paper deserving credit for its editorial-page stands on the Nicaraguan situation. Time and again the *Times* saw through the Reagan administration's baseless charges and misleading statements. The Minneapolis *Star Tribune* was another of very few papers whose editorials showed that someone was consistently paying attention to critical reports from the region. Moreover, the *Star Tribune*'s op-ed page occasionally carried reports from average Minnesotans who had been in Nicaragua; most op-ed pages granted access only to persons with demonstrated authority. The *Seattle Times* was another that went out of its way to gather extra information, publishing special reports prepared by an interested staffer.

While it is true that a handful of Washington-based investigative reporters could claim stories in the early and mid-1980s pinning the CIA to illegal Contra activities, it is a sad commentary on the whole news system to note that if Eugene Hasenfus had died in November 1980 when his cargo plane was shot down, it is likely that the Oliver North wing of the Iran-Contra scandal would not have been discovered for some time. The AP's Parry was the first to publicly identify North as White House contact man with the Contras. That story broke in June 1985. He and his partner Brian Barger carried their investigation deeper, including travel in Central America, and on June 10, 1986, reluctant AP editors allowed their comprehensive story on North's management of a private network to run.[41] Barger was taken off the story and quit the AP in late 1986, while Parry persisted until early 1987, when he resigned after 13 years of service and joined *Newsweek*. Suffering from similar self-censorship problems there, he left and became a strong critic of "establishment journalism."[42]

While working for the AP, Parry fell under increasing pressure from the State Department's Latin American Office of Public Diplomacy, headed by former Miami businessman Otto Reich, and others in the administration. On one occasion in 1986, *Miami Herald* reporter Alfonso Chardy, one of those few chasing the North story, warned Parry: "They're trashing the hell out of you," and advised him to stay off trail for a while for his own good.[43]

At *Newsweek*, though, I would discover that the CW [Conventional Wisdom] supporting the Reagan intervention in Central America was more deeply rooted than I had understood. Too many important figures in the upper echelons of American politics and journalism had committed themselves to the rightness of the cause. These were not men and women who readily admitted error.[44]

It was safe for reporters everywhere to jump onto the story after Hasenfus parachuted to safety and his list of contacts was discovered in the wreckage. On October 31 the Beirut magazine *Al Shiraa* revealed the arms-for-hostages deal, causing a worldwide sensation, and reporters began putting the Middle Eastern and Central American pieces of this puzzle together. On November 25 Attorney General Edwin Meese held a press conference and admitted that some of the arms sale profits had gone to support the Contras.[45] At that point the Iran-Contra scandal became a permanent part of American history.

Regarding the general problem of maintaining access to important sources, it should be noted that most of the major field correspondents felt the rather natural pressure to keep lines open. Few succumbed to the temptation to please by deliberately balancing copy, but it was clear that reporters openly skeptical of Contra claims were not welcome at the Honduran border camps, nor were reporters who were outspoken in their suspicions of the Sandinistas given much interviewing time in Managua. One press association veteran disagreed about the amount of pressure, however, arguing that the Contras and Sandinistas needed the major journalists and gave access to those who were not lopsided in their coverage.[46]

It must be said that, while leading journalists took criticism from the liberal left for not hitting hard enough, they also were targeted by conservatives for reporting the other side at all. Held up for example were Stephen Kinzer's features about the suffering in the villages and barrios, the funerals of children, and the determination of the people to resist what Kinzer at times clearly described as U.S.-sponsored aggression. Kinzer's experiences were shared by many of his colleagues, and in a general sense, he spoke for others when he offered explanations of the challenges and frustrations.

In July 1989, a few months after he ended his Nicaraguan adventure, Kinzer allowed a bit of his private side to show, and only for a few minutes. In this remarkable burst of candor—a critic later labeled it "unrecognized self-criticism"—Kinzer reflected on "one of the exigencies of what is known as objective journalism." Talking with a reporter for the *Cape Cod Times*, Kinzer offered this as an example of how stories would read if reporters were allowed to make strong interpretive judgments as well as dutifully reporting official statements:

> President Reagan today denounced the Sandinistas for having converted Nicaragua into a "totalitarian dungeon"—another of his [Reagan's] wild exaggerations that ignore the abuses of the Guatemalan colonels, Salvadoran death squad leaders, and Argentine torturers, with whom he is so friendly.[47]

Kinzer added, "You can't put that in a story but that is sometimes what is crying out to be said." Then why did he not find ways to work in these ideas more often? Perhaps the best answer came from the writer Joe Klein, who said Kinzer worked with what he called "rigorous self-censorship," a "restraint, enormous caution."[48] There is a practical side to this debate as well, one that nonjournalists might not fully appreciate.

Kinzer's strength as a writer was in hard news and analysis. The in-depth feature stories that might have revealed more about his understanding of the Nicaraguan people—not the government—ended up getting a lower priority for reasons of space, time, and perhaps writing ability. Few foreign correspondents are recognized as literary giants. Kinzer was a fine reporter and a clear writer for what he and his editors chose to emphasize. His dilemma was explained best by Bill Gentile, the region's most experienced photographer and a professional who, like Kinzer, refused to mythologize leaders with whom he had natural sympathies. "It was easy in 1979 . . . it was black and white. Good guys and bad guys. But then you began to get some grays in there, and now [1986] it's all gray, darker and lighter shades of gray and much more difficult to pick your way to the truth."[49]

Kinzer's 1986 view: "I think it is good for Americans to receive news from Nicaragua from as many different kinds of sources as possible. In fact, if those sources seem to give them conflicting information they probably are finally coming to understand the complexities and the difficulties of the situation here . . . I'm not disillusioned with the complexity of it. In fact, I find the complexity of it to be particularly intellectually stimulating. And it is that intellectual challenge that is one of the things that makes covering this story so interesting. This is a story which doesn't come to a final conclusion, which doesn't lend itself to absolutes, and requires a little more sophisticated appreciation." He felt his colleagues working for major U.S. newspapers were "sophisticated and hard-working and intelligent—I think it's a good group that by and large understands the complexity of the situation and tries to make a good effort to convey that."[50]

Kinzer did not change his mind about this over the years. In late 1992, while covering the destruction of Bosnia for the *Times*, he took time out in a telephone interview with this writer to reflect on his experiences in Nicaragua. He disputed the notion that U.S. journalists were so attuned to Washington-generated pressure that they "bent over backwards" to include anti-Sandinista information. "I never felt an obligation as an *American* reporter to be fair to *American* policy," he said.[51] Obviously there was a difference of opinion on this question of how reporters reacted to the pressure in the air.

THE POWER OF THE HOMETOWN GATEKEEPERS

Far away from the newsroom politics, Stephen Kinzer was well aware of the penchant of *Times* editors to understate news running counter to the current consensus as principally determined by Washington image-makers. Admit it or not, he and the majority of his colleagues had a feeling for the basic strain of conservatism cutting through the United States that always had made it next to impossible for mainstream journalists to inform the reader of the mountains of disinformation separating reporter and audience.

In addition to being aware of his own emotional and physical limits, he was aware of the unspoken but recognized limits at the *Times*; he was aware of the disturbing recall of Ray Bonner, the *New York Times* correspondent in El Salvador brutally criticized for his reporting of a massacre of civilians by Salvadoran troops (see the section of this chapter dealing with El Salvador). Only Kinzer and his editors know how hard he pushed against editorial decisions that distorted his reporting. His 1991 book, *Blood of Broth-*

ers: Life and War in Nicaragua, gives but a few clues to the internal strife at the *Times*.

In one instance Kinzer described how in March 1983 he and freelance photographer Ken Silverman were the first journalists to actually locate one of the Contra camps being set up by the CIA in Honduras. Silverman's candid photo of Kinzer with armed Contras and Kinzer's account of finding U.S.-supplied arms contradicted Washington's line that the Contras were an independent force and that there were no camps supported by the CIA and the government of Honduras.

He briefly noted how, instead of boldly proclaiming the embarrassing discovery, a headline writer said: "At a Border Camp in Honduras, Anti-Sandinistas Are Wary of Visit." Kinzer wryly said his March 28 story had been "classically understated" but was "potent nonetheless." It was—official Washington was turned on its ear and the external support for the overthrow of the Nicaraguan government could no longer be hidden.[52]

Throughout his stay in Central America, which ended in January 1989 when he turned over the *Times* bureau to Mark Uhlig, Kinzer had frequent access to President Daniel Ortega, Costa Rican President Oscar Arias, and other Central American leaders. He was in a commanding position, or so it seemed to outsiders. But in reality Kinzer—like many foreign correspondents before him—came to the point of knowing too much, of seeing the minuses in leaders as well as the pluses, of being exposed to too many deaths and too much political turmoil. Like others in Managua, he was bothered by the intellectual arrogance of some of the Sandinista *comandantes*, the top leadership; he noted how—too often, in his judgment—Sandinista ideology collided with a chance to make an economic or political breakthrough; he knew firsthand the evil of the Contras and the demoralizing effects of the war on the Nicaraguan population.

By early 1988 Kinzer and some of his colleagues were emotionally spent. He wrote later:

> Having lived among Nicaraguans during such a searing period of their history, and having seen so much tragedy and death reporters posted in Managua could not help but be emotionally involved in the drama unfolding around them. Many of us found the first months of 1988 the worst period of our assignments there. Hopes for peace seemed to be slipping away, and the prospect ahead was for more war and more repression. In six years more than thirty thousand Nicaraguans had died violently . . . besides the emotional toll the war took on me and other

correspondents, the physical risks began to seem greater as time passed. I had been exposed to my share of danger in Nicaragua, but I had always felt that fortune was with me. Now I began to fear otherwise.[53]

His instincts were correct. In March of 1988 he and a handful of journalists, including the AP's Bryna Brennan and the *Washington Post's* Julia Preston, traveled by helicopter to the Honduran border area. The Sandinistas wanted to show how they had driven Contras back across the Coco River in a massive display of force that Washington propagandists called an "invasion." To his horror, a Honduran Air Force plane bombed the riverbank area, forcing Kinzer and colleagues to dive for cover and then run to their helicopter for a hasty retreat. Then in July he was knocked unconscious by a Sandinista policeman at Nandaime, during a clash between anti-Sandinista protesters and police. Adding to his misery, his coverage of the causes of the violence was bitterly criticized by Sandinista supporters in the United States.

While Kinzer went on to become a *Times* reporter in Germany, again to witness mind-boggling changes there and in Yugoslavia, it fell to others to report the freest election in Nicaraguan history and the aftermath of Ortega's shocking defeat in February 1990 by Violeta Chamorro, widow of Pedro Joaquín Chamorro Sr., the martyred publisher of the anti-Somoza newspaper *La Prensa*.

That election provided one of the most memorable moments of this writer's Central American travels. It came on February 26, the morning of President Daniel Ortega'a concession to Violeta Chamorro. The press corps gathered at dawn to witness an emotional end to this chapter of Nicaraguan history. I was only a few feet from Ortega and could see the pain as he spoke. Members of the press corps certainly had mixed feelings about the Sandinistas, but there was a feeling of profound respect and sympathy in the room as he courageously accepted defeat. In the preceding hours reporters were at both Sandinista and Chamorro headquarters. The scene at the Chamorro party also was memorable because the stage was filled with all of the characters of the past, Contra leaders and anti-Sandinistas of every stripe, including exiles from Miami.

Few journalists had predicted the Chamorro win, and their world had turned upside down. One who had predicted it was Juan Vasquez of CBS, who told me in the morning that Ortega would lose. I did not believe him, but within a few hours there was a strange excitement in the air. Our trips to polling stations in previously pro-Sandinista areas revealed a big turnout for Chamorro. By early evening there was talk of a possible upset. Minutes after the first returns it was clear that Chamorro was on her way; the press corps bolted from election headquarters and headed for her headquarters. Later that following morning there was considerable excitement as Ortega appeared at a rally to reassure followers that FSLN principles would not die. On March 1 Marc Cooper and I had breakfast at the home of Foreign Minister Miguel D'Escoto, whom I had met on previous trips. Bitter about the U.S. government's pro-Chamorro actions, he told us how he felt enough voters had finally said "Uncle" and given up in the face of a continued war. He also predicted that promises of massive U.S. aid would not be kept, and he was correct. "The United States really doesn't care about us [now that the United States has gotten its way]," he said.[54] As our interview ended D'Escoto said Ortega was on his way over to talk about the loss and the future. As it turned out, the Bush administration kept Chamorro under great pressure and used aid as a weapon, but to Washington's dismay the Sandinistas maintained legislative power and control of the military leadership.

As the Sandinistas became the first revolutionary government in Latin American history to turn over power at the ballot box, the effects of the Contra war on the deteriorating economy and morale faded from the collective memory of the news media. Sandinista inefficiency and repression were listed as the reasons for Mrs. Chamorro's win, in President George Bush's Washington and in the copy of many of the U.S. correspondents forced to come up with an answer. Mark Uhlig's long account failed to mention the major contributing factor for the peace vote—U.S. sponsorship of the war.

THE CIA INFLUENCES THE WAR COVERAGE

In defense of all journalists in the field, it is clear that the full extent of CIA influence, although suspected, was hard to determine on the spot. In the case of Nicaragua, in the early 1980s the Sandinistas wore journalists and visitors out with their claims that the Catholic Church and *La Prensa* were beneficiaries of CIA propaganda funds—and thus reasonable targets for harassment. *La Prensa*'s funding of hundreds of thousands of dollars from the National Endowment for Democracy put the newspaper into a legitimately suspect category; after all, editor Jaime Chamorro did lobby for $100 million for the Contras in a 1986 *Washington Post* op-ed piece.[55]

Perhaps the most damaging testimony against the CIA and the Reagan administration came from the former spokesman for the Contra Directorate, a Nicaraguan exile skilled in public relations named Edgar Chamorro. When Chamorro fully realized how the CIA was attempting to "internationalize and antisovietize" the conflict to gain U.S. public support for the anti-Sandinista effort, he balked.[56] His testimony to the World Court at the Hague helped lead to its June 1986 decision that found U.S. aggression against Nicaragua to be in gross violation of international law.

Chamorro's story contained anecdotes about the CIA's attempts to manipulate U.S. journalists into writing pro-Contra stories. The goal was to create an image that the FDN (Nicaraguan Democratic Force) was legitimate, filled with true representatives of the people willing to live on the edge of death to retake Managua. Reagan in 1985 called them "the moral equivalent of our Founding Fathers and the brave men and women of the French Revolution."[57] To kick off its propaganda campaign, in early 1983 the CIA tricked a *Stern* magazine team into a favorable article and used it to stimulate interest within the U.S. media. Soon it became fashionable to interview Contra leaders and eventually to visit Contra camps.[58]

Arguing against the conventional line that the Contras simply popped over the border in 1981 and asked for U.S. assistance, Edgar Chamorro described how as early as fall of 1980 more than 50 of Somoza's former National Guardsmen were being trained in Argentina—by experts in terror who carried out their own "dirty war"—and how these Nicaraguans were moved into Miami to train others.[59] Vital to this story of deception and attempts to drag U.S. journalists into the web of lies was the cover story told Congress in 1982 that the United States had no plan to overthrow the Nicaraguan government but was concerned about how to interdict alleged arms flows from Nicaragua to insurgents in El Salvador.

Chamorro later clearly stated that CIA Director William Casey's original plan was to attack Nicaragua and to build up the Contra force.[60] It is important to note that in July 1985, while Washington still blamed the Ortega government for the insurrection in El Salvador, the U.S. military attaché to the U.S. Embassy in Managua told this writer that there was no truth to Washington's claims, saying that any arms flow was "insignificant."

The fully decorated attaché was one of hundreds of guests at a party given by the Sandinista government the evening before the celebration of the sixth anniversary of the revolution. Away from the main crowd, the North American debated Comandante Tomás Borge in Spanish within a circle of a dozen young Sandinistas who followed each verbal thrust with great excitement.

This writer was the only journalist and one of two North Americans watching. When Borge asked the U.S. officer when Nicaragua would be left alone, the stern reply was: "When you learn to behave and respect your neighbors." To the crowd's delight, Borge shot back: "Is that what you say to [Chilean dictator] Pinochet?"

It was like a boxing match. Borge had a cigar in one hand and a drink in the other. He bobbed and weaved before the tall, erect officer. Borge then said the Sandinistas were aware of U.S. contingency plans to invade Nicaragua. He pledged to send U.S. troops home in body bags and said the Sandinistas would fight from the hills as they had in the past—that Managua would fall easily but the war would be a long one. When the match ended and the Sandinistas had departed, the officer asked me if I wanted a drink. Over a *Nica Libre* (the old *Cuba Libre*, or rum-and-coke, to the rest of us) I learned the gentleman's opinion about the allegations of massive Sandinista supplies going to El Salvador. The information was in amazing contrast to everything being reported from Washington. He simply said that while the United States had its differences with the Sandinistas, there had not been much arms-traffic action since 1981. I appreciated his candor and thought he had more than a little brass to fight the war with the only surviving founder of the FSLN on the old guerrilla leader's home grounds.[61]

Incidentally, former CIA analyst David McMichael told the World Court the same thing shortly afterward—that there had been no credible evidence of a significant flow of arms from Nicaragua to El Salvador for four years.[62]

Two *Miami Herald* reporters who smelled a good story, Juan Tamayo and Alfonso Chardy, in February and June of 1983 linked the increased Contra activity to a deepening involvement of the Reagan administration and the CIA.[63] As noted, Kinzer had been the first to find a U.S.-supplied Contra camp. The CIA's involvement became more clear in 1983–84, when the agency mined Nicaragua's Puerto Sandino and harbors on both coasts and then got caught publishing a psychological operations manual for the Contras.

Although the cover story was that independent Contras had been responsible for the minings, the truth emerged. Brian Barger's Pacific News Service account of the "psyops" manual tipped the CIA's hand in July of 1984, and major organizations finally picked up the story in October. This led to the passage on October 12 of another Boland Amendment, prohibiting further aid of any kind to the Contras (Note: the first Boland Amendment, signed into law on December 21, 1982, merely prohibited the overthrow of the Sandinistas but had easy-to-find loopholes). This then set the stage for the 1985–86 maneuvers by the Reagan administration to bypass congressional intent, most of which were missed by the mainstream news media. CIA officials admitted later that there were always two tracks, one the publicly explained CIA objective of interdicting weapons to Salvadoran guerrillas, and the other—the real goal—the overthrow of the Sandinista government.

Sandinista charges of widespread CIA interference, made throughout this period, later were supported in 1988 by John Spicer Nichols, a journalism professor at Pennsylvania State University, who conducted a year-long investigation. Looking at documents obtained through the Freedom of Information Act or from congressional committees, Nichols wrote: "*La Prensa* has received covert funding not only from the Central Intelligence Agency, but also from the secret network coordinated by Lieutenant Colonel Oliver North, the former National Security official and central figure in the Iran-Contra scandal."[64]

Despite the hypocrisy of defending a newspaper that fronted for the bombers of health centers and schools, U.S. Embassy officials in Managua continued to get media attention with their claims that the Sandinistas were "undemocratic." The CIA and State Department knew full well that a cry of "press freedom violation" would get the attention of any red-blooded U.S. editor, particularly if he or she were a member of the Society of Professional Journalists or the Associated Press Managing Editors, groups dedicated to panel discussions on press abuses. There is a bit of irony here, though, because there were press freedom violations on both sides.

When the intrepid Costa Rican–based freelancer Martha Honey reported to readers of the *Columbia Journalism Review* in 1987 that the CIA had bribed a number of Costa Rican and Honduran journalists to distort news in favor of the Contras, the revelation did not shock journalists who had been in the region, and no one else seemed to care. Little attention was given her findings, even though it was obvious the CIA had skirted its own 1977 regulations barring "any paid or contractual relationship" with U.S. journalists, including freelancers. In that year a Senate Select Committee discovered that the agency had been paying up to fifty American reporters over a number of years.[65] Speculation continues that the CIA's payoffs to foreign journalists remain part of its covert action program.

The role played by freelance journalists in exposing the CIA's role in the Central American story is an interesting one. University of Arizona journalism professor Jacqueline Sharkey provided one of the early comprehensive looks at the CIA's role, writing for *Common Cause* in the fall of 1986.

She outlined the agency's anti-Sandinista media campaigns, not only inside Nicaragua but also in neighboring Honduras and Costa Rica.[66] One might logically wonder why these heavy reporting tasks fell to freelancers and not to the highly paid regulars.

When it came to the Catholic Church, it was even easier for the embassy to lay out a trail of deceit about Sandinista "religious freedom abuses." For one thing, the head of the church in Nicaragua was Archbishop (later Cardinal) Miguel y Bravo Obando, who had played a major role in bringing down Somoza. Kinzer and others spent a considerable amount of time trying to figure out the truth in this emotional free-for-all. The Sandinistas ending up looking bad, closing down the church radio station and censoring its publications.

There was little attention given to the fact that Obando said his first Mass as a cardinal for the Contras in Miami, on his way home from Rome. Nor was there much understanding or curiosity about how many dollars were being funneled into the church's accounts. Overworked field correspondents cannot be expected to develop stories like these alone; their success depends upon the curiosity and cooperation of home editors and reporters who too often lack the knowledge or interest needed to assist.

There later was confirmation of the CIA's illegal dealings with the church. A 1992 *New York Times* story dealing with the trial of former CIA official Clair E. George revealed that in the middle 1980s "among the covert operations the agency was running in Nicaragua at the time was a program to finance elements of the Catholic Church to serve as political counterweights to the Nicaraguan government."[67]

In one notable case, the March 6, 1984, visit to Managua of Pope John Paul II, the CIA exploited an unfortunate incident that occurred during the celebration of the Mass to make it appear that the Sandinistas, rulers of a Roman Catholic country, lacked respect for the man whose photo was on every other living-room wall. The Pope was interrupted by cries and protests against Reagan's activities, particularly from mothers of dead soldiers, but when the Pope's irritation was shown on television, there was an implication that the Sandinistas could have prevented the outbursts but chose not to. According to Edgar Chamorro, nothing could have been further from the truth, but the Sandinistas lost this round in the propaganda war.[68] From this point the U.S. government perpetuated the falsehood that there was widespread religious persecution in Nicaragua, a notion never adequately clarified by correspondents.

The CIA also conducted a transparent but nevertheless successful anti-

Sandinista, anti-peace campaign in Costa Rica. This writer became acquainted with it in December 1985 while reporting on the March for Peace, an assemblage of 350 persons from more than 30 nations who went from Panama to Mexico. I was one of several journalists with the group in Costa Rica and Nicaragua, including a week stalled at the Honduran border when U.S.-trained Honduran troops blocked the border crossing. The bulk of the group eventually reached Mexico City by flying to Guatemala and skipping Honduras and El Salvador.

While in San José, Costa Rica, the group was attacked for hours by a mob organized by Costa Rica Libre, a notorious right-wing organization. I reported the incident for CBS radio by calling from a pay phone across the street from the rock- and bottle-throwing in which a dozen persons were hurt. My story led off at least one CBS national broadcast, but otherwise there was little attention given this international incident in the United States. The Associated Press story written in San José whitewashed the violence to the extent that an AP reporter in Nicaragua privately apologized for it. Working hard, the CIA planted stories and advertisements against the peace march throughout the region. It came to light during the Iran-Contra investigation that Benjamin Piza, the government official who pulled away his guardsmen so that the mob could attack us, was working with the CIA. The San José station chief, Joe Fernandez, was one of the key links to Oliver North's operations.

It is a small world—the North group had its eyes on everything. *Peace* was a dirty word in Central America. It also was a dirty word in New York. Two weeks later, just before New Year's Eve, I called CBS radio with a story about how dozens of heavily armed U.S.-trained Honduran military, flanked by jeering civilian Contras, prevented the peace group from crossing the border. It was extremely tense as the marchers stood nose to nose with the nervous troops, waving their passports and singing their native songs. The news editor said I should call back if anyone were hurt or killed. When the marchers finally reached Mexico City they received a tumultuous welcome downtown but little press coverage outside of the region.[69]

THE LA PENCA BOMBING AND THE CHRISTIC INSTITUTE CASE

While the journalists' behavior generally was understandable, even to their critics, at times it was confusing. One prime example: Insiders familiar with the Iran-Contra scandal and the Christic Institute lawsuit against a number of the Iran-Contra participants were mystified at the reluctance of a number of correspondents to learn more about one key event, the blowing up of a press conference at La Penca, Nicaragua, on May 30, 1984. For example, Stephen Kinzer told this writer in 1986 that he had not cared to read a detailed report of the bombing prepared by Costa Rican–based journalists Martha Honey and Tony Avirgan—about the time that their investigation was becoming well known. Avirgan was one of more than 20 journalists injured in the explosion, which killed three of their colleagues, including Linda Frazier, an American writing for San José's investigative English-language paper the *Tico Times* and wife of Joe Frazier, the Associated Press's bureau chief.

In a strange bit of irony, Martha Honey, Avirgan's wife, was stringing for the *New York Times*. She had written a page-one story for the May 31 edition, reporting CIA pressure against former Sandinista leader Eden (Commander Zero) Pastora, who was refusing to merge his Costa Rica Contra group with the mainline elements in Honduras. Little did she know that same page would carry a United Press International story from San José about the La Penca bombing, where Pastora escaped the death someone had planned for him. Honey was dropped from the *Times* freelance list the next day, without explanation.

Kinzer's page-one story of June 1 reported Pastora's earlier claims of CIA pressure but also quoted him as blaming the Sandinistas for the attack. Costa Rican President Luis Alberto Monge, who worked closely with U.S. intelligence agencies, echoed the same line while on a visit to Spain. Within hours of the bombing, the CIA's anti-Sandinista version was "leaked" to U.S. journalists in New York and Washington. The next day Pastora switched his opinion, blaming the CIA. The contradiction was underscored by Kinzer in his June 2 follow-up, which contained Pastora's definite statement, "This attack is punishment for not yielding."[70]

Unlike the UPI version of the bombing that appeared in the May 31 *New York Times*, which avoided any mention of responsibility, the *Los Angeles Times* morning final edition carried a UPI story with a lengthy charge of Pastora spokesmen that the CIA had planted the bomb "in retaliation for the rebel leader's refusal to join his forces with U.S.-backed rebels fighting from havens in Honduras." However, in the late final edition this quote was gone, replaced by a statement that Pastora's followers blamed the CIA and the Costa Rican government blamed the Sandinistas. As happens often with foreign stories, the merger of UPI and AP copy eliminated the thrust, or at least the most controversial part, of the story.[71]

The following day the *Los Angeles Times* carried a lengthy item under William Long's byline. The *Times* quoted a Contra communiqué blaming the Sandinistas, a lame statement from Contra leader Brooklyn Rivera that either Sandinistas or extreme rightists were guilty, and Secretary of State George Schultz's apparently baseless insinuation that the Sandinistas were responsible. In a wonderful example of agenda-setting, Schultz was en route to El Salvador for the inauguration of President José Napoleón Duarte. In the airborne interview he "denied" CIA involvement, "doubted" Contra participation, and thus implied Sandinista guilt. Asked if this were his implication, he used the opportunity to say, "Not on the record." The CIA threats against Pastora, part of the original record, already were forgotten.[72]

In his book Kinzer said that after the bombing "the Central American press corps lived through its worst tragedy of the 1980s."[73] It turned out that one of the severely injured, a British-born *Newsweek* reporter named Susan Morgan, had worked closely with Kinzer and Rod Nordland, then with the *Philadelphia Inquirer*, Christopher Dickey of the *Washington Post*, and others, and they took a personal interest in her welfare.

According to Kinzer, Morgan and some of the survivors came to believe that Pastora's Contra enemies, perhaps working with the CIA, planned the bombing. But in his cautious style he says, "Those who were seriously interested in finding the truth, including the victims, did not have the resources for an exhaustive probe. Those who had the resources apparently lacked motivation."[74] He did not specify who had the resources—the U.S. government obviously did—nor did he mention the endless and exhaustive investigation begun by Honey and Avirgan and later joined by a Washington organization called the Christic Institute headed by lawyer Daniel Sheehan, although he did cite one of Honey and Avirgan's works in a footnote. He told this writer, "To give absolute credibility to a report produced by two people—whoever they are—is something that I am not prepared to do." He said his instincts were guided by the judgments of some persons within the La Penca survivor group and families of those affected, who doubted anyone could learn who did it.[75]

Sheehan crossed the nation to hold rallies and celebrity fund-raisers in support of a lawsuit filed jointly by the journalists and the Christic Institute against more than two dozen persons linked to covert activities in Central America. Calling for the impeachment of Ronald Reagan and later George Bush for withholding knowledge of the arms shipments to Iran and the diversion of the illegal funds to the Contras, he and his lieutenants recited the alleged crimes of a secret team of former U.S. military and CIA officers who, they said, had been involved around the world with drug-running, assassinations, and other activities since the 1960s. Honey and Avirgan often spoke as well, updating Costa Rican aspects of the case and reliving their experiences in reporting U.S. attempts to subvert the region to its will. In doing so they assumed great personal risks, and in fact their lives were threatened and disrupted several times.[76]

Oliver North's notes indicated that he was well aware of Honey and Avirgan. The CIA went to great lengths in Costa Rica to drive the pair from the country. Personal attacks were part of a coordinated media strategy. On one occasion in San José I interviewed a Costa Rican working with the CIA who was leading the media attacks. After a testy interview, during which he condemned Honey and Avirgan, he relaxed and proudly displayed a picture of himself and others with President Reagan in the White House.

One *New York Times* correspondent working on the Iran-Contra story told me in 1987 that his section editor had informed him that the words "Christic Institute" would never appear in the newspaper, even though a Florida court had accepted its case against prominent anti-Communists like Richard Secord, John Singlaub, and others. He was correct; the *Times* ignored the story. Editor Abe Rosenthal's paper had no stomach for a complicated story about drug-running, arms-smuggling, and murder, despite similar charges made public by CBS's *West 57th St.* magazine show, *New Republic, Common Cause*, and others in the 1985–86 period.[77]

Also ignored by the U.S. press was the Costa Rican government's indictment of John Hull, an American with ties to the CIA and Lt. Col. Oliver North who owned a ranch in Costa Rica, and Felipe Vidal, an anti-Castro Cuban. Hull and Vidal were charged with involvement in the La Penca bombing in concert with Contras and elements of the CIA. Vindicated to a great degree by the Hull and Vidal indictments, which were central to their story—if not Sheehan's more wide-ranging charges—Honey and Avirgan were dismayed and angered when, again, major news media paid little if any attention.

A former associate of Hull told this writer in 1991 that Hull, then avoiding the Costa Rican charges, certainly had worked for the CIA, along with other ranchers living along the Costa Rican–Nicaraguan border. He said there was jubilation in his circle of friends the night of the La Penca bombing—toasts were freely made. During the conversation he was protective of Hull and argued that Hull had not been active in drug flights. As for the bombing itself, he added a new theory to the list. Without offering any additional explanation or documentation, he said there was a "consensus around here" that Israeli Mossad agents were instrumental in the killings, doing dirty work for the CIA as they had in the Middle East. This, of course, would be extremely difficult for journalists to prove. Besides, one person with possible knowledge of this and other Central American covert operations, Israeli "counter-terrorism" official Amiram Nir, was silent. He had died in a mysterious plane crash in Mexico in 1988.[78]

After six years of frustrating legal battles, internal squabbling, government harassment, Sheehan's declining credibility, and almost no coverage from establishment journalists, the Christic Institute closed its doors in 1992. The lawsuit and a subsequent appeal had been lost. On top of everything else, a bond of more than $1 million was ordered to be forfeited and distributed to the defendants. Sheehan then locked horns with Honey and Avirgan in a bitter battle over ownership of documents, which the couple won in 1994.

As Kinzer suggested, perhaps journalists will never learn the truth about La Penca, or about the entire Iran-Contra investigation, whose final report was issued in late 1993 after more than six years of controversy. And if not, it will be because some persons with power, including some in the news world, really did not want to know. Regarding La Penca, Kinzer did not include himself in that category, but he added, "This is the region of the triple and quadruple doublecross." Kinzer told me, "You can't imagine how Byzantine the political labyrinth in this part of the world is."[79]

His words were prophetic; in August 1993 Juan Tamayo, by then the *Miami Herald*'s foreign editor, published the results of a long investigation claiming that the La Penca bomber was a leftist Argentine trained by Nicaraguan security forces, for the most part pinning the crime on the Sandinistas. He left a slight opening for the possibility that the bomber was a right-wing agent who infiltrated the Argentine organization and moved on to Nicaragua to work with a CIA-Contra group. Honey and Avirgan, checking into the Argentine connection, used a third party to assist Tamayo with some aspects of the identification of the bomber. While arguing that much of the story remains unclear—that this could have been a setup and that the CIA still may have been involved—they also called on Sandinista leaders to reveal any knowledge of the incident. Meanwhile the Costa Ricans stuck with their contention that the CIA was involved. In 1994, a decade after the bombing, the arguments continued.[80]

INTRODUCTION: EL SALVADOR

The popular struggle against repression in El Salvador parallels that of Nicaragua, a never-ending battle for survival of the poor whose thumbs were
tied behind their backs by powerful landlords and businessmen. Unlike Nicaragua, however, El Salvador has a more intense history of labor organizing
and protests, a deeply entrenched tradition that directly affects today's politics. Salvadorans of age recall the 1932 Matanza, when Army troops slaughtered thousands of rebellious Pipil Indians who were being exploited on cof-
fee plantations. Agustín Farabundo Marti, the revolutionary organizer of
both Indians and city workers, was executed, leaving a martyr for the ages.
Fear gripped the nation and the government banned urban labor organizing until 1948, keeping a lid on rural activities.

All of this broke loose in the 1970s when disparate leftist guerrilla groups
began to unify in the face of increased government crackdowns against organizing. The government-sanctioned death squads, the *escuadrones de
muerte*, began their killings in the mid-1970s, following the pattern of systematic extermination in Guatemala spawned by the CIA's 1954 overthrow
of the democratically elected government of Jacobo Arbenz, the man who
pledged to institute land reform. Then in March of 1980, Joaquin Villalobos
and other guerrllla leaders united their self-identified Marxist-influenced elements to form the Farabundo Marti Liberation Front (FMLN).

The increasing tensions in El Salvador occasionally made headlines in the
United States in the late 1970s. As in Nicaragua with the assassination of
Chamorro in 1978 and the driving out of Somoza in 1979, it took dramatic events to attract more U.S. journalists to the scene. The first occurred
March 24, 1980, when Archbishop Oscar Romero, a powerful critic of the
military and advocate of social reform, was assassinated while saying Mass
in a hospital chapel.[81] On December 2 four U.S. churchwomen, three of
them nuns, were raped and murdered by government security forces. Despite the horror of this story, U.S. military aid to El Salvador was halted
only for a few weeks.

Thus began a decade of killing during which 40,000 Salvadorans died,
some through a continuation of death-squad activities. There were widespread retaliations by the FMLN, the indiscriminate bombing of the countryside by government planes and helicopters, and a campaign within the
United States for an end to U.S. financial support. The decade ended with
the 1989 murders of six Jesuit priests, an act tied to the military that again
brought world attention to El Salvador. The Jesuits had provided the intel-

lectual framework for decent reform measures, drawing the wrath of right-wing political and military leaders who accused them of fostering Communism.

In the middle of this were members of the San Salvador press corps. As noted, many of this group used El Salvador as a base for covering all of Central America, just as Kinzer and some of his Managua-based colleagues occasionally headed to El Salvador's killing fields, Oscar Arias's office in Costa Rica, the Contra camps in Honduras, or the Indian villages of Guatemala. The El Salvador–based journalists were caught in a no-win trap, unable to satisfy the host government, its U.S. ally, and conservative critics at home unless they ignored the human rights abuses. There was no middle ground. More often they alienated liberal critics by treading lightly on the U.S. connection to the death squads.

When the fighting ended with the first steps toward reconciliation in the early 1990s, and the FMLN ran candidates in the 1994 national election, arguments over the U.S. role faded. They flared briefly in 1992 when details of a 1982 massacre of civilians were substantiated, contradicting official U.S. statements made at the time and vindicating two journalists who covered that story. In retrospect El Salvador continued to be a tougher assignment than Nicaragua because the host government and wealthy landowners posed more problems for peace than the former guerrillas. The fighting may have ended, but the terror had not been eliminated.

THE SAN SALVADOR PRESS CORPS

Like his colleague Stephen Kinzer, *New York Times* correspondent James LeMoyne was subjected to years of bitter accusations, particularly from U.S. progressives who felt that he had not consistently explained the linkage between U.S. corporate interests, the Salvadoran power structure, and the death squads that had terrorized the nation for most of a decade. Instead, they said, he had spent too much time finding fault with the Farabundo Marti National Liberation Front (FMLN) guerrillas who obviously threatened U.S. financial interests. To his credit, LeMoyne made numerous dangerous trips into the countryside to get stories from the guerrilla side and was one of the most knowledgeable reporters there. He was chief of the *Times* San Salvador bureau from 1984 to 1988.

As in Nicaragua, women correspondents provided a good share of the war coverage. They woke up to the news of more death-squad murders in

San Salvador's outskirts, spent days driving into the countryside to see the war from the FMLN side, and attempted to penetrate the myths perpetuated by the government and the U.S. Embassy about El Salvador's human rights record.[82]

One prominent woman byliner who joined others to shatter the stereotype in El Salvador was Shirley Christian, one of the most influential journalists in the region. In September 1979 she switched to the *Miami Herald* from the Associated Press bureau in Santiago, opening the *Herald*'s first Central American bureau in San Salvador in early 1981 and winning that year's Pulitzer Prize and the George Polk Award for her Central American coverage. A year later she threw most of her colleagues into a rage when she wrote an article for the *Washington Journalism Review* accusing in particular the *New York Times*, the *Washington Post*, and CBS of biased reporting in favor of the Sandinistas. Riding and DeYoung were singled out for heavy criticism and responded in another issue of *WJR*. She later wrote *Nicaragua: Revolution in the Family*, generally critical of the Sandinista regime.[83]

In one of those ironic twists, when she joined the *New York Times* in 1985 it was over the protests of a number of staffers who were bothered by her political connections. After a stint in Buenos Aires and a year in Washington, she became the main *Times* correspondent in Central America in 1991, with a home base in El Salvador. As could be expected, her perceptions had not changed. In late 1992, in a story that contained a bit of explanation about the history of Managua, this is how she reconstructed the cause of the Contra war, neat and simple, even throwing in the rationalizing term "civil war."

> Over the next few years [after the 1979 toppling of Somoza] reconstruction received little more than lip service as political instability worsened, eventually plunging into the civil war pitting the Sandinista Government against the United States–backed Contras.[84]

RAY BONNER AND ALMA GUILLERMOPRIETO: EL MOZOTE

The experiences of Raymond Bonner of the *New York Times* provided the classic case of the reporting problems, personal frustrations, and dangers described in this chapter. While most of the El Salvador veterans sparred with embassy personnel and took nerve-jangling trips into the country, none was subjected to the abuse that Bonner endured. An aggressive former Marine officer who had served in Vietnam, Bonner briefly practiced law before deciding to head for South America, where he reported mainly from Peru and Bolivia as a major stringer for *Newsweek* and National Public Radio (NPR). Bonner also did a few pieces for the *Wall Street Journal* before he headed north in late 1980 and Riding arranged for him to work as a stringer in Central America. The *Times* had no Central American bureau, and Riding, whose name now appeared on a Salvadoran death-squad hit list, was headquartered in Mexico City. Bloody times were ahead; in December the four U.S. churchwomen were murdered. The discovery of their bodies brought El Salvador into focus in the United States. Bonner's main task was the El Salvador coverage, but he was expected to roam the region and his first two stories were from Guatemala. Rewarded for his hard work, he became a regular *Times* staff member in January 1981. Although assigned to the Metro Desk, as was the practice with new hires, he was able to make several trips to El Salvador that year. In November he went down for what he supposed would be a short trip but stayed until the following August. Because of his persistent attempts to discover the truth, he soon found himself in repeated conflicts with U.S. Ambassador Deane Hinton and Salvadoran officials. Eventually some of his own editors joined the fray.

In August 1982 *Times* editor Abe Rosenthal recalled Bonner from his San Salvador position, reassigning him to the business desk. When it became apparent that he would not be given another foreign assignment or a position in Washington, he resigned. Bonner's dilemma is described in his book *Weakness and Deceit: U.S. Policy and El Salvador*. Rosenthal's side of this bitter episode is found in Joseph Goulden's *Fit to Print: A. M. Rosenthal and His Times*.[85] It is instructive to read Goulden's account, which describes Rosenthal's personal difficulty in dealing with criticisms of Bonner's work and Bonner himself.

The most significant dispute centered around Bonner's reporting of the deaths of hundreds of civilians at El Mozote and several neighboring villages in remote eastern El Salvador. Bonner and the *Post*'s Alma Guillermoprieto entered the area separately in January 1982. They counted numerous mutilated bodies, interviewed survivors, and wrote that Salvadoran soldiers had committed the massacre during a sweep through the region that began in mid-December. Bonner accompanied a guerrilla unit with photographer Susan Meiselas while Guillermoprieto traveled with another group. On separate days they interviewed one of the few survivors of the Mozote village killings, Mrs. Rufina Amaya, whose husband, son, and three daughters had been murdered.

Bonner already was in trouble with some of his editors because of a story published on January 11 under the four-column headline, "U.S. Advisers

Saw 'Torture Class,' Salvadoran Said."[86] This account, based on the testimony of one apparent witness, was carefully attributed. In it Bonner acknowledged his lack of individual confirmation of the torturing of young FMLN prisoners. The story had been held up for weeks and edited several times. Its publication generated considerable heat from Bonner's growing list of detractors in the State Department and provided additional ammunition when the El Mozote controversy developed. Bonner later stated that he should not have submitted this story without additional sourcing, a rare admission for a correspondent.

On January 26 the *Times* published the first of three page-one articles based on Bonner's two weeks of hiking with the guerrillas. The headline, "With Salvador's Guerrillas in Combat Zone," caught the spirit of his trip, during which he reported the setting up of schools and health clinics, recruitment sessions, and the capture of territory. For the first time readers saw a bit of the other side. Then came the shocker. Bonner's article the next day was headlined, "Massacre Hundreds in Salvadoran Village." The lead was:

> Mozote, El Salvador—From interviews with people who live in this small mountain village and surrounding hamlets, it is clear that a massacre of major proportions occurred here last month.[87]

The killings had taken place during a 13-day sweep in Morazan Province by the notorious Atlacatl Battalion, an élite U.S.-trained unit known for brutality during search-and-destroy missions. In his fifth paragraph Bonner inserted the traditional denial, this time of a spokesman for the Salvadoran National Guard who said the massacre story was "totally false" and was fabricated by "subversives." Ironically, on the jump page of Bonner's story there was a report of how the ACLU and Americas Watch had condemned El Salvador for human rights abuses.[88]

That same day the *Washington Post* carried Guillermoprieto's story in a bold page-one box: "Salvadoran Peasants Describe Mass Killing." She ran the government's obligatory denial, or conventional lie as this turned out, in the third paragraph. Her lead was:

> Mozote, El Salvador, Jan. 14 (delayed)—Several hundred civilians, including women and children, were taken from their homes in and around this village and killed by Salvadoran Army troops during a December offensive against leftist guerrillas, according to three survivors who said they witnessed the alleged massacres.[89]

Bonner filed his stories after leaving the rebel zone in mid-January.

Guillermoprieto had just arrived in the company of guerrilla forces, so she stayed on after arranging to have her handwritten massacre story taken back to San Salvador for transmission. It is remarkable that the stories appeared the same day, but it is unknown whether one paper's plans led to pressure on the other to match the coverage. The *Post* prominently displayed one of Meiselas's photos of a grave site and a long sidebar by John Dinges on the U.S. Embassy's dilemma in keeping track of the rising civilian body count and in attributing the deaths to various groups. As of September 1980 there had been 7,372 bodies discovered.[90]

The immediate effect of the twin stories was to cause chaos in the State Department, because President Reagan had chosen that moment to give his blessing to the Duarte government's human rights progress. To say the least, the news was embarrassing.

Bonner's third story was similar to his first—there was no real linkage between the three. Headlined "In Salvador Class, Martial Arts and Marxism," this was a long feature on the guerrillas and their strategies, including their deliberately mild treatment of government prisoners. The next day, however, the Washington agenda-setters were in action. Charles Mohr reported that in response to a rebel attack on a Salvadoran air base, Reagan was ready to offer aid. In doing so the President had "certified to Congress that the military-civilian junta in El Salvador was making a 'concerted' effort to protect human rights." How did Mohr and the editors relate this to colleague Bonner's Mozote story? In the final two paragraphs Mohr mentioned the ACLU and Americas Watch comments and how a State Department spokesman discounted the U.S. government's ability to determine responsibility for civilian deaths. "He was responding to questions and news reports of a massacre of major proportions in eastern El Salvador that local residents attributed to government troops."[91] Goodbye, Mozote.

The following day saw Mohr's page-one story, "Salvadoran Peasants Praise Land Policy." Although not entirely pleased because of continued right-wing attacks, leaders of the peasant organization somehow showed up in Washington in order to praise Duarte's efforts. Again there was no mention of how anyone felt about Mozote.[92] Christopher Dickey, in El Salvador, handled the *Post*'s stories about the attack on the air base and the predictable reaction.

The Mozote stories, of course, brought denials from the State Department's Thomas O. Enders and embassy officials in San Salvador. Elliott Abrams, Assistant Secretary of State for Human Rights and Humanitarian Affairs, was the point man for the government's lies in this case, as he was throughout this period. The *Wall Street Journal* joined the fray with a vicious editorial on February 10, 1982, that brought great embarrassment to *Times* publisher Punch Sulzberger and Rosenthal. Warning about the dangers of "journalistic romanticizing of revolutionaries," the *Journal* cited Herbert Matthews's early coverage of Fidel Castro and Sydney Schanberg's reports from Cambodia as examples of *Times* reporters failing to see evil in the future script (Note: Schanberg won the Pulitzer Prize for his work). The *Journal*'s point was that the "overly credulous" Bonner was repeating these alleged reporting errors in El Salvador and the *Times* should be held accountable.[93]

ENTER REED IRVINE: READY, AIM, FIRE

Incredibly, at this time, media critic Reed Irvine, founder of the ultraconservative Accuracy in Media (AIM), had Sulzberger's ear about Central American coverage and was focusing on Bonner. Sulzberger, in turn, pressured Rosenthal, who for several years had been ignoring Irvine's criticism of *Times* foreign coverage. In *Fit to Print* Joseph Goulden maintains that in the beginning Rosenthal railed against AIM, as he always defended his paper from outside criticism,[94] but that a trip to the region shortly after the Mozote controversy, which included a meeting with Ambassador Hinton, convinced him that Bonner had erred in a number of ways.[95]

In addition to his uneasiness about Bonner's reporting of government atrocities, Rosenthal believed he should have been concentrating on U.S. and Salvadoran allegations that high levels of Communist aid were being smuggled to the FMLN. In accepting Hinton's word on this, Rosenthal bought into the administration's arguments for pushing the Contra war in Nicaragua—to stop a flow of arms to El Salvador—and for unequivocally supporting the Duarte government, despite its toleration of right-wing abuses. From that point Bonner's days were numbered. Goulden's negative assessment, which generally corresponded to that of Rosenthal and the State Department, was that the relatively inexperienced Bonner had "burned" the *Times.* Goulden suggested that the paper should have told its readers that "the pillage at Mozote may not have been a deliberate slaughter by Salvadoran soldiers."[96]

Of course there was no reason in Bonner's mind to completely whitewash the story as Goulden and others would have liked. It was not good enough for his critics that he acknowledged to his readers his inability to *independently* confirm how many died or who killed them. Instead he stuck to a description of the carnage, interviewed eyewitnesses, and linked this event to the army's pre-Christmas activity in the region, which had been mentioned in San Salvador newspapers.

News of Bonner's recall and the accompanying gossip about the reason for Rosenthal's decision had an immediate chilling effect on coverage of El Salvador. The greatest impact was on younger correspondents covering their first major conflict, men and women uninitiated in the devious ways of the State Department. Those who had covered Vietnam, Cuba, Haiti, or the Dominican Republic were less inclined to be influenced. Nevertheless, the combination of attacks from within the profession, particularly the *Wall Street Journal* editorial and Christian's article, and continuation of the sniping about Bonner's work from embassy and State Department sources, took its toll. The U.S. government's goal was to gain public support for Duarte's "moderates," to help them win the war instead of concentrating so heavily on death squads and bombings in the mountains. Stories began to center more on this "positive" aspect. Regarding pressure from the hometown gatekeepers, Bonner learned that the foreign editor of a major newspaper sent copies of the editorial to several of his correspondents in the region. The implied message was "Let's not let this happen to us."[97]

As the controversy continued in 1983, some reporters privately criticized Rosenthal for surrendering to embassy attacks. While Bonner's colleagues universally admired his courage and credited him with exposing the U.S. government's disinformation campaign, some confessed feelings of uneasiness, saying he had become too personally involved or was guilty of crossing the line into advocacy journalism. These reporters considered him a committed journalist who pushed so hard against the system to report the truth that he hurt himself.[98] In saying so they clearly revealed their awareness of the limits within their own organizations. It appears that some of them had been "chilled" before they arrived in El Salvador, while others never had an inclination to buck U.S. actions even if it had been permissible. And, in fairness, some like Dickey charged on without hesitation to report military ties to the death squads.

TEN YEARS LATER: VINDICATION OF A SORT

In one of those few moments of justice for controversial journalists, Bonner was exonerated on October 22, 1992, in a page-one *Times* story written by Tim Golden, by then one of the paper's top Latin American writers. The dramatic account, accompanied by a photo of a mass grave, was headlined: "Salvador Skeletons Confirm Reports of Massacre in 1981." The photo caption read: "In the village of El Mozote, El Salvador, forensic experts have uncovered a site holding the skeletons of 38 children who were among the 792 local villagers reported massacred in 1981 by American-trained soldiers."[99] Guillermoprieto's original reporting also was cited. A *New York Times* editorial followed up four days later, again mentioning the two reporters and pointedly recalling the *Wall Street Journal*'s criticism of Bonner for accepting the accounts of peasants. "The peasants did not exaggerate," the *Times* said, thumbing its nose at the old critics without having the honesty to at least briefly admit that some of Bonner's critics were internal and that he was unfairly treated by all concerned.[100] The *Times* also praised the government of President Alfredo Cristiani for moving ahead with "courageous determination," when in actuality it took tremendous pressure from the nation's U.N.-backed Truth Commission to allow the bodies to be exhumed. Golden put everything in perspective by reporting about past Salvadoran response to human-rights complaints: "Only one senior official has ever been convicted."[101]

"The bones have emerged as stark evidence," Golden wrote, "that the claims of peasant survivors and the reports of a couple of American journalists were true." He interviewed Mrs. Amaya, by then 51, who said, "Maybe if everyone sees these things clearly, they will have to do justice."[102] He added, "Government officials denied that such a massacre had taken place or blamed the rebels for the killings, and United States officials hotly disputed reports from the scene by Raymond Bonner of the *New York Times* and Alma Guillermoprieto of the *Washington Post*."[103]

There are several other points about the Bonner story. While it may appear that he was vindicated in most journalists' eyes by 1983, this was not the impression of some who served in the region. There also was disagreement about how long any chilling effect lasted. After all, the "new wave" of journalists (middle 1980s) were not in the region when he was recalled and only heard secondhand stories, some portraying him not as a hero but as a liar who deserved what he got. It took the 1992 stories to turn around one veteran of the 1984–89 period who had seen the Bonner case as "journalists policing their own . . . time and again one of the reporters would refer to that liar Bonner . . . the embassy was always asking why we didn't police our own as we ask the government to do, and judging by what journalists said, I thought we had . . . one thing, some of the journalists hated each other . . . in Bonner's case some had probably responded to 'rockets' [blunt messages from the home desk] referring to his work and they probably said he was lying . . . those people weren't chilled by what happened to him."[104]

After leaving the *Times* Bonner wrote a second book, about U.S. foreign-policy maneuverings in the Philippines,[105] gained attention as a popular figure on the speaker circuit, and later became a staff writer for the *New Yorker*. "It's hard to write against the prevailing wisdom in Washington, no matter who is in power," Bonner said later, adding, "The real problem was that my reporting didn't fit the tenor of the times, or the *Times* under Abe Rosenthal."[106] Critics of the U.S.-sponsored state terrorism in Central America put him in the league of Dr. Charles Clements, who wrote a blistering behind-the-scenes account of the Salvadoran guerrilla war,[107] and former CIA agents David MacMichael, John Stockwell, and Phil Roettinger. But as Bonner pointed out to me in November 1992, he was not an "advocate" like the others mentioned. "I'm a journalist. The recent Mozote developments further establish that Hinton et al., including some at the *Times*, tried to brand me as an 'advocacy journalist.'" He also said he felt only "partially" vindicated.

The Mozote massacre story and the attacks that followed were the beginning and the end of my career at the *New York Times* and as a daily journalist. But that's not important. I can hardly have been considered to have "suffered" too much—after all, I am a staff correspondent at the *New Yorker* [he left that post in 1992 and, of all things, was hired by the *Times* for special assignment work]. Besides, it's part of the turf. As journalists we give lumps, and we have to be prepared to take them. And when it comes to vindication, you know what is really meaningful vindication? The stories that Alger Hiss was not a spy. That's vindication. Sure, I took some hits, but Alger Hiss was *destroyed* by ideologues. With the Cold War over, we might think that there are no lessons from all this, from letting ideologues destroy individuals in the name of fighting an enemy. I fear, however, that it will rise again, with the "enemy" becoming Islamic fundamentalism, the "ism" now replacing communism in our fears. Look what happened to Peter Arnett when he tried to report out of Baghdad . . .

Looking back, I really have little to say . . . maybe this telex message from the great John Kifner does: "Ray, Galileo and Bonner, still right after all of these years. Kif."[108]

A FREELANCER FIGHTS THE PACK

Those readers generally familiar with the Bonner story might be surprised to know of a footnote to this tale of hypocrisy. The Mozote story was not broken first in the *New York Times* and *Washington Post* but instead a month earlier, by Pacifica radio station KPFK, Los Angeles. News director Marc Cooper and his assistant Tony Calvin were informed of the killings by human-rights and pro-opposition sources cultivated on earlier visits.

Cooper recalled later that between his December 28 report and the Bonner-Guillermoprieto stories of late January, "the Mozote story was well-known inside the community of persons familiar with the Salvador story."[109] Cooper said that after the report was aired on KPFK and sister stations in Washington, D.C. and Berkeley, California, he was informed that the allegations of atrocities by the Atlacatl Battalion had been made available to the home offices of the *New York Times* and *Washington Post*. In Bonner's case, he had planned his trip to the guerrilla area of Morazan Province for more than a year, and a December adventure had been postponed because of the government's search-and-destroy operations. He was in New York for Christmas and did not have an opportunity to get into the mountains until early January.

Cooper, full of praise for Bonner's work, said that in January 1982, when Bonner and Guillermoprieto gained attention, "We [those who had known of the story] didn't think of them as heroes; we saw them as establishment-minded reporters slow to understand and report a major story."[110] Cooper's explanation for the reluctance of responsible journalists and government officials to deal honestly with a number of massacre reports—Mozote was only one—was that "this story spin didn't fit in the acceptable range of American opinion." In other words, stories of U.S.-sponsored state terrorism clashed with the underlying assumption that massive U.S. aid to Salvador was necessary to stave off the Communist threat.

By putting both Nicaragua and El Salvador in an East-West context, instead of focusing on the age-old class differences and exploitation, reporters and government officials alike shut the door to the Bonners and the Coopers who made the unpopular second assumption: that U.S. aid to the right-wing governments supporting death squads and massacres was morally wrong. Cooper agreed that Bonner's removal had the desired effect on reporters, but that many of them already were reluctant to dig deeply for fear of offending home editors or government sources.

Cooper's own story is an interesting one. His first exposure to Latin America was in Chile during the Allende years. Nearly a decade of various freelance activities followed before he found his niche in Central America. Following the KPFK success he went to San Salvador, where he covered the 1982 elections. He co-authored two *Village Voice* pieces with future CNN correspondent Ronnie Loveler, a five-part series for the *San Diego Union*, and a week's worth of award-winning 15-minute radio shows for a number of public radio stations linked by satellite. He teamed with Tim Frasca in Washington, D.C., for the radio shows.

By 1982 Cooper had become one of the lone voices raising doubts about the veracity of the elections and of U.S. policy in general. His scholarly analysis of the 1984–85 election period deserves attention, if for no other reason than that it helps us understand reporting and editing methods. Cooper's review of more than 800 articles from five major newspapers revealed that from March 1984 through October 1985 "the Salvadoran story was no longer being reported as one of repression, escalating war and massive human-rights violations, but rather as one of hope for peace and democratic renaissance." As noted, Washington officials did their best to muddle any tough reports from the field about FMLN successes or human-rights abuses. Now, according to Cooper's analysis, Washington would have an easier time with the San Salvador press corps seeing Duarte as a "moderate" and even a "liberal."[111]

Cooper chided his fellow reporters for uncritically accepting Duarte as a democrat and not researching his record. "That Duarte had presided over the government junta during the bloodiest period of state terror in Salvadoran history was not seen as a possible impediment to his self-proclaimed role as reconciler and reformer," Cooper wrote. Slacking off a bit in his criticism, Cooper was understanding of the pressures reporters find themselves under, in addition to sorting out the complexities. Unfortunately home editors were prone to see Salvador as another East versus West, Communism versus democracy, moderate versus extremist situation.

The pressure to produce the often-mocked but always delivered "bang-bang" accounts was part of the picture. Cooper saved a telex sent from the New York AP office which read: "Will need stepped up volume of photo copy from Salvador, particularly violence related. View increasing number of those killed, getting pressure from major countries for more pix." Most important, though, Cooper explained the ideological pressures felt by reporters. He put it this way:

> Reporters run in packs and have much more in common with each other than with the people they cover. Commonly held viewpoints among reporters can easily be confused for universal truths. Perceptions are confirmed and re-confirmed with every conversation they have with colleagues. Moreover, the reporter who breaks from the chorus is more likely to be held suspect by superiors than lauded for taking initiative.[112]

This, of course, is what every reporter knows but gives little thought to because of a dozen reasons why it is important to collaborate, to be part of that pack, to share experiences. Reporters usually do write alone and are secretive about their final product. And, yes, they often do disagree strongly about the meaning of a story. But Cooper's generalization about reporting behavior is well taken because it breaks with an underlying assumption that reporters can distinguish between breaking news elements and the true meaning of why there is a story in the first place.

In contrast to Washington's hope that massive aid to the Duarte government would stem the tide of the FMLN, the war continued and the guerrillas mounted several strong offensives. In March 1988 Cooper was co-producer and correspondent for a *Christian Science Monitor* television report, "El Salvador: Frontline of a Forgotten War." This grew into a June 1988 segment for PBS's *Frontline* series, "The Forgotten War." FMLN leader Joaquin Villalobos consented to his first, long detailed interview for this show, conducted by Cooper.[113] Then in March 1989 he co-produced with Richard O'Regan a segment for CBS's *West 57th St.*, which for the first time showed the urban strength of the guerrillas and more or less predicted the assault on San Salvador that shocked everyone in November 1989. With that show of force the guerrillas demonstrated the necessity for negotiations. In early 1994 Cooper put the Zapatista revolt in Chiapas, Mexico, into perspective, telling his *Voice* readers that millions of Mexicans demanded democracy and opposed the global market system that threatened to continue their exploitation.[114] Later that year he was in Cuba, joining other Central American veterans who reported on the "rafters" and Fidel Castro's battle of wits with the Clinton administration. From there a number of regulars and freelancers went to Haiti for the September showdown with the ruling junta.

PENETRATING THE LIES AND THE DISTORTIONS

Cooper figured in another incident revolving around media criticism. James LeMoyne reported the killing by guerrillas of two male villagers because they possessed new voting cards. The story gave the impression that LeMoyne had entered the village and interviewed people when he hadn't. Cooper and other San Salvador freelancers investigated the story and found it to be false. LeMoyne's article apparently was based on information in a San Salvador newspaper that had attributed it to a press release distributed by the Salvadoran armed forces. Cooper's account was published in the *L.A. Weekly*, which in turn resulted in an unusually long correction by the *Times*. Freelancer Chris Norton, who wrote often for the *Christian Science Monitor*, Chris Hedges of the *Dallas Morning News*, and Frank Smyth, best known for his CBS radio work, were among those who distinguished themselves by trying to get behind the smokescreen.

Penetrating myths proved nearly impossible for the correspondents for major U.S. organizations, man or woman. For example, while everyone suspected that Roberto D'Aubuisson's Republican National Alliance party (ARENA) was linked to the pro-government violence and that U.S. embassy staff and advisers hid behind a bush of lies, it was difficult to state these relationships as fact. In D'Aubuisson's case, in 1985 he was implicated in death-squad activities and the murder of Archbishop Romero, but the Reagan administration showed its unhappiness with D'Aubuisson only after congressional threats to cut off aid to El Salvador. D'Aubuisson died of cancer in 1992, and about a year later more than 12,000 intelligence documents were released by the State Department, Defense Department, and CIA after congressional pressure. These revealed how throughout the 1980s the Reagan and Bush administrations had detailed information about the complicity of Salvadoran military officers in the killings but continued to support them.[115] Among the correspondents who discussed this were the *Washington Post*'s Douglas Farah, who reported from El Salvador in the 1985–90 period, and freelancer Norton, who began his reports in 1986. Norton said the Reagan administration used a "docile Washington press corps to publish its disinformation on Central America as fact," while U.S. embassy officials punished reporters who questioned policy and maintained "especially cozy relationships" with selected television reporters.[116]

Some of the old hands returned in 1992 when a formal treaty ended the fighting. At the same time some of the old problems remained. Golden, for example, said the treaty ended "a 12-year civil war that turned [their] tiny Central American nation into the most violent theater of East-West conflict in the hemisphere."[117] Boudreaux of the *Los Angeles Times*, soon headed for a new assignment in Moscow, saw it almost exactly the same way, calling the conflict "the Western Hemisphere's bloodiest legacy of the Cold War."[118] It was as if the government's White Paper on Communist arms had never been discredited. The Reagan administration justified its massive aid on the bogus claim that the fighting was another East-West struggle, hoping that more than 60 years of class strife would be ignored. The government was successful to a great extent.

Boudreaux even reported that guerrilla leaders "declared triumphantly the treaty's terms vindicated their Marxist-inspired insurgency which cost an estimated 75,000 lives, wrecked the country's economy and civilian institutions and displaced one-fifth of its 5 million people." This rewriting of history failed to mention the bulk of those who died were killed by government bullets or bombings.

LeMoyne and Marjorie Miller produced significant Sunday magazine pieces for their respective newspapers that in a sense summed up their judgments about the past. LeMoyne wrote:

> The sad truth is that only war could budge the clique of army officers and oligarchs who dominated the country in a militarized, colonial form of capitalism. And the only ones willing to wage that war were the Marxists, radicalized priests, organized peasants, trade unionists and angry students who formed the five groups making up the guerrilla Farabundo Marti National Liberation Front.[119]

LeMoyne recounted the killings of the Jesuits, Archbishop Romero, and thousands of others at the hands of the government. He also interviewed Villalobos, who "admitted to 'errors' in tactics, said he 'regretted' some rebel killings and spoke with apparent conviction of the need for democracy based on fair laws, elections and social welfare." Miller caught up with Villalobos also, offering an intimate profile of the rebels' "best and meanest military commander" who now "found himself at receptions with businessmen who almost certainly had funded paramilitary death squads in the early 1980s—and might be willing to do so again."[120]

In 1994 it was an open question whether Salvador's élite could agree to fundamental changes in the nation's authoritarian culture. There would have to be economic changes in order to prevent more fighting. But, as LeMoyne pointed out, guerrilla leaders demonstrated striking changes in attitude, so perhaps there was some hope for the other side. "While some Americans still sport bumper stickers demanding 'U.S. Out of El Salvador,'" he wrote, rebel officials now wanted the U.S. military group to stay, "to help in the transition to peace."[121]

As bizarre as this may have seemed to readers who had followed the war, such statements did not surprise those veteran correspondents who knew and respected the basic desire for peace found everywhere in Central America. Daniel Ortega often told his people that all Nicaragua wanted from the United States was to be paid 10 cents for a pound of bananas, instead of a penny, and to live in peace.[122]

Chapter Seven

The Middle East:

In the Eye of the Storms

Jordan's Crown Prince Hassan meets reporters at 1987 Arab Summit in Amman; the scene is typical of the rush for news anywhere in the world. Michael Emery photo.

INTRODUCTION: THE PALESTINIAN QUESTION

The best advice anyone could give a correspondent headed for the first time to Israel and the Occupied Territories would be to realize there are two oral histories of this land, each reflecting thousands of years of experiences. Second, the newcomer should become intimately familiar with the post–World War II history, including those variations, because nearly every conversation starts with either "Before 1948 . . . " (Palestinians) or "After 1948 . . . " (Israelis). The other quick history lessons are pegged to the benchmark date of 1967.[1] Lastly, there is a required trip to Hebron in what now is the West

Bank, to visit the tomb of Abraham, the historical father of both Arabs and Jews. At this point everything should become clear. These Semitic people are related—like it or not, they are cousins.

In pointing toward their own frustrating condition, some Palestinians grudgingly acknowledge the pain suffered in the Jewish diaspora prior to the declaring of Israel's statehood on May 14, 1948. This time around it was the Palestinians who were suffering, in their diaspora and in the Occupied Territories. The striking similarities between the Israelis and Palestinians include a long tradition of education, skill at business and technology, a penchant for politics, strong personal and geographic identity, and an effectiveness at guerrilla and psychological warfare. Israeli determination to defend the existing state is matched by the Palestinian drive to create their own independent state. In late 1994 the Israelis still held most of the cards.

This chapter has two parts. The first focuses on the coverage of the Israeli-Palestinian struggle, with a special emphasis on the *Intifada* which began in 1987. The second, which has its own introduction, deals with the wars in the Gulf region from 1987 to 1991, including Operation Desert Storm. In both cases the purpose is to put the coverage into historical context and to make judgments about the overall quality of the information received in the United States. The Middle East is riddled with age-old rivalries with the potential for war, but the core problem is the Israeli-Palestinian conflict, which we will look at first.

The peak of Israeli dominance in this grinding struggle was reached June 7, 1967 when troops gained control of the Old City of Jerusalem, including the Wailing (Western) Wall, the only remaining section of the Second Jewish Temple destroyed A.D. 70. The correspondents' leads were filled with religious significance.

Robert Toth of the *Los Angeles Times* wrote:

> With the hollow bleat of a ram's horn for which Jews have listened for 2000 years, Israelites Wednesday morning took back their most sacred shrine, the Wailing Wall in the old city of Jerusalem, formerly held by Jordan.[2]

Arthur Veysey of the *Chicago Tribune* stood nearby and this was how he summed up that pivotal day:

> Jews sang the praises of the Lord Almighty beside the great square stones of Solomon's temple today for the first time in 19 years, and one of them, a young paratroop corporal, paid with his life.[3]

The "eye for an eye, tooth for tooth" tradition was maintained when the sniper who killed the young Israeli was hunted down and killed, while those singing at the Wall barely noticed the violent acts taking place a few feet away.

One Associated Press bulletin to the world on June 7 read:

> Israel proclaimed victory tonight in the Sinai Peninsula campaign against the United Arab Republic. On the eastern front both the Old City of Jerusalem and Bethlehem were captured from the Jordanians.[4]

Terrance Smith of the *New York Times* also was caught up in the emotion of the hour:

> Israeli troops wept and prayed today at the foot of the Wailing Wall— the last remnant of Solomon's Second Temple and the object of pilgrimage of Jews throughout the centuries.[5]

A compilation of press association dispatches produced this lead for the *Washington Post*:

> The Israeli officer stood among his sweaty men in the heat of the midmorning and radioed back the news. "I am in possession of the Temple Mount—I repeat—I am in possession of the Temple Mount."[6]

Israel had become a world military power, respected by Western nations not only for military prowess but for a tremendous demonstration of civilian courage and cooperation. From that magic moment of jubilation and thanksgiving, Israeli fortunes began to slide—slowly at first, following the 1973 war, and then rapidly in the 1980s, as the combined pressures of the West Bank and Gaza occupation, hostility of the Arab world, and internal stress took a heavy toll. It is clear that in those early days, from the war of 1948 through the 1973 Yom Kippur war, the bulk of the foreign press corps was more or less "cheerleading" for Israel. The reasons for this bias demonstrate how the news coverage of any region may be shaped. In this case it is particularly important to note how the coverage of the crucial Israeli-Palestinian conflict, the core of the larger Israeli-Arab struggle, lacked essential elements from the beginning and made future peace-making efforts all the more difficult.

It was natural for Americans to support the Jewish effort to have security in an independent state. The post–World War II Jewish rebellion against British rule in Palestine gained considerable attention in the U.S. press and the sickening horrors of the Holocaust became a major part of this emerging story. In most minds this added a great justification for Jewish demands. Steeped in the Judeo-Christian tradition and woefully ignorant of Middle East history, geography and cultures, most fair-minded Americans were ill equipped to evaluate the details of decisions being made. As usually happens in fast-moving situations, future consequences were not foreseen because most observers lacked the ability to place events in a historical perspective. On the cynical side, politics played a role, too. President Truman was among those who briefly favored placing Palestine within a U.N. Trusteeship. Then the realities of Cold War competition with the Soviets and the 1948 election came into focus. In his memoirs, Truman explained the pressures that caused him to switch to support for an independent Israeli state. In short, the Western view of Arabs was negative, while traditional Western prejudice against Jews was suspended by emotion, guilt and a Crusader-like attitude about redeeming the Holy Land.[7]

However, Arabs had opposed Jewish immigration to Palestine throughout the British Mandate period (September 1923–May 1945) and were not about to capitulate. I. F. Stone, one of the chroniclers of Israel's founding, succinctly described the Arab viewpoint years later when he said, "The Palestinian Arabs, from the beginnings of Zionism, foresaw the danger of being swamped and dislodged by Jewish immigration. Neighboring Arab states feared that this immigration would stimulate a continuous territorial expansion at their expense and create a Jewish state powerful enough to dominate the area."[8] Acting on their fears and bitter resentment, the Arabs rejected a 1947 United Nations partition plan that would have created separate Jewish and Arab states, with Jerusalem under international control. Jews, who by this time numbered about 33 percent of the population and occupied 6 percent of the land, would have received about 55 percent of the land. While Jewish leaders had reservations about the proposed borders and the status of Jerusalem, they pushed for the plan and were supported by both the United States and the Soviet Union. The Soviets had their own agenda for the region and awaited the withdrawal of their traditional nemesis, the British. The British abstained from the U.N. vote, the Arab and Muslim states voted no, but the plan was adopted by a 33–13 vote. With the end of the Mandate coming on May 15, the Jews prepared for their declaration of independence.

Between 1948 and 1988, when they gained worldwide status by declaring their independence and recognizing the State of Israel, Palestinians fought for their identity. One reason for the easy dismissal of Palestinians was their own lack of leadership. The press played a role in this as well, as we will see. Until the Palestine Liberation Organization (PLO) appeared in 1964 and Yasir Arafat took the helm, the Palestinians did not have a voice. Instead Prime Ministers David Ben-Gurion and Golda Meir took every step to eliminate the Palestinian image. Meir even denied their existence as a people. In the first years after the 1948 war hundreds of Palestinian villages were leveled. The Arab nations did little to help their Palestinian brothers and sisters.

During Jordan's occupation of the West Bank (1948–67) Palestinian nationalists chafed under the tight and sometimes brutal Jordanian rule. Jordan's King Abdullah, said to be in close cooperation with the Israelis prior to the outbreak of fighting, removed the word "Palestine" from official maps and documents in 1950. He came to an agreement with the Jewish Agency a few days before Israeli independence that his forces would not attack territory partitioned for Jews and that he wanted to occupy the balance of Arab lands within Palestine.[9]

Keeping in mind that U.S. politicians, beginning with Harry Truman, learned how to court the Jewish vote and that American-Jewish leaders learned how to gather immense amounts of money for those politicians (later the main organization was known as the American Israel Political Action Committee), it is reasonable to conclude that the U.S. public was treated to a one-sided version of Israeli-Arab affairs. This was particularly true when Lyndon Johnson and Richard Nixon were in office, from 1963 to 1974, and again during most of Ronald Reagan's years, 1981–88, with the exception of negative coverage during the 1982 invasion of Lebanon and beginning again in 1987 with the outbreak of the *Intifada*.

Prior to the late 1960s few correspondents were assigned to the Middle East on a full-time basis. As usual, the press associations and a handful of major newspapers dominated the coverage. More than half of the members of the foreign press corps were Israelis working for foreign publications. Then came the 1967 war which received attention similar to the peak of the Gulf War, with long stretches of continuous television coverage and frequent news bulletins. More newspapers set up offices in Tel Aviv, Jerusalem, Cairo, and other cities, establishing a pattern familiar in the 1990s. Television coverage was more spotty. Between conflicts the network television crews operated from their European bureaus or from the United States. In 1993 full-time network teams were based in Israel but there were cutbacks in overall Middle East television coverage. While the concentration here is on print journalists, the contributions of the broadcast correspondents are noted. They sometimes shaped the print coverage in that home editors, like everyone else, formed strong viewpoints from the nightly news footage.

THE WAR OF 1948: A DIVIDING LINE IN HISTORY

There was heavy violence on both sides during the winter months of 1947–48, with Jewish forces seizing territory ceded to the Arabs by the ill-fated Partition Resolution. There is strong evidence that the Jewish forces had no intention of living within the boundaries they had previously accepted. More than 200,000 Palestinians fled from their homes in the December– April period. On April 9 forces of the Irgun and the Stern Gang, two underground terror groups headed by future Prime Ministers Menachem Begin and Yitzhak Shamir, slaughtered about 250 unarmed Palestinians at Deir Yassin near Jerusalem.[10] This single well-documented act accounted for a great deal of the panic among Palestinians that continued after the May 14 declaration of Israeli independence. Later it was learned that the outlaw groups collaborated with the regular Jewish force, the Haganah, whose commandos provided covering fire during the massacre.[11] In May about 20,000 soldiers from neighboring Arab states began coming to the assistance of the almost defenseless Palestinian Arabs who could field at the most a few thousand poorly armed fighters. The Haganah numbered about 40,000 and these were backed up by an estimated 30,000 to 50,000 other second-line personnel in settlements, youth battalions and the Irgun and Stern Gang units.[12] Many of the front-line troops were British trained.

Correspondents covering the 1948 war overwhelmingly adopted the Israeli version of events. The general assumption was that, despite the military might of neighboring Arab states, Israel prevailed in a good and just cause. After strenuous debate over the question of U.N. trusteeship, the White House assumption came to be that, with the British retreating from the Eastern Mediterranean, it was vital to thwart whatever gains the Soviets might make in the region. One way to signal toughness was to support the Jewish state.[13] Another way to look at the events is to say Israel took advantage of Arab disunity and weakness to engage in "ethnic cleansing," forcing as many as 800,000 Palestinians from their homes and seizing far more territory than specified by the United Nations plan.[14] The officer who ordered the expulsion of about 50,000 Palestinians from Lydda and Ramleh in mid-July 1948 was Lt. Col. Yitzhak Rabin. Hundreds of civilians were killed as Israeli forces provoked the panic.[15] Ben-Gurion, who said, "Israel is the country for the Jews and only the Jews,"[16] later frankly admitted that Jewish forces stole the Palestinian lands to build and expand their own state.[17] From this early point Palestinian refugees became invisible.

The 1948 war was immediately romanticized and mythologized for the U.S. audience by correspondents, propagandists, religious leaders, and politicians. Eventually filmmakers got into the act with movies such as *Exodus* leaving everlasting memories of Jewish freedom fighters and Arab murderers. Within years Israel was known as this nation's "strategic ally." The use of this term has sparked fierce debate between Israeli supporters and those who claim that a succession of U.S. administrations succumbed to political pressures. In 1989 I met George Ball in Washington. A White House adviser during the Kennedy-Johnson years, Ball said that if JFK had lived "there probably would have been a more even-handed policy in the Middle East. LBJ sold the farm." Ball said Kennedy was becoming irritated with the pressure from the Jewish lobbying group AIPAC (American Israel Public Affairs Committee).[18] The Soviets, early friends of Israel, soon joined with the Arab nations. The United States, eager to maintain control of Middle Eastern oil, saw Israel as a potential military partner in any future showdowns. The year 1948 already had seen a clampdown in Czechoslovakia, there was chaos in Greece, and Germany was headed for a crisis later in the year. Thus began a powerful convergence of strategic, economic and religious interests that went sour in the late 1980s and early 1990s because of disagreements involving the Iran-Contra scandal, the Israeli push for settlements in the Occupied Territories, and brutal treatment of Palestinians living under occupation.

One way to judge the accuracy and comprehensiveness of Israeli-Palestinian coverage would be to look at how U.S. journalists recorded the steady Israeli acquisition of Palestinian land following independence. In 1994 few Americans knew that about 92 percent of all the land in Israel was owned by the state and the Jewish National Fund (JNF), an internationally registered philanthropical organization to which U.S. citizens could make tax-deductible donations.

This is the history that got lost in the aftermath of a popular victory. The Jewish National Fund was founded in 1901 as an offshoot of the World Zionist Organization. The goal was to collect funds from around the world to purchase lands in Palestine for Jewish people. By the 1948 war, however, the JNF held title to only 3.5 percent of Israel, so a mechanism had to be established to acquire homes and land for farming. The original Arab fears cited by Stone were justified. When the fighting ended, Palestinians were forbidden to return to their homes. Instead they witnessed the innovative use of a Custodian of Absentee Property, who had the authority to declare Palestinian homes and lands to be "abandoned." This illegal activity, which fueled generations of Palestinian hatred and disgust, was ignored by press and politicians alike. The JNF charter specifies that its property belongs to the "Jewish nation," not the "Israeli nation," and that Arabs living in Israel may not purchase land. In fact, no one actually owns land in Israel, but rather deeds are made out to either the state or the JNF.

Thus the State of Israel, assumed to be following the legal and moral norms of the secular Western societies supporting its existence, actually was creating a "Jewish state" by dispossessing or segregating the existing Palestinian population. The JNF expanded its activities in the Occupied Territories following the 1967 war; by 1992 more than 60 percent of the West Bank had been officially confiscated for "security reasons" and title to about 80 percent of Arab water rights had been transferred to Israel. A web of Israeli real estate companies was involved in a complex system of covenants and private but commonly held understandings designed to put property in the hands of Jews without having any of this incorporated into Israeli law.

The biggest of these firms, the Heimanuta Corporation, was founded in 1938 as a subsidiary of the JNF. Also involved with clearing land titles was the Israel Land Authority (ILA), an arm of the Ministry of Agriculture. The powerful ILA was controlled by a board, half of whose members were from the JNF and half from the Israeli government. The ILA adopted the racially restrictive charter of the JNF. Finally, officials of all of these organizations were closely linked with the right-wing settler movement which pressured for evictions of Arabs from their homes in the Old City and East Jerusalem. Ignored in mainstream U.S. press coverage, some of this came to light in early 1992 when armed settlers illegally seized homes in East Jerusalem. The most comprehensive journalistic look at the history of the JNF and the continued illegal land confiscation schemes was published by the *Village Voice*, which described these acts as barriers to success in the Middle East peace negotiations.[19] The Israeli magazine *Challenge* subsequently published a series of similar articles which for the most part were ignored by the U.S. media.

THE 1967 WAR: MYTHS AND REALITIES

In recent years there has been a good deal of revisionism regarding some of the myths surrounding Israel's wars. One of the leading scholars in Israel, military analyst Uri Milstein, has written extensively about Israel's wars, reevaluating the legends and controversies.[20] Others have looked at the 1967 war, including the killing of 34 sailors aboard the U.S.S. *Liberty* by Israeli pilots and boat gunners,[21] as conveniently fitting into Israel's long-term goal of achieving "*Eratz Israel*" or "Greater Israel," which to some included southern Lebanon, the Jordan River Valley, and the Sinai and for others simply meant the land "from the Nile to the Euphrates."

The common assumption was that Israel, ready to be attacked on three sides, jumped ahead and wiped out Egyptian, Syrian, and Jordanian aircraft before assaults could be launched. The world shook with excitement when news came of the spectacular Israeli success—it was Pearl Harbor in reverse. But there is another assumption, one that continues to be studied. It is that the Arabs had no centralized plans for an immediate attack, but rather blundered into a situation where Israel, planning for years to expand its territory and water supply, took advantage before there could be any Western-ordained mediation. This position holds that in 1967, as during the Suez crisis of 1956, the Arab forces were deployed defensively and that their military responses to Israeli attacks, although ineffective, were enough to give Israel grounds for claiming the Arabs had hit first. Speaking to this point in 1982, Prime Minister Begin told a National Defense College audience in Jerusalem that the war of 1967 was not "a war of necessity" but a war of choice: "Nasser did not attack us. We decided to attack him."[22]

Corroborating testimony from Israelis included Prime Minister Levi Eshkol's observation, "The Egyptian layout in the Sinai . . . testified to a military defensive setup." General Rabin said, "I do not think Nasser wanted war. The two divisions he sent to Sinai in May [1967] would not have been sufficient to launch an offensive against Israel. He knew it and we knew it." General Mattityahu Peled was more explicit: "The thesis . . . that Israel was fighting for its physical existence . . . was born and developed after the war . . . By falsifying the causes of the war [the Government] is trying to get the Israeli people to accept the principle of . . . annexation of territories."[23] There is a unusual degree of candor in Israel about potentially embarrassing events, found in newspaper reports there and in Europe. Little of this is reflected in U.S. press reports.

Kennett Love, the *New York Times* Middle East correspondent who covered the 1956 Suez crisis, produced a massive history of that Egyptian-Israeli conflict and its relationship to the 1967 fighting. Love was no stranger to media manipulation that favored the Israelis. "For reasons never satisfactorily explained," *Times* editors ignored his exclusive June 2, 1955, interview with Egyptian President Gamal Abdel Nasser, which ran counter to Israeli claims that Nasser was intent on war.[24] Love later saw the 1956 war as a rehearsal for 1967, both requiring only "favorable circumstances and a political decision to be put into action."[25]

One of the key events leading to the war occurred November 13, 1966, when Israel razed 40 homes in Jordanian villages in what was said to be reprisal for Syrian shelling from the Golan Heights area. Every bit of this is shaded by controversy. U.N. observers and veteran missionaries later said the Israelis deliberately encroached by moving into the area, in a sense knowing they would be "drawing fire." Israelis denied this, claiming the right to protect settlers living within Syrian artillery range. This tense standoff, marked by raids by both sides, escalated on April 6 when Israel shot down six Syrian jet fighters in a wild dogfight.[26] Anthony Lukas told *New York Times* readers on June 6 in a historical backgrounder, "The Arabs apparently felt taunted."[27] The Syrians and other Arabs then called on Egypt's

President Gamal Abdel Nasser to be bold, to ask U.N. peacekeeping forces to get out of the way so he could move his army up to the Israeli border. This was accomplished on May 19, and on May 23 he closed the Gulf of Aqaba, an international waterway. During these days Nasser crowed that Israeli would be defeated. It also should be recorded that on both May 25 and May 26 Nasser placed his comments about the destruction of Israel in the context that "the Jews threaten war" and "if Israel embarks on an aggression."[28]

Nasser, finally realizing his personal goal of unifying the Arab world under his leadership by standing up to Israel, walked into a setup partially of his own making. The Israelis had decided to break the deadlock. On the morning of June 5 Israeli fighter-bombers swept low across the Sinai and obliterated hundreds of Egyptian planes. Jordan's King Hussein then complicated history by making a fatal mistake. Apparently believing reports of an early Egyptian victory, or feeling he had no choice but to honor his pact with Egypt, he ordered his forces to fire into West Jerusalem.[29]

This is exactly what the Israelis wanted. They swept across the old Green Line (the 1949 armistice line that cut Jerusalem in two), seizing East Jerusalem and all of the West Bank. To the horror of the Palestinian residents, Israeli troops captured their cities, Bethlehem, Ramallah, Hebron, Nablus, Jenin, and Jericho. In one incident Israeli forces under the overall command of Chief of Staff Yitshak Rabin expelled 5,000 Palestinians from their villages inside of Israel and destroyed their homes. It is alleged that a "large number of civilians" were killed by napalm bombing as they fled through the desert area between Jerusalem and Jericho.[30] These horrors went unreported in the U.S. press. To the south the Gaza Strip was taken from Egypt. More than one million Palestinians fell under Israeli rule, many of them members of the same families who had lost their homes in 1948. Hundreds of thousands ended up in Jordanian, Syrian or Lebanese refugee camps, where they remain today.

The Israelis annexed East Jerusalem and placed the West Bank and Gaza under military rule. In November 1967 the U.N. Security Council unanimously passed Resolution 242, a British-sponsored plan linking Arab world recognition of Israel with Israeli withdrawal from "territories occupied in recent conflict." The immediate hang-up was the deliberate omission of any definitive word(s) (a, the, all, some of) before the word "territories." The United States and the United Nations regarded the annexation of East Jerusalem as illegal and insisted that it be part of lands considered "negotiable" in any future peace conference. For that reason the United States and most nations refused to move their embassies to Jerusalem. The Israeli position was that Jerusalem would never again be a divided city and would be exempt from negotiations.

THE CORRESPONDENTS SCRAMBLE, FROM CAIRO
TO THE GOLAN HEIGHTS

As the buildup began for what became known as the Six-Day War, Joe Alex Morris Jr. of the *Los Angeles Times* was in Cairo. On May 31 he quoted "informed sources" who said, "Arab nations planned a quick knockout blow before the West can intervene militarily." Within the next days Morris reported from Amman, the Mt. Scopus area of Jerusalem, the road to Bethlehem, and eventually Beirut.[31] Robert Toth wrote from Jerusalem for most of the week but ended up under fire in the Golan. Don Cook was in Cairo with the dispirited Egyptians. With several major areas left uncovered, the *Times*, as did the majority of U.S. papers, depended heavily on AP and UPI for breaking news and overviews. Several stories from Israel written by the *Washington Post*'s Alfred Friendly got good play. On June 5 the AP bulletined the news that Israeli pilots had destroyed 374 enemy planes. Toth reported from Tel Aviv the Israeli contention that the war began when it responded to "approaching" Egyptian aircraft and the shelling of three Israeli settlements from the Gaza Strip. Cook reported the Egyptian version, that the war began with the Israeli attacks.[32]

James Reston, former Washington bureau chief for the *New York Times* and a widely respected columnist, was in Cairo during the first days of June. In a dispatch dated June 4 he said, "An enormous fatalism seems to be settling over this city."[33] When the fighting broke the following day he was in Tel Aviv, where he defended the Israeli bombing raids, saying Washington, the British, and the United Nations had been of no help as the crisis grew.[34] *Times* byliners from the region were Eric Pace, Charles Mohr, Henry Tanner, Henry Kamm, Robert H. Phelps, Juan de Onis, James Feron, Thomas Brady, Dana Adams Schmidt, and Neil Sheehan of Vietnam fame, who was posted on the U.S.S. *America* in the eastern Mediterranean. On the home front, the veteran correspondent Drew Middleton's job was to tie everything together. At this point in newspaper journalism history, all eyes were on the *Times* and its huge reporting staff. The paper's overall coverage, extensive in number of column inches, paralleled that of major competitors when it came to insight and perspective. For the most part this was another black-and-white event, with good guys and bad guys.

The initial *Times* reports in its June 5 Late City edition were a jumble of confusion. The lead cited a communiqué from Tel Aviv that claimed heavy fighting had broken out on the eastern border "between Egyptian armored and aerial forces which moved against Israel and our forces which went into action in order to check them." Meanwhile, Cairo radio was reporting Israeli air strikes, the *Times* said.[35] All of this preceded the heavy air strikes that by most accounts opened the war. It is difficult to reconstruct these days event by event, but it is clear that propaganda played a heavy role in preparing the U.S. public for this conflict. It is probable that some of these events never happened. There was plenty of surprise within the press corps, too. On June 5 the AP's Garven Hudgins wrote how Don Cook of the *Los Angeles Times* and other Western correspondents were having breakfast around a Cairo swimming pool, speculating on when they might be leaving for home, when they heard supersonic booms and antiaircraft fire over Cairo.[36]

When news of the war hit Chicago the *Tribune* blared: "Jews, Arab War!" The bulletin story on Israeli air attacks came from Reuters' Paris bureau. Veysey, the *Tribune's* only correspondent, went with the Israeli forces on their push into Jordan. Incidentally, the Egyptians asked all U.S. correspondents to leave Cairo following the bombing raids, curtailing coverage from that angle. There were casualties in the press corps, also. Paul Schutzer, a photographer for *Life,* was killed in the Sinai area and Ted Yates, a producer NBC News, was shot to death at the King David Hotel in Jerusalem.

The *Washington Post* team included Friendly, columnist Flora Lewis, and Bernard D. Nossiter. Chalmers Roberts in Washington wrote the lengthy war leads that dominated the top of page one. Friendly reported the Israeli reaction from Tel Aviv and ended up in the Golan area, while Nossiter followed Israeli troops east and saw the capture of Bethlehem. Some of the most exciting writing came from Lewis, who saw war open in Jerusalem on the 5th:

> The first shell came at a little after 11 a.m. Since then it has not stopped. Rifle and machinegun fire has continued and the occasional sound of shells gets louder.
>
> Early this morning we all heard the fighting had begun in the Sinai but there was no sign of anything here . . . (A shell just landed in front of the [King David] hotel).[37]

She had been on the Jordanian side of the famed Mandelbaum Gate the previous evening and had walked back across; she was probably one of the last to do so before it was closed. The gate was the historic divide between Israel and the Arab world.

It was on June 8 that Israel set up its military rule in the "occupied West Bank," a term that came into play that day in at least one story. Morris of the *Los Angeles Times* wrote: "Israel set up a military government for the occupied West Bank area of Old Palestine Thursday."[38] As the stories poured out of the region, few mentioned the plight of the Palestinian refugees who again had been rendered invisible. Morris did report that "U.S. diplomats have discussed with Israelis the question of feeding several hundred thousand Arab refugees in camps on the West Bank."[39] Harry Trimborn reported from Jerusalem for the *Times*, while William Coughlin was in Beirut and William Tuohy got the Sinai assignment. Tom Lambert also was in Lebanon.

With an irony that only could be appreciated in the 1990s when Israelis and Palestinians sat down at peace tables, Sydney Gruson of the *New York Times* wrote on June 8 from Tel Aviv:

> The observers here believe the Israelis may be persuaded in a peace conference but in nothing less to accept a line running south from Jenin to Nablus to Jerusalem [splitting the territory in half, keeping the heights] . . . while the west bank of the Jordan would be the natural and rightful frontier, a compromise involving the territories now being held in the west bank . . . may have to be accepted for the sake of the larger issue of peace.[40]

June 8 also was the day the U.S.S. *Liberty*, an intelligence ship, was attacked by the Israelis some 20 miles off the Egyptian coast near the Gaza Strip. Thirty-four crew members died and 171 suffered wounds, many serious. The *Los Angeles Times* ran a page-one report from its Washington bureau: "Israeli jets and torpedo boats mistakenly attacked a U.S. Navy communications ship in the Eastern Mediterranean early Thursday." Deeper in the story the *Times* said the ship "was flying U.S. colors" and that there had been six strafing runs and a torpedo boat attack.[41] The details of this first report cast considerable doubt on the commonly accepted version from Tel Aviv and from the Johnson White House that there had been a "mistake." William Beecher's June 9 page-one story in the *New York Times* was headlined "Israel, in Error, Attacks U.S. Ship." Beecher reported, "An American naval vessel was mistakenly attacked by Israel planes and torpedo boats today in international waters." Later in the story he told the reader the U.S. flag was displayed. A photo caption also referred to the "mistake."[42]

Over the years the issue of the *Liberty* attack was kept alive by survivors and supporters who demanded the truth. An authoritative eyewitness account and investigative report by crew member James M. Ennes Jr. laid it bare in 1979. The attack lasted more than two hours—not just a few minutes—and the Israelis left 821 rocket and machine-gun holes in the ship. Israelis machine-gunned the *Liberty's* life rafts in the water. Only the belated sending of Sixth Fleet aircraft saved the ship from further attacks. Prior to the assault Ennes himself ordered a clean, large flag hoisted, to float freely for all to see. Incredibly, during the previous hours, as the ship sat offshore, there had been discussion among crew members about the possibility of an Israeli attack.[43] There are many opinions about why the Israelis would try to sink a U.S. "spy ship."[44] Ennes denied that the *Liberty* had long-range radio monitoring capabilities, but said the ship was kept within sight of land fighting near El Arish below Rafah (the current Egyptian-Israeli border). The U.S.-Israeli coverup worked—no one will ever know exactly what the *Liberty* was up to or why the Israelis tried to blow it to pieces.

The most intriguing speculation was that the Israelis fabricated communications from Nasser to King Hussein early in the fighting, to mislead the Jordanians into thinking the Arabs were winning and that it would be safe to enter the war from the East. This unsubstantiated line of reasoning goes on to assert that the Israelis feared that the *Liberty*, with its huge antenna, may have discovered the trick that they crafted to give themselves the chance to conquer the West Bank. So they tried to destroy all evidence. A second and more plausible reason is that the Israelis were about to launch their still secret all-out attack on the Syrian-held Golan area and thought the ship had learned of those plans. Israel wanted to finish its expansion without giving Washington a chance to interfere.

STEREOTYPING THE ARABS AND JEWS

The job of any good news organization is to put the hodgepodge of daily news stories into some sort of perspective. Reporters in the field like to write these "think pieces" if given enough time, but the home office has the overall responsibility. At the end of the Six-Day War, Philip Geyelin in Washington prepared an unusually realistic perspective piece for the *Post*. The headline was "David Fights Goliath in a Desert Mirage."

> A great many Americans see a gleaming pool and a patch of green called Israel in a baking desert inhabited by hostile elements. They are all stereotypes. Israel is David and Goliath is the Arab world . . . An Israeli is a sturdy, tenacious pioneer, as well as a victim of oppression and atrocity, rightly entitled to a homeland of his own. If American news media are any test, Israelis are also bronzed, industrious and strong. They smile, and ride off to war singing songs with a pretty girl in fetching uniform.
>
> An Arab is also part of the American experience—in this context. His role is that of the American Indian, slothful, weak; they scowl, their eyes are dark and menacing. And they ride to war in heavy Soviet tanks. This

is extreme, of course, but it is difficult to deny that most Americans see Israel as a bold and imaginative experiment in the creation of a dynamic, democratic modern nation, while the Arab world appears as downright savage, if Cairo radio is any test . . .

There is some truth in any stereotypes. The trouble with them is that they ignore some hard realities . . . Already there are a quarter of a million Arabs in Israel. Hundreds of thousands more inhabit territory which the Israelis now have overrun, on the Gaza Strip and on Jordan's West Bank. As the Israelis are certain to realize, the addition of these Arabs to their country would so upset the ethnic balance that it would cease, for all practical purposes, to be a Jewish state—quite apart from the security problems.

But the Arabs cannot be driven off their land without complicating a refugee problem which, 20 years after the first Arab-Israeli war, is still a festering sore. This suggests that, for all its increased bargaining power from its military victory, Israel will be under added pressure to confront the problem of Arabs displaced by creation of a Jewish state.[45]

Remarkably, 25 years later Daniel Williams of the *Los Angeles Times*, reporting the election campaign between Prime Minister Yitzhak Shamir and former Prime Minister Yitzhak Rabin, saw the same cultural and political dimension. Nothing had changed, except there were more Palestinians to take care of.

Beersheba, Israel—A look at the kickoff television election ads for the ruling Likud Party and the Labor Party, its main challenger, might lead viewers to believe that Israel is mainly a garden of ruddy farmers happily toiling in a generous land.

Likud's promo shows a strong-armed worker bailing golden hay on a well-manicured field. Oddly enough, so does the ad for Labor. Its farmer looks remarkably like the Likud's, all forearms and heavily tanned. The twin images of rural bliss are meant to evoke one of the basic national symbols of Israel: the new Jewish Man at home with the land. Never mind that these days, a farmhand is just as likely to be an underpaid Palestinian day worker as an Israeli, or that masses of Russian newcomers have no intention of shoveling manure on some kibbutz. You would never guess that Israel is rapidly moving toward a high-tech economy encased in air-conditioned laboratory complexes . . .

Parties continue to make hay with symbols such as the joyful farmer—not to mention a heavy use of the blue-and-white Israeli flag . . . The main difference between the two men centers on how to treat the 1.7 million Palestinians who live there.[46]

Geyelin, of course, correctly saw the full dimensions of the problem caused by Israel's expansion into every square inch of "Old Palestine." Lewis told her readers how Israelis, heady with such an outcome, slowly began to realize the implications of becoming "the major Middle East power." She passed along Moshe Dayan's idea of an Israel-Jordan federation to settle the security, frontier, and refugee problems.[47] Again, the Israelis, many Arab leaders, and the press reporting their strategies failed to remember that the Palestinians were more than a "refugee problem" to be absorbed by the drawing of another boundary line. They were the original inhabitants of the land taken from 1948 to 1967 and at this early point they lacked a voice.

BUILDUP TO ANOTHER WAR: THE SCARE OF 1973

The years between the Six-Day War and the 1973 Yom Kippur War were marked by numerous group or individual acts of violence. There was continued agitation in Israel's northern border area, the PLO leaders dedicated themselves to retribution for the seizing of Palestinian land, and finally in 1972 eight Israeli athletes were murdered at the Munich Olympic Games after being held hostage by Arabs. In the early 1970s the PLO and its various splinter groups hijacked airliners and engaged in numerous violent acts against Israelis designed to focus world attention on their plight. The most active organization was the Popular Front for the Liberation of Palestine (PFLP), led by George Habash. While all of this was happening—and Arabs were getting a black eye because of the violence—Israeli officials felt free to continue the merciless West Bank and Gaza occupation and to conduct raids of their own on Palestinian camps in southern Lebanon.

General war came again on October 6, 1973, when Israel was taken by surprise on the Yom Kippur holy day. Egyptian forces rolled across the Suez Canal area and forced the Israelis to abandon their positions. Some of the old hands from the 1967 war had moved on to other posts, but others like Jonathan C. Randall of the *Washington Post,* moved in. Randall had roamed the world for the previous 16 years for UPI, the *International Herald Tribune* and the *New York Times.* Philip Caputo, the Rome correspondent for the *Chicago Tribune,* was sent in to cover the fighting. A former Marine officer in Vietnam, Caputo was one of the few to reach the Sinai front in the opening days.[48] The *Tribune* also had Donald Kirk, an eight-year veteran of Vietnam, reporting in Lebanon and Syria.

The mood was set on October 10 when the *Post's* Bernard D. Nossiter reported the grim news: "The Israeli command acknowledged Tuesday that it has abandoned most of its Bar-Lev defense line on the Suez Canal and warned the country that it faces a long war."[49] But assisted by massive U.S. aid and a quick turnaround in fortunes on the battlefields, the Israelis soon were chasing the Egyptians back across the border. Israeli forces also crashed into Syria, pushing President Hafiz al-Assad's forces back toward Damascus. Israel's eastern border with Jordan was safe; King Hussein did not enter this particular war and the West Bank was not involved in the conflict.

Following the 1973 victory, attention turned northward to Lebanon. The leadership of the PLO had moved there in 1970 following its removal from Jordan in the Black September catastrophe. For several years the PLO had used Jordan as a base for attacks on Israel, but in 1970 King Hussein ordered his troops to attack PLO elements who had in effect attempted to set up a "state within a state" in Jordan. The king's units shelled some of the Palestinian refugee camps, killing several thousand persons and causing an everlasting hurt.[50] Driven out of Jordan, Arafat had for a last refuge only Lebanon, which itself was fragmented by internal strife. Israeli strategy was to support certain armed Christian elements against the Muslims. Lebanon, considered part of Greater Syria by the totalitarian Assad regime, was close to collapse. Finally, in 1975, a civil war broke out that led to greater Syrian and Israeli involvement and the disintegration of the Lebanese society. During this struggle the Syrians turned on the PLO and drove Arafat's units to southern Lebanon.

ISRAEL'S VIETNAM: THE QUAGMIRE IN LEBANON

In mid-June 1982 Prime Minister Begin and Defense Minister Ariel Sharon decided to crush the PLO, wipe out Syrian missile sites in the Bekaa Valley, and form a tight alliance with Lebanese Christian militiamen.

Newsweek's Steven Strasser was the lead writer for a June 21 "special report" on the invasion which contained his eyewitness account:

> In a bright yellow Dodge taxi, I was trying to get from Damascus to Beirut when the first explosion shook the car . . . "Look, mister!" my driver cried as another missile burst just to the left. Israeli warplanes circled high above the snow-flecked mountains that dominate the valley. Then one wave after another swooped down, the sun at their backs, firing missiles at the SAM batteries. Syrian MiG-23s, hugging the valley floor, rushed in pairs to intercept the attackers. Bombs began dropping near us faster and faster. Miraculously, they always fell slightly behind us. "Yalla! Yalla!" I shouted at my driver. "Move!"[51]

The Israeli land forces numbering about 60,000 quickly secured a 25-

mile zone in southern Lebanon and then moved toward Beirut. They joined with Christian Phalangist allies to surround West Beirut where 6,000 PLO fighters and some 1,500 Syrians were trapped. The Israeli attack on Beirut caused worldwide concern and a switch in tone of U.S. coverage. Critical comments from high-level Reagan administration officials, angered by what they considered a double cross after Begin and Sharon promised a limited campaign, fueled the negativity. At one point NBC's John Chancellor labeled the bombardments the actions of an "imperial Israel," not the Israel Americans knew. His comments drew a heavy protest from viewers, as did other critical print and broadcast analyses.[52] Bowing to U.S. pressure and having achieved most of their goals, the Israelis agreed to a cease-fire. A political agreement allowed the PLO forces to be evacuated, giving Arafat another chance to regroup. Eventually, Tunisia became the PLO headquarters, far from Israel and the Occupied Territories.

On August 23, 1982, when the PLO departure from West Beirut was under way, CBS News commentator Bill Moyers summarized the situation for viewers of Dan Rather's evening news show. His harsh denunciation of the PLO and criticism of Israel's "war machine" typified the view of a growing number of observers bothered by PLO intractability and, to a lesser degree, by Israeli arrogance. His assumption, based on a traditional pro-Israel foundation, was that if the PLO accepted the existence of Israel, and the Arab states stopped using the Palestinians as pawns in their campaign against Israel, the problems would be solved. Moyers apparently gave little thought to Israel's responsibility for the refugees. In late 1994, long after the PLO had swallowed its pride and other Arab nations in one way or another had acknowledged Israel's presence, there was little evidence that justice would be served to Palestinians. Nevertheless, this pointed observation came from Moyers in 1982:

> Watching scenes of the Beirut evacuation this weekend, I was struck by how it is possible for the cameras to magnify a lie. These Palestinian troops left town as if they'd just won a great victory. Arafat, they praised as a conquering hero. In fact, they are leaving town in defeat. And, in fact, Arafat led them to this cul-de-sac where they made their last stand behind the skirts of women and among the playgrounds of children. The only victory they won was to give General Sharon an excuse for total war and so to bring upon Israel the condemnation of world opinion and to many Jews, a tormented conscience. But the world was condemning Israel even before Beirut, and will for time to come. And the anguish of Jews at the suffering caused by their own war machine comes from the bitter experience of having learned that those who die by the sword must live by the sword. Carnage, indeed, and no one's hand too clean. But it

could have been otherwise if Arafat and his allies accepted the reality of Israel, if they had not established within Lebanon a terrorist state sworn to Israel's destruction, and if Arab governments had not found it useful to nurture the PLO in the bloody illusion that Israel can one day be pushed into the sea. Argue as you might about the events leading up to the establishment of Israel. Weep as you must for the Palestinian refugees. But a fact is a fact, and Israel is a fact, yet the guerrillas leaving Beirut are vowing to fight on until victory. Well, there will be no peace in the Middle East until the Arabs stop asking their young men to die for a lie.[53]

Taking another point of view, *Time's* Roger Rosenblatt accurately predicted the future in late June:

> Nor will an Israeli victory in Lebanon settle the issue of a place for the Palestinians to live. The U.S. position is not greatly enhanced by all this either. It has the perennial task of proving to the Arab states that it is not exclusively eager for Israel's pre-eminence in the area, and it may also assume a new political and financial burden of policing a reviving Lebanon.[54]

The United States did enter the picture, sending a contingent of Marines as part of an international peacekeeping force to guard the Beirut airport and to provide general security for the Gemayel government while the Israelis began withdrawal to their newly established security zone. This U.S. involvement ended on a bitter note for all concerned in October 1983 when 241 Marines were blown up in their barracks by a pro-Iranian unit and the U.S.S. *New Jersey* gained notoriety by shelling innocent Lebanese villages with bombs as big as automobiles. This was a giant setback for both U.S. and Israeli images around the world, bringing scorn to the Reagan administration's pro-Israeli policies.[55] Years later young Palestinians in refugee camps, well versed in recent history, would mention "the *New Jersey*" as evidence that the United States should not be trusted, while Israelis pointed to the withdrawal of the Marines as their evidence that the United States could not stick it out in a tough situation.[56]

SABRA AND SHATILA: THE PRESS TELLS THE TRUTH
ABOUT A MASSACRE

The biggest story related to the Lebanese invasion came in September 1982, three months after the initial drive across the border. It brought a shared

Pulitzer Prize to Tom Friedman of the *New York Times* and Loren Jenkins of the *Washington Post*. It also brought heartbreak to Palestinians world-wide and shock to Israelis, many of them in a growing antiwar movement led by members of Peace Now. Hundreds of Palestinians were massacred in the Sabra and Shatila refugee camps near Beirut by right-wing Christian Phalangists, allies of Israeli forces who provided access to the camps. In his 1989 book, *From Beirut to Jerusalem*, Friedman related the horror he felt as a Jew when he learned the degree of Israeli complicity. The only full-time Jewish correspondent in the Middle East, Friedman felt distrusted by both Arabs and Jews. This was the most sensitive story any of these corre-spondents would ever have to write, and they did not flinch from their ob-ligation to tell the truth, despite the natural pressure to be softer with the Israelis than to Arafat's PLO or to any of the warring factions in Lebanon.

On September 17 Jenkins was with the Israeli forces in West Beirut. His story that day, published on Saturday, September 18, gave a clue as to what was going to happen, detailing how the IDF (Israeli Defense Force) units cordoned off that sector of the city "and began a systematic hunt for Leba-nese and Palestinian sympathizers of the now evacuated Palestine Libera-tion Organization." He went on to describe how "plainclothes security agents, carrying lists of names, led squads of soldiers through the streets in search of presumed enemies to interrogate."

> Armed members of the Lebanese Forces, the Christian rightist militia that is allied with the Israelis, entered Palestinian refugee camps on the city's southern outskirts and went house to house arresting Palestinian males. In several instances Christian and Moslem militiamen exchanged rockets and gunfire. Cordons of Israeli tanks surrounded the Shatila, Sabra and Burj al Barajinah camps as the Christian militiamen, feared and hated by the Moslem population since the 1975–76 civil war, car-ried out their work.[57]

He continued with this observation: "But it was not the futile fighting that most worried West Beirut's half-million residents. It was instead the prospect of a sectarian crackdown on the Moslem population by Israel and its Lebanese Christian allies." He recalled the July 1976 slaughter of 3,000 Palestinians at the now-razed Tel al-Zaatar camp by the Christian militia-men, the "Kataeb" led by Bisher Gemayel, the president-elect assassinated earlier that week. Gemayel's men had been equipped with Israel weapons with IDF markings.[58] He also reported that Israelis were keeping outsiders from entering the camp but that a foreign television crew got into Gaza Hospital in the Sabra Camp and filmed badly wounded people. Reporting the denial of a Lebanese Forces spokesman that any Christian militiamen had entered the camps, Jenkins ended this first day's story with:

> But this correspondent, after evading Israeli Army roadblocks and making two separate visits to Shatila during the day, saw the militiamen operating openly there.[59]

Colin Campbell and Ihsan Hijazi were in Beirut with Friedman for the *New York Times*. Campbell's story for the Saturday edition described how Israel was increasing its stranglehold on Beirut.

> Beirut, Lebanon—More Israeli armored forces poured into West Beirut today, increasing the Israeli grip on the predominately Moslem sector, and Lebanese Christian militiamen entered Palestinian refugee camps in the southern suburbs to arrest guerrilla suspects.[60]

He continued, "With Israeli tanks standing guard outside, Israeli-backed Phalangist militiamen moved by foot and by jeep into the battered Sabra and Shatila camps." After describing the sounds of gunfire inside and recalling the "bloody siege" of Tel al-Zaatar, he finished with this:

> To many Moslems and Palestinians, what they had long feared happened today: Phalangists, their longtime bitter foes, followed the advancing Israelis and with Israeli tanks standing guard, were able to get into camp areas to hunt for enemies.

The Sunday edition carried Friedman's confirming report. Arriving in Beirut on Friday, September 17, 1982, after a vacation in the United States, he immediately picked up rumors that Phalangists had entered the camps. His impression was that no one had gotten inside; he didn't know that Jenkins had succeeded. Roberto Suro of *Time* told Friedman that he had talked with some Phalangists outside of Shatila and that gunfire could be heard inside the walls, as Campbell reported. Friedman recounted later that the Phalangists had been killing from Thursday, September 16, through early Saturday, when their Israeli friends "discovered" them and ordered them out.[61]

Friedman and others identified the militiamen who entered the camps with Israeli permission as belonging to units commanded by Major Saad Haddad, armed and trained by Israel.[62]

Friedman's lead, for a story that was accompanied by a strong sidebar from Campbell, read:

> Beirut—Lebanese Christian militiamen massacred scores of Palestinian men, women and children in a refugee camp on this southern edge

of West Beirut Friday night, according to witnesses and reporters who visited the camp.[63]

Timothy McNulty of the *Chicago Tribune* told his readers on September 19:

> Beirut—Christian militiamen massacred hundreds of men, women and children in two Palestinian refugee camps Friday night while the Israeli army stood outside, witnesses said.[64]

McNulty told of reporters seeing the Israeli troops outside the camp on Friday and ended with the tale of 3,000 dead Palestinians at the Tel al-Zaatar camp.

Meanwhile, Jenkins continued his relentless reporting and for the Sunday edition wrote a story that confirmed his Saturday scoop:

> Beirut—Lebanese gunmen belonging to right-wing Christian militia units killed hundreds of men, women and children in two undefended Palestinian refugee camps overnight, according to accounts by survivors given to correspondents who counted scores of corpses lying in the streets of the camps today.[65]

After identifying the men of Major Haddad, Jenkins added: "This correspondent saw men wearing the uniforms of both Gemayel's and Haddad's units in Shatila on Friday . . . this correspondent counted 46 bodies lying in the open in Shatila before being overcome by nausea." President Reagan expressed "outrage and revulsion" when he received these accounts, the *Post* reported, "using what appeared to be the angriest language ever directed at Israel by an American president."[66]

Two reporters for the *Los Angeles Times*, David Lamb and J. Michael Kennedy, shared the byline on September 19. Lamb, a UPI staffer in Vietnam, had recently taken over the Cairo bureau after five years in Africa and numerous other assignments for the paper.[67] He reported Israeli troops moving through the camps as early as the 16th. The scramble for news included the *Times* using a BBC staffer's photo, sent via the AP. Their lead, more specific about the times of the attacks than others, had strong impact:

> Beirut—Hundreds of Palestinians, many of them women and children, were massacred in the Sabra and Chatila refugee camps here Thursday night, Friday and early Saturday by Lebanese Christian militiamen despite the presence of Israeli troops just outside the camps.[68]

All papers carried more details on September 20, making the link between the Israelis and the Phalangists even more clear and knocking down

Israeli claims of ignorance of what was happening a few feet away. It is difficult to imagine how these killings could have been allowed. Friedman tried to explain the often violent convergence of Arabs and Jews in his widely praised book, just as *Times* Jerusalem correspondent David Shipler explored the two cultures in his equally impressive work, *Arab and Jew: Wounded Spirits in a Promised Land.*[69] Others, like Chomsky, found consistent patterns of corrupt political behavior into which stories like that of Sabra and Shatila fit rather easily; that is, the Israelis had not just suffered a lapse of judgment but rather the massacre was part of a punitive plan. Friedman later described Order Number 6, which was given to the troops in Beirut: "Searching and mopping up the camps will be done by the Phalangists and Lebanese army."[70]

Beyond that Friedman said, "Many Israelis had so dehumanized the Palestinians in their own minds and had so intimately equated the words 'Palestinian,' 'PLO,' and 'terrorists' on their radio and television for so long actually referring to 'terrorist tanks' and 'terrorist hospitals,' that they simply lost track of the distinction between Palestinian fighters and Palestinian civilians, combatant and non-combatants." These attitudes caused Israeli officers not to respond when informed of Phalangist actions during the first round of camp killings. Citing the Kahan Commission, the government inquiry board that uncovered evidence that the Israelis could have prevented the massacre, Friedman said: "Sabra and Shatila was something of a personal crisis for me. The Israel I met on the outskirts of Beirut was not the heroic Israel I had been taught to identify with. It was an Israel that talked about 'purity of arms' to itself but in the real world had learned how to play by Hama Rules [referring to Assad's killing of anywhere from 10,000 to 25,000 of his own people at the city of Hama in February 1982] like everyone else in the neighborhood. The Israelis knew just what they were doing when they let the Phalangists into those camps."[71]

During the furor over the killings, which accelerated the peace movement in Israel and led to some large demonstrations, Sharon sued *Time* for a report directly linking him to the killings. In early 1985 a New York jury ruled in a Solomon-like fashion, saying the report had been "false and defamatory" but had not been published with "actual malice." So *Time* was off the hook, but not without some embarrassment.

REVOLT IN THE TERRITORIES: THE WHOLE WORLD IS WATCHING

There was enormous press reaction to the outbreak of the Palestinian *Intifada* in Israel's Occupied Territories. The Arabic word means to "shake off something unpleasant," like an animal shaking water off its back. The *Intifada* was more than an "uprising," an occasional flare-up of protest against oppression; rather it was an organized, systematic, and philosophically based reaction to 20 years of Israeli occupation. This emphatic and symbolic statement, endorsed by the great bulk of the population, completely rejected the general Israeli assumption that Palestinians under occupation had no choice but to accept their fate. This wholesale revolt was aimed not only at Israelis but at anyone else, including Arabs, who might be opposed to Palestinian independence. As it spread to nearly every Palestinian family, the *Intifada* accelerated the already changing role of women and encouraged initiatives in education, health care, and food production. Palestinians saw the underpinning of the *Intifada*, the networking of nonviolent activities, as proof that they had the intellectual and organizing skills to maintain their own state.

Much of the research for this chapter was conducted in Israel and the Occupied Territories. I interviewed the Palestinian's chief spokesperson, Hanan Ashrawi, several times there and in Los Angeles before she became world renowned, and I met numerous others active in the *Intifada*. On the Israeli side I had the great fortune to meet journalist and security analyst Uri Milstein and journalists and political figures from the left to the extreme right. On one memorably hot July day in 1987, Uri drove me from Tel Aviv to the Lebanon border and across Israel's northern road, giving me the chance to see what it is like to live in that tense area. That night we had dinner in a restaurant filled with both Jewish and Arab families; Uri said softly, "This is the way it should be." My photographer colleague Jim Lukoski and I spent several days in the homes of West Bank settlers and on one occasion stood on a windy hilltop with Prime Minister Shamir as he was denounced by settlers for being a "traitor." One other person deserves a mention, the one and only Alya Shawa, owner of Marna House, where journalists stayed in Gaza. One day, while she showed off her voluminous pile of journalists' cards, I asked her who did the best job. "The Americans," she said with a conviction based on experience. "They go right for the story. They are very courageous."

The *Intifada* began in the Gaza Strip on December 9, 1987, after an Israeli military truck rammed into a van carrying Palestinian workers, killing four and injuring others. Palestinians assumed the act was a deliberate retaliation for the recent killing of an Israeli. Thousands rioted throughout the 28-mile-long Gaza Strip. Within hours Israeli troops had shot dozens of Palestinian demonstrators, killing several. News of the killings spread quickly to Nablus, other West Bank cities and occupied East Jerusalem. The reader should be aware, however, that stone throwing and violent retribution were nothing new. Actually there had been a constant *Intifada* since the late 1960s, with major flare-ups in the 1970s, but never did it have the scope and depth of the 1987 revolt. Never before had there been such intensity and determination. This is what shocked the Israelis and impressed foreign observers.

By December 12 the world's television cameras were on the story, as were Jerusalem-based reporters like Dan Fisher of the *Los Angeles Times*, who wrote:

> Gaza, Israeli—Occupied Gaza Strip—"Young people, go at them!"urged the amplified voice from the tower of the mosque across the street from the city's main hospital."
>
> "Don't be afraid!" the voice shouted in Arabic as scores of Palestinian youths hurled rocks and Molotov cocktails at armed Israeli troops on the streets below. "Don't back down!"
>
> Mahmoud Sakhli, 22, and Ibrahim Daqar, 23, followed that advice to their deaths Tuesday, two of at least four fatalities here during the bloodiest day yet in a weeklong orgy of violence that a ranking U.N. official said has become "a popular uprising."[72]

Gradually it dawned on PLO leaders outside of the Territories that this was developing into one of those moments that should not be missed. Over a period of time a sophisticated communications network evolved that allowed "the people outside" and "those fighting from inside" to coordinate statements, strike activities, and different forms of support. As the violence spread in late December the Israelis also realized that it would take an enormous effort to quell the disturbances. They braced themselves for the worst, resorting to widespread beatings, tear gassings, and shootings.

The sheer volume of print and broadcast coverage led to severe media criticism from supporters of Israel, while the lack of historical context bothered those in sympathy with the Palestinians—the same complaint of those interested in the underdogs in Central America and elsewhere in the world. The Israeli contention, clearly expressed in a booklet distributed by the *Jerusalem Post* entitled *Israel in Medialand*, is that "as the result of the restraint exercised by its army in putting such rioting down, the Palestinians achieved early successes—not so much in operational terms as in scoring points with the international media. This in turn brought the Palestinians to regard the Israelis as weak, which encouraged them to further acts of violence and to aggravated abuse . . . Israel, anxious to avoid shedding blood, issued its forces with these non-lethal police tools [nightsticks or billy clubs] . . . but the media, for reasons of its own, chose to interpret the matter as heralding a policy of 'brutal beatings,' thus turning world opinion against Israel."[73]

It was emphasized earlier that there are two versions to every story involving Arabs and Jews. The Israeli viewpoint also was forcefully made in *The Media's Coverage of the Arab-Israeli Conflict*, a series of essays edited in 1989 by Stephen Karetzky and Norman Frankel. There are 15 rebukes to coverage of the *Intifada* and another seven dealing with other events in the 1980s. The *New York Times* received a thrashing for its coverage, as did all television networks and other newspapers. One universal criticism was that Israeli abuse of Palestinians received attention far out of proportion to other violent events in the world.[74]

Former Secretary of State Henry Kissinger endorsed a military order by Defense Minister Yitzhak Rabin that Israeli soldiers should "break their bones" and suggested that the Israelis ban all television cameras from the Occupied Territories because they encouraged the rioters and were hurting Israel's image. In February 1988 Kissinger met with prominent American Jews at an off-the-record breakfast where he urged that Israel take these steps. According to a memo in which his comments were paraphrased, he said, "The insurrection must be quelled immediately, and the first step should be to throw out television, à la South Africa. To be sure, there will be international criticism of the step, but will dissipate in short order."[75] Larry Tisch, CBS's chief executive officer, agreed with Kissinger, placing his news division in a precarious position. Throughout this period gossip about behind-the-scenes arguments between network executives and news bosses over coverage led to additional caution on the desks.[76]

The power of television was enormous, as was the interest it created in all parties to the conflict. For good or for bad, Arabs and Jews listened to each other's comments, while journalists tuned in to see what they had missed. The Israeli Defense Ministry estimated that three quarters of West Bank and Gaza homes had television, about the same percentage as Israelis. BBC reports from Cairo could be picked up in Gaza and southern Israel; Jordanian news could be received throughout the area in Arabic, French, English and Hebrew; the Israelis broadcast to the region in Hebrew and Arabic. Satellite-dish antennae could bring in CNN, Eurovision, East European and Soviet, and Middle Eastern shows.[77]

In addition to the usual disputes about accuracy and fairness, questions remained about whether the U.S. audience fully realized the depth and scope of the Israeli occupation. The first step in examining this was the author's detailed analysis of 10 major newspapers from November 6, 1987—when tension in the region was reaching a boiling point—to January 6, 1988, when the *Intifada* was known worldwide. These 10 newspapers gave 10 percent of foreign news space, or 551 stories, to *Intifada* coverage. Competing for headlines were the Gulf tanker war, demonstrations and elections in South

Korea, the war between Iran and Iraq, and the peace gestures in Central America. This entire study, one of the most comprehensive of this type ever attempted, showed some surprises in coverage.[78]

Some editors, undoubtedly caught unaware by the widespread upheaval, devoted unusual attention to the flow of stories. The *Milwaukee Journal*, a relatively thin paper with no foreign correspondents, devoted 12.8 percent of its foreign news space to *Intifada* stories, while the resource-rich *New York Times* gave 6.8 percent to its readership. The other leaders were the *Boston Globe* (12.7%), with Mary Curtius in Jerusalem; the *Miami Herald* (12.6%), represented by Juan Tamayo; the *Chicago Tribune* (11.9%), its office manned by Jonathan Broder; and the *Los Angeles Times* (10.6%), with Dan Fisher in charge.

In terms of column inches, the most generous coverage was in the *Los Angeles Times,* which gave prominent attention to Fisher's on-the-spot reporting from both Gaza and the West Bank. Fisher, previously a bureau chief in both Warsaw and Moscow, came to Jerusalem as chief in 1984. His editors gave his initial stories front-page play. In contrast, it took the *New York Times* several days to put this story in front-page perspective. Charles Wallace, then stationed in Nicosia, joined Fisher to give the *Times* added coverage. The Jerusalem–Tel Aviv press corps was rich in experience. The highly regarded Curtius had covered the Middle East for the *Christian Science Monitor* prior to moving to the *Globe* and had been familiar with the region since a 1979 university internship in Jerusalem under the guidance of the late Dial Torgerson. She later joined the *Los Angeles Times* in Jerusalem. George D. Moffett III took Curtius's *CSM* job. A Harvard Ph.D. with government service in the international area during the Carter years, he was well grounded when he arrived. Tamayo, of course, had covered the extreme violence of Central America and was undaunted. In May 1988, Tamayo gave advice to Roberto Ceniceros and me about how to drive through the West Bank to Nablus, "by looking up at any overhangs where someone might be waiting to throw down a big rock." Driving in the Territories was unpredictable. Israeli soldiers resented seeing the "press" sign in Arabic, and Palestinians were suspicious that Israelis might be posing as journalists. Glenn Frankel, a bold reporter with a flair for descriptive writing, represented the *Washington Post*, and Marc Duvoisin was there for the *Philadelphia Inquirer*. (Author's note: In November 1992 Israel had the tenth largest foreign press corps in the world, with 270 foreign news associations; the United States was represented by 56 different news or feature agencies, and Germany by 51.)[79]

The *New York Times* was in a period of transition. Friedman was in Jerusalem until February when he took a leave of absence to finish his book.

In January 1989 he was named the paper's chief diplomatic correspondent in the Washington bureau. Friedman's intellectual news analyses and long pieces for the *New York Times Sunday Magazine* drew attention because of his ability to balance—there's that dreaded word again—his interpretations. His fairness was debated by both sides, and many Palestinians were not convinced of it, but some of Israel's strong U.S. supporters had problems with him as well because some of his pieces included evidence of glaring deficiencies in the Israeli system. Like Kinzer in Managua, he was the man in the middle, and his readers should have known what to expect when the *Intifada* broke out in 1987.

While Friedman had his critics and walked a thin line at times, the reporters who incurred more wrath in their local Jewish communities were Tamayo, Frankel, and Fisher. This writer learned that the blasts against Tamayo and threats to cancel advertising in the *Miami Herald* far exceeded anything thrown at the paper by Cuban and Nicaraguan exiles in the Nicaraguan war days. Frankel endured an enormous amount of pressure and threats, while in Los Angeles an angry and powerful pro-Israel community pounded away at Fisher, Dan Williams, and Michael Parks, equally observant and tenacious. To the credit of their editors, as well as those in Boston, Philadelphia, and other cities, the frontline journalists were protected from the nonjournalistic pressures. But they felt them nevertheless, just as they felt pressure in Israel where they had to deal with the institution of strict censorship, the frequent denial of access to troubled areas, and a generally hostile attitude.

While Friedman kept his eye on the Israeli-Palestinian dilemma from Washington and returned to it many times, others now were in the field, notably Joel Brinkley, Jerusalem chief from April 1988 to August 1991, when he also was assigned to Washington. Sabra Chartrand reported for the *Times* from Jerusalem. Others who assisted included the veteran John Kifner, who filled in for Friedman during the opening days in Gaza and provided graphic descriptions of the worst violence. Francis X. Clines was another. By 1990 many of the names had changed on the mailboxes in Beit Argon, the government press center.[80]

In the television news world, Bob Simon of CBS, Dean Reynolds of ABC, Martin Fletcher of NBC, and Mike Greenspan of CNN were the main correspondents. All four network correspondents strongly criticized Israeli actions at times, while also reporting any violent Palestinian reactions, like firebombings or bus attacks. Greenspan ran into problems with the Israelis and was removed by management. Of the other three, the hard-nosed Simon appeared to receive the most negative feedback. CBS was both praised and damned for showing lengthy footage of four Israeli soldiers using rocks to beat two Palestinians. While the crew was hailed for its powerful exclusive, shown worldwide, the Israeli government said the soldiers involved were punished and the Palestinians were not seriously injured. Bill Seamans, chief of ABC's Jerusalem bureau, put the complaints about television coverage in perspective. "I've been on the scene of every major terrorist attack [in the Middle East] since 1967. And we did nothing differently then [in coverage] than what we're doing now. But nobody ever complained then the way they are complaining now."[81] There were numerous skirmishes with Israeli authorities. Fletcher had his credentials temporarily revoked in April 1988 for violating a security regulation. He reported on Israel's assassination in Tunisia of Khalil al-Wazir (the famed Abu Jihad), Arafat's top strategist for the *Intifada*. Frankel also had his credentials lifted.

All of the evening news anchors had covered Middle East events and weathered disputes, but ABC's Peter Jennings, an award-winning foreign correspondent with 15 years experience in covering Europe and the Middle East, was best prepared to explain both sides of the Israeli-Palestinian struggle. While he generally gathered praise for his fairness, pro-Israeli supporters long considered Jennings "pro-Arab." NBC's Tom Brokaw and CBS' Dan Rather avoided major criticism. Brokaw's team drew some fire from Israeli supporters for a bold documentary in July 1987 that foreshadowed the *Intifada*; Rather once was attacked by Arab-Americans for his prominent participation at a Jewish fund-raising dinner involving Kissinger.[82]

Hundreds of incidents were reported involving local and foreign journalists in the first years of the *Intifada*. Israel's Foreign Press Association estimated that by May 1988 nearly a hundred journalists had been attacked by Israeli soldiers. There were many examples. A week after the CBS broadcast of the Nablus beatings, troops ganged up on a CBS crew that was filming them beating a young Palestinian in Gaza. ABC crew members filming a beating in Ramallah were grabbed and abused. Another CBS crew was stopped in Hebron and a cameraman was hit in the head with a rifle butt. In July ABC News President Roone Arledge protested to Israeli officials that security forces in a West Bank village had posed as an ABC News crew to arrest a Palestinian.[83]

Conditions continued to be tight and in October freelance journalist Neal Cassidy was shot in the leg in Nablus and hospitalized. He had the distinction of being the first foreign journalist to be hit by a bullet. In an odd case, Reuters news photographer Jim Hollander was granted $780 in an Israeli court after a reserve soldier was charged with breaking his camera and threatening him.[84] Two Reuters correspondents, Steven Weizman and Paul Taylor, and Andrew Whitley of the *Financial Times* (London) had their credentials suspended in October 1988 after reporting the activities of army undercover units. Whitley wrote that undercover troops used Arab cars and posed as journalists to detain suspects. The units also had the authority to shoot Palestinian organizers. In other words, some of these units were "death squads."

In December 1988 photographer Jim Lukoski and I saw four beer-drinking, armed Israeli soldiers in civilian dress riding in a car with blue license plates in Ramallah about 10 miles north of Jerusalem (West Bank Palestinians have blue plates; Israelis, including settlers in the territories, have yellow, and Arabs in Gaza have white). They stopped next to us while we were talking with an Israeli officer, who then acknowledged their presence. "Everyone knows we have soldiers in civilian clothes driving around at night in Arab cars," he said, "but no pictures." That same dark night we also saw a blue-plated car with four armed soldiers in military dress and a command vehicle with a man wearing an Arab headdress. Lukoski photographed the uniformed soldiers harassing several Palestinians. Palestinians interviewed before and after this incident said the Israelis used the blue plates to enter neighborhoods, driving people away for beatings or arrests. This was part of the ugly underside of Israeli attempts to supress the *Intifada*, not normally seen by reporters. During the next few years there were scattered stories about these units following numerous complaints from Palestinians and human-rights organizations.[85]

The Israel Defense Force routinely closed areas of the West Bank and Gaza to journalists, particularly during curfew periods but also after any violent incidents. The Israelis also tried to limit access by arresting many of the Palestinian journalists who were serving as interpreters and stringers. Jawdet Manna, who worked with numerous journalists through his Bethlehem Press Service, was arrested, beaten into unconsciousness, and put into prison. By March 1988 at least 21 others were in prison, including Radwan Abu Ayyash of the popular Palestine Press Service, which was closed down. The Committee to Protect Journalists (CPJ) protested the arrests to the Israeli government and the U.S. State Department. Arab newspapers in East Jerusalem were subject to closure throughout the *Intifada* and authorities even shut down two small newspapers with distribution within Israel, the Hebrew *Derech Hanitzotz* and its Arabic counterpart *Tariq A-Sharara*. Both were highly critical of security force activities in the Territories. To the credit of the main Israeli press, the closures and arrests were reported.

U.S. PRESS COVERAGE AND REACTION TO ISRAEL'S *INTIFADA* CRACKDOWN

Stirred by the dramatic coverage of their correspondents and the television footage, all 10 of the newspapers that I studied focused strong editorial-page criticism on Israel's heavy use of force to deal with what the journalists saw as a political problem. They had a point: By July 1992 it was estimated that 1,045 Palestinians had been killed by Israeli forces, the vast majority by gunshots (several hundred others said to be Israeli collaborators also died); more than 120,000 had been hospitalized; 66 had been expelled; more than 2,100 homes had been demolished by military order; many thousands had been held in prison under the provision of "administrative detention," which required no formal charges, and in 1992 about 15,000 remained in prison; 24-hour curfews had been ordered for towns of more than 10,000 population more than 11,000 times; almost 150,000 trees had been uprooted as a form of punishment; and about 2 percent of West Bank land was being confiscated monthly.[86]

The quotes give an idea about the tone of the coverage. The *Philadelphia Inquirer* quoted Israeli author Amos Elon, who called Gaza "the Soweto of the State of Israel." A sister paper in the Knight-Herald chain, the *Miami Herald*, said: "Thoughtful Israelis foresee—and shudder at—their nation becoming analogous to South Africa, keeping those Arabs in perpetual inferiority akin to that of blacks in South Africa." The *New York Times* warned: "As long as Israel occupies these territories it is accountable for the lives of the Palestinian civilians who live in them." The *Milwaukee Journal* joined in with a reference to the "transfer" suggestion [advocated by the right wing led by Sharon]: "For Israel to force Palestinians to evacuate their lifelong homes and flee to a country like Jordan could destabilize the Jordanian government while leaving a moral blot on Israel that will add to its alienation."

The *Washington Post* noted the "routine of a 20-year occupation," while the *St. Louis Post-Dispatch* called for the Reagan administration to "lean hard" on Israel, the *Los Angeles Times* noted the excess force that "the U.S. and other governments have rightfully condemned," and the *Christian Science Monitor* asked how Israel would free itself "from its role as the suppresser." The *Chicago Tribune* was unhappy with the leadership on both sides but aimed a dart at Israelis who used complaints of "anti-Semitism" to duck responsibility for their actions. Finally, it was left to the *Boston Globe* to put all of this into perspective when it said: "The Palestinian teenagers throwing rocks at soldiers have not changed the balance of power in the Mideast. But they may have changed the ways Palestinians and Israelis see the future."[87]

It was clear from many conversations with U.S. journalists in Israel and some of their Israeli, Arab, and European counterparts that no one doubted the severity and cruelty of the Israeli occupation. U.S. journalists, working within their traditional parameters, were not "pro-Arab" in outlook but rather expressed their dismay and disappointment at Israeli practices. Progressive Israeli journalists pointed to their own reporting of some of the worst aspects. Conservative Israelis and government spokesmen claimed that the U.S. media ignored violent Arab-vs.-Arab oppression elsewhere, such as in Syria, and were overblowing the Israeli use of force. They feared that excessive or unfair criticism would hurt the chances for renewed U.S. aid funds. Europeans said their newspapers and broadcast systems were more open to covering the excesses than the U.S. news media. Arabs, in the Occupied Territories and in Jordan, constantly expressed surprise at the number of stories being published that they considered "anti-occupation" but doubted that the news could overcome the power of Jewish politics in the U.S. In the Arab world the image of the American Israel Political Action Committee (AIPAC) loomed over the United States like a steel shield protecting Israel from any bad publicity. It was as difficult telling an Arab that AIPAC's influence was exaggerated as it was telling an Israeli that mainstream PLO supporters, the moderates who dominated peace-talk efforts, fully recognized Israel's need for security and had no desire to argue about pre-1967 properties lost to Israelis.

Despite the evidence of solid traditional reporting and uninhibited editorial page criticism, it was apparent that the home editors (and television producers) did not tackle some of the underlying issues. Overall, there was little background offered about the events in the Territories leading up to the December 1987 outbreak: the stone throwing, arrests, detentions and expulsions dating to the late 1960s; Israel's expansion of settlements dating to 1977 with Begin's Labor Government; arguments over water rights dating to 1948; the constant seizure of land; continual crackdowns against dissent; and the discrimination against Palestinians everywhere, in Israel and in the Territories. There are dozens of books written in English, Hebrew, and Arabic detailing all of this turmoil.

A SECOND DECLARATION OF INDEPENDENCE: FORTY YEARS LATER

The Palestinians eventually were taken seriously. On November 15, 1988, Arafat read the Palestinian Declaration of Independence in Algiers. In December he announced that the Palestinians recognized Israel, including her right to exist, eliminating that long-standing bone of contention. The Palestinians recognized U.N. Resolution 242 and renounced violence. While the *Intifada* continued, more positive steps were taken which led to the

Middle East negotiations beginning in 1991. It was recognized that these talks, directly involving Secretary of State James Baker, evolved at the end of the Gulf War because of U.S. political needs. The war had ended badly, with Saddam still in power, Kuwaitis driving out Palestinians, and the Kurds in danger. One thing within the New World Order administration's grasp was the ability to push for at least partial resolution of Palestinian-Israeli difficulties.

One of Arafat's top deputies told me in June 1991 that if the Israelis gave an indication of "readiness to withdraw [from the Occupied Territories] *in principle,* the doors would open for both sides to sort out the various modalities [related to mutual security, economic guarantees, military weapons, etc.]." He said the Palestinians were looking for "Israeli reciprocation of the 1988 verbal Palestinian statement of recognition." The Israelis, the United States, and anyone else involved would have to accord the Palestinians the U.N. guarantee of the "right to self-determination." If this happened, he said, the following might develop: (1) the long-awaited Arab world recognition of Israel; (2) the end of the economic boycott, then new trading relationships; and (3) a demilitarized Palestinian-controlled area.[88]

As for Israeli withdrawal in return for security and economic guarantees, the high-ranking PLO official said withdrawal "could take place over months or even years" if necessary, and the vacuum could be temporarily filled by a loosely knit Jordanian-Palestinian confederation designed to lead to complete Palestinian control. Another idea was to have the West Bank and Gaza fall under U.N. trusteeship during the transition period, whereupon there would be free elections to choose leaders of the new state. He said the high command of the PLO was ready to discuss any proposals related to the achievement of mutual recognition. One hangup to any real chance for a breakthrough was the presumed U.S. "policy" (originally Henry Kissinger's personal position) not to allow an independent Palestinian state and particularly one with East Jerusalem as its capital. Knowing they could rely on this dead end to Palestinian aspirations, the Israelis had the upper hand in negotiations, suggesting various half-measures like "autonomy" for Palestinians who would continue to live under Israeli laws. In late 1992 it became clear that if the U.S. abandoned the old Kissinger rule and created an "open-ended policy" (no prohibitions against any final resolution of the problem) there might be a chance for the parties (including the Jordanians) to break out of their stalemate.

A major breakthrough occurred in Oslo, Norway, on August 30, 1993, when Israeli and Palestinian negotiators set the stage for the mutual recognition that occurred on September 13 when President Clinton hosted Israeli Prime Minister Yitzhak Rabin and PLO Chairman Yasir Arafat in Washington, where a Declaration of Principles (DOP) was signed. Officially recognizing the PLO for the first time, Israel agreed to transfer governing authority to Palestinians in Gaza and the historic West Bank town of Jericho as the first step in a multiyear withdrawal plan. Arafat agreed to accept limited autonomy during the transition period, deeply disappointing many of his most devoted supporters in the Occupied Territories who felt the basic Palestinian right to self-determination had been compromised. By mid-1994 Arafat had appointed the majority of positions in a National Authority. Palestinian policemen patroled Gaza and Jericho streets, the World Bank was ready to assist with the rebuilding process, and national elections were pending. After months of speculation about Arafat's difficulties in making the transition from resistance leader to head of a government, the PLO chairman returned "home" for the first time in 27 years on July 1. A worldwide television audience saw this smiling symbol of Palestinian independence greeted by a tumultuous crowd in Gaza. But reporters pierced the euphoria by noting the struggles that lay ahead with both Palestinian fundamentalists and the Israeli right wing. Many obstacles remained to a legitimate peace, but at least the Israelis and the Palestine Liberation Organization were openly dealing with each other after nearly three decades of bloody hostility. Hopes then rose for Israeli agreements with Syria and Jordan. In October 1994, Clinton presided at an Israeli-Jordanian peace conference and traveled to Syria to push for an Israeli-Syrian settlement.

Sticking within the context of the Israeli-Palestinian aspect and ignoring the larger Arab-Israeli picture, in which the Palestinians evaporate, it is important to focus this discussion on fear. Simply put: The Israelis feared that they would somehow lose their state; Palestinians feared they would never get one. Everything that happened took place within this box: the racism, jealousies, petty angers, killings, of both Arab and Jew. During the *Intifada*, as the press corps pointed out by their descriptions of the "Children of the Stones," the Israelis had the raw power and automatic rifles. The Palestinians had much more to fear from a physical standpoint, and symbolically they became the David while Israel was the frustrated Goliath. In reality, the Israelis had deep fears for the future of their own financially strapped, racially and religiously fragmented nation. In a sense the Palestinians had become the scapegoats—just as Jews had, by others—for the Israelis, who had overextended themselves. But, in fairness, reporters were successful in separating the Israeli people from the Begin and Shamir governments and to appreciate the pressures upon the typical Israeli family, just as they learned to separate the average Palestinian from the acts of certain Palestinian fringe groups.

On a larger front, that was no serious journalistic examination of the unique U.S.-Israeli relationship and the concept of Israel being a "strategic ally" to be spared U.S. government and news media criticism for its handling of the Palestinians. As noted, this began changing during the Lebanon invasion of 1982 but without much explanation. In other words, it was likely that the reader of recent *Intifada* news (1988–95) would understand the basics of the situation but would not have much understanding of the frustrating years of occupation that preceded it. Nor, by the way, would the reader learn much about the Israeli retributions carried out in private, sometimes by execution squads. Yet the same reader probably would recall the acts of terrorism against Israel and her citizens—and there were many of these—because, as they checked their facts and judgments, the correspondents in the field, their desk editors, and the opinion chiefs made sure to include enough references to past Arab sins.

Being in the middle of the *Intifada* may have seemed like a black-and-white story to some, with all of the violence, but it was amazingly complicated because of the ignored history, outside influences from the United States and the Arab world, and the seeming hopelessness of a situation in which neither cousin wanted to smile first.

When Israeli forces shot 17 Palestinians to death in Jerusalem on October 8, 1990, there was worldwide coverage of the bloodiest day of the *Intifada* and a question arose whether efforts to encourage Saddam Hussein to leave Kuwait should be linked to solving the Palestinian Question. The United States, Great Britain, Israel, and other nations said there should be no linkage, and beyond that, Iraqi withdrawal was unconditional. While not officially endorsing the invasion, Arafat came down on Saddam Hussein's side. Both he and King Hussein opposed the use of outside force to solve what they called "an Arab problem." Arafat rejected appeals from close supporters not to get involved with Saddam's power politics but to "sit it out" for the sake of the Palestinians post-war agenda. Instead he said enough to encourage Palestinians to cheer for Iraq, including when Scud missiles flew over Jordan and the West Bank into Israel. The Israeli response was to put the West Bank and Gaza under continuous curfew. The Palestinian situation did return to the forefront once the Gulf War ended on February 27, 1991.

HARAM AL-SHARIF TO THE ARABS, TEMPLE MOUNT TO THE JEWS: OCTOBER 8, 1990

The shootings occurred on the grounds of the Muslim holy site called Haram Al-Sharif (Noble Sanctuary), known to Jews as the Temple Mount. Mayor

Teddy Kollek said later it was the worst day in Jerusalem since the Israelis seized the Old City and East Jerusalem in the June 1967 war. Unfortunately, to this day major news organizations, including the *New York Times* and *Los Angeles Times*, have not apologized for, or even substantially corrected within subsequent stories or photo captions, their erroneous reporting of that day's events. Apologies are rare, we know, and not necessary if there is correction.

Unbelievable as it seemed to observers familiar with the facts, in subsequent references to the violence major media offered the wrong cause-and-effect chronology. The reader was given to understand that hate-filled Palestinians threw rocks *at Jews worshipping at the Western Wall, triggering the terrible but almost understandable Israeli overreaction.* It was one of the biggest collective journalism goofs in many years, and the ramifications were astounding.

As the journalist who originally broke the story that the media had misreported a world-shocking event, I had been continually bothered by the stubbornness of reporters and editors to get this straightened out. For me this was symbolic of what was wrong with our overly competitive, holier-than-thou news business.

The Haram Al-Sharif killings flared up for me again on June 7, 1992, when Dan Williams of the *Los Angeles Times*, whom I often have praised for his level-headed, courageous reporting, said the following in a long profile of Palestinian leader Faisal Husseini, who had been prominent on October 8:

> . . . incited by a sudden release of tear gas, the *anxious* Palestinians threw rocks *on the scattering Jewish worshippers below* the mosque at the Western Wall (emphasis added).

In a polite letter to the *Los Angeles Times Magazine* where the piece appeared, I praised Williams's piece but said, "the much-publicized rocks, actually aimed at Israeli police, fell into the empty plaza . . . not one Jewish worshipper was hurt by a rock at the Wailing Wall. *I can tell you Husseini would not be pleased* [with the misrepresentation]. *Palestinians were shot to death inside the mosque grounds before one rock went over the wall.*" (Emphasis added.)

The last and most important line, emphasized above, showing a different sequence of events, was cut from my letter. A response followed, saying I was in error in stating that the plaza was empty and citing testimony gathered by Judge Ezra Kama in "an independent probe" that showed there were "hundreds of worshippers below and that a handful, perhaps 10, were slightly injured."

The most important thing, however, was that Judge Kama concluded on July 18, 1991, after a nine-month investigation, that the police, not the Palestinians, initially provoked the violence, which was the heart of my complaint about the coverage. This finding contradicted those of a government-appointed commission which in October 1990 justified the shootings—and much of the early news reporting.

Privately owned videotapes from that day obtained by this writer were the basis for my November 13, 1990, *Village Voice* story that unscrambled the chronology [Chicago's nationally distributed alternative newspaper *In These Times* also carried my story that week]. For the record, the tapes were shot by a Jewish tourist from New York and a University of Iowa graduate student who happens to be neither Jewish nor Arab. A December 2, 1990, *60 Minutes* segment, reported by Mike Wallace and based on the *Village Voice* account, offered dramatic proof that indeed the original story had been turned on its head. The main points:

1. At least one and probably several Palestinians were mortally wounded by live ammunition inside the Haram Al-Sharif grounds *before* the rocks sailed over into the Western Wall plaza area. Inside the grounds, tear gas had been carelessly or deliberately used by Israelis against a group of Palestinian women, inciting Palestinian men to throw rocks. Border police began firing while being forced out of the grounds by the stone-throwing crowd.

2. The hail of rocks featured prominently on world television was aimed *at the Israeli border police*, who had been forced to retreat through the gate. Because of the seven-meters-high wall that surrounds the grounds, *those standing beneath it inside could not see into the Western Wall plaza*. Police firing through slits in the gate kept them at a distance. Many of the rocks were hurled at a couple of border policemen, crouching atop the wall, who were seen on television.

3. Israeli border police stormed back inside and assumed control of the area after opening fire on unarmed Palestinians, some of whom were shot in the back from long-range distances. Hundreds of rounds were fired and the sounds are audible on the videotapes.

4. There had been several thousand Jewish worshippers for mid-morning services at the Western Wall. The vast majority had left prior to the outbreak on the grounds of Haram Al-Sharif. The firing of tear gas, shouting and finally the initial shooting could be heard in the plaza below. The remaining persons were urged by authorities to leave the vicinity of the Wall and they did, driven by fear and the noise. The plaza is huge; some Jewish persons may have remained in the

general area to watch the police take action. Rooftops were crowded with onlookers.

5. Attempts by numerous journalists to locate injured Jewish persons failed. If anyone had been seriously injured by a rock, Israeli authorities would have made sure that television crews found them. The simple reason is that Palestinians did not throw rocks at Jews as they worshipped at the Wall. The *60 Minutes* team later spent several days attempting to locate anyone injured and came up empty. I was told of reports that several persons suffered minor injuries while running from the area, falling down or bumping into someone. Several policemen were injured by rocks.

6. Jewish persons seen on television and in newspaper photos running from the Wall area actually had been hiding during the rock-throwing in rooms adjacent to the Western Wall. None of them were injured by rocks but careless or opportunistic television editing gave the impression that the rocks were falling as they fled. A CBS editor in New York said to me when he learned of the private videotapes, "You mean that we got the story backwards?"

Yes! They certainly did. This is a sample of what mainstream print and broadcast journalists reported in October 1990:

Sabra Chartrand, *New York Times*: ". . . during an hourlong battle outside Al Aksa Mosque between Israeli policemen and thousands of Arabs *hurling rocks and bottles at Jews praying at the Western Wall below*" (page one, October 9).

Joel Brinkley, *New York Times*: ". . . when more than 3,000 Palestinians on the plaza outside the mosque rioted, raining stones and bottles on Jewish worshippers at the Western Wall below" (page six follow-up, October 10).

Daniel Williams, *Los Angeles Times*: ". . . Palestinians who were *raining down stones on Jews* worshipping in Jerusalem's Old City." (page one, October 9).

Associated Press: ". . . The clash erupted after Palestinians threw stones from the Mount *at thousands of Jews worshipping below* at the Wailing Wall, Judaism's most holy site, witnesses said" (Urgent, October 8).

Peter Arnett, Cable News Network: "The severity of police behavior against the Palestinians has shocked many Israelis. Some newspapers have charged that police were ill-equipped for an event they had advance warning about and *consequently over-reacted when thousands of demonstrators threw stones.*" (October 9).

Dean Reynolds, reporting for ABC's *Nightline* show: ". . . the Palestinians let fly with a barrage of stones, hoping it would keep them [the Temple Mount Faithful marchers shown earlier] away. The *stones fell on Jews* who were making no claim on Moslem shrines but simply *praying peacefully* at the Western Wall" (October 9).

An Agence France-Presse photo which received wide play showed Jewish women running across a rock-strewn plaza "as they were pelted with rocks thrown by demonstrators at the mosque above."

Another AFP caption for a photo of tear gas exploding inside the mosque grounds said that police fired tear gas "to break up a crowd hurling rocks at Jews praying at the Western Wall, below the mosque." The women running were featured in both the *New York Times* and *Los Angeles Times* of October 9 and the New York paper added the tear-gas photo to its huge inside page display.

Many of the so-called witnesses, I later learned, were persons set up by Israeli agents or were agents themselves. This dawned on one Reuters correspondent who had been called by persons living a distance away, claiming to have been present. Israeli propaganda units had a field day, ending up with a bogus story debated on editorial pages worldwide that Saddam Hussein plotted with Palestinians who had packed away tons of rocks for the occasion.

These accounts were accepted as fact. Propagandists then took advantage of the collective ignorance. *New York Times* columnist William Safire's imagination combined with Brinkley's erroneous reporting to create this lie on October 11: "A crowd of 3,000 Arabs, many carrying stones brought with intent to throw, took up positions overlooking the worshippers at the wall. Amid shrieks of hatred inciting the mob to violence, the bombardment of rocks began. The congregation fled in terror; 28 of those in prayer were reportedly wounded." The old double standard was at work here—if anyone had *erroneously* reported that 3,000 Danes or Australians had done something horrible they wouldn't have survived the day, but after all these were Arabs.

Never mind that one of Jerusalem's chief rabbis confirmed to Mike Wallace that no one was injured in the rock throwing. "It was a miracle," he told the *60 Minutes* audience. Never mind that no Jerusalem-based journalist reported meeting anyone injured that day. At this point it looks like those that Williams and others said were "slightly injured" were those who fell down and scraped their knees.

What about the 17 shot to death inside, the 300 or more injured by gunshots, most of it live ammunition from high-powered weapons? What of the rumors that the Temple Mount Faithful, the right-wing group that began the disturbance early in the morning by demanding to place the cornerstone for the Third Jewish Temple near two Arab mosques (Dome of the Rock and Al Aqsa), was hoping for violence to gain support for future actions?

What about reports that high Israeli officials, perhaps Prime Minister Yitzhak Shamir himself, authorized the storming of the grounds to show the Palestinians who was boss—that those doing the shooting knew they had the highest of blessings? That the Israeli govenment, frustrated by the lack of U.S. action against Saddam at this point, wanted to provoke him into an anti-Israeli act—and what better way than to take advantage of a violent situation and kill some Palestinians? The rumors flew, but reporters for major news groups did not return to the scene of the crime.

Gershon Salomon's Temple Mount Faithful pledged to make future marches to the Haram Al-Sharif area. How will the massacre of 1990 be recalled if that happens? This group had an intimate tie to the religious settler movement behind the seizure of Arab property in the Old City and neighboring Silwan—actions designed to interfere with the U.S.-Israeli-Arab peace talks.

The 1991 anniversary of the massacre was followed by nighttime raids on Arab homes in Silwan that did distract from the ongoing talks. The one-year anniversary also saw the *New York Times* repeat its error in a photo caption. The massacre was only one in a long string of Jerusalem tragedies. It is obvious that, unless the three holy sites (add the Church of the Holy Sepulcher for Christians) were protected, there would be no peace in Jerusalem, the West Bank, or Gaza.[89]

The violence at Haram Al-Sharif was an immensely important story that deserved to be correctly passed from newspapers to history books. It was one of those defining moments, like the 1994 massacre of Palestinians at a mosque in Hebron where a right-wing Jewish settler upset the ongoing Israeli-Palestinian negotiations. Both events showed how the people in power treat those under occupation. The Haram Al-Sharif killings temporarily took world focus from the Gulf War buildup. Both caused U.N. debates on the treatment of Palestinians. Mainstream journalists in Jerusalem, many of whom I greatly admired, as well as their hometown editors who think the Associated Press never errs, did us a terrible disservice by misreporting the Haram Al-Sharif story. They did better on the Hebron killings, but only after Israeli witnesses contradicted the IDF's original explanation of how an armed settler could enter a guarded holy place and kill innocent worshippers. In neither instance did the regular reporters put the history of the settlements into perspective and show the link to constant anti-Arab harassment and violence. The most incisive long-term reporting was done by Robert I. Friedman in the *Village Voice* and in his books, including *Zealots for Zion: Inside Israel's West Bank Settler Movement* and *The False Prophet: Rabbi Meir Kahane—From FBI Informant to Knesset Member*. Friedman began his Middle East reporting in 1977. In 1994 he was at full steam, writing about CIA and Israeli links to one of the World Trade Center bombers, and the threat of a civil war in Israel with Jew pitted against Jew in the West Bank and Gaza.

Obtaining the videotapes was quite another story. When I heard the first news of the shootings I called a colleague who I knew would be informed. He told me the streets near Makassad Hospital on the Mount of Olives had been full of ambulances and private cars carrying the dead and wounded. He also said that he met a fellow who had been videotaping from the well-known tourist lookout overlooking the eastern side of the Old City. This turned out to be Matthew Bergman, an adventuresome Iowan with an interest in the Middle East. Feeling the buildup of tension, he was there with his camera, ready for anything. However, he said later he had no idea what to expect. The first frames of his tape show his hand screwing on a telephoto lens. He was breathing heavily and an "Oh, my God!" could be heard. For the next 29 minutes the viewer hears hundreds of shots and the voices of sheiks in the mosque calling for an end to the killing and urging the young people to run for protection. Also on the screen are numerous tear-gas bursts, the ambulances arriving to pick up victims, and people running back and forth. Without knowing what might be on that tape, I decided that someone had to find it.

At about the same time, a Jewish tourist and his friend, both of whom will be anonymous here, were on a rooftop in the Jewish Quarter of the Old City. They were looking out at the Wailing (Western) Wall, filming people worshipping there. After most of the worshippers had left the plaza area, yelling could be heard from inside the Haram Al-Sharif area. Then there was a burst of gunshots from an automatic weapon. No one knew it then, but the bullets ripped into several Palestinians, killing at least one and perhaps several. There were other scattered shots, and police retreated from a gate in the wall. After that this tape and another one made by an Israeli film crew showed a hail of rocks coming over the Wall—the rocks seen and remembered by the world! A few days later a *New York Times* story from Jerusalem mentioned the existence of this tape. I read that story as my plane left Kennedy airport for Amman, Jordan. I had decided several days before to go to Jerusalem to see what had really happened.

Once in Jerusalem I began to make the rounds of persons who might know of the Mount of Olives tape. As it turned out, Bergman first offered the tape to a Visnews crew (affiliated with BBC and NBC). He edited the long version down to highlights but said the Israelis on the crew were disinterested. To his horror, Deputy Foreign Minister Benjamin Netanyahu later turned up with the edited copy and used it as evidence that someone had edited it or, in other words, distorted it. That was after a copy made its way to the United Nations, where it was shown to the General Assembly. But back in mid-October it was hard to find a copy.

Persistence and luck combined a few days later and I saw the tape. It was an amazing experience, seeing an entirely different view of such an historic event. Within hours I reached Joel Brinkley at the *Times* office and offered to show him the tape (I now had my own copy) in return for seeing the Jewish Quarter tape. He agreed and the next day he and his wife, Sabra Chartrand, picked me up at the American Colony Hotel in East Jerusalem, one of those favorite places for journalists. At this point I did not have an assignment from any publication. I did not know anyone at the *Village Voice*. I told Brinkley and Chartrand that I was a professor and a freelance journalist who had done stories for various publications, including one for the *Los Angeles Times* from the Central American peace talks in Costa Rica, and hoped to see what might come out of these tapes. That seemed fine with them, so we drove to the Jewish Quarter and met a man who had custody of various tapes. We watched three of them—mine and two shot from the Jewish Quarter.

When we were through, our host and I began negotiating for an exchange of materials, which was completed via the mails a few weeks later. My colleagues were anxious to get back to their office. Little was said between us on the return drive. I appreciated their cooperation and hoped that they had appreciated mine. As far as I was concerned, if they wanted to write a story about the tapes, they could. I still did not have my own story angle developed very well but my mind was whirling with the knowledge that the story had not been reported accurately. As it turned out they declined the opportunity to use the information, which was their decision. Meanwhile, I had the further good luck to meet several persons with intimate knowledge of what had occurred up on the Haram Al-Sharif grounds. At one point I accidentally met a storekeeper in the Old City who took me to a rooftop where I interviewed members of a religious community who said Israeli snipers used the area for firing into the crowds below. I met another man, a non-Arab non-Jew who must remain anonymous, who was on the grounds that day. After the shooting he had begun an extensive interviewing process that produced drawings of where each Palestinian had been shot.

More interviews produced other new information. This finally led to the production of a rough chronology of events. Then, by comparing the sights and sounds on the tapes with the eyewitness testimony, I was able to come up with a fairly close approximation of the events. Again I was assisted in this by my anonymous source, who as it turned out was quite accurate. A few days after my return to Los Angeles I received a call from Dan Bischoff, an editor for the *Village Voice*, who had been tipped to the existence of my story. He excitedly began to plan for immediate publication. We hit the streets of New York a few days later, on a Tuesday, and within minutes a copy was on a desk in the CBS newsroom. Rather's people thought it was too complicated for them and passed it on to the *60 Minutes* office.

A few days later, after a flurry of meetings and calls between the *Voice* and Mike Wallace, who saw the tapes, I received a call from Wallace. He said he was on his way to Jerusalem and wanted to be certain that *60 Minutes* could use the tapes. I had obtained them with the condition that I would use them only "as a journalist," so I felt it would be proper to pass them along to another journalist. To keep everything clean, there were no financial considerations.

When Wallace arrived in Jerusalem he met with producer Barry Lando, who was busy preparing a feature on some aspect of the *Intifada*. Wallace had told me he hoped to change Lando's mind about the thrust of the Jerusalem story. When I talked with Wallace a few days later, awakening him at his American Colony room, he told me that his taped interview with an injured Palestinian nurse had convinced Lando to devote the entire segment to the shootings.

Lando apparently said that Wallace's interview with Fatima, her arm nearly severed by a bullet fired through the ambulance window, was one of the most riveting in his *60 Minutes* experience. Wallace later said the story was one of the two most satisfying in his long career. After shooting extensively and investigating the points made by the *Voice* and other observers, Lando's team went back to Paris for editing, while Wallace returned to New York. At one point I was asked to air special a better quality version of one tape.

I happened to be on the phone with one of the Paris staff when the final version was being viewed in New York by Don Hewitt and others. Their voices could be heard over the squawk box and I nervously asked, "What are they saying?" "They're loving it, they're loving it," she said with a big burst of relief. It went on the air that Sunday and the reverberations went through New York television. I talked with Wallace once more, a few days after the show. He said there had been quite a few complaints but nothing to worry about. He was used to the pro-Israel crowd bombarding his office. Not long after this Wallace and Hewitt were attacked at a New York party by ABC's Barbara Walters, Mort Zuckerman of *U.S. News & World Report*, and others who felt the show had been unfair and "anti-Israel." Hewitt walked out in a huff, leaving Wallace to defend the ship, which he did with his usual bluntness. The *Jerusalem Post* also attacked Wallace in its media review columns, calling him a "self-hating Jew." All I can add to this debate is that I found Wallace completely faithful to the facts as we knew them, honest in his evaluation of the people involved, and courageous in his telling of this bizarre incident. The entire team did a highly professional job, from start to finish, and I am not saying this only because I agreed with their editing choices. They indeed were a pleasure to work with: tough and decisive.

INTRODUCTION: THE GULF WARS

For most Americans the name Saddam Hussein was lost in a crowd of other Arab names in 1987. Readers and listeners knew that Iraq and Iran were fighting in the Gulf and most of those who cared about this conflict were cheering for Iraq because the fundamentalist Iranians had thumbed their noses at the United States after taking power in 1979. The 444-day hostage crisis ruined the Carter presidency and stuck in America's craw. Iran was considered an outlaw nation; the Arab States were worried sick that Iran would foment religious uprisings by Shiites living in the Gulf states; the Western states and Japan worried out loud about the future of oil prices. We knew little about the new Iranian leaders, and despite his many years in high office, we knew little of Saddam Hussein, whom Americans often confused with the other and better-known Hussein, the King of Jordan. It again was left to a few foreign correspondents to unravel some of this for us.

The Iran-Iraq War exploded on September 22, 1980. It was the first modern war fought in the Gulf area, the "politically unstable region that provides 40 percent of the non-Communist world's oil" and "is a cockpit of superpower rivalry."[90] Even before the war settled into a deadly stalemate in the middle 1980s, the United States tilted toward Iraq, which made the first strike after getting a green light from Washington. A number of startling revelations in 1992 showed that the Bush administration favored the Iraqis with loans and credit right up to the eve of Hussein's August invasion of Kuwait. U.S. interest in the conflict escalated in 1987 when President Reagan committed the U.S. Navy to escort Kuwaiti ships through the narrow waters. The U.S.S. *Stark* was severely damaged by an Iraqi jet that year with heavy loss of life.

In addition to details about coverage of U.S. involvement in what was dubbed "the tanker war," this section includes a description of the most important Middle East political event of that year, the Arab Summit Conference hosted in Amman by King Hussein. A number of developments there affected the outcome of the war as well as the future Israeli-Palestinian relationship. The main goal, which was achieved, was to convince Syria to discontinue its support of Iran—to split that axis. Understanding these Middle East power plays puts the 1991 Operation Desert Storm in better perspective. I arrived in Amman from London on November 1 as part of a two-month around-the-world look at foreign correspondence. My goal was to report on some of these events myself and also to talk with journalists about their experiences in getting out the news. Don Bremner of the *Los Angeles Times* foreign desk was gracious enough to notify a handful of *Times* people in different places about my trip.

THE ARAB SUMMIT: A FRONT-ROW SEAT TO POWER

Los Angeles Times reporter Charles Wallace was not too sure about talking with a fellow wearing two hats, and in retrospect I do not blame him. I told him people would have to trust that I would not tattle on their private attitudes while working with them and discussing reporting problems. So far I have not. Wallace, one of the many former "Unipressers" working for major newspapers (he was in the Soviet Union and Africa for UPI), had logged a lifetime of experiences in his four years of Middle East journalism. His impressive professional profile was similar to others there in their mid-30s, a list of bureau assignments associated with major events. He was in Beirut when the AP's Terry Anderson was kidnapped in 1985;[91] he was one of the few to report from Iran; he covered Vice President Bush's 1986 trip to Israel and Jordan; and he had flown in from his base in Cyprus for the Amman meetings. Wallace generously offered tips on covering the region, particularly the Gulf, where I soon would be headed.

Five hundred U.S., European, Asian, and Arab world journalists were in Amman, among them Friedman, Curtius, Moffett, Tamayo, Simon, and others of the Jerusalem corps. Joining Friedman to give the *New York Times* an unbeatable one-two punch was the Paris-based Youssef M. Ibrahim, one of the area's most highly respected interpreters of events. Trudy Rubin of the *Philadelphia Inquirer*, another knowledgeable veteran, was one of the specialists there. Warren Richy, the *Christian Science Monitor*'s Gulf correspondent, flew in to work with Moffett, giving the *CSM* a formidable team. The government of Saudi Arabia outfitted the elaborate press area, complete with broadcast editing booths, huge spaces for television production, separate facilities for each major press association, and facilities for telephoning or telexing stories. Media briefings were held in an adjoining and especially plush auditorium where television crews representing the entire world jammed into the front space.

Typical of such occasions, everyone grabbed the latest reports from Petra (the Jordanian news agency) made available in the press area. Back at the Intercontinental there was a constant huddle around a Reuters printer that clicked away around the clock. John Rice, trained in California journalism, was the AP man on the spot; Louis Toscano from Jerusalem UPI, the old Central America hand, was joined by the amazing Magma Abu-Fail from the Cyprus bureau, who could work in 10 languages. The Reuters bureau chief was the well-respected Alistair Lyon. The press association people, including those from DFP (Germans), AFP (French), KUNA (Kuwait), and Xinhua (People's Republic of China), worked themselves into exhaustion. The Xinhua crew of 10 put everyone to shame with its language abilities: At the end of a session the team would send out the same story in Arabic, English, and Chinese. Down in the television area, Simon of CBS tinkered with his copy, a model of concentration. Christopher Dickey, now with *Newsweek*, prowled around looking for a clue to the private negotiations among the Arab heads of state. There was no question about the sheer talent in the press area.

There were three media highlights for me. One was King Hussein's final day news conference, in which he explained the significance of the Arab world solidarity demonstrated by the Syrian decision to go along with the Saudis and Jordanians in helping Iraq. The old angers over Egypt's go-it-alone 1979 treaty with Israel and its subsequent isolation had not surfaced. The king was delighted with his personal success. Earlier that day I had joined news photographers and television camera people for one of the week's two major "photo opportunities." We waited four hours and endured several security checks before being led into the private, brightly lighted conference area. There they were, sitting in a huge semicircle—Hussein of Jordan, Assad of Syria, Hussein of Iraq, Arafat of Palestine, and the other leaders and confidants. Each small photo group was allowed five minutes. In that brief time one newsmagazine photographer on deadline shot two and one-half rolls with two cameras, an amazing feat under pressure, while I shot off 18 memorable photos.

The next evening a small group of reporters waited for hours before meeting with Arafat at the Plaza Hotel. It had been a bad day for the PLO chairman. Not only had the Arab leaders ended their Summit without focusing on the Palestinian Question but, as I later learned in some detail, Arafat had suffered through an unsuccessful meeting with King Hussein. Entering the room with smiles and jokes, Arafat soon found himself in a dispute with journalists over the wording of a Summit communiqué. Flanked by one of his close assistants, Basam Abu Sharif, Arafat stuck to his positions regarding Palestinian aspirations, leaving those present somewhat frustrated by the shadings of meaning and the problems with communication—a wonderful example of the difficulties in covering the Middle East.

Mid-November 1987 was the last time the Arab leaders had a sense of common good feeling. Little did they know that the turned-off Palestinians would begin their *Intifada* in about three weeks, or that the Iran-Iraq War would lead right into a greater conflict. Regarding the escalating Palestinian problem, journalists headquartered in Jerusalem were aware of the increasing number of incidents in the Territories. I recalled that Toscano told me he was writing "this is how it is to live in Gaza" stories; "that's [Gaza] still the story as far as I am concerned." He was right. Later Palestinians said they were keenly aware of the lack of commitment to their issue at the Summit and that this added to their isolation and anger. During a quick five-day trip to Israel and the Occupied Territories following the conference, I was reminded of the high tensions there that I had felt on another visit in August—particularly in Nablus, where in the gloom of the early winter evening my taxi drove in heavy traffic alongside an Israeli patrol. The grim-faced soldiers moved along quickly, in and out of the hateful stares of shopkeepers and residents, and finally became dark figures in the rearview mirror.

THE TANKER WAR: THE PRESS ASSOCIATIONS' BATTLE FOR PRESTIGE

A few days later I was walking along the edge of Failaka Island, off Kuwait City out near the middle of the Gulf. The Iran-Iraq battlefield was another 25–30 miles off in the distance. A local man told me, "at night we can hear the cannons." Kuwait City residents could hear the battle noise when the wind was blowing from the north. Earlier in the year the island had been the first Iranian missile target. While in Kuwait I learned that people there had lived in a growing state of tension for the past four to five years. There was a fear that Shiites under the control of the Ayatollahs would bomb public buildings and oil facilities. Of the population of 1.6 million, about 1 million persons were from other nations, about a third Palestinians and others from Pakistan, India, Sri Lanka, and other Arab States. About 150,000 of the 600,000 Kuwaitis were Shiites and only a minority were considered dangerous, but people still were afraid.

My feeling was that anything could happen there at any moment. The air was tense and the people were nervous. First, the Iranians had several kinds of long-range missiles. The heat-seeking kind was good for hitting tankers; another reportedly was guided from a plane or helicopter by a homing device. They also had the ability to just lob a missile in, with no specific target (that's the one to worry about). There was strict press censorship there, about as bad as the Saudi Arabian brand. At least the Kuwaitis occasionally ran photos of women. But the press was forbidden to criticize the emir's family or anyone with whom they associated—that is to say, half the country. Of course the censorship was there for security reasons as well. I was informed by one local journalist that in May 1987 Bedouin firemen bravely put out a fire within a liquid petroleum tank started by an explosive device. The tank, containing an estimated 500,000 gallons, was drained off so that only the burning top remained. If a missile had hit that area, the source said, the explosions would have jarred the entire city. They had kept the fire story private, he said, to avoid giving information to those behind it. One missile did slam into the loading area, causing extensive damage and a great deal of panic.

There were few foreign journalists in Kuwait; the majority were in Bahrain and Dubai, much closer to the action. The U.S. and British television crews provided spectacular coverage of the Iranian attacks on Gulf shipping, further heightening interest. By the time of my visit in late November 1987, that phase of the war was in full swing. The Pentagon instituted a pool system to allow for coverage from Navy ships; otherwise journalists flew in and out of Bahrain, where the Navy docked, or Dubai, which had more open communications and was a little closer to the upper Gulf area.[92] A few journalists were allowed into Iraq during the war for quick tours to the front, but for the most part the land war was covered from a distance. To illustrate the isolation of events from reporting, it should be noted that in 1987 NBC's Rick Davis was the only U.S. network television correspondent permanently based in the Islamic world. Martin Fletcher from the Tel Aviv office was NBC's man in the Gulf; ABC sent in Mike Lee from London; CBS had the veteran Alan Pizzey on hand. In these early days CNN did not play an important role in the Gulf; that was to change quickly.

The press associations and networks relied on an elaborate radio monitoring system to keep track of the latest Gulf incidents. The distribution varied, but London offices monitored Radio Tehran and Iranian News Agency reports and fed the texts by computer back to bureaus. Monitoring stations in Nicosia, Cyprus, also were important. UPI, Reuters, and AP offices in Bahrain and Nicosia all received monitoring feedback. Another key source was the Lloyd's of London intelligence service, which immediately issued reports on ships that had been hit. Lloyd's was used by every major organization (although NBC eventually dropped it).

The press association competition was ferocious. While in Bahrain I had the good fortune to meet the AP bureau chief, Aly Mahmoud, and his talented assistant, Nabila Megalli, responsible for the war theater. The bureau had six full-time persons, including chief correspondent Richard Pyle, then at sea with the U.S. Navy, and William Murray, the AP–Dow Jones reporter. There was one stringer in Kuwait and another in Dubai. The staff had learned early in the war that Iranian radio reports of Friday sermons in Teheran gave clues to events. The monitoring of salvage-ship radio reports along the coast was another way to get a jump on a story. Mahmoud and Megalli were well-known Egyptian journalists: Mahmoud, who joined AP in 1960, had interviewed many Middle East leaders; Henry Kissinger once refused to start a press conference until Megalli arrived. At one point during an afternoon filled with stories about Gamal Abdel Nasser (who once threw him in jail), Anwar Sadat (who released him), and King Hussein, Mahmoud said with characteristic enthusiasm, "The AP [from the Gulf] is faster than the CIA."[93] While the Middle East and particularly the Gulf was considered prime territory for the British and French news agencies, the AP made strong inroads during the two Gulf Wars.

Mahmoud's main rival was Reuters correspondent Graham Stewart, whose wall was covered with a huge map filled with pins marking the latest shipping attacks. In some areas there was little space left. Stewart's assistant was Youssef Asmeh. Several other full-time writers on an "internationalized" staff included people from Britain, the United States, Norway, Turkey, Egypt, and Bahrain. The Australian-born Stewart, who had joined Reuters in 1968, was quietly competitive, intent on fighting off pressure from AP and AFP by maintaining not only fast news reports but also his agency's growing reputation for financial news. The United Press International operation was barely hanging on in the Gulf, with minimal coverage provided by a small Bahrain bureau and a few stringers.

This competition was displayed on Thanksgiving Day 1987 during coverage of a tanker attack off Dubai. I was visiting the AP's top "contract" photographer, Greg English, when we heard the attack begin while listening to a shortwave radio beamed to a shipping channel. The captain of what he said was a "Romanian tanker" (later there was a story saying it was a Kuwaiti tanker decked out as a Romanian) described threats from an "Iranian warship." English sped to the airport while I stuck with the radio.

While English's helicopter flew over his Gulfside apartment house, I heard the tanker captain yell that his ship was on fire, that the Iranian had attacked. During the next 10 hours, until dark, I monitored the Iranian frigate chasing the Romanian tanker for about 80 miles, until they were only 10 miles off Dubai. I could see black smoke on the horizon through my binoculars. All the while I was phoning reports from the radio back to Mahmoud and Megalli in Bahrain. Their stringer in Dubai heard the initial threat but was unable to dictate running quotes. The Iranians backed off and the ship docked in Dubai. In this instance the AP beat Reuters, which mistakenly said the Iranians attacked by speedboat. My role in reporting the incident was mentioned in the AP report and appeared in my parents' hometown Minneapolis paper the next day. Meanwhile, English had shared the helicopter with an AFP man and they had secured closeup photos of the fire. English's photos, developed in his bathroom and transmitted from there as well, received wide play in the United States. At midnight I was on my way to China, flying over the Gulf of Hormuz and all of the chaos inside of it.[94]

In retrospect it was clear that the Western news agencies each spent a fortune to bring home stories and pictures from the Gulf. News managers correctly perceived the widespread interest in this event. The costs were enormous, up to $8,000 per day even for chartering a small boat to chase tankers. Helicopters cost several thousand dollars per day and were shared if possible. The BBC, Reuters, and Visnews shared, but the U.S. networks had to fly separately. While much of the coverage was similar to "cops and robbers," the U.S. public began to receive considerable information about the Gulf region, its people, and to some extent its history. More information was needed on the long history of Western financial and military interests in the area (U.S. ships had been in the region since 1938). Islamic Fundamentalism, with all of its complications, remained a dark and intimidating story.[95]

In all fairness, the editors and reporters in the field did a solid job of reporting both the Iran-Iraq War and the accompanying Tanker War. Again, if more interpretation was needed to allow the U.S. public a chance to decide about the wisdom of escorting Kuwaiti tankers and risking engagement with Iranian ships, point toward the hometown editors. The Reagan administration had its reasons for a U.S. presence: The Soviets had a big base at Adan in nearby South Yemen and were hoping for a Western breakdown in the area; U.S., European, and Japanese dependence on oil demanded that we protect the lifelines (would we have been there if they grew strawberries?); the weak southern Gulf areas needed to be protected from Iran; and, in the wake of several hostage crises, the United States needed to present a strong image to the Iranians and to the world.

While the correspondents were toiling on the surface, the diplomats and intelligence agents were working belowdecks. One wonders about the world's reaction had it been revealed that only a few months before, in early August 1986, Vice President Bush had encouraged Saddam Hussein to unleash heavier bombing raids on Iran, to panic the Iranians into buying more weapons as part of the arms-for-hostages deal. Fearing that Iran might win, and needing a speedup of both cash and the release of hostages, the U.S. government advocated an escalation of the war.[96] Punishing Iran eventually made the conflict spill over into the Gulf shipping lanes, with the possibility of direct U.S. confrontation with the Iranians or even the Soviets.

"WOW, HOLY COW": THE BOMBING OF BAGHDAD

ABC's Gary Shepard was talking to anchor Peter Jennings and an ABC television audience from his room in Baghdad's Al-Rashid Hotel. It was 6:35 P.M. Eastern Standard Time, January 16, 1991. Suddenly, Shepard said:

> I am looking directly west from the hotel and through the entire sky, there are flashes of light. It appears to be some sort of anti-aircraft fire. Couple of flashes on the horizon, something is definitely under way here . . . It's like fireworks on the Fourth of July, multiplied by 100.[97]

CNN's Bernard Shaw and producer Robert Wiener saw a flash of red exploding in the sky. Then came the barrage of antiaircraft fire from surrounding rooftops. Cameraman Mark Biello crawled toward the camera by the window, followed by Peter Arnett. A few seconds later John Holliman crouched beside them. The rest is broadcast history.

> Peter Arnett, join me here . . . Let's describe to our viewers what we're seeing . . . The skies over Baghdad have been illuminated . . . We're seeing bright flashes going off all over the sky . . . Peter . . . Well, there's anti-aircraft gunfire going into the sky . . . We haven't heard the sound of bombs landing, but there's tremendous lightning in the sky, lightning-like effects . . . Bernie . . . This is extraordinary. The lights are still on. All the streetlights in downtown Baghdad are still on . . . Peter . . . We're trying to get the lights out in our hotel room . . . The firing is continuing and the sirens are continuing . . . Here with us now is John Holliman . . . Good evening, gentleman, or rather good morning . . . Wow, holy cow (hitting the floor) that was a large airburst that we saw . . . It was filling the sky . . . (Arnett) . . . You may hear the bombs now. If you are still with us, you can hear the bombs now. They're hitting the center of the city.[98]

A few minutes later ABC and other organizations lost their telephone connections when bombs hit the telecommunication center, but CNN continued to broadcast live, thanks to its foresight in arranging for a special

telephone line to Amman that hooked into a satellite relay. Broadcast stations around the world dropped their own coverage and picked up CNN.
In the United States the Atlanta-based organization was tied to 84 independent stations and 130 others affiliated with NBC (53), CBS (45) and
ABC (32). Many of these faded away from Brokaw, Rather, and Jennings.
In fact, later that first evening NBC itself tuned in to CNN so that its viewers could hear reports from all three reporters. Afterward, Brokaw paid the
ultimate tribute to CNN, telling Shaw, "CNN used to be called the little
network that could. It's no longer a little network."[99]

Booming black headlines were in the morning papers. "WAR in GULF."
The Knight-Ridder Newspapers service reported to its clients:

> Washington—The United States and its allies went to war Wednes-
> day night against Iraq, battering Baghdad with wave after wave of fighter-
> bombers in hope of routing Iraq from occupied Kuwait.[100]

Jack Nelson, Washington bureau chief for the *Los Angeles Times*, said
it more simply:

> Washington—War with Iraq began today as hundreds of American,
> British, Kuwaiti and Saudi Arabian warplanes bombed strategic targets
> in Iraq and occupied Kuwait.[101]

That evening Bush spoke to the largest audience for a single news event
in television history, an estimated 61 million households. The President
promised that the war "will not be another Vietnam . . . Our troops will
not be asked to fight with one hand tied behind their back." He warned
that Saddam Hussein was building "an infinitely more dangerous weapon
of mass destruction, a nuclear weapon ."[102] Within the space of a few days
the White House moved from a passive position to one where the President raised the specter of Saddam Hussein becoming a new Hitler.

In those first hours the AP's Edith M. Lederer bulletined from Saudi
Arabia:

> Central Saudi Arabia—The United States and its allies followed up
> devastating pre-dawn air strikes with daylight attacks today in furious
> bid to drive Saddam Hussein's armies from Kuwait and break his mili-
> tary might.[103]

ABC broadcast the first pictures of the air attack from Amman on Friday. The tape was shot by a WTN cameraman and carried out by Shepard
when he, CBS's Alan Pizzey, and other journalists left for Jordan in a cara-
van. By January 20 almost the entire press corps was gone, leaving behind
in Baghdad Arnett, Wiener, and technician Nick Robertson for CNN, re-

porter Tom Aspell and a small NBC crew, the BBC's John Simpson, Brent Sadler of ITN, Patrick Cockburn of the *Independent* (London), and a few other print journalists. On January 25 CNN announced it had been granted "a half-dozen visas" and the right to bring in a portable satellite unit. Once installed, Arnett began sending his live broadcasts.[104]

THE PRESS COVERS THE BUILDUP TO WAR

Between Iraq's August invasion of Kuwait and the January bombing, foreign editors of major U.S. newspapers and press associations accelerated their plans for rapid deployment of reporters and photographers in the event of all-out fighting. The *Los Angeles Times* had the most ambitious "war plan," which eventually led to an overwhelmingly comprehensive report. The paper gave assignments to nine foreign correspondents, nine Washington bureau reporters, nine business reporters, and one media critic. The overseas contingent was augmented during the fighting so that at one point the paper had 12 persons in Saudi Arabia. Douglas Jehl and Kim Murphy led the Saudi contingent, which at different times included David Lamb, John Broder, and Tracy Wilkinson, while Nick Williams Jr. took the Jordan flank and Dan Williams stayed in Israel. Another *Times* reporter, Mark Fineman, was the first Western newspaper correspondent to get into Iraq after the August invasion, arriving there on August 25, 1990.

R. W. "Johnny" Apple took the lead for the *New York Times*, joined in Saudi Arabia by Malcolm Browne, James LeMoyne, Chris Hedges, and others, while Joel Brinkley covered Israel and Alan Cowell remained with his Amman beat. Geraldine Brooks and Tony Horowitz earned considerable credit for their *Wall Street Journal* stories as did a large team from the *Washington Post* for their work. A number of women correspondents were active, continuing the tradition of the Central American reportage. The *Washington Post*'s Molly Moore, who had accompanied U.S. Marines to the front, was the only woman to witness the opening of the ground war. She had covered the Pentagon since 1986, at the time the only woman doing so [by 1991 she had been joined by Suzanne Schafer of the Associated Press and Melissa Healy of the *Los Angeles Times*]. Women on television included PBS's Charlayne Hunter-Gault, CBS's Martha Teichner, ABC's Linda Pattillo, and CNN's Christiane Amanpour, Margaret Lowrie, and Linda Scherzer.[105]

A few of the television correspondents temporarily became folk heroes or at least emerged as characters in this drama: CNN's Charles Jaco through his self-deprecating Scud missile coverage from Saudi Arabia (he admitted he knew when it was time to get off camera); Richard Blystone, CNN's man in Tel Aviv, who calmly acted as though a Scud alert were no more serious than a rainfall prediction; and three other "Scud-watchers," ABC's Reynolds, CBS's Tom Fenton, and NBC's Arthur Kent, the "heartthrob" of millions. NBC's veteran Israel correspondent Martin Fletcher also was active, while Forrest Sawyer, Koppel's backup *Nightline* anchor, was in the thick of the action.[106]

David Lamb put all of this into a nostalgic historical perspective, comparing the "mint-on-your-pillowcase, marbled retreat" in Dhahran to the Caravelle in Saigon, the Commodore in Lebanon, the Camino Real in San Salvador—places that provided "the war correspondents' staples: communications, information, alcohol and safety—generally in that order . . . the stiffest drink in Dhahran is a kandana fizz, orange juice and nonalcoholic sparkling white wine in a martini glass . . . the Saudis' rigid visa controls have kept the groupies at bay, and the alcohol ban has produced what must be the most conservative and well-behaved buildup of journalists—and soldiers—in military history."[107]

On a serious note, several journalists faced extreme danger. Caryle Murphy of the *Washington Post* hid in Kuwait for nearly a month after the invasion, phoning out reports. She eventually escaped and won the Pulitzer Prize.[108] Bob Simon and his CBS crew were captured near the Kuwait border after breaking free from pool restrictions. They sat out the war in an Iraqi prison, telling later how during the 40-day period Iraqis beat them with canes and interrogated them as spies.[109] The only journalist killed during the war and the period immediately following was Gad Schuster Gross, freelancing for *Newsweek* in the Kurdish area of northern Iraq. Gross, a native of Romania and a Harvard graduate, was killed March 29, 1991, while traveling with Frank Smyth of the *Village Voice* and CBS and Alain Buu of Gamma-Liaison. His colleagues were captured and taken to Baghdad before being released three weeks later.

Smyth and I worked closely together in Amman in mid-February. We spent my last evening talking about Central America, of all places, and our experiences there. Smyth had strong views about the failures of the press in El Salvador. One day we attended a King Hussein news conference together. So when he disappeared on March 1 and was feared dead I was personally affected, along with all of his *Village Voice* and CBS friends. The Iraqis received a blizzard of requests for his release and we were delighted when someone, probably Saddam Hussein, gave in. Journalism blood flows thickly, particularly in the foreign corps.

In those early days of the crisis Ted Koppel, Dan Rather, and Tom Brokaw reported from the region as part of a frantic scurrying for ratings points and prestige. Koppel scored the first coup, bringing his ABC *Nightline* team into Iraq on August 14. The highlight was an interview with Foreign Minister Tarik Aziz.[110] Shortly afterward Rather secured a midnight interview with Saddam Hussein, the first for Hussein since the invasion. Brokaw reported from Saudi Arabia, as did Sam Donaldson. The ABC documentary, *A Line in the Sand*, allowed Peter Jennings to bring his Middle East experiences into focus, although this September 11 show to some extent, like most of the network-produced specials and interview programs, was criticized for its almost exclusively pro-Washington viewpoint.

SETTING THE AGENDA FOR THE HOME FOLKS

Many of the so-called military and political experts interviewed on television about the Gulf War were lobbyists for points of view associated with particular think tanks. Discussion was limited; the growing crisis was portrayed simply as a test of wills between defenders of peace and democracy and an evil man. The historic origins of the conflict were ignored, Arab world culture and traditions were considered irrelevant, and spokespersons from the anti-intervention side were virtually nonexistent. The small but significant antiwar movement was marginalized—worse, trivialized—by national and local news media.[111]

One of the most extensive compilations of opinions about the war coverage was published by the Freedom Forum Media Studies Center. In a debate over whether the press adequately pressed the government to clarify its goals, one critic stated that "with some notable exceptions, the media chose to ignore clear and early signs that the administration was preparing for a full-scale war against Iraq—and when that prospect could not be denied, they helped make it appear to be inevitable through the business-as-usual transmission of the war whoops of the administration."[112] Regardless of whether peace got a fair hearing, it is clear that as August became December, those who gave priority to economic sanctions got less print and broadcast attention. In one study of the 25 largest newspapers between August and mid-November only one—the *Rocky Mountain News* (Denver)—opposed military action as a last resort. The *News* said it was right to draw a line at Saudi Arabia but opposed the "liberation of Kuwait."[113]

There was a fear of heavy U.S. casualties because the Iraqi army was being touted as "the fourth largest in the world" by administration spokesmen justifying the sending of troops to Saudi Arabia. On August 8, the day after the first contingent was sent, the *New York Times* said the reason was to "deter an attack on Saudi oil fields and to intimidate President Saddam Hussein of Iraq."[114] The *Los Angeles Times* sketched the battle for Saudi

Arabia in a page-one story.[115] As the buildup continued, the stated U.S. goals shifted.

Later the seriousness of the Iraqi threat against Saudi Arabia was strongly questioned. But at the moment it seemed real, and once armed forces from the 28-member coalition were in the Desert Kingdom, an all-out war was inevitable. Neither president was going to budge. The Iraqi neck had been in a noose since August 2 and President Bush and Prime Minister Thatcher were not about to let it out. There would be a hanging, but only at the appropriate time. Little did the Allies know that one particular Iraqi, Saddam Hussein, would wriggle free at the end, remaining in power long after Thatcher and Bush left office.

On September 11, 1991, President Bush announced four objectives: (1) unconditional Iraqi withdrawal from Kuwait, (2) restoration of Kuwait's legitimate government, (3) assurance of the stability and security of the Gulf area, and (4) protection of U.S. citizens abroad.[116] The U.N. Security Council repeatedly endorsed these goals. The question for future historians was whether the United States, which for all practical reasons controlled the U.N. coalition and the Security Council, gave any serious diplomatic effort to achieving its first objective. There is considerable evidence that the United States was hell-bent for war. Bush skillfully used World War II rhetoric to avoid the impression that Iraq and Kuwait were only "feuding neighbors." Many Americans held that opinion of the Iran-Iraq war, despite the concern about oil production and prices. Bush succeeded in putting Kuwait into a larger perspective.[117]

Leading a futile counterattack against the overwhelmingly one-sided presentation were such diverse individuals and groups as Noam Chomsky, his partner in analysis Edward Herman, a handful of local media critics, writers in the alternative press, commentators on Pacifica Radio, heads of Arab-American organizations (particularly the American-Arab Anti-Discrimination Committee and the Arab American Institute), the magazine *Washington Report on the Middle East*, and the organizers of the PeaceNet computer "bulletin boards" and "conferences."

Edward W. Said, professor of English at Columbia and prominent Palestinian spokesman, said in January 1991 that many Arabs opposed Iraq's aggression but also resented the U.S. buildup. He said, "The tragedy, then, is that there is a convergence between an imperialist American will to war against an upstart third world state and an almost equally remorseless Arab propensity to violence and extremism that began with Iraq's invasion against Kuwait and continues in the Iraqi-Kuwaiti-Saudi-Egyptian drive to war."[118]

ARNETT IN THE MIDDLE OF TROUBLE

During the increasingly tense days between the January 16, 1991, attack on Baghdad and the February 23 all-out assault, Peter Arnett and some of his colleagues became objects of hostility. Although for the most part Arnett made it clear that his reports were made with a censor at his side, he was accused of being a traitor. At times some of the CNN anchors in Atlanta seemed leery of his reports, as if they were supposed to feign discomfort. On one occasion Arnett was clearly irritated with one of those "But are you sure, Peter, how do you know?" questions. His reply was a curt "Because I'm here" type of reply.

Praised by the majority of his colleagues for his fairness and calm assessment of the situation, Arnett occasionally contradicted Pentagon claims about bombing raids. The term "collateral" (accidental) damage was often used by the Pentagon in its briefings at the U.S. Central Command Center in Riyadh, Saudi Arabia, to dismiss the hitting of nonmilitary (civilian or industrial) targets. The glitzy, high-tech nature of this computer-driven war, with all of its show-off components, brought "wows" and "holy cows" from all quarters, press and home audience alike. This was a "clean" war with few U.S. casualties; the enemy was not seen and there were no guesses (body counts) about how many enemies died in the "surgical strikes." There was little speculation about how many of the "smart bombs" were off target, but a few questions did emerge—such as, if only 10 percent of the bombs were "smart," then what damage did the 90 percent of the "dumb" bombs do?[119]

One of Arnett's two biggest flaps came when he reported the bombing of what Iraqis claimed was a "baby milk factory." The Pentagon said it was a chemical warfare plant. Former Attorney General Ramsey Clark later visited the bombed building and concluded in a video interview that there was no evidence the building had been used for anything other than producing milk. Incidentally, that tape, shot by freelance journalist Jon Alpert, which also showed close-ups of home damage in the Basra area, was kept off the air by NBC executives despite enthusiasm in the newsroom for its showing.[120] The second Arnett incident came when two bombs from a U.S. Stealth fighter-bomber incinerated more than 300 Iraqi civilians in a Baghdad shelter. While the U.S. command said the shelter was used for military purposes, Arnett and other journalists concluded otherwise. This was a major exception to the coverage and even here the U.S. propaganda machine managed to blur the lines on the bomb-shelter story. Otherwise, the U.S. audience got few clues as to the extent of Iraqi suffering, which included thousands of dead and injured civilians, destruction of water and electrical facilities, and widespread damage to the nation's infrastructure. The actual number of civilian deaths was not determined by outsiders or admitted by the Iraqi government, but television tapes shown in Jordan and other countries showed considerable damage in nonmilitary areas. The number of Iraqi military deaths was placed at between 100,000 and 200,000, but again there was considerable doubt about the estimates.

The crisis was escalated on January 17, 1991, when Iraqi Scud missiles slammed into Israel. Martin Merzer of Knight-Ridder saw the dimensions of the story:

> Tel Aviv, Israel—Carrying out the threats of Saddam Hussein, Iraq fired three or four missiles into civilian areas of neutral Israel early today, threatening to widen the Persian Gulf war but failing to provoke an immediate Israeli response.[121]

Israeli censors did their best to restrict specific coverage of the Scud attacks related to security, but there was dramatic television footage of damaged buildings, crying victims, angry politicians, empty streets, air-raid sirens, and journalists wearing gas masks. The threat of chemical warfare was raised daily, adding to the growing pressure not only to liberate Kuwait but to "destroy Saddam." The question of possible Israeli retaliation was raised about as often, with "Israeli restraint" becoming code words for "don't push them any further." The legitimate U.S. fear was that Israeli intervention would break apart the anti-Saddam Arab coalition.

ARGUMENTS OVER THE POOL SYSTEM

Between the August troop buildup and the February ground war, more than 1,400 journalists showed up in Saudi Arabia, staying an average of seven weeks and averaging 47 stories apiece. An enormous amount of material flowed through computer modems, satellite hookups, and fax machines. A few even dictated to the home office as in the days of old.[122] However, the bulk of the information originated either from military briefings, from interviews arranged by the military, or through pool activity. Bob Davis of the *Wall Street Journal* said the pool reports were "90 per cent junk."[123]

While most of the correspondents agreed that pools were necessary to keep some kind of order, there also was a consensus that the pools were not helpful. That's the polite way of admitting that the correspondents were victims of the most skillfully orchestrated media manipulation in the twentieth century. They should have known it was coming. During the 1982 Falklands campaign the British military allowed 27 reporters into the war zone, censoring their reports before their transmission over a British marine radio system. Taking the clue, the Pentagon devised an unprecedented censorship of the 1983 Grenada invasion, when 300 reporters were kept in Barbados 150 miles from the action. When it was time to invade Panama in 1989 a pool team of 12 did land at the U.S. air base there only four hours after hostilities began. And that's where they stayed until it was deemed safe for them to get into the streets. To this day no one knows the extent of the bombing damage in civilian neighborhoods; Operation Just Cause was a sham.[124] In late 1992 Panamanian civilians were involved with lawsuits aimed at investigating charges that numerous mass graves had been used to cover up the number of deaths. So there was a precedent for the Gulf censorship.[125]

Only 150 journalists were allowed into the pool system and only half of them were out with the troops at any one time.[126] At times there were as few as 16 newspaper journalists covering the 514,000 Americans under arms. There were a number of oddities. The *New York Times* did not get a correspondent into a pool until February 10, three weeks after the war started. The progressive (to some "left-wing") magazine *Mother Jones* had its visa application rejected, but the fashion magazine *Mirabella* was represented in a pool slot. More than 300 European and Asian journalists were told to share three pool positions. *Los Angeles Times* correspondent John Balzar was shown videotapes of Apache helicopter attacks where Iraqi soldiers were blown to pieces; he wrote an article about the deaths and thereafter was barred from visiting the Apache units. Douglas Jehl, also of the Los Angeles paper, reported that 50 U.S. military vehicles were "missing"; he was ordered out of his pool. James LeMoyne's interview with General Norman Schwarzkopf was canceled after he quoted enlisted men's criticisms of President Bush and the U.S. presence in the Gulf.

Reporters complained much more about not being granted access than they did direct censorship, but there were numerous examples of reports being altered or stopped. One wire-service reporter said only seven of his 27 stories made it through unscathed. The most frequently cited incident involved a *Detroit Free Press* reporter who was not allowed to say that returning U.S. pilots were "giddy" with success. Instead the censor said they were "proud." That pales in comparison with numerous reports of journalists being put under military arrest or held at gunpoint for alleged pool violations. Others were verbally abused or had their credentials confiscated by U.S. or Saudi soldiers. *Time*'s Wes Bocxe was blindfolded and held at gunpoint, and questioned about spying for Iraq. Angry about all of this, the AP's Mort Rosenbaum said, "I've covered wars for 25 years and the first time I'm held prisoner is by my own military."[127]

Daniel Fesperman of the *Baltimore Sun* summed up the opinion of many in Dhahran, calling the pool system "basically a stupid system . . . designed primarily to spread disinformation."[128] David Lamb said: "At the best of scenarios, pool reporting dulls initiative and dilutes a writer's ability to give shape and forms to his observations and words. In the worst, it creates a product that is bland and homogenous. If World War II had been covered by pools [author's note: It was, at times] there never would have been a national treasure named Ernie Pyle."[129] The public saw this differently, however. On January 31 a public opinion survey showed that 79 percent of persons responding said military censorship was a "good idea" and 57 percent said they would favor greater control. At the same time 78 percent said the press coverage was good or even excellent.[130]

THE "MOTHER OF ALL BATTLES": A 100-HOUR GROUND WAR

On February 22, 1991, Soviet President Mikhail Gorbachev announced that Iraq had agreed to a "full and unconditional withdrawal" from Kuwait. This news spilled across the world and those hoping to avoid the ground war, including correspondents with the U.S. troops preparing to rip into the Iraqi lines, took a deep breath. Instead, Bush gave Hussein one day to start pulling out, an impossible demand to meet.[131] War was only a few minutes away. An intense bombing of Iraqi positions was heard nightly by the *Washington Post*'s Molly Moore and 10 male colleagues. They were with U.S. Marine forces who were about to make the heaviest armored attack in their history. An eyewitness to a commanding general's every decision, Moore brilliantly reconstructed the war in *A Woman at War*. Ironically, she was prevented from immediately reporting her battlefield observations because of her remote position and communication problems. So it all ended up in a book.

In the final hours before the ground attack an awful fear enveloped the front. Heavy casualties were expected. No one knew what the Iraqis might throw back. Admittedly very frightened herself, Moore wrote:

> Loud booms bounced across the desert outside . . . The nightly bombing raids had become commonplace . . . I wondered how many young Iraqi soldiers were dying with each bright flash . . . this long-distanced, high-technology war was being waged out of eyesight of every war correspondent in Saudia Arabia. We saw only the bloodless, antiseptic tapes that General Norman Schwarzkopf decided to release . . . As I stood atop the sand berm the human costs of the war suddenly came into sharp

focus . . . I wondered, like so many of the troops whom I had interviewed, if returning Kuwait's oil supplies to its monarch and wealthy citizenry was worth the lives it would cost both sides.[132]

"Ground War Launched," screamed the *Los Angeles Times*. The deck read: "Bush Acts After Iraq Scorns Deadline." The paper's reporting team said in this story bylined by James Gerstenzang in Washington and Nick Williams Jr. in Amman:

> One of the most violent battles in the history of modern warfare began on the wind-swept desert beside the Persian Gulf today as the United States and its allies launched their threatened ground assault against Iraqi forces to drive them out of Kuwait.[133]

The following day Apple of the *New York Times* wrote this bit of history:

> Allied troops drove into Iraqi-occupied Kuwait on Sunday, reaching the outskirts of Kuwait City before nightfall . . . to the West, powerful armored columns and a huge fleet of helicopters stormed into Iraq, heading northeast toward Basra in an effort to isolate Iraq's elite Republican Guards.[134]

Kifner of the *Times* was one of the journalists with the helicopters, writing: "More than 2,000 American air assault troops plunged at least 50 miles into Iraq at first light today in the largest helicopter-borne operation in military history. The attack . . . established what is essentially a giant, fortified gas station."[135] Other reporters were not as lucky. Balzar of the *Los Angeles Times* also flew in a lead helicopter, but he was unceremoniously dropped off six miles from any action and told to walk. The former U.S. Marine did, burning mad at the deliberate mistreatment.[136]

When the ground war began on February 23, those journalists who broke away from their U.S. military escorts went into the combat zone with Saudis, Egyptians and Kuwaitis, a strange commentary considering the closed nature of those societies. Yet most of this discussion of censorship was lost when U.S. television brought home scenes of Kuwait's liberation. Leading the way was CBS, which had trailed in the war ratings. Bob McKeown scooped his colleagues with a live broadcast from Kuwait City at 6:00 P.M., Kuwait time, Tuesday, February 26, 1991. Sawyer's ABC team arrived at midnight, while NBC, ITN, CNN, and others ran into trouble at roadblocks. The official pool reporters did not arrive until late on the 27th. A few print reporters, like Paul McEnroe of the *Star Tribune* (Minneapolis), risked their lives by driving across the desert, beating the main group by hours. By that time the story was worldwide—the airwaves were filled with the whoop and holler of the Kuwait liberators and the liberated. As the news of the rout in southern Iraq came in, the coverage became tinged with a smug satisfaction that "we whipped 'em."

Journalist Robin Andersen said later:

> The Mother of all Battles was little more than a sweep against a defeated army in retreat . . . one pilot said the road to Basra filled with the withdrawing Iraqi army looked like "spring break at Daytona Beach" as he bombed the congested line. No images from the ground which might have sobered up the college metaphor were provided. Americans were allowed to see only uplifting footage of the Liberation of Kuwait and grateful prisoners kissing the hands of their "liberators." What became clear as the ground war pressed on to "total victory" was that one of the main targets for destruction . . . was actually the spectre of the Vietnam war . . . when U.S. television did show pictures of dead civilians, viewers were invited not to feel concerned because they were part of Hussein's "psychological war against the American public." Over graphic videotape of the charred bodies of dead children, NBC's Faith Daniels says, "What they do show is that Saddam Hussein's propaganda machinery continues to function." And after airing a few moments of civilian casualties, the *MacNeil-Lehrer News Hour* called the footage "heavy handed manipulation." *Time* magazine defined "collateral damage" as "dead or wounded civilians who should have picked a safer neighborhood."[137]

Larry Grossman, the former head of NBC News, said after the war that "there is no question that in war, reporters tend to be cheerleaders for their own side and their own country. They are patriots like everybody else and tend to have very conventional views of what is going on. But certainly in this war, which lasted for such a short time and was so intense, I think there was no question that we saw an unusually patriotic, supportive journalistic corps."

It was Grossman's contention that this perception was "exacerbated by television." Of course it was, with all of the "Hi, Mom" messages being flashed back as if from the sidelines of a football game. To Grossman the most interesting aspect of the war was the government's dominance of the television screen. "The issue was not so much keeping things away, but how much from one perspective dominated the screen. This was the ultimate in the cheerleading war." Former CBS broadcaster Marvin Kalb chimed in with this criticism: "Unfortunately . . . the American people were short changed, in part because the press engaged in that most dangerous of professional practices, namely, patriotic journalism."[138]

In a sense the coverage was a throwback to the World War II period when in American culture war was, in the words of author Dan Hallin, "a manly, exciting adventure with very little sense of the human costs." Looking at the role of television during a post war review, he said: "As soon as it became clear that the country was strongly behind this war, television became very vary of being caught on the wrong side of that consensus. It pushed television away from treating the war as a political policy and toward treating it as a kind of national celebration—like a moon shot or something."[139]

The administration did its best to keep a shadow from falling over the image of total victory. But with the Iraqi army rampaging against the Kurds in the north and Kuwaitis brutalizing local Palestinians, it was hard to keep the record clean. During a televised "All Star Salute to Our Troops," Bush said that during the war Americans had regained confidence in the nation's "*special decency*, courage, compassion, and devotion to principle."[140]

A voluminous literature on the causes and effects of the Gulf War developed within months of its ending. George Gerbner, Douglas Kellner, Herbert I. Schiller, Alexander Cockburn, George Black, and others joined Chomsky and Herman in dissecting media coverage and putting the war into either a broad cultural perspective or in cold-blooded political terms.[141]

Chomsky simply contrasted Washington's handling of the breakup of the Soviet Union, where Bush had little impact on Soviet developments, with the president's "insistence upon sole authority in the crucial energy-producing regions of the Middle East." As the Iraqgate scandal developed in 1992, it became clear how the concept of U.S. "tilting" from Iran (the Shah was our Gulf policeman up to his 1979 exile) to Saddam was accompanied by corruption and scandal. Freelance journalist Murray Waas and Douglas Frantz of the *Los Angeles Times* were coauthors of coverage that outdistanced all others in the 1992 Iraqgate coverage.

From military strategy to arguments against press censorship, the experts had their say, in print and on radio and television. Peter Arnett, CNN's star reporter in Baghdad, was on a speaking tour, preparing a book; Ramsey Clark, a war opponent, also wrote his account and conducted a war crimes tribunal;[142] some journalists went into Iraq to assess war damage unavailable to them before.[143] But important questions remained about the conduct of Bush administration officials during the August-February period. The major one: was the war necessary or did President Bush and British Prime Minister Margaret Thatcher maneuver to keep Saddam Hussein in a self-made trap from which he could not escape?

A SEPARATE VIEW: SECRET DOCUMENTS AND AN INTERVIEW WITH KING HUSSEIN

On February 19, 1991, five days before Bush unleashed the ground war, I was in Amman for the sole purpose of interviewing King Hussein about the origins and conduct of the war. Both the *Los Angeles Times* and *Village Voice* had indicated interest in the interview, which took place in a large sitting room in the palace working area. The material appeared in a full-page display in the *Times*'s March 3 Opinion Section and as the *Voice's* March 5 cover story, "The War That Didn't Have to Happen."

The king, generally disappointed with Western news media coverage portraying him as the weak man in the middle, granted few interviews after the August buildup. The week before my visit ABC's Diane Sawyer had conducted a casual and inconsequential chat with the royal couple. After the war Judith Miller of the *New York Times* was granted a session, out of which came a solid look at postwar Jordan. My story peg was to interview the king as part of an investigation of how U.S. and British officials scuttled Arab-nation efforts to prevent Saddam Hussein's August invasion and another attempt to induce him to leave Kuwait.

Rumors had been flying around the Middle East since early August 1990 of how Bush and Thatcher had strong-armed President Hosni Mubarak of Egypt to influence the course of events. My four-month investigation was based on information from diplomats, senior officials of several Arab governments and persons with ties to Middle Eastern intelligence agencies. It was corroborated by documents purportedly seized by the Iraqis in Kuwait and shared with various parties.

King Hussein told me that beginning in August 1988, the time of the Iraqi-Iranian cease-fire, he began to hear rumors from Western visitors headed home from the Gulf that Saddam Hussein had extensive military ambitions in that region. A personal investigation led the king to believe that "some intelligence agencies" were putting out disinformation. Throughout 1989 and 1990 Iraq was at odds with the Gulf States over the issues of war reparations and the Iraq-Kuwait boundary. A series of meetings in the summer of 1990 had produced no results. When the Iraqi moved troops to the Kuwait border in July 1990, King Hussein became alarmed and took actions to stop an invasion.

There has been considerable speculation about the role of April Glaspie, U.S. Ambassador to Iraq, who on July 25 failed to give Saddam Hussein a tough warning about the consequences of invading Kuwait. One official statement to the Iraqi leader was: "We have no opinion on the Arab-Arab conflicts."[144] Treated like a pet by visiting U.S. officials for years, and particularly in the 1988–90 period, Saddam Hussein may or may not have been given the green light. It is clear, however, that the Bush administration did nothing to stop his buildup and then joined with others to ruin any chances that the Arab nations had of settling their own differences short of war.

My sources indicated the possibility that a two-pronged U.S. policy may have been in effect (1) on a higher level to continue supporting Iraqi financial and strategic needs as the great buffer against Iran, but also (2) on the lower intelligence agency level, to begin to plan for a "tilting" away from Iraq to ensure continued U.S. and British power in the relatively unprotected and oil-rich Gulf States.

So, I asked the king, how in the first few days of August 1990 did Saddam Hussein "go from nothing to Hitler"? Before I could finish my question the king interjected, "Margaret Thatcher!" His Majesty explained in great detail a series of meetings and telephone calls occurring between July 30 and August 3 that in his judgment made all-out war almost inevitable. On July 30 the king and a group of advisers flew to Kuwait, where he met with the emir and his advisers met with Kuwaiti counterparts. A crucial meeting was to be hosted the next day by the Saudis at Jiddah. The Jordanians, who would not be involved directly, encouraged the Kuwaitis to soften their hardline attitude toward Iraqi demands for war reparations.

I learned—from a highly placed European source with knowledge of communications between King Fahd of Saudi Arabia and Saddam Hussein—that a deal had been agreed upon. The Saudis and Kuwaitis were to pledge $10 billion each toward reaching a total of about $30 billion that had been demanded by Saddam Hussein at an angry May meeting. King Hussein said he was not familiar with the specifics of the agreement, but he did authenticate the signature of the Kuwaiti emir on one of the stolen documents— King Fahd's invitation to the emir for the July 31 meeting. The text referred to a recent communication and agreement between the emir and Saddam Hussein and read, in part: "I have full confidence in your judgment and wisdom *in fulfilling all that we are looking for* in overcoming all of the obstacles . . ." (emphasis added). The Middle Eastern rule of thumb was that the Saudis did not attend meetings unless they knew the outcome in advance. This strong wording fit the pattern. The emir's signature was on the invitation because in passing it on to his representative at Jiddah, the foreign minister, he ordered him to disregard King Fahd's comments and the Iraqi demands, remembering instead the advice of "our friends in Washington, London and Cairo."

At the July 30 meeting the Jordanians were shocked to hear the Kuwaiti foreign minister make sarcastic remarks about the Iraqi soldiers poised near his border. According to a Jordanian official who was present, the Kuwaitis were warned about the serious consequences of not being flexible. Instead, the foreign minister (Sheik Sabah Ahmed al-Jaber al-Sabah) said, "We are not going to respond to Iraq . . . if they don't like it let them invade . . . we are going to bring in the Americans." He hesitated for a moment, adding: "Well, you know what is embarrassing about this . . . what is embarrassing is the Israeli-American dimension." I later was told that in the same week the Kuwaiti crown prince told senior military officers that in the event of an invasion, they only had to hold off the Iraqis for 24 hours, time for the Americans and British to arrive.

The next day's meeting at Jiddah lasted only two hours. Living up to their word, the Kuwaitis insulted Iraqi Vice President Izzat Ibrahim. They reportedly offered $500,000. The meeting broke up with great anger and Iraq invaded two days later. On the morning of August 2, King Hussein was awakened by a 6:00 A.M. telephone call from King Fahd, who informed him that Saddam Hussein's tanks were nearing Kuwait City. King Fahd wanted the Jordanian leader to call Saddam Hussein, to tell him to stop and get out. King Hussein reached Foreign Minister Tariq Aziz, who said the Iraqis would stop if immediate agreement could be reached for another meeting at Jiddah, on August 5. A few minutes later Saddam Hussein told the king the same thing. Armed with this little bit of hope, King Hussein said that he and his group flew immediately to Alexandria, Egypt, where the king met with Mubarak.

The essence of the meeting was that King Hussein needed 48 hours to see Saddam Hussein personally, to ensure his retreat from Kuwait, in return for Mubarak's promise that the Iraqi actions would not be condemned at the Arab League foreign ministers' conference being held in nearby Cairo (they had met with Mubarak outside of Cairo to avoid drawing attention).

King Hussein said Mubarak agreed, and that President Bush called the Egyptian during the meeting. According to the Jordanians, Bush raised two points: (1) he was worried about Americans in Kuwait, and (2) he wanted Iraq to withdraw. He said nothing about the sending of troops to the Gulf. King Hussein informed Bush that he would fly to Baghdad the next morning. Numerous attempts to reach King Fahd failed. The Saudi monarch, supposedly the host of the August 5 meeting, was unresponsive—an ominous sign. Nevertheless, in the morning King Hussein was in Iraq. Saddam Hussein was in a nearly apoplectic rage, storming about the selfishness of the Gulf States leaders. The king admitted being alarmed over Saddam Hussein's behavior, but he managed to get through a negotiating session. In the end the Iraqis agreed to begin a withdrawal if the August 5 meeting met with their satisfaction. The Kuwaitis would have been taught a lesson and negotiations could continue on disputes over an oil field and the northern boundary.

King Hussein flew toward Amman about 6:00 P.M., thinking he may have preserved the Middle East peace. But within minutes he learned from his foreign minister at the Cairo conference that Mubarak had broken his pledge not to condemn Iraqi. The king admitted that his reaction was, "Oh, my God, now the conspiracy is complete." Mubarak had been pressured to pass the anti-Saddam measure by 5:00 P.M. on August 3 in order to coincide with the presentation of the U.S.-drafted Security Council resolution calling for economic sanctions against Iraq. Diplomats attending the Cairo meeting later confirmed how the Egyptians aggressively pushed for condemnation, aided by the Saudis. There would be no meeting at Jiddah, the Iraqis would stay in Kuwait, and the Americans would come. The king later confronted Mubarak, blaming him for the crisis. "It's your fault," he said. Mubarak complained about pressure from King Fahd and the media, saying, "I'm so tired, I can't think." King Hussein's angry response: "When you can think again, call me back."

In the Jordanian view, this was a "setup" to ensure long-range American and British control of the region. But what about the Iraqi threat to the Saudis? I asked the king if Saddam Hussein had those intentions and he responded sharply, "No way!" As proof, he offered a story of how on August 7 he had received a visiting Saudi official, offering him "half of the Jordanian army" if a threat actually existed. He was told firmly that there was no need for help. Within 30 minutes of the guest's departure he learned that the first Americans had arrived in Saudi Arabia. The king maintained that the Saudis "hit the panic button" when Secretary of Defense Dick Cheney flew in with CIA photographs of Iraqi tanks near the Saudi border. The king said he had seen some of the same photos and found them unconvincing.

This brings Thatcher back into the story. The king related with a chuckle that after the troop buildup was under way, he engaged in what he described as a "loud argument" with the Prime Minister in London. "It was one of the rowdiest discussions that I ever had with anybody. She was very strong on her side and so was I . . . very strong language . . . but one thing came out. She said troops were halfway to their destination before the request came for them to come." In another conference, November 20, 1990, in Geneva, Thatcher tried to back away from her comments, the king said, but he did not accept her explanation. "[Her original statement] was very clear," he said. There are accounts also of Thatcher's visit to Colorado with Bush in the first days of August, when she reportedly twisted his arm, telling him what she told King Hussein: "He *cawnt* get all of the oil!"

During the middle of this two-hour session we were interrupted by one of the king's advisers, who said he had important news to share. The Americans had rejected Soviet proposals for Iraqi withdrawal, although the Soviets said their ideas were in line with United Nations resolutions. The king sat silently and slumped noticeably. He murmured to himself in Arabic. I asked him what this meant and he said, "I think a ground war will take place soon . . . I believe it is imminent . . . Obviously it goes way past the liberation of Kuwait." Four days later, on February 23, 1991, Bush officially rejected the final Soviet plan, but it was clear all along that there would be no compromise.

King Hussein's insistence to both Bush and Thatcher that he not join the coalition cost him dearly. Not only was the king personally hurt by the Western perception that he had junked his responsibilities and thrown in his lot with Saddam Hussein, but Jordan was put into the middle of the pressure cooker, with Iraq on one side and Israel on the other. U.S. jets bombed Jordanian trucks and cars on the Baghdad-Amman highway; Jordan was informed that if Israel did enter the war, the Israelis expected to fly over Jordanian territory for bombing missions and that interference would not be tolerated; Jordan was made an outcast among the Arab nations, its commerce slashed by the Saudis; Jordan's postwar economy suffered even more when 300,000 Palestinians were expelled from Kuwait and ended up in Jordan.

Only some of this was understood by journalists covering Amman. They reported that the king, beholden to his Palestinian population, supported Iraq to maintain their allegiance.[145] It is true that during the war the king's popularity with all of his people never was higher, but this was due in part to his fierce stance against a renewal of colonialism. That is one area where the king and all of his people saw eye-to-eye—the Americans were the New Crusaders following in the Middle East footsteps of the British and French. Unlike Americans, the people of the Middle East see events in terms of history. When U.S. planes bombed Iraq, Middle Easterners remembered how the British had used chemical gas shells against Iraqis in 1920. Winston Churchill authorized "using poisoned gas against uncivilized tribes."[146] Another word that is used often in the Middle East when referring to the West is *hypocrisy*. That has to be considered and understood.

As for my investigation and King Hussein's recollections, it remains one of those stories that did not get into the U.S. mainstream flow. The *Times* version was syndicated worldwide and was published in Europe and Asia. Perhaps the war could have been avoided. We'll never know. The Soviet plan was the best chance. Instead—the popular view prevailed, that a reluctant Bush, at first unsure of the significance of the Iraqi invasion, decided to defend Saudi Arabia and then slowly moved toward action, taking many diplomatic steps until it was clear that diplomacy would not work. The press and the public didn't know much about the policies of "tilting" and the double-dealing of Iran and Iraq dating to the 1970s that pushed events out of control.

The countdown to the ground war was in its last few hours when I left Amman on February 23. When we arrived in Cyprus the crew huddled around a radio but there was no news. When we arrived in Amsterdam there still was no word. The plane was filled with anxious and upset Jordanians, fearing that the war would spread across their borders.

Finally, out over the dark Atlantic, a crew member came by my seat and said simply, "It started." My thoughts flashed to the Gulf, where I imagined huge flashes of light and many deaths, and then to Amman, where correspondents at the Intercontinental Hotel would be filing. I wondered about some of the people with whom I had only hours before shared a meal or drinks—Nick Williams Jr., Frank Smyth, Mike O'Connor. As I began to transcribe King Hussein's comments word for word, I couldn't help thinking about all of the people caught in the middle.

Conclusion

When this book was near completion, I described some of the main events to a friend, who surprised me by asking, "Who are your heroes in this story?" I responded that, because there were so many correspondents with admirable traits, it would be difficult to list only a few as my favorites. But it is possible to put together a composite of the ideal foreign correspondent and here it is: This person would have the curiosity of Negley Farson, the physical courage of Keyes Beech and Marguerite Higgins, the intellect of Theodore White, the dramatic flair of Dorothy Thompson, the professionalism and integrity of Edward Price Bell, Anne O'Hare McCormick and Sigrid Schultz, the sensitivity of Neil Sheehan, the news judgment of David Halberstam, the historical knowledge of Harrison Salisbury, the honest patriotism and decency of Edward R. Murrow, the adventurousness of Richard Harding Davis, the writing ability of Homer Bigart, and the high-level consistency and perseverance of Peter Arnett.

An overall analysis of the correspondents' work suggests that for the most part the men and women of the U.S. press corps are fairly well educated, reasonably well trained, serious about their work, and generally successful at getting their stories into the reader's living room. Among the regulars there was little evidence of corruption, misuse of power, unchecked bias, or grossly unethical behavior. Sure, some drank too much and others were lazy and uncaring, but this is not a profession for the faint-hearted and those of weak character. Rather, for the most part foreign correspondence has been the choosing of men and women of stamina, heart, and healthy self-confidence. For example, CNN viewers will recognize these traits in Christiane Amanpour, good-natured in the face of one crisis after another from the Middle East to Bosnia to Haiti, always in the center of action with insightful reporting.

Over the years the level of education rose, including foreign-language ability. However, few correspondents had sufficient appreciation of the role of a particular culture in their work—a serious deficiency that needs to be overcome if stories are to be framed in the proper context without unconscious stereotypes being passed on to the reader or viewer. It is one thing, as reporters say, "to live in the culture." It is another step to realizing how one's own assumptions quietly become part of the story.[1] One glaring example: The rise of Islamic Fundamentalism was a phenomenon barely understood by reporters and less by the general public. Few U.S. journalists had permanent assignments in the Muslim world, but when Muslims were implicated in New York's World Trade Center bombing, journalists worldwide were asked to write reaction pieces that included explanations of the Muslim viewpoint. That was a story that only a few could do well.

Within this critique there are many exceptions, of course, not only in terms of Pulitzer Prize–level achievement but also in lapses of judgment and failure to overcome some of the barriers to the flow of foreign news. Even the best-known journalists have their bad days, make big mistakes, and suffer the wrath of the home bosses and angry sources. Sometimes, for a combination of reasons, the entire press corps in a city misses the essence of a story, as discovered in the chapter on Stalin. Over the years those with unfamiliar bylines plunge on, day after day, with mixed success—at the mercy of those government officials and others trying to create a different truth, as learned in the section on El Salvador. The cliché is that journalism is the first draft of history. In some cases the page-one story or newscast is the final draft, right on the mark at the magic moment: Davis writing from Belgium in 1914 on the German invasion; Murrow describing the Battle of Britain for a radio audience in 1940; the television reporters racing through the streets at the fall of the Philippines' Ferdinand Marcos in 1989, and describing the raising of the new flag in South Africa in 1994.

But in most cases the typical foreign news story offers only a skimpy look at one segment of a complex situation, facts and observations deserving a deeper interpretation than might be possible at the moment and subject to unexpected changes. Despite the advances in technology, there is little that can be done about this. Space, time and financial limitations dominate. A steady flow of print or broadcast reports could be considered adequate if supplemented by independently prepared background reports, including maps and graphs. To their credit, major news organizations offered hefty news packages during the biggest news events of this century. At times both quantity and quality were outstanding. But the news media frequently came up short in two areas: the historical background piece needed to put the event in some perspective and, to a far greater extent, something which could be dubbed "the alternative viewpoint story," in which the reporter goes outside of what Robert Parry called "conventional wisdom" and looks at the event from a different and probably unpopular angle. This would be the true "other side." As mentioned at the outset, the villains here are those who adhere to the corporate mindset that dictates so many of the news and opinion pieces about foreign affairs, particularly those written in the Washington, D.C., bureaus and in the home offices.

Then there is the problem of public apathy. The extensive print and broadcast coverage of Bosnia between 1991 and 1994, including the merciless Serbian bombardment of Sarajevo, gave the U.S. public abundant facts and imagery. Yet, as noted earlier, there was little pubic reaction here to the "ethnic cleansing." In addition to a natural reluctance to plunge into another foreign adventure lacking a clear ending, there were other factors that will continue to hinder public involvement in U.S. foreign policy. Danny Schechter, co-producer of the film *Sarajevo Ground Zero* and executive producer of human-rights material for Globalvision, put it this way:

> The American television network brand of "sound-bite journalism" is especially superficial when it comes to reporting on people with foreign-sounding names and thick accents. The Bosnians might as well have been from another planet . . . TV news becomes a numbing blur of charge and countercharge. At a certain point the sheer madness of it becomes too much to bear. We become desensitized. There is no way to digest it at all because so little context is offered to advance comprehension. Is it a surprise, then, that many tune it out? . . . It is one major reason why Americans don't seem to care.[2]

Despite good intentions, on a typical day-in, day-out basis, most news media organizations fail to adequately supplement their foreign reports. The most notable exception is the *Los Angeles Times World Report,* a special section produced weekly with emphasis on a theme that ties into breaking news. On television CNN has its outstanding *World Report* show, where uncensored reports from foreign television services are featured. In the radio world National Public Radio and Pacifica feature long interpretative stories. Ironically, computer bulletin boards carry volumes of information not available from regular sources. This is encouraging because in our modern period the avalanche of skewed information from paid consultants and other partisans in the form of op-ed pieces and talk shows diminishes the effect of the news product and creates the illusion that the public—a public already at the mercy of the peddlers of news in the form of entertainment—is receiving enough information.

Nevertheless, the experiences discussed here at length offer a number of valuable lessons for the public as well as today's foreign journalists—particularly those early in their careers—and their editors and managers of news organizations. For one thing, the fragility of the nation's foreign correspondence system is laid bare. As noted in the Introduction, fewer than a thousand U.S. citizens patrol the world as our first line of defense, reporting and processing news that might affect all of us. The long-range fate of the foreign correspondent seems to be in doubt. In this age of financial cutbacks, improved technology, and quick transportation, there is a greater dependence on foreign nationals to shoulder the load. Network exchange agreements have lessened the need for competition and on-site correspondents.

While Western European cities and Tokyo have remained havens for healthy numbers of U.S. journalists, there is a clear pattern. Throughout the century, huge areas of the world have had little U.S. representation: China and Southeast Asia, the Indian Subcontinent, most of Africa and Latin America, Iran and the Gulf States, and the former Soviet Republics. At a crucial time in U.S.-Mexico relations—including the assassination of that nation's leading presidential candidate—our neighbor hosted few full-time U.S. reporters. World coverage followed traditional economic lines and moved to the underdeveloped nations in times of war or political upheaval—or, in the case of Mexico, a temporary flash of excitement about the North American Free Trade Agreement or a masked rebel named Marcos. But if, for example, U.S. business benefited from NAFTA and more major corporations had major offices in Mexico, there would be incentive for news organizations to post additional staffers there.

In the year 2000 Mexico City will remain the largest city in the world, according to the Population Fund, with a population of 25.6 million—up 5.4 million from the 1990 count, when Tokyo was second with 18.1 million, followed by São Paulo (17.4), the New York area (16.2), Shanghai (13.4), the Los Angeles area (11.9), Calcutta (11.8), Buenos Aires (11.5), Bombay (11.1), and Seoul (11.0). The question is, what will be the quantity and quality of coverage from these cities, as well as from the Caucasus, Azerbaijan, Karabakh, Armenia, Kashmir, Tibet, East Timor, Kurdistan, and the other neglected places on the globe? The post–Cold War world will be confusing to Western news executives because a standard guidepost for news is missing: the U.S.-Soviet competition. There is a concern that, as in the past, many significant Third World stories will not receive coverage unless major powers demonstrate self-interest. The "shrinking world" concept and the marvels of instant communication do not count here. The only guarantee of coverage will be if someone sends in troops, as in Somalia, Rwanda, or Haiti.

The financial constraints on news organizations were so severe during the heavy Bosnian fighting in 1993 that at times U.S. networks used reporters in London to do voice-overs of videotape shot in Sarajevo. While the Associated Press assumed major responsibility for foreign news delivery with about 400 U.S. citizens, the networks and daily papers came up short. NBC, CBS, and ABC had fewer than 20 correspondents each, while CNN had 30. The *New York Times* (32) and *Los Angeles Times* (27) maintained a total of about 60 correspondents, but fewer than 25 of the 1,700 U.S. dailies had even one foreign reporter. About 25 percent were women, an increase from previous years. By 1994 women were firmly established within the foreign press corps, but men continued to dominate in sheer numbers whenever front-page bylines were counted or airtime was tabulated.

George Krimsky, a former Associated Press correspondent who headed the Center for Foreign Journalists in Reston, Virginia, expressed continued concern about a perceived drop in both quality and quantity in foreign reporting. On the other hand, Professor Emeritus Ralph E. Kliesch of Ohio University has observed that the U.S. foreign correspondent corps was "larger and more equitably distributed than any in recent decades." Krimsky doubts whether increased numbers, if accurate, truly reflect greater media attention to the real world out there.[3]

The academic debates and the overall concerns aside, a number of conclusions can be made about the state of foreign correspondence, first in the area of censorship. Japan's systematic control during its war with Russia in 1904–05 was the first model of the century, to be brought to a peak of sophistication in the mix of propaganda, media manipulation, and access control by the United States during the Gulf War (1990–91). This followed the British experience in the Falklands War (1982) and the U.S. experiments in Grenada (1983) and Panama (1989). However, the most pervasive use came during the First World War. That first war was a lie from beginning to end, as was the period immediately following when the Great Powers drew boundaries in Europe and the Middle East that spawned future conflicts. As for Vietnam, this disillusioning era began with "media management" by the Kennedy administration and led to the widespread lies of the Johnson and Nixon administrations, particularly regarding the bombing of North Vietnam and Cambodia.

Regarding the period studied, 1962–63, Neil Sheehan's assessment is generally accepted here, that the Washington policy planners and most of the Vietnam commanders were deluded with their own ideas and had not yet established the pattern of systematic lying so well developed later. It is clear that the Ap Bac case was one of a number of exceptions, however, because there was a defeat in front of the journalists' eyes and no excuse for U.S. spokesmen to arrogantly claim a victory. Sheehan gave his opinions at a small dinner party in Los Angeles in 1989 where he described his early experiences with Halberstam and the others. In a gloomy moment he told of Richard Nixon affecting the lives of hundreds of thousands of Asians as if playing chess, and after the session he bluntly told me his belief that any president, given that enormous power, would use cruel force to ensure foreign policy gains. This was a stern warning not to underestimate the capacity for brutality in our highest officials in foreign actions. Various correspondents wrote their books of reminiscence and revisited the scenes of their past stories, including a disillusioned Louis Fischer, but Sheehan's Vietnam flashbacks in *After the War Was Over* were the most poignant.

Censorship is repugnant and condemned by all journalists, but it also is an established part of modern governmental life. It is to be expected. The greater evil and one far more disappointing is self-censorship, the unnecessary and cowardly act of stomping on your own correspondent's work in order to bow to one's biases, to curry favor with a higher boss, or to placate an ill-informed but critical public element. In this study self-censorship did not appear to be a major problem until the focus shifted to Central America and the Middle East. Prior to that there were plenty of arguments over assignments and news play—the summer of 1914 saw some good examples of home-desk ignorance fouling up life for the correspondents. But certainly the years of conflict in Central America produced some of the worst examples. The Ray Bonner story is remarkable for the dishonesty and callousness displayed by New York and Washington journalists who knew the truth. Robert Parry's experiences were equally disillusioning. There was considerable self-censorship during the Gulf War.

The same criticism of self-censorship can be leveled at those at home who sidetracked any honest appraisal of Israel's treatment of the Palestinians. This one-sidedness was one factor in the long delay in the peace process—the U.S. media played a major role in Israeli foreign policy. As noted in the text, the Israelis could do whatever they wanted because for too many years the resident press corps served as cheerleaders for Israel and ignored the Arab-world viewpoint. To their credit reporters like Tom Friedman and Loren Jenkins reported the invasion of Lebanon with hard truths, to be followed by others who generally played the Palestinian *Intifada* down the middle. It is safe to say that historic Israeli-PLO agreements would not have been possible without the improved press scrutiny of the entire Palestinian situation.

There are a number of disturbing episodes in this story, but perhaps the most bothersome was one that was not mentioned in the main text. It involved the role of multinational public-relations firms in working closely with the U.S. government to affect foreign policy decisions. With the revolving door open, there is a steady flow of personnel back and forth between these firms and government. It was well documented that the powerful Hill & Knowlton firm waged a propaganda battle for its Kuwaiti clients during the late 1990–early 1991 buildup to all-out war. On October 10, 1990, the firm arranged for a 15-year-old Kuwaiti to testify that she saw Iraqi soldiers take babies from incubators and leave them on the floor to die. This became a worldwide story that reached foreign correspondents in the Middle East. Some referred to the "incubator story" in their own stories. In 1991 when the Congress voted for war, several Senators said their opinion was influenced by the testimony of the young woman. After the war it was revealed that she was not an ordinary Kuwaiti, as presented to the House Human Rights Caucus, but the daughter of the Kuwaiti ambassador to the United States and that she had lied. No babies had been killed. This was a carefully orchestrated event set up by the White House and Hill & Knowlton that directly affected media coverage. There is every reason to believe that international PR firms will continue to influence foreign coverage. This is one thing correspondents working in previous eras did not have to worry about.

In retrospect it seems that the *New York Times* was the one paper that put itself and its correspondents on the spot during the early stages of a major event, while others failed to make the necessary financial and physical commitment. One thinks of Walter Duranty in Moscow, one of a handful of reporters; then there was Herbert Matthews in Cuba, Homer Bigart and David Halberstam in Vietnam, and Stephen Kinzer in Nicaragua. They all were singled out for bitter criticism, much of it undeserved. With the exception of Duranty, their stories were available in the field to backbiting competitors and sensitive news sources. They carried tremendous individual responsibility—something that diminished considerably for print journalists in the television era. Continuing in this tradition, John Burns of the *Times* won the Pulitzer Prize for Bosnian coverage that by its descriptive quality almost cried out for U.S. action. But this time the government and public were not opposed to the message. They just paid no attention. In fact, over the years the personal *ideology* of reporters seems to have had little effect on their editors and the government, in contrast to any rifts caused by correspondents telling the truth.

Skillfully writing the truth—the best you can—that is what the job is all about. Some of the men and women recalled here were blessed with an unusual degree of candor. One highlight was the determination of the 1962–63 Vietnam crew to buck the authorities. But given the time period and the desperateness of the situation, the ability of the Korean War writers to bitterly criticize U.S. unpreparedness was remarkable. The U.S. public did not want to read that American boys threw down their rifles and ran, but this is what Beech, Bigart, Lambert, Higgins, and others told them, along with reports of the successes that followed.

There was great pressure to produce in each time period studied, but it appears that the Moscow group of 1928–29 suffered the worst collective mental agony. There is considerable evidence that they all knew Stalin's excesses were worse than imagined and certainly more than any one of them reported. It is one thing to pillory Duranty, but the fact is that they all failed, for a number of good reasons discussed in Chapter 2. If William Henry Chamberlin had to wait until 1934, when he knew he would not return to Russia, to write an open account of Stalin's crimes, it is easy to see why others were unsuccessful.

Each chapter is filled with the excitement of "scoops," but one of the most dramatic and pressure-packed was Max Jordan's Munich victory over William L. Shirer. Edward R. Murrow may have been the master news organizer, and H. V. Kaltenborn the analyzer, but it was correspondents like Jordan and Shirer, pushing for opinions in the streets and news from the diplomats, who were the real stars of September 1938, just as today's most valuable players are the men and women whose bylines or broadcast sign-offs we quickly forget.

In September 1994 satellite technology allowed CBS's Dan Rather an exclusive live broadcast from Haiti seconds after President Clinton's nationwide address in which he threatened an invasion if military leaders refused to step down. Amazingly enough, Rather was sitting next to Haiti's junta chief, who told the U.S. audience he was not prepared to give in to Clinton's threats. Murrow would have been impressed.

As noted here, freelancers are often some of the most knowledgeable people at the scene of a story. Many a full-timer owes a story tip to a U.S. or local freelance journalist. In the broadcast field, freelance television crews supply a great deal of the work, and radio news would not survive without regular reports from freelancers. Finally, freelancers or "independent" journalists provided the lion's share of the "alternative viewpoint" stories argued for above. These appeared in newspapers like New York's *Village Voice*, Chicago's *In These Times*, and San Francisco's *Bay Guardian,* as well as magazines and journals. Of these the *Village Voice* clearly led the way. Often criticized for being "left-wing" organs, these publications appear to be radical because their coverage clashes with the official Washington line and the editorial stand of most newspapers and broadcast stations. In reality, however, these accounts are jarring because the writers have experienced firsthand the corruption and hypocrisy that underscores U.S. involvement in too many of the world's poverty-stricken areas. They write with the anger and passion of Carleton Beals—and sometimes with a point of view—but in doing so frighten readers and fellow journalists who, in this era of Iran-Contra, BCCI, the fake Star Wars program, and Iraqgate, should be much more skeptical and probing. We have not forgotten the photographers, either. In recent years the daring James Nachtwey's outstanding work in *Time* and other magazines has served as the model for the next generation of overseas photojournalists.

It is interesting to note, however, that the deepest anger about hypocrisy and deception in foreign affairs found in this book came from top-flight establishment journalists. Yes, there are references to the work of Noam Chomsky and Edward Herman, two forceful and articulate critics in the progressive wing, and to Reed Irvine and others on the right. But the most damaging comments about self-censorship and poor media performance came from Sheehan, Halberstam, Parry, and Bonner—*New York Times* and Associated Press, true-blue Establishment. These were the tough, straight-shooting young reporters, sent out to tell the truth, who ended up disillusioned to the core. We can learn from them and should not ignore their criticisms and experiences. Their words remind us of our tradition of news-media criticism, of how that great reporter Will Irwin spoke sharply about the practices of his time, as did George Seldes. We also are reminded of Murrow's warnings about the possibilities for abuse of power in his television field, how the medium could be used to dominate thought (as during the Gulf War) instead of offering true diversity. It should be made clear, however, that not all news managers are ignorant villains. Some print and broadcast executives were correspondents first, and most have some overseas travel experience.

Nevertheless, one theme running through the correspondents' experiences was the sense of provincialism at home and too often in their own newsroom. From the classic United Press cable of 1914, "Simms down hold warscare upplay Caillaux" to the CNN anchor desk's suspicious questioning of their own Peter Arnett in Baghdad, those at the home end have irritated their roving colleagues. Sometimes there is an honest difference of opinion; field reporters easily can think they are producing the only important story. But like those correspondents who filed stories to please the desk—and it is silly to think that the desk should not be pleased—some editors heard imaginary footsteps up in the executive suite and edited or arranged stories accordingly. That's human nature, but it is not good journalism.

Looking into the future, here are some suggestions. There should be continued concern about the financial strength of the world's four largest press associations. While the Associated Press was running strong, United Press International was on its deathbed. Its demise would leave a giant hole for those who believe in competition. Fortunately, the checks and balances system works when papers receive syndicated reports from the New York Times Service, the Los Angeles Times–Washington Post Service, the Knight News Tribune (KNT) wire, and others. But the old competitive idea of a "deadline every minute" was gone. There should be scrutiny of the diversification of resources within Reuters to greatly boost its financial services at the expense of the news division and of financial problems within Agence France-Presse (AFP), the large French agency. After all, many U.S. outlets get supplementary foreign news from the British and the French.[4]

This means that major newspapers and broadcast organizations will have to find ways to increase the number of foreign correspondents. The CIA ran into trouble by not having enough agents "on the ground with the people." The news business has the same problem and it will get worse if future managers opt to pool resources and cut back on the volume. There are some big storms brewing in a world divided by economics and tradition. The rich-versus-poor, North-versus-South problem is easy to see. But West-versus-The Rest is harder to imagine. From China to Iran, this involves an insistence that the West, including its media, understand and respect differences in religion, culture, and lifestyle. Coping with fundamentalism in the Islamic World is part of this picture. Dealing with the Chinese in 1997, when they assume control over Hong Kong, is another; avoiding conflicts with North Korea and Iran fits in too. The relationship with Russia and the former Republics is in its beginning stage, fraught with peril. Europe is at a crossroads: economically strapped, crammed with refugees, and lacking military credibility. Central America could flare up at a moment's notice; the end of war brought only more instability. U.S. trade with Latin American nations is bringing more wealth but only to large companies, as the poor continue to be left behind.

There also should be more discussion about the possible influence of news technology on foreign policy and military decisions and the responsibilities carried by both government and media personnel. Two recent examples make the point. Television pictures from Mogadishu in 1993 showed laughing Somalians dragging the body of a dead U.S. soldier along a street and caused an immediate national cry to bring U.S. forces home. Walter Goodman of the *New York Times*, reflecting on how such horrible images can erase the complexity of issues, wrote: "What sort of policy making is it to have Washington's actions decided, even in part, on the latest affecting pictures on the evening news?"[5] The swiftness of television reports, particularly over Cable News Network, certainly gives government planners far less time for maneuvering. This works both ways, of course. During the Haitian crisis of 1994, former President Jimmy Carter gave an interview to CNN before he briefed President Clinton on his negotiating mission, knowing full well that Haitian leaders would be watching. He used the opportunity to offer moderate comments, trying to offset heavy criticism of the Haitian leadership made by President Clinton the previous evening. On the positive side, the television networks did not broadcast the lift-off of U.S. planes headed for Haiti, even though their powerful zoom lenses gave them the pictures. Here they drew the line in favor of protecting U.S. lives.

Despite an occasional buildup of crisis atmosphere, there is reason to believe that America has been disengaging from the confusing world scene for some time and if allowed would continue to do so. Almost a decade ago the journalist Sanford J. Ungar wrote: "The United States is estranged from that complex world—separate, aloof, more alone than even the most cynical or pessimistic observers might have predicted in the heyday of American postwar power. The symptoms are obvious everywhere . . . Although it often emerges in the form of bravado or contempt for others, the unease is also deeply felt inside the United States. It is a phenomenon that extends across party and ideological lines."[6] Nothing has changed in intervening years. Results of a 1994 poll by the Times Mirror Center described the public as "angry, self-absorbed and unanchored politically," with a deepening distrust of the federal government.[7]

The author carried a sense of this growing disenchantment while on a trip to Yugoslavia in December 1991, for interviews with President Milosevic of Serbia and Tudjman of Croatia. My *Village Voice* lead called for the sending of United Nations peacekeepers to Bosnia before the war spread there. It was not hard to imagine that happening, and a few months later it did. But there was a sense of futility in that story opening, as if it were clear the United States would not flex its moral muscles. In late 1994 the Balkan story was far from over, but the work of a number of outstanding correspondents seemed to fly into the wind, like this *Newsweek* piece by the trustworthy Charles Lane in besieged Mostar, Bosnia:

> "You want to see hell, Mister?" Dzevad asks. "Come, I'll show you hell." He steps gingerly down a staircase into the pitch-black basement of a ruined apartment building in the Muslim held eastern quarter of Mostar, southern Bosnia. Sniper fire and mortar rounds rattle and boom in the distance. As we round a corner, the dull glow of a red lamp breaks through the midnight gloom. There, on the floor of a tiny four-room cellar, 100 haggard Muslim refugees—women, children and old men—lie huddled together, trying to sleep . . . "Because of our religion they took our houses, our cars and our property," moans one old woman. "And now we are refugees."[8]

Given the temptation to fall into isolationist patterns, it was heartening to read a six-page memo from Bernard Gwertzman, of the *New York Times*, to his foreign staff, written in November 1992, "in a year when Americans clearly signaled that they had largely decided to turn inwards." Giving an "unambiguous yes" to the question of whether foreign news still was important to the *Times*, he said:

> In many ways, we are asking more and no less from our correspondents, even though the proportion of front page hard news stories from

overseas may have dropped in the past year . . . What is new is not that we are covering foreign news less, but that we have to cover it differently. We have to be as flexible and multi-talented a corps of editors and correspondents as ever existed . . .

The television networks in the United States have in effect given up trying to cover overseas news on a regular basis. It may be a vestige of the past, but we still want to be first with the most important news around the world. Scoops will be rewarded . . . Every correspondent must make a very major effort to become literate in economic affairs . . . I suspect that in coming years this will be a prerequisite for becoming not only a foreign correspondent but a local one as well.[9]

Urging a new degree of diversity in reports from individual countries, he said, "We are interested in what makes societies different, what is on the minds of the people in different regions. Imagine you are being asked to write a letter home every week to describe a different aspect of life in the area you are assigned." The spirit of this memo was undoubtedly shared by many print and broadcast foreign-desk chiefs. Only time would tell if there was enough of an industrywide commitment to maintain and diversify the foreign news flow.

The memo also serves as a challenge to those in journalism education to further internationalize their curricula, to stress language skills and economic knowledge, and to push harder than ever for strong writing skills. Members of the Association for Education in Journalism and Mass Communications (AEJMC), their allies in the nation's community college system, and other instructors who produce more than half of the nation's print and broadcast journalists have the increased responsibility of preparing all students better in the international area. It is hoped that more will go into journalism's foreign service or at least be better prepared to handle foreign news coming into the newsroom.

This assessment of the current state and future of foreign correspondence may seem gloomy. But occasionally something happens to offer reassurance that we will continue to be represented in a timely fashion by men and women of high standards. I looked for some of those examples for this book's ending. It was refreshing to read that the dedicated Christiane Amanpour, cited for her outstanding Gulf War and Bosnian coverage, turned down more lucrative offers from three rival networks to stay with CNN, where she was comfortable with her story assignments and airtime. It also was gratifying to see a foreign correspondent in high demand instead of an television anchor, entertainment star, or athlete.

Then a story appeared that revived images about the ideals that we've been stressing in this book: assuming personal risk; teaming with observant editors to alert the public about a distant event which at the moment might have little apparent interest to readers and viewers; noting contradictions; and poking holes in conventional wisdom. This story was transmitted from Rwanda, where uncounted thousands had been slaughtered in a civil war that the world's major governments and media systems generally ignored until the French sent in forces in June 1994. It was written by Raymond Bonner and the headline brought reminders of his El Salvador adventures: "Grisly Discovery in Rwanda Leads French to Widen Role."[10]

> Bisesero, Rwanda, June 30—Four hundred sick and frail Tutsi, including scores of people suffering from grenade, machete and gunshot wounds, were rescued today from marauding Hutu forces near this town in western Rwanda . . .
>
> The carnage is another reminder that despite the recent French intervention, killings of Tutsi go on. Some American and human rights organizations have called the massacres genocide . . . It was not until journalists alerted French troops to the ragtag band of 400 that a patrol was dispatched. The French soldiers were clearly unprepared for what they found . . . "This is not what we were led to believe," said a non-commissioned officer at the French camp in Bisesero. "We were told Tutsi were killing Hutu, and now this."

Bonner's stories from these new killing fields were featured throughout the summer, often on page one. In time Rwanda's pain finally was registered so that thousands of lives were saved by a U.S. airlift and the work of international agencies. Some credit for this must go to Bonner and his colleagues, who risked sickness and death to witness one of the worst human disasters of the century. The tragedy grew to such proportions, with more than two million persons fleeing to neighboring lands, and the scenes of starvation and disease were so ugly, that veteran journalists were, in the words of ABC's Ted Koppel, "shattered" by their experiences. Once the television crews arrived in Africa the home audience got a look at what the print journalists had been describing.

John Balzar of the *Los Angeles Times* joined the press corps in the camps and, like Bonner and others, left behind a string of memorable stories. From all of his words these stand out as evidence of what it is like to be a foreign correspondent:

> Much has been written about the dead in this horrible scene, perhaps so much as to numb the senses . . . the smell, the teeming crush, the sickness, the pawing children who want only attention, the long fast slide

from civilization churn up a dizziness that no Dramamine can prevent. The impulse to flee climbs up the neck.

So a visitor climbs into a dirty car, engulfed by refugees. The driver screeches on the horn . . . but the way is blocked by a pile of lava boulders. From out of the crowd two skinny, barefoot boys in filthy rags dart forth. Together they lift the razor-sharp rocks from the car's path and then instantly blend back into the crowd. Inexplicably, those in so much need of help still found help to give.[11]

It was one more occasion when a foreign correspondent had a front-row seat to the world.

Notes

NOTE FOR THE INTRODUCTION

[1]James McCartney, "Rallying around the Flag," *American Journalism Review* (September 1994), p. 42. McCartney, a syndicated columnist for Knight-Ridder Newspapers, covered the Cuban missile crisis for the *Chicago Daily News*. Similar media criticism is found in Ken Silverstein's "Follow the Leader," *American Journalism Review* (November 1993). "The media's approach lets the president frame the nation's foreign policy agenda for the Third World. It also misinforms the public and undermines democratic policy-making . . . " (p. 31). Silverstein was an Associated Press reporter in Rio de Janeiro from 1989 to 1993.

NOTES FOR CHAPTER ONE

[1]Mark Sullivan, *Our Times* (New York: Scribner's Sons, 1932), vol. 4, pp. 5–9.

[2]Paul Scott Mowrer, *The House of Europe* (Boston: Houghton Mifflin Co., 1945), pp. 217–21.

[3]*Los Angeles Times*, June 29, 1914, p. 1.

[4]William D. Bowman, *The Story of The Times* (London: Geo. Routledge & Sons, Ltd., 1931), pp. 42–47.

[5]Edmond Taylor, *The Fall of the Dynasties* (Garden City, N.Y.: Doubleday and Company, Inc., 1963), pp. 1–2.

[6]*New York Herald*, July 19, 1914, p. 1.

[7]*New York Herald*, July 22, 1914, p. 10.

[8]*New York Herald*, June 28, 1914, p. 9 III.

[9]*New York Herald*, July 16, 1914, p. 10; July 18, 1914, p. 9; July 20, 1914, p. 9.

[10]*New York Herald*, July 28, 1914, p. 8.

[11]Joe Alex Morris, *Deadline Every Minute* (Garden City, N.Y.: Doubleday and Company, Inc., 1957), p. 61.

[12]*New York American*, July 14, 1914, p. 8.

[13]Linda Enochman, University of Minnesota journalism history student, unpublished manuscript, summer 1967.

[14]*New York American*, July 16, 1914, p. 8.

[15]Frederic William Wile, *News Is Where You Find It* (Indianapolis: Bobbs-Merrill Co., 1939), p. 239.

[16]Mowrer, *The House of Europe*, pp. 165–66.

[17]Will Irwin, *The Making of a Reporter*, (New York: G. P. Putnam's Sons, 1942), p. 244.

[18]Ibid., pp. 244–45.

[19]James W. Barrett, *Joseph Pulitzer and His World* (New York: Vanguard Press, 1941), p. 345.

[20]Irwin, *Making of a Reporter*, p. 244.

[21]Ibid., p. 245.

[22]Theodore E. Kruglak, *The Foreign Correspondents* (Geneva, 1955), p. 55.

[23]Reuters (1851) still exists; Agency Havas (1836) became Agence France-Presse after World War II; Wolff (1849) was replaced after the Nazis's 1933 takeover of all media. The AP did not escape entirely from the cartel's restrictive clauses until 1934, allowing rival United Press (1907) to make big inroads in Latin America and Asia. United Press became UPI in 1958, when it merged with International News Service (1909).

[24]Kent Cooper, *Kent Cooper and the Associated Press* (New York: Random House, 1959), p. 64.

[25]Irwin, *Making of a Reporter*, pp. 242–43.

[26]Philip Knightley, *The First Casualty* (New York: Harcourt Brace Jovanovich, 1975).

[27]J. L. Hammond, *C. P. Scott of the Manchester Guardian* (New York: Harcourt Brace and Co., 1934), p. 173.

[28]Ibid., p. 179.

[29]Wile, *News Is Where You Find It*, p. 252.

[30]The most authoritative work on Bell is James D. Startt's *Journalism's Unofficial Ambassador* (Athens: Ohio University Press, 1979). This biography of Bell, 1869 to 1943, gives full treatment to Bell's outstanding reporting and news organization during WW I, including his detailed correspondence with colleagues and political figures. He was a man of high integrity and enormous news-gathering skills.

[31]This argument raged during the war and immediately afterward as "revisionism" began. Harvard historian Sidney Bradshaw Fay (*The Origins of the World War*, New York: Macmillan Company, 1930) summed up the original revisionists' arguments when he cited documents from 1919 and the 1920s that contradicted the general assumption that Germany and Austria should receive exclusive blame. He said all major powers contributed in significant ways to the mobilizations. Later a highly significant work by German historian Fritz Fischer (*Germany's Aims in the First World War*, W. W. Norton Company, Inc., 1961, English translation 1967) documented Germany's plans for world domination beginning with her pre-1914 policies.

[32]Wile, *News Is Where You Find It*, p. 129.

[33]Ibid., p. 132.

[34]*New York Times*, June 27, 1914, p. 3.

[35]*New York Times*, June 29, 1914, p. 2.

[36]Wile, *News Is Where You Find It*, p. 246.

[37]Ibid., p. 246.

[38]Ibid., p. 249.

[39]Ibid., pp. 251–52.

[40]Ibid., p. 253.

[41]*Chicago Tribune*, June 28, 1914, p. 1 II.

[42]*Chicago Tribune*, July 12, 19, 26 and August 2, 1914, p. 1 II.

[43]Mowrer, *House of Europe*, pp. 128–30.

[44]Ibid., p. 70.

[45]Ibid., p. 137.

[46]*Chicago Daily News*, July 24, 1914, p. 3.

[47]Mowrer, *House of Europe*, pp. 223–24.

[48]Irwin, *Making of a Reporter*, pp. 204–05.

[49]E. Alexander Powell, *Adventure Road* (New York: Doubleday and Company, Inc., 1954), pp. 141–43.

[50]Ibid., p. 144.

[51]Nicholas Roosevelt, *A Front Row Seat* (Norman: University of Oklahoma Press, 1953), pp. 57–58.

[52]H. V. Kaltenborn, *Fifty Fabulous Years* (New York: G. P. Putnam's Sons, 1950), pp. 75–76.

[53]Willis J. Abbot, *Watching the World Go By* (Boston: Little, Brown and Company, 1933), pp. 301–04.

[54]Frederick Palmer, *With My Own Eyes* (Indianapolis: Bobbs-Merrill Company, 1932), p. 298.

[55]Emmet Crozier, *American Reporters on the Western Front, 1914–1918* (New York: Oxford University Press, 1959), p. 16.

[56]Wythe Williams, *Dusk of Empire* (New York: Charles Scribner's Sons, 1937), pp. 1–4. Also see his *Passed by the Censor* (New York: Dutton, 1916).

[57]Barbara Tuchman, *The Guns of August*, p. 1.

[58]Williams, *Dusk of Empire*, p. 9.

[59]A number of key persons on major newspaper staffs were Europeans. Ernest Marshall was assisted by Orton Tewson, also an Englishman but one who had worked in New York. Fred Grundy of the *Sun* was a Britisher, but his assistant was a Bostonian named Ambrose Lambert. Another Englishman, George Allison, was an assistant on the *Herald* and later became Hearst's European chief.

[60]Williams, *Dusk of Empire*, pp. 24–30.

[61]Ibid., pp. 37–39. Historian George Malcolm Thomson said Caillaux could have regained the premiership, that there would have been an end to Poincaré's personal diplomacy, the Russians would have been discouraged from their fatal mobilization, the English would have looked with suspicion at the other Entente members, and Caillaux—an arrogant, brilliant, unscrupulous man—would have tried to repeat his 1911 success of the Agadir crisis. Thomson, *The Twelve Days* (New York: G. P. Putnam's Sons, 1964), p. 98.

[62]Sidney Fay, *Origins of the World War* (New York: Macmillan Co., 1930), vol. 2, pp. 183–290.

[63]*New York American*, July 23, 1914, p. 8.

[64]*New York World*, July 19, 1914, p. 5E.

[65]*New York World*, July 24, 1914, p. 3.

[66]*New York Herald*, July 24, 1914, p. 10.

[67]*Chicago Tribune*, July 24, 1914, p. 1.

[68]*Times of London*, July 24, 1914, p. 7. As further illustration of the press's shortcomings, consider the following: The *San Francisco Chronicle*, the most distinguished newspaper in the West, carried only one short story pertaining to the crisis between July 7 and July 25; that was on July 9, when it was reported that Berlin police were investigating members of the Servia Students Club for possible Pan-Slavism conspiracies. Surveys of the *Minneapolis Tribune* show that the ultimatum came as a complete surprise and that in this interval this member paper did not publish any European news from the AP related to the oncoming crisis. The *Chicago Herald* and the *Baltimore Sun* paid no attention. Wile's July 22 dispatch was the only hint that *New York Times* readers received. The *Chicago Daily News* was worried about its coverage of the Chicago delegation investigating European railroad terminals, and the *Chicago Tribune* was content to run Wile's two-week-old feature stories. The only major American magazine that tried to interpret European events at this time was the *Literary Digest*, which in April 1914 commented on the Russo-German press war and some mobilization of Russian troops for duty on the Western front. The *Digest* also reprinted articles from leading European newspapers. *Collier's* first comment on the war situation came on August 15, when an editorial read: "Aside from such reflections as may be uttered upon our happy immunity from Europe's war, we know nothing to say upon the crisis more important than the following words." The magazine offered advice from an English economist who said this was America's chance to prosper, selling food and supplies to European nations.

[69]*New York Times*, July 24, 1914, p. 1.

[70]*Times of London*, July 24, 1914, p. 8.

[71]*New York Times*, July 24, 1914, p. 1.

[72]Taylor, *Fall of the Dynasties*, pp. 211–12.

[73]Ibid., pp. 218–19.

[74]*New York Times*, July 26, 1914, p. 1.

[75]Ibid.

[76]Tuchman, *Guns of August*, p. 25.

[77]*New York Times*, August 1, 1914, p. 1.

[78]*New York World*, August 1, 1914, p. 1.

[79]*New York Times*, August 1, 1914, p. 1.

[80]Tuchman, *Guns of August*, pp. 115–22.

[81]Williams, *Dusk of Empire*, p. 50.

[82]*Chicago Tribune*, August 1, 1914, p. 1.

[83]*Chicago Daily News*, August 4, 1914, p. 3.
[84]*Chicago Daily News*, August 3, 1914, p. 4.
[85]Mowrer, *House of Europe*, pp. 251–52.
[86]Crozier, *American Reporters*, p. 14.
[87]Palmer, *With My Own Eyes*, pp. 300–37; Crozier, *American Reporters*, p. 73.
[88]*New York World*, August 9, 1914, p. 3; *New York Times*, August 9, 1914, p. 3;
Wile, *News Is Where You Find It*, pp. 292–309.
[89]Irwin, *Making of a Reporter*, pp. 209–22.
[90]Crozier, *American Reporters*, p. 46.
[91]Ibid., p. 44.
[92]Irwin, *Making of a Reporter*, p. 227; Crozier, *American Reporters*, p. 42.
[93]Irwin, *Making of a Reporter*, pp. 225–36.
[94]*New York Tribune*, August 24, 1914; Sullivan, *Our Times*, pp. 21–26. Frederick
Palmer wanted to see the Germans move through Brussels, too, but since he was the
only American accredited with the British Army, he risked capture as a spy. "But you
have the job that will pan out," Davis told him. "I wish I had it. Good luck." With that
Davis went to collect an all-time story. "He was like that," Palmer wrote. Palmer, *With
My Own Eyes*, pp. 304–05.
[95]*New York Tribune*, August 31, 1914; Sullivan, *Our Times*, pp. 28–29.
[96]Hohenberg, *Foreign Correspondence*, p. 220.
[97]Joseph Mathews, *Reporting the Wars* (Minneapolis: University of Minnesota Press,
1957), p. 169. In the final days of the war Martin Egan, the 1904–05 colleague of
Palmer, Davis, and others, asked if he could go under enemy fire. Palmer took him—the
last time he was to see action. Palmer, *With My Own Eyes*, pp. 375–76.

NOTES FOR CHAPTER TWO

[1]*Time*, October 13, 1967, p. 104 (Gilmore's obituary; the 32–year AP veteran died
at age 60 of a heart attack in England).
[2]Walter Duranty, *I Write As I Please* (New York: Halcyon House, 1935), pp. 5–6.
[3]George F. Kennan, *Russia and the West* (Boston: Little, Brown and Company,
1961), pp. 64–79.
[4]Eugene Lyons, ed., *We Cover the World* (New York: Harcourt, Brace and
Company, 1937), p. 76.
[5]Lyons, *We Cover the World*, p. 184. Correspondents Bessie Beatty and Rheta
Childe Dorr covered the Revolution and its aftermath. See Zena Beth McGlashan,
"Women Witness the Russian Revolution: Analyzing Ways of Seeing," *Journalism
History* XII (Summer 1985).
[6]Lyons, *We Cover the World*, p. 76.
[7]Duranty, *I Write As I Please*, p. 14.
[8]Robert Desmond, *The Press and World Affairs* (New York: D. Appleton-Century
Company, 1937), p. 265. Also see Arthur Ransome, *Crisis in Russia* (New York: B. W.
Huebsch, Inc., 1921).
[9]Emery and Emery, *The Press and America* (Englewood Cliffs, N.J.: Prentice-Hall,
Inc., 1992), p. 262.
[10]Walter Lippmann and Charles Merz, "A Test of the News," *New Republic*
supplement, August 4, 1920.
[11]*News Agencies: Their Structure and Operation* (UNESCO, 1953), p. 56.
[12]Desmond, *The Press and World Affairs*, pp. 270–71. The first press "decree"
appeared on October 27, 1917, announcing the closing of opposition newspapers.
Lenin supervised the liquidation of the bourgeois press, Stalin expanded the control,
and censorship of dispatches was included from the beginning. Also, pp. 78–79 of the
unpublished "Mass Communication in East European Countries," prepared by Dr. G.
H. Mond, Institut Français de Presse, visiting professor at University of Minnesota,
1967.

[13]Edwin L. Hullinger, "Battling for News in Soviet Russia," *Editor & Publisher*, January 7, 1922; F. A. McKenzie, "Getting the News Out of Soviet Russia," *Editor & Publisher*, March 7, 1925.

[14]Isaac Deutscher, *Stalin* (New York: Vintage, 1961), pp. 313–14.

[15]Duranty, *I Write As I Please*, pp. 122–25.

[16]Ibid., pp. 166–67.

[17]Ibid.

[18]Ibid.

[19]S. J. Taylor, *Stalin's Apologist: Walter Duranty, The New York Times' Man in Moscow* (New York: Oxford University Press, 1990).

[20]James William Crowl, *Angels in Stalin's Paradise* (Washington, D.C.: University Press of America, 1982), p. 43. Whitman Bassow briefly makes similar criticisms about Duranty's early 1930s coverage in his *Moscow Correspondents* (New York: Morrow, 1988). He claims (p. 71) that "the first comprehensive report on the famine" was done by Chamberlin in 1934 after he had left Russia for good.

[21]Crowl, *Angels in Stalin's Paradise*. See pp. 2–3 for analysis of inferiority and p. 199 for charges that Duranty was allowed to remain at his post because of the alleged incompetence of his boss, Edwin L. James, chief of European correspondents.

[22]Emery and Emery, *The Press and America*, p. 314. Also see section on Duranty and the Mowrer brothers, pp. 313–16, with mention of other foreign correspondents active in the 1920s and 1930s.

[23]Crowl, *Angels in Stalin's Paradise*, pp. 166–67.

[24]Duranty, *I Write As I Please*, pp. 198–200.

[25]Walter Duranty, *The Kremlin and the People* (New York: Reynal & Hitchcock, Inc., 1941), p. 34.

[26]Robert C. Tucker, *Stalin As Revolutionary, 1879–1929* (New York: W. W. Norton Co., 1973), p. 283. In a chapter on Stalin's conflicts with Lenin, Tucker speculated that Lenin's death freed Stalin from fear of his power. Lenin was the most important person in Stalin's life—there was deep hero-worship—and his passing allowed the widely reported public veneration that for subconscious reasons maintained the intimate tie and lay the groundwork for Stalin's own cult.

[27]Duranty, *I Write As I Please*, pp. 95–96.

[28]Robert Payne, *The Rise and Fall of Stalin* (New York: Avon Books, 1965), pp. 410–12.

[29]Tucker, *Stalin as Revolutionary*, p. 420.

[30]Deutscher, *Stalin*, pp. 312–22.

[31]Duranty, *I Write As I Please*, p. 287.

[32]*New York Times*, October 21, 1928, p. 3 III.

[33]*New York Times*, October 21, 1928, p. 15.

[34]Hryhory Kostiuk, *Stalinist Rule in the Ukraine* (New York: Praeger, 1953). This work is an authoritative study of the years 1929–29 and would help with understanding the post–Cold War situation there. Robert Payne, in *The Rise and Fall of Stalin* (New York: Avon, 1966), cited the incredible figure of 10 million peasants and 120 million horses, cattle, pigs, and sheep as the loss suffered by Russia during the collectivization period, mainly from 1929 through 1934 (p. 417). The livestock statistics were from an official handbook; the exact number of peasants killed, starved, or put in prison camps will never be known.

[35]*New York Times*, November 1, 1928, p. 14.

[36]*New York Times*, November 5, 1928, p. 16.

[37]Kostiuk, *Stalinist Rule*, pp. 8–9, 33–34.

[38]*New York Times*, December 4, 1928, p. 9.

[39]*New York Times*, December 9, 1928, p. 3 III.

[40]*New York Times*, December 16, 1928, p. 5 II.

[41]*New York Times*, December 23, 1928, p. 3 III.

[42]*New York Times*, January 1, 1929, p. 1; January 5, 1929, p. 6.

[43]*New York Times*, January 1, 1929, p. 1.

[44]*New York Times*, January 13, 1929, p. 4 III.

[45]*New York Times*, January 6, 1929, p. 19.

[46]*New York Times*, January 12, 1929, p. 12.

[47]Dorothy Thompson, *The New Russia* (New York: Henry Holt & Co., 1928). The greater part of this book appeared as a series of articles in the *New York Evening Post*. She covered the Tenth Anniversary celebration on November 7, checked notes with journalists like Junius Wood of the *Chicago Daily News* and Paul Scheffer of the *Berliner Tageblatt*, and completed a whirlwind trip.

[48]Duranty, *I Write As I Please*, p. 298. For an explanation of practical reasons why Stalin may have been preparing his people for future sacrifices, while moving clumsily and crudely with Lenin's program, see Theodore Von Lane, *Why Lenin? Why Stalin?* (London: Weidenfeld and Nicolson, 1966), pp. 208–17.

[49]Duranty, *I Write As I Please*, pp. 277–78.

[50]Negley Farson, *The Way of a Transgressor* (New York: Harcourt, Brace & Company, 1936), pp. 394–97.

[51]Ibid., pp. 530–31.

[52]*Chicago Daily News*, December 3, 1928, p. 2.

[53]Farson, *Way of a Transgressor*, pp. 514–15.

[54]*Chicago Daily News*, December 4, 1928, p. 2.

[55]*Chicago Daily News*, December 5, 1928, p. 2.

[56]*Chicago Daily News*, December 7, 1928, p. 2.

[57]*Chicago Daily News*, December 6, 1928, p. 2.

[58]*Chicago Daily News*, December 11, 1928, p.2.

[59]*Chicago Daily News*, January 7, 1929, p. 2; January 12, p. 2.

[60]*Chicago Daily News*, January 25, 1929, p. 2.

[61]*Chicago Daily News*, January 28, 1929, p. 2.

[62]Others made important contributions in Moscow during 1928–29. Eugene Lyons manned the United Press desk from 1928 to 1934. For the Associated Press, Jim Mills was chief from 1924 to 1926; Walter Whiffen returned (he had served from 1914 to 1917) for the 1926–28 period but died; William Reswick continued through 1929.

[63]*Christian Science Monitor*, January 5, 1929, p. 1. While Duranty had trouble making page one and in fact did not get past page two during the period of study, Chamberlin did receive at least a few page-one placements.

[64]*Christian Science Monitor*, January 7, 1929, p. 12.

[65]American magazines apparently most interested in Stalin were *Living Age* and *Literary Digest*. Between 1924 and 1928 each ran three articles, and from 1929 to 1932 nine more appeared, another deadlock. *Collier's* offered a seven-part series running from December 1931 through January 1932, that magazine's total contribution during the nine-year period. "Red Czar" was the title. They, like most of the other articles, focused on Stalin the man of mystery, man of steel, Russia's strongman who emerged from the political struggle with Trotsky. *Current History* ran five articles on Stalin over the period. *The Nation* magazine had one article, *New Republic* had two, *World's Work* had one, *Foreign Affairs* had one. Pictures of Stalin were rare, too. As far as can be determined, approximately only a half-dozen appeared in U.S. publications between 1924 and 1928. Perhaps a dozen were run between 1929 and 1932. The majority of these were in the limited-circulation, more intellectual type of magazine or journal, such as *Current History, Outlook and Independent*, or *Review of Reviews*.

[66]Jerome Davis, "Joseph Stalin—Russia's Ruler Today," *Current History*, March 1929, 29:961–68; M. A. Aldanov, "Stalin," *Contemporary Review*, May 1928, 133:605–12; *Living Age*, February 1929, 335:420–22.

[67]W. H. Chamberlin, "Peasant Progress in Soviet Russia," *Current History*, October 1925, 23:82–88.

[68]Chamberlin, "Djugashvili, Alias Stalin, New Ruler of Russia," *The Literary Digest*, August 7, 1926, 90:42–44. Chamberlin's "Stalin, Heir of Lenin" was published in *Asia*, July 1926.

[69]W. H. Chamberlin, *The Russian Enigma* (New York: Charles Scribner's Sons, 1944), p. 19.

[70]Louis Fischer, "Who's Who in Soviet Russia," *Current History*, June 1925, 22:392–401.

[71]Fischer, "The Passing of Trotsky," *The Nation*, December 1927, 125:703–05. Fischer, "Why Stalin Won," *The Nation*, August 1930, 131:174–76.

[72]Stalin talked to few foreign journalists. He met with Japanese newsmen in 1926 and again in the 1930s, dates unknown; Fischer's group in 1927; Anne O'Hare McCormick on September 9, 1927; three newsmen in the fall of 1930. First was Eugene Lyons of the United Press ("Stalin Interview Won After Year's Work," *Editor & Publisher*, November 29, 1930), and then Walter Duranty, on December 1, 1930. Duranty said Stalin opened up "thrice" that month, indicating that another writer had gained an interview (see *Duranty Reports Russia*, New York: Viking Press, 1934, p. 235). German author Emil Ludwig had a three-hour interview on December 13, 1931 (see Payne, *The Rise and Fall of Stalin*, p. 429). Roy W. Howard of the United Press was granted an interview on March 1, 1936. The renowned interviewer Edward Price Bell never interviewed Stalin. The last man to be granted direct information was James Reston of the *New York Times*, whose typed questions were answered on a sheet signed "Stalin" in 1953, shortly before the dictator's death. Eugene Lyons (*Stalin Czar of All the Russias*, New York: J. B. Lippincott Co., 1940), p. 197, claimed that up to 1940 the only foreign photographer allowed a private close-up shot was James E. Abbe, an American. The date was not known.

The full account of Fischer's interview was published in pamphlet form by the Workers' Library, New York; this was called the first American Trade Union delegation, and others present in addition to those mentioned in the text were Frank Palmer, editor of *The Colorado Labor Advocate*; James Fitzpatrick, president of Actors and Artists of America; and Albert Coyle, executive secretary of the All-American Cooperative Commission. Matthew Woll, AFL vice president, commented on it in the February 1928 *Current History*, p. 691.

[73]Louis Fischer, *The Life and Death of Stalin* (New York: Harper and Brothers, Publishers, 1953), pp. 100–106.

[74]Ibid., p. 106.

[75]Fischer, "The Passing of Trotsky," *The Nation*, December 1927.

[76]Fischer, *The Life and Death of Stalin*, pp. 21–22.

[77]Sherwood Eddy, *The Challenges of Russia* (New York: Farrar & Rinehart, Inc., 1931), p. viii.

[78]Eddy, *Challenges of Russia*, p. 129.

[79]Ibid., pp. 13–14.

[80]Desmond, *Press and World Affairs*, p. 274.

[81]*Chicago Tribune*, January 25, 1929, p. 19.

[82]As reported in *The Literary Digest*, January 14, 1928, p. 19.

[83]*Time*, February 11, 1929, p. 25.

NOTES FOR CHAPTER THREE

[1]The German ambitions are explained in enormous and engrossing detail by John W. Wheeler-Bennett, *Munich: Prologue to Tragedy* (New York: Duell, Sloan and Pearce, 1963).

[2]H. Stuart Hughes, *Contemporary Europe: A History* (Englewood Cliffs, N. J.: Prentice Hall Inc., 1961), p. 298.

[3]Winston S. Churchill, *The Gathering Storm* (Boston: Houghton Mifflin Co., 1948), p. 287.

[4]Arthur S. Link, *American Epoch* (New York: Alfred A. Knopf, 1959), p. 63.

[5]Ibid., p. 464.

[6]Emery and Emery, *The Press and America* (Englewood Cliffs, N.J.: Prentice Hall Inc., 1992). For the development of overseas news operations, including Munich coverage, see pages 322, 325–27. See also, Mitchell V. Charnley, *News by Radio* (New York: Macmillan Co., 1948), and Sydney W. Head and Christopher Sterling, *Broadcasting in America*, 5th ed. (Boston: Houghton Mifflin, 1987). For a compact history of early radio news and the development of the foreign coverage, see David H. Hosley, *As Good as Any: Foreign Correspondence on Radio, 1930–40* Westport, Conn.: Greenwood Press), 1984. The author provides excellent biographical information on the important participants, a number of whom were interviewed.

[7]*World Almanac,* 1939, p. 430.

[8]*Life,* September 26, 1938, p. 24 (Lynn Fontanne, one of several personalities returning from Europe).

[9]H. V. Kaltenborn, *I Broadcast the Crisis* (New York: Random House, 1938), p. 23. NBC used a "phone" for the airing of a two-way conversation as an anniversary stunt in 1935, but it was CBS broadcaster Kaltenborn who successfully used the device after the crisis progressed. See Francis Chase, *Sound and Fury* (New York: Harpers & Brothers Publishers, 1942), p. 168. Otherwise the CBS system consisted of consecutive reports from various capitals. The radio telephone itself was put into use in 1927, and in 1930 the *New York Times,* AP, and INS used it for covering the Argentine revolution. On March 12, 1935, Webb Miller of UP became the first to radio-telephone a story from Europe to Japan, which went from London to Tokyo. By 1937 photographs were transmitted between continents. Press Wireless, Inc. began to operate on transoceanic bands September 15, 1929. Original members were the *Chicago Tribune, Chicago Daily News, Christian Science Monitor, Los Angeles Times,* and *San Francisco Chronicle.* Hearst papers obtained independent bands that same year. See Robert Desmond, *The Press and World Affairs* (New York: D. Appleton-Century Co., 1937), pp. 128–37.

[10]William L. Shirer, *Berlin Diary* (New York: Alfred Knopf, 1941), pp. 126–27.

[11]*New York Times,* September 13, 1938, p. 1.

[12]*World's Press News,* September 15, 1938, p. 3.

[13]Kaltenborn, *I Broadcast the Crisis,* p. 25.

[14]Ibid., p. 34.

[15]Francis Chase, *Sound and Fury* (New York: Harper and Brothers, 1942), p. 163.

[16]Paul W. White, *News on the Air* (New York: Harcourt, Brace and Co., 1947), pp. 45–46.

[17]Despite the public demand for news during the Munich Crisis, when Murrow, Shirer, and Thomas Grandin met in London in June 1939, they were the entire CBS European staff. In the next few weeks they persuaded foreign broadcast directors, prospective staff members and "stringers" to be ready at the outbreak of war. One of these was Eric Sevareid, then working days for the Paris *Herald* and nights for United Press. "I don't know very much about your experience," Murrow told him, "but I like the way you write and I like your ideas. There's only Shirer, Grandin and myself now but I think this thing may develop into something."

Among other correspondents in Europe during the crisis: Ferdinand Kuhn Jr. was the *Times* man in London, Guido Enderis was also stationed in Berlin, Arnaldo Cortesi was in Rome, Clarence Streit held the Geneva post, P. J. Philip was in Paris, and Emil Vadnay (the former Austrian soldier who had guarded the dead Archduke's body) and G. E. R. Gedye reported from Prague. Alex Small was the *Chicago Tribune* correspondent in Prague, Edmond Taylor was in Paris, David Darrah went to London after being expelled from Mussolini's Italy, Donald Day was still in Riga, and Sam Brewer was in London.

Paul Scott Mowrer had returned to America in 1934 to become editor of the *Chicago Daily News,* but his brother Edgar Ansel and son, Richard, carried on for him in Paris. William Stoneman was the London correspondent, M. W. Fodor and John T. Whitaker would be in Prague during the crisis, and Frank Smothers was in Rome.

The *New York Herald Tribune* boasted of Walter B. Kerr in Prague, John Elliott in

Paris, and Joseph Driscoll in London, and it exchanged news with its Paris office. DeWitt MacKenzie, J. A. Bouman, Melvin Whiteleather, Edouard Traus, Whit Hancock, Larry Allen, John Lloyd, Fred Vander-Schmidt, Ray Porter, Edward Kennedy (to become infamous at the end of World War II for the premature release of the German surrender story), Jack Stark, Edward Shanke, and R. F. Schildbach were other Associated Press men active in Europe. Webb Miller, Ed Beattie, Richard D. McMillan, Harold Ettlinger, Reynolds Packard, Hans Thomas, Robert Best, Ralph Forte, and Edward DuPury were chief United Press writers. International News Service staffers included the dean, Karl Von Wiegand, William Hillman, Kenneth Downs, Pierre J. Huss, Charles A. Smith and H. R. Knickerbocker. Demaree Bess and Everard C. Coates covered the crisis for the *Christian Science Monitor* and dozens of other men and women wrote for other newspapers and magazines.

[18]A.M. Sperber, *Murrow: His Life and Times* (New York: Freundlich Books, 1986), p. 126. A brief treatment of the Munich Crisis is included in Sperber's encyclopedic study of the complicated Murrow's professional and private lives. The high-strung Murrow, alternately moody or jovial, became personally involved with his stories and spent hours talking with colleagues and friends about the experiences.

[19]NBC publicity brochure, 1938, p. 7.

[20]Kaltenborn, *I Broadcast the Crisis*, pp. 41–47.

[21]*Broadcasting*, October 1, 1938, p. 45.

[22]*Life*, September 26, 1938, p. 24.

[23]Kaltenborn, *I Broadcast the Crisis*, p. 48.

[24]NBC brochure, p. 8.

[25]Kaltenborn, *I Broadcast the Crisis*, pp. 50–51.

[26]Ibid., p. 54.

[27]NBC brochure, pp. 8–9.

[28]Kaltenborn, *I Broadcast the Crisis*;, p. 65.

[29]Ibid., pp. 74–75.

[30]Shirer, *Berlin Diary*, p. 134.

[31]NBC brochure, p. 9.

[32]Kaltenborn, *I Broadcast the Crisis*, pp. 76–88.

[33]NBC brochure, p. 10.

[34]For a vivid description of the Czech determination at the moment of "sell-out," see *London Daily Herald* correspondent Alexander Henderson's "Czechoslovakia: Operation without Anesthetics," in *Foreign Correspondent*, edited by Wilfrid Hindle (London: George G. Harrap & Co., 1939).

[35]Kaltenborn, *I Broadcast the Crisis* pp. 93, 97–98.

[36]Published in *Time*, September 26, 1938, pp. 15–16.

[37]NBC brochure, p. 10.

[38]Kaltenborn, *I Broadcast the Crisis.*, p. 100.

[39]Ibid., p. 111.

[40]Chase, *Sound and Fury*, p. 168.

[41]Kaltenborn, *I Broadcast the Crisis*, pp. 135–138.

[42]Ibid., p. 140.

[43]NBC brochure, p. 11.

[44]Shirer, *Berlin Diary*, pp. 138–39.

[45]*New York Herald Tribune*, September 24, 1938, p. 1.

[46]Kaltenborn, *I Broadcast the Crisis*, pp. 166–67.

[47]*Chicago Daily News*, September 25, 1938, p. 7.

[48]*Chicago Daily News*, September 24, 1938, p. 1.

[49]NBC brochure, p. 12.

[50]Kaltenborn, *I Broadcast the Crisis*, pp. 178–81.

[51]*New York Herald Tribune*, September 26, 1938, pp. 1–2.

[52]Ibid., p. 1.

[53]*Broadcasting*, October 1, 1938, p. 63.

[54]*Chicago Herald Examiner*, September 25, 1938, pp. 1–2.

[55]Shirer, *Berlin Diary*, pp. 142–43.

[56]Kaltenborn, *I Broadcast the Crisis*, pp. 210–11.

[57]Ibid., p. 206.

[58]*New York Times*, September 27, 1938, p. 1.

[59]Kaltenborn, *I Broadcast the Crisis*, pp. 210–11.

[60]*New York Herald Tribune*, September 28, 1938, p. 7.

[61]Ibid., p. 1.

[62]*New York Daily News*, September 28, 1938, p. 15.

[63]Kaltenborn, *I Broadcast the Crisis*, p. 214.

[64]Ibid., p. 218.

[65]*New York World Telegram*, September 28, 1938, p. 1.

[66]*Chicago Daily News*, September 28, 1938, p. 1.

[67]Indeed, no one has forgotten the agony of those days. President George Bush invoked the image of Munich prior to ordering the 1991 attack on Iraq. The long memory also was evident during the Yugoslavian crisis of the early 1990s when there was Western reluctance to stop the "ethnic cleansing." Journalists and diplomatic observers frequently mentioned that a precedent for appeasement had been set at Munich. The world watched Serbs and Croats attack Bosnian Muslims at will, just as it once watched Hitler.

[68]Kaltenborn, *I Broadcast the Crisis*, p. 229.

[69]*New York World-Telegram*, September 28, 1938, p. 3.

[70]Kaltenborn, *I Broadcast the Crisis*, p. 231.

[71]*Chicago Tribune*, September 29, 1938, p. 1. Schultz was one of the mainline U.S. reporters, providing page-one stories throughout the crisis. Born in Chicago in 1893 and raised in Europe, the *Tribune* hired her as a translator at the end of WWI. In 1924 she became the first woman elected to the board of directors of the Foreign Press Club in Berlin and in 1925 she was named the first woman foreign bureau chief for a major U.S. newspaper. Contemporaries were the *New York Times* roving European reporter Anne O'Hare McCormick and columnist Dorothy Thompson. Of the three Schultz was the daily journalist, responsible for breaking news stories. Margaret Bourke-White became famous as a *Life* photographer. For a comparison of the work of Schultz and McCormick see the unpublished M.A. thesis by Silvia Knight of California State University, Northridge, 1995.

[72]*Chicago Herald Examiner*, September 29, 1938, p. 1.

[73]NBC brochure, p. 18.

[74]Max Jordan, *Beyond All Fronts: A Bystander's Notes on This Thirty Years War* (Milwaukee: Bruce Publishing, 1944), pp. 218–22.

[75]Shirer, *Berlin Diary*, pp. 145–46.

[76]*New York Evening Post*, September 30, 1938, p. 2.

[77]*Chicago Daily News*, September 30, 1938, p. 1.

[78]*New York Times*, September 30, 1938, p. 1.

[79]*New York Herald Tribune*, September 30, 1938, p. 1.

[80]*Chicago Tribune*, September 30, 1938, p. 1.

[81]*Chicago Tribune*, September 30, 1938, p. 1.

[82]*Chicago Daily News*, September 30, 1938, p. 6.

[83]*Christian Science Monitor*, September 30, 1938, p. 1.

[84]*Chicago Daily News*, September 30, 1938, p. 1.

[85]Shirer, *Berlin Diary*, p. 148.

[86]Charnley, *News by Radio*, p. 19, 51.

[87]Llewellyn White, *The American Radio* (Chicago: University of Chicago Press, 1948), p. 470.

[88]*Broadcasting*, October 1, 1938, p. 63.

NOTES FOR CHAPTER FOUR

[1]*New York Herald Tribune*, June 22, 1950, p. 14.

[2]*New York Times*, June 20, 1950, p. 20.

[3]*Chicago Daily News*, June 30, 1950, p. 2.

[4]The CIA released the files to the public on September 30, 1993. *Los Angeles Times,* October 1, 1993, p. 4. Other files included an analysis of the possible use of nuclear weapons against China during the Korean War and against the Vietnamese following their defeat of the French in 1954.

[5]David Rees, *Korea: The Limited War* (New York: St. Martin's Press, 1964), p. 14. For details of political and military strategy, see also Clay Blair's 1136–page *The Forgotten War: America in Korea 1950–53* (New York: Times Books, 1987); and Callum A. MacDonald's *Korea: The War Before Vietnam* (New York: Free Press, 1986).

[6]*Chicago Daily News*, June 20, 1950, p. 2.

[7]*Chicago Daily News*, June 21, 1950, p. 2.

[8]*New York World-Telegram and Sun*, June 5, 1950, p. 2.

[9]*New York Herald Tribune*, May 31, 1950, p. 1.

[10]Rees, *Korea*, p. 9.

[11]Ibid., pp. 11–13.

[12]Louis J. Halle, *The Cold War as History* (New York: Harper & Row, Publishers, 1967), p. 200.

[13]Ibid., pp. 205–206.

[14]Rees, *Korea*, p. 9.

[15]*New York Times*, February 17, 1950, p. 13.

[16]*New York Times*, May 11, 1950, p. 19.

[17]*New York World-Telegram and Sun*, May 10, 1950, p. 2.

[18]*New York Times*, April 26, 1950, p. 17.

[19]*New York Times*, May 20, 1950, p. 7.

[20]*New York Times*, May 30, 1950, p. 18.

[21]Rees, *Korea*, p. 3.

[22]Joe Alex Morris, *Deadline Every Minute* (Garden City, New York: Doubleday Company, 1957), pp. 319–20.

[23]*Editor & Publisher*, July 1, 1950, pp. 30–31.

[24]*New York Times*, June 25, 1950, p. 1.

[25]*Broadcasting*, July 3, 1950, p. 35.

[26]Morris, *Deadline Every Minute*, p. 320; *Editor & Publisher*, July 1, 1950, p. 11.

[27]*Editor & Publisher*, July 1, 1950, p. 11.

[28]*World's Press News*, July 6, 1950, p. 4.

[29]*New York Times*, June 26, 1950, p. 3.

[30]*Chicago Tribune*, June 26, 1950, p. 1.

[31]*New York Herald Tribune*, June 27, 1950, p. 6.

[32]*San Francisco Chronicle*, June 27, 1950, p. 1.

[33]*Chicago Tribune*, June 27, 1950, p. 1.

[34]Marguerite Higgins, *War in Korea* (Garden City, New York: Doubleday & Company, 1951), pp. 15–30.

[35]*New York Times*, June 29, 1950, p. 3; *Editor & Publisher*, July 1, 1950, p. 11; *Life*, July 10, 1950, p. 23.

[36]*Chicago Daily News*, June 28, 1950, p. 1.

[37]Rutherford M. Poats, *Decision in Korea* (New York: The McBride Company, 1954), p. 2.

[38]*Chicago Tribune*, June 29, 1950, p. 5.

[39]*Broadcasting*, July 3, 1950, p. 35.

[40]Rees, *Korea*, p. 77.

[41]Higgins, *War in Korea*, p. 31.

[42]*Chicago Daily News*, June 29, 1950, p. 10.

[43]*New York Herald Tribune*, June 30, 1950, p. 1. While Beech and Higgins shared a passion for covering combat, Maggie's intense competitiveness bothered her colleague. On one occasion *Time*'s Frank Gibney told Higgins, "Korea is no place for a woman." Beech, who generally agreed with Gibney, blurted a double-edged retort : "It's okay for *her*." See Antoinette May's *Witness to War: A Biography of Marguerite Higgins* (New York: Beaufort Books, Inc., 1983), p. 136. The author met Beech in Los Angeles at a 1983 conference on Vietnam. Asked about Higgins, the old warrior apparently had retained his mixed feelings. He said only, "Oh, yeah, Maggie."

[44]*Chicago Tribune*, June 30, 1950, p. 1.

[45]*Chicago Daily News*, June 30, 1950, p. 2.

[46]Ibid., p. 1.

[47]Ibid.

[48]Rees, *Korea*, pp. 36–37.

[49]*New York Herald Tribune*, July 1, 1950, p. 1.

[50]Higgins, *War in Korea*, p. 62; *New York Herald Tribune*, July 6, 1950, p. 1; *Life*, July 17, 1950, p. 47; *Chicago Daily News*, July 5, 1950, p. 2 (Tom Lambert of AP); Carl Mydans, *More than Meets the Eye* (New York: Harper & Brothers, 1959), pp. 294–97.

[51]Higgins, *War in Korea*, p. 62.

[52]Rees, *Korea*, pp. 460–61.

[53]*World's Press News*, July 6, 1950, p. 4.

[54]Higgins, *War in Korea*, pp. 49–50.

[55]*World's Press News*, July 21, 1950, p. 17; *Editor & Publisher*, July 15, 1950, p. 6. The Japanese Telegraph Administration opened a telegraph circuit from Pusan to Tokyo about July 15, by cable under the Japan Sea. But the circuit went through several relays, and the fastest transmission any correspondent received was 12 hours, with delays up to 29 hours. Also, Pusan was far from the front at this point. The Army promised to set up a radio-teletype circuit to Tokyo but was slow and although Mackay Radio, RCA, and Press Wireless were authorized to bring in their own mobile units, they hesitated because the Army said it could not provide assistance in setting up the heavy equipment.

[56]Higgins, *War in Korea*, p. 82.

[57]Higgins, *War in Korea*, p. 51. For a concise profile of Higgins's life, see Barbara Belford's *Brilliant Bylines* (New York: Columbia University Press, 1986), chapter 19.

[58]*Editor & Publisher*, July 1, 1950, p. 11.

[59]*Editor & Publisher,* July 22, 1950, p. 6.

[60]Ibid.

[61]*Editor & Publisher,* July 8, 1950, p. 7.

[62]*New York Herald Tribune*, July 3, 1950, p. 3.

[63]*Editor & Publisher*, July 22, 1950, p. 7.

[64]Keyes Beech, *Tokyo and Points East* (Garden City, N.Y.: Doubleday & Co., 1954), p. 172.

[65]May, *Witness to War*, p. 158. She offers a slightly more formal version of the Beech quote.

[66]Letter from Whitelaw Reid to Prof. Marion Marzolf, Department of Communication, University of Michigan (September 30, 1977).

[67]*New York Herald Tribune*, July 12, 1950, p. 1; *Editor & Publisher*, July 15, 1950, p. 7.

[68]*Chicago Herald-American*, July 10, 1950, p. 1.

[69]As the action increased the wire services and many newspapers began making plans for sending other correspondents. Jack James of UP had suffered a foot injury during an air attack at Suwon and was replaced at the front by Peter Kalischer. Ralph Teatsorth of the Manila bureau arrived to assist Hoberecht in Tokyo, World War II writer Frank Tremaine flew from Los Angeles, and Charles Moore, Gene Symonds, Charles Cordry Jr., Robert Vermillion, Murray Moler, and Robert Bennyhoff also were on their way during the first week of July.

Don Euth had joined the AP staff managed by Russ Brines. Summoned were Wendell (Leif) Erickson from Honolulu; Milton Marmor, a roving correspondent in Asia; Relman Morin, a New York bureau executive; and photographers Frank "Pappy" Noel and Max Desor. Later other World War II veterans would arrive, among them Hal Boyle and Don Whitehead. Foreign editor John Martin of International News Service flew in to coordinate his service's coverage. With Ray Richards dead, INS chief Howard Handleman's staff consisted of reporters John Rich and Frank Emery and photographer Charles Rosecrans, who also contributed stories.

The *New York Times* former Seoul correspondent, Richard Johnston, was on his way to assist Tokyo bureau chief Lindesay Parrott, and Hong Kong bureau chief Walter Sullivan was transferred to the war area, also. Fred Sparks of the *Chicago Daily News* was welcomed by Keyes Beach, and others like George Grim of the *Minneapolis Tribune* showed up to provide hometown coverage for their readers. Another prominent writer was Harold Martin, covering for the *Atlanta Constitution* and the *Saturday Evening Post*. See *Editor & Publisher*, July 8, 1950, p. 7.

[70]*Life*, July 10, 1950, p. 20.

[71]*Life*, July 17, 1950, pp. 28–31.

[72]*New York Herald Tribune*, July 11, 1950, p. 1.

[73]*Chicago Daily News*, July 10, 1950, p. 3.

[74]Higgins, *War in Korea*, p. 91.

[75]*New York Times*, July 12, 1950, pp. 1, 4.

[76]*New York Times*, July 13, 1950, p. 3.

[77]*New York Herald Tribune*, July 15, 1950, p. 1.

[78]*Chicago Herald-American*, July 15, 1950, p. 2.

[79]*Chicago Herald-American*, July 15, 1950, p. 2.

[80]*Chicago Daily News*, July 17, 1950, p. 1.

[81]After the Chinese entry in late 1950, the Soviet Union provided half of the planes fighting the United States. It was revealed in 1993 that U.S. and Soviet pilots engaged in a secret air war for two years. The Soviet pilots were disguised as Chinese, but a former Soviet air commander said the Americans were aware of the deception. These secrets and others regarding the Korean War were released from Soviet archives. See *U.S. News & World Report*, August 9, 1993, p. 45.

[82]*New York Herald Tribune*, July 19, 1950, p. 1.

[83]*Chicago Tribune*, July 20, 1950, p. 3.

[84]*Chicago Tribune*, July 21, 1950, p. 1.

[85]Philip Deane, *I Was a Captive in Korea* (New York: W. W. Norton & Company, Inc., 1953), p. 33.

[86]See *General Dean's Story*, as told to William Worden (New York: Viking, 1954) and *Editor & Publisher*, July 29, 1950, p. 7.

[87]*Chicago Daily News*, July 20, 1950, p. 3; *New York Herald Tribune*, July 21, 1950, p. 1.

[88]*Chicago Daily News*, July 21, 1950, p. 2.

[89]Roy E. Appleman, *South to the Naktong, North to the Yalu* (Office of the Chief of Military History, Department of the Army, U.S. Govt. Printing Office, 1961), p. 247.

[90]Rees, *Korea*, p. 39.

[91]*Chicago Sun-Times*, July 19, 1950, p. 2.

[92]*New York Herald Tribune*, July 19, 1950, p. 1.

[93]*New York Times*, July 13, 1950, p. 4. In line with President Truman's decision to intervene in Korea and to help combat Communist aggression in the Philippines and Indochina (*New York Times*, June 28, 1950, p. 1), the United States sent eight C-47 transport planes into Saigon during the first week of July. A military study group was there to make recommendations. The U.S. government did announce that no Americans would be sent to reinforce French troops, but combat aircraft and a wide variety of military supplies were en route (*New York Times*, July 21, 1950, p. 4.).

[94]*Broadcasting*, July 24, 1950, p. 18.

⁹⁵*Broadcasting*, July 17, 1950, p.11.

⁹⁶Ibid., p. 35.

⁹⁷*Broadcasting*, July 24, 1950, p. 69.

⁹⁸*Broadcasting*, August 7, 1950, p. 54.

⁹⁹*Broadcasting*, July 24, 1950, p. 19.

¹⁰⁰*Broadcasting*, August 7, 1950, p. 15.

¹⁰¹*Broadcasting*, July 24, 1950, p. 18.

¹⁰²Rees, *Korea*, pp. 41–44.

¹⁰³Appleman, *South to the Naktong*, p. 477.

¹⁰⁴Higgins, *War in Korea*, p. 116.

¹⁰⁵Letter from L. Engleking, former sub-editor at the *Herald Tribune* who hired Higgins in 1942, to Prof. Marion Marzolf, Department of Communication, University of Michigan (September 17, 1977). She wrote: "Everybody knew that M.H. went upstairs and next thing Higgins was on her way. Simple as that—of course a bit chancy to go 'out of channels.' but most everybody had the itch to get into the big show, and certainly Mrs. Reid was all in favor of women." Helen Reid, already a strong figure in journalism circles, assumed control of the paper upon her husband's death in 1947. This account was substantiated by her son, Whitelaw, in another letter to Prof. Marzolf · (September 30, 1977). "I am quite sure that she somehow greased the wheels for her first overseas assignment—following some special pleas, such as you suggest, from Marguerite." See Prof. Marzolf's treatment of Higgins's career in her *Up From the Footnote : A History of Women Journalists* (New York: Hastings House Publishers, 1977), pp. 76–78.

¹⁰⁶Knightley, Philip, *The First Casualty* (New York: Harcourt Brace, 1975), p. 339.

¹⁰⁷Higgins, *War in Korea*, pp. 116–29.

¹⁰⁸Ibid., p. 131.

¹⁰⁹*Editor & Publisher*, August 5, 1950, p. 9.

¹¹⁰*Editor & Publisher*, August 5, 1990, p. 10.

¹¹¹*Editor & Publisher*, July 29, 1950, p. 7.

¹¹²*San Francisco Chronicle*, July 15, 1950, p. 4.

¹¹³*Editor & Publisher*, August 12, 1950, p. 7.

¹¹⁴Ibid.

¹¹⁵*Chicago Daily News*, July 24, 1950, p. 1.

¹¹⁶Higgins, *War in Korea*, p. 144.

¹¹⁷Rees, *Korea*, p. 94.

¹¹⁸*Time*, August 21, 1950, p. 50.

¹¹⁹*Life*, August 7, 1950, p. 32.

¹²⁰*Editor & Publisher*, September 9, 1950, pp. 7–8.

¹²¹*New York Times*, July 31, 1950, p. 4.

¹²²*Editor & Publisher*, November 4, 1950, p. 13.

¹²³*Editor & Publisher*, November 4, 1950, p. 13.

¹²⁴*Editor & Publisher*, October 21, 1950, p. 12.

¹²⁵*Editor & Publisher*, October 21, 1950, p. 12.

¹²⁶Morris, *Deadline Every Minute*, pp. 321–22.

¹²⁷Higgins, *War in Korea*, p. 27.

¹²⁸Notes of telephone call from Beech to Prof. Marion Marzolf, Department of Communications, University of Michigan (November, 1977). In a letter to Prof. Marzolf dated November he wrote: "I enclose a book that I wrote many years ago in which there is a chapter on Maggie. It wasn't a very good book, but what I wrote about Maggie still stands. As Pete Lisagor, who knew her during her Washington period, once said, 'Whatever else she may have been, she was an original.'" See Beech's *Toyko and Points East* (Garden City, N.Y.: Doubleday & Company, 1954), pp. 167–83. In these pages he demonstrated his admiration for her journalistic toughness and her personal courage, while at the same time frankly admitting, "I could think of no man or woman who could bring out the S.O.B. in me more quickly than Higgins."

[129]Higgins, *War in Korea*, p. 195.

[130]I. F. Stone, *Hidden History of the Korean War* (New York: Monthly Review Press, 1952).

[131]Philip Knightley, *The First Casualty* (New York: Harcourt Brace Jovanovich, 1975), p. 347.

[132]Ibid., p. 348.

[133]Ibid., p. 349.

[134]David Halberstam, *The Fifties* (New York: Villard Books, 1993), p. 73.

NOTES FOR CHAPTER FIVE

[1]*Life*, March 16, 1962, p. 39.

[2]The first American serviceman killed on active duty in Vietnam was Specialist Fourth Class James T. Davis of Livingston, Tennessee. He died December 21, 1961, while riding with a detachment of South Vietnamese troops in a truck ambushed ten miles west of Saigon (two U.S. sergeants shot by terrorists in a movie theater in July 1959 were the only others killed by Communist gunfire between the end of the French war in 1954 and 1961). By the end of 1962 combat deaths among advisers, helicopter crews, and T-28 and B-56 pilots had reached 21 (perhaps as many died in various accidents). And in 1963, 76 more Americans were to die in combat, during a year when the complexion of the American commitment would be more obvious. By 1964 "only" 250 Americans had died in combat. So the total for 1961–64 was about the same as the weekly totals of the worst days of 1967 and 1968.

[3]*Life*, March 16, 1962, p. 39.

[4]Concisely written background information on the post–World War II period in Indochina, including brief highlights of Diem's career, coverage of the French-Indochina War, and the Kennedy administration's buildup of advisers is found in John Hohenberg's *Between Two Worlds* (New York: Praeger, 1967), pp. 31–43 and 311–12. Discussion of Vietnam was a small part of a large-scale study of "policy, press and public relations in Asian-American relations." The early period is included in William M. Hammond's *Public Affairs: The Military and the Media, 1962–68* (Washington, D.C.: Army Center of Military History, 1989). The author showed sympathy and respect for the reporters' situation. Also see Peter Braestrup's *Big Story* (New Haven: Yale University Press, 1983), containing an overview of the press corps in the opening chapter.

[5]The most detailed report on the assassination and terror attacks is found in Stephen T. Hosmer's *Viet Cong Repression and Its Implications for the Future* (Lexington, Mass.: Heath Lexington Books, 1970). The killings and abductions, about 400 to 600 per year in 1958–59, jumped to 5,000 in 1966 and more than 9,000 in 1967. (See pp. 5–6.) While there was some press attention given to this prior to 1965, there was little coverage as the war grew in scope and intensity. Robert Shaplen's *New Yorker* pieces were an exception. See the Hong Kong–based roving reporter's collections. Also see *Aggression from the North: The Record of North Viet-Nam's Campaign to Conquer South Viet-Nam*, Department of State publication, Far Eastern Series, released February 1965.

[6]*Newsweek*, April 2, 1962, p. 32.

[7]*Newsweek*, April 2, 1962, p. 33.

[8]Peter Arnett, *Live from the Battlefield* (New York: Simon & Schuster, 1994), p. 92. Arnett's fascinating autobiography includes a detailed look at these early days.

[9]See Milton E. Osborn, Data Paper No. 55, Southeast Asia Program, Cornell University (April 1965).

[10]*Newsweek*, April 2, 1962, p. 32.

[11]*Newsweek*, April 30, 1962, p. 43.

[12]Ibid.

[13]Ibid.

[14]*Newsweek*, May 14, 1962, p. 56.

[15]*Newsweek*, May 28, 1962, p. 40.

[16]Harrison E. Salisbury, *Without Fear or Favor* (New York: Times Books, 1980), p. 40.

[17]*New York Times*, July 21, 1962, p. 1.

[18]*New York Times*, July 25, 1962, pp. 1–2.

[19]Ibid.

[20]Ibid.

[21]Malcolm W. Browne, *The New Face of War* (Indianapolis: The Bobbs-Merrill Company, Inc., 1965), p. 60.

[22]*New York Times*, July 25, 1962, p. 2.

[23]When Bigart died at age 83, his obituary in the April 17, 1991, *New York Times* (C23) said: "His articles remained taut, witty and astringently understated, even when created under deadline pressure and the appalling working conditions imposed by war and famine, even when they concerned mundane events that lesser reporters regarded as routine. Mr. Bigart knew that what counted most was not the place but the poetry, and that a reporter could create memorable prose from even the most unremarkable happening."

[24]*New York Times*, July 29, 1962, p. 13.

[25]*New York Times*, July 27, 1962, p. 4.

[26]Bernard Fall, *Street without Joy* (Harrisburg, Pa.: The Stackpole Company, 1961). See revised edition, 1963, p. 349.

[27]Fall, *Street without Joy*, p. 353.

[28]John Mecklin, *Mission in Torment* (Garden City, N.Y.: Doubleday & Company, Inc., 1965), p. 24.

[29]See Stanley Karnow's *Vietnam: A History* (New York: Viking Press, 1983). The author relied on his many years of Asian reporting experience to produce this mammoth history, the basis for PBS's *Vietnam: A Television History*. Chapter 7 explains the splits in U.S. and Vietnamese objectives.

[30]Columbia Broadcasting System radio news report, April 6, 1972.

[31]*Newsweek*, August 20, 1962, p. 41.

[32]Ibid., p. 40.

[33]*Newsweek*, September 17, 1962, p. 68.

[34]*Newsweek*, September 24, 1962, p. 30.

[35]Ibid., pp. 31, 34.

[36]*Newsweek*, December 10, 1962, p. 41.

[37]See Arnett, *Live from the Battlefield*, p. 312.

[38]Neil Sheehan, *After the War Was Over* (New York: Random House, 1992), p. 60. This was confirmed by Harrison E. Salisbury in his *Without Fear or Favor*(New York: Times Books, 1980), p. 40.

[39]David Halberstam, *The Making of a Quagmire* (New York: Random House, 1964), p. 157; Pierre Salinger, *With Kennedy* (Doubleday & Company, 1966), p. 324.

[40]Halberstam, *Making of a Quagmire*, p. 147.

[41]Ibid., p. 155.

[42]Ibid., p. 72.

[43]Karnow, pp. 259–60. For an analysis of Vann's flawed personality, see Neil Sheehan, *A Bright Shining Lie: John Paul Vann and America in Vietnam* (New York: Random House, 1988). For better understanding of the U.S. dilemma, see David Halberstam, *The Best and the Brightest* (New York: Random House, 1972). Also see the second revised edition of Bernard Fall, *The Two Viet-Nams: A Political and Military Analysis* (New York: Praeger, 1967), considered the most important study of the war's swiftly changing nature.

[44]See Arnett, *Live from the Battlefield*, p. 98.

[45]See Reston's *Deadline: A Memoir* (New York: Random House, 1991). He devotes

an entire chapter to "The Reporters of Vietnam" and sympathetically recounts the bitter criticism of Halberstam, Sheehan, Mohr, and others. See pp. 327–28 for his defense against the attacks of Marguerite Higgins and Joseph Alsop and pp. 315–16 for more from Alsop about Sheehan's coverage of the Ia Drang Valley defeats. Also see Salisbury's *Without Fear or Favor* for the linkage between Sheehan's 1962–63 Saigon experiences and his role in the 1971 Pentagon Papers case. Another interesting rundown of those days is found in Glenn MacDonald's excellent *Report or Distort* (New York: Exposition Press, 1973). Edwin Emery provided an interpretive summary of the first 10 years of coverage in "The Press in the Vietnam Quagmire," *Journalism Quarterly* (No. 4, Winter 1971).

[46]Arnett had deep respect for Gallagher's courageous actions. See *Live from the Battlefield*, p. 173. To the AP's credit, controversial stories were rarely halted.

[47]Neil Sheehan, *After the War Was Over* (New York: Random House, 1992), p. 60. Vann died in a 1972 helicopter crash, and his funeral at Arlington was, in Sheehan's words, "*the* funeral of the war." It took him 16 years to finish his book about Vann. Then he was able to return to Vietnam to produce his poignant and critical retrospective.

[48]*I. F. Stone's Weekly*, October 28, 1963.

[49]Halberstam, *Making of a Quagmire*, p. 159–60.

[50]Marguerite Higgins, *Our Vietnam Nightmare* (New York: Harper & Row, Publishers, 1965), p. 127.

[51]Russ Braley, *Bad News: The Foreign Policy of the New York Times* (Chicago: Regnery Gateway, 1984), p. 238. See Chapter 9, "The Halberstam-Higgins War," where he gives support to Higgins, Beech, and others who disagreed with Halberstam, Sheehan, Robert Shaplen of the *New Yorker*, and those criticizing the war strategies.

[52]Keyes Beech, *Not without the Americans* (Garden City, N.Y.: Doubleday & Company, Inc., 1971), p. 311.

[53]*Time*, September 28, 1962, p. 30.

[54]*Newsweek*, January 21, 1963, pp. 24–26, 29.

[55]Mecklin, *Mission in Torment*, p. 16.

[56]Ibid., pp. 16–19.

[57]Mecklin, *Mission in Torment*, p. 42. For an assessment of the effects of propaganda on the public and press, see Milton E. Osborne, Data Papers No. 55, Southeast Asia Program, Cornell University (April 1965). "The history of the United States involvement in Vietnam has been marked by encouraging official statements which have subsequently had to be withdrawn or modified very considerably . . . The optimism which has been recorded . . . contrasts strongly with the 1964 assessment that 'It was apparent that many of the provincial chiefs . . . would employ any measures (because of fear of Ngo Dinh Nhu) . . . false reporting to achieve the quantitative goals set.'"

[58]Mecklin, *Mission in Torment*, 153–56.

[59]*New York Times*, May 8, 1963, p. 10.

[60]*New York Times*, June 3, 1963, p. 9.

[61]*New York Times*, June 5, 1963, p. 1.

[62]Ibid., p. 2.

[63]Higgins, *Our Vietnam Nightmare*, p. 83.

[64]Ibid., pp. 88–103.

[65]Mecklin, *Mission in Torment*, pp. 153–54.

[66]Browne, *New Face of War*, pp. 256–57.

[67]Halberstam, *Making of a Quagmire*, p. 211.

[68]*New York Times*, June 11, 1963, p. 6.

[69]*New York Times*, August 22, 1963, pp. 1–2.

[70]Russ Braley, in his *Bad News: The Foreign Policy of the New York Times*, claims (p. 212) that while the Buddhist crisis was building, Halberstam, Sheehan, and Mert Perry of *Time* were working on an in-depth analysis showing "a serious deterioration of

the military situation in the delta." Braley said the *Times* ran the piece on August 15, 1963, at the height of the crisis, after a long delay, implying some sort of manipulation. Nevertheless, it is no wonder that President Kennedy became irritated with Halberstam's stories and once asked *Times* Publisher Arthur Ochs Sulzberger if he had thought of transferring Halberstam. Fortunately, the answer was no.

[71]*New York Times,* August 23, 1963, pp. 1–3.

[72]*New York Times,* August 24, 1963, p. 2.

[73]*New York Times,* August 27, 1963, p. 1.

[74]See "Cablegram from State Department to Ambassador Henry Cabot Lodge in Saigon," August 24, 1963, as published in Sheehan et al., *The Pentagon Papers* (New York: Quadrangle Books, 1971).

[75]*Time,* September 20, 1963, p. 32.

[76]*Time,* August 31, 1963, p. 26.

[77]*Newsweek,* October 7, 1963, p. 98.

[78]Salinger, *With Kennedy,* pp. 325–26.

[79]Halberstam, *Making of a Quagmire,* p. 267.

[80]Salinger, *With Kennedy,* p. 328.

[81]Salinger, *With Kennedy,* p. 325; Halberstam, *Making of a Quagmire,* p. 268.

[82]Halberstam, *Making of a Quagmire,* p. 270.

[83]Ibid., pp. 269–72.

[84]*Time,* September 20, 1963, p. 32.

[85]Halberstam, *Making of a Quagmire,* p. 272 (see also *Nieman Reports,* January 1964).

[86]*Time,* September 20, 1963, p. 62.

[87]Ibid., p. 62.

[88]Halberstam, *Making of a Quagmire,* pp. 273–75. Halberstam put the Mohr incident into perspective in his *The Powers That Be* (New York: Dell Publishing Co., Inc., 1979), pp. 639–51.

[89]*Time,* October 11, 1963, p. 55.

[90]Halberstam, *Making of a Quagmire,* p. 269.

[91]Sheehan et al., *The Pentagon Papers,* pp. 216–19.

[92]*Newsweek,* October 14, 1963, p. 46.

[93]Halberstam, *The Best and the Brightest,* p. 562. Arnett, in a private conversation with the author in Dallas, November 1972, described the "early days"; how the AP group of himself, Browne, and Faas teamed up while Halberstam and Sheehan were a team in a sense; how Halberstam "took Sheehan under his wing," being more experienced at that point; how it wasn't until Diem's death that the correspondents fully realized the extent of future U.S. involvement, that America was going to be sending more money, helicopters, and men; and how, following a "peace settlement," the situation would likely revert to the days of 1960–61, when terrorism, assassination, and propaganda dominated; how he himself, after a dozen years, had no home except Vietnam and did not regret it. For Arnett's life story, including his 1962–75 Vietnam experiences, see his *Live from the Battlefield.* Those expecting much interpretation of events from Arnett will be disappointed, however. He was candid and descriptive, just like a good AP and CNN reporter. For Browne's views of this period, see his *Muddy Boots and Red Socks* (New York: Times Books, 1993). Browne was the *Times's* last bureau chief in Saigon when the city fell in 1975. In May 1994 he returned (as the paper's senior science writer) to revisit the battle scenes for a series of page-one reports (see "Battlefields of Khe Sanh: Still One Casualty a Day," May 13, 1994).

[94]See Arnett, *Live from the Battlefield,* p. 111.

[95]Edwin Emery, "The Press in the Vietnam Quagmire," *Journalism Quarterly* (Winter 1971) p. 621.

[96]Halberstam, *Making of a Quagmire,* p. 275.

[97]Salisbury, *Without Fear or Favor,* p. 42. He cited a January 27, 1947, Saigon report from Trumbull, who predicted a French defeat. He said Trumbull's "low-keyed

words write an epitaph *in advance* to the three decades that were to follow."

[98] The discussion with Salisbury took place in 1983 at a conference on Vietnam held at the University of Southern California. For a full discussion of the correspondents' retrospective attitudes, see Michael and Edwin Emery, *The Press in America* (Englewood Cliffs, N.J.: Prentice Hall, Inc., 1992), "Vietnam Reconsidered: Lessons of the War," pp. 453–54. Also see Halberstam's comments about Richard Nixon's role in encouraging the development of the Vietnam conflict and delaying its conclusion in "Richard Nixon's Last Campaign," *Columbia Journalism Review* (July-August 1994), p. 35. At age 60, the veteran correspondent pulled no punches. He was particularly disappointed that while covering Nixon's 1994 funeral some commentators credited the former president with ending the war.

NOTES FOR CHAPTER 6

[1] *The Nation*, February 22, 1928, p. 204 (vol. 126, no. 3268).

[2] *The Nation*, April 11, 1928, p. 406 (vol. 126, no. 3275).

[3] *The Nation*, March 14, 1928, p. 281 (vol. 126, no. 3271).

[4] For a revealing cover story about Anastasio "Tacho" Somoza, see *Time*, Nov. 15, 1948, pp. 38–40, 43. In 1939 President Franklin Roosevelt read a "long solemn memo about Somoza and Nicaragua" sent by Sumner Wells. FDR reportedly wisecracked that much-repeated line: "As a Nicaraguan might say, he's a sonofabitch but he's ours."

[5] For historical background, see: "Sandinista Foreign Policy: Strategies for Survival," in *NACLA Report on the Americas* XIX (May/June 1985), 18, which includes a historical introduction and a generally unreported explanation of the role of "Sandinismo"; John Britton, "Carleton Beals and Central America after Sandino: Struggle to Publish," *Journalism Quarterly* LX (Summer 1983), 240.

[6] See Stephen Kinzer, *Blood of Brothers: Life and War in Nicaragua* (New York: Doubleday, 1971).

[7] This interview on July 21, 1986, coincided with the Sandinistas' week-long celebration of the seventh anniversary of the revolution (July 19). I was accompanied by Latin American specialist Phil Otis. On July 20 we separately interviewed William Long of the *Los Angeles Times* and Tim Golden, then of the *Miami Herald*. The war was at a crucial stage, there were many rumors, and Kinzer felt the Contras would open a phase of urban warfare in Managua. He made his point by describing the vulnerability of Sandinista oil storage facilities to Contra attacks. Instead, the Contras were kept at bay in the mountains. Regarding his own vulnerable position, he said it was "fine" for a large number of journalists to chase around Nicaragua digging up different opinions, but "only one person has to report for the *New York Times*."

[8] Kinzer interview, July 21, 1986.

[9] Interviewed by telephone October 16, 1992, Hunt said his "guess" was that Kinzer's behavior was guided by his critical 1982 book on U.S. activities in Guatemala, *Bitter Fruit*, and that once he was with the *Times* he "went out of his way to make sure he wouldn't be perceived as a leftist journalist."

[10] For example, see Kinzer's review of Nicaraguan poet Rubén Darío's work in *The New York Times Book Review* (January 18, 1987), p. 3. Darío dazzled Europe with his talent from 1888 until his death in 1916, and Kinzer put his career into modern perspective.

[11] Interview with Diederich, October 14, 1992.

[12] The source asked to remain anonymous. A point could be made here about the camaraderie that still exists among those who covered "the early days," the events leading up to the fall of Somoza. They all took risks and they enjoy talking about them. Getting the story straight and getting back safely was more important than competition. Riding later reported from Europe. He covered some of the Bosnian negotiations, filing from Geneva in 1993, and otherwise had general assignments.

[13]The former president's memoirs and other sources indicate what little attention was given the Sandinista revolution in comparison to the Begin-Sadat meetings, the Iranian hostage crisis, and America's energy crisis. During the 1990 elections the author met Carter in Managua and observed his efforts to protect the Sandinistas against charges that the election process was unfair. Carter had come a long way, as he had in his perceptions of the Middle East. Fair or not, it seemed that he was making up for mistakes made in 1979–80 that had played into the hands of those who created the Contras. (Note: The Contras were *created*, with great help from the Argentinians and the Hondurans; the force also grew naturally as conditions within Nicaragua worsened. But there is a distinction to be made.)

[14]Bernard Diederich, *Somoza and the Legacy of U.S. Involvement in Central America* (Maplewood, N.J.: Waterfront Press, 1989), pp. 277–78. (Note: First published in 1981 by E. P. Dutton; that edition is out of print).

[15]*Washington Post*, July 11, 1979, p. 10. One of those rare stories that show the emotion of the press corps when dealing with a difficult situation. See also, Richard Dudman, "Lessons from Bill Stewart's Murder," *Washington Journalism Review* (September-October, 1979), p. 36.

[16]See Milton Jamall and Margo Gutierrez, *It's No Secret: Israeli Military Involvement in Central America* (Association of Arab-American University Graduates, Inc.: Belmont, Mass., 1986), which documents how Israel supplied arms, ammunition, technology, and counterinsurgency techniques to Central American regimes and right-wing movements. Also see the writings of Jane Hunter of *Israeli Foreign Affairs*, Charles Clements, Cheryl Rothenberg, George Black (*The Nation*), and others familiar with Central American intrigue. See Hunter's "Cocaine and Cutouts: Israel's Unseen Diplomacy," *The Link* (published by Americans for Middle East Understanding), January-March, 1989. Israeli agent Michael Harari's Central American network, including his relationship with Gen. Manuel Noriega, is the centerpiece of this research.

[17]Telephone interview with Don Bohling, October 14, 1992. Bohling, with an encyclopedic memory, recalled *Miami Herald* staffers of the past and some of his own experiences. He began covering Central America in 1964, to be joined by William Montalbano and later William Long. The latter two moved on to the *Los Angeles Times*, but Bohling stayed with the *Herald*, where he began serving as Latin American desk editor in 1968.

[18]*Los Angeles Times*, July 18, 1979, p. 8.

[19]*Los Angeles Times*, July 20, 1979, p. 1.

[20]*Chicago Tribune*, July 18, 1979, Sec. 2, p. 2.

[21]*Chicago Tribune*, July 20, 1979, p. 1.

[22]*Washington Post*, July 20, 1979, p. 1.

[23]*Washington Post*, July 22, 1979, p. 14.

[24]See her book of photographs, *Nicaragua: June 1978–July 1979* (New York: Pantheon, 1981). She shared the editing of *El Salvador* (New York: Writers and Readers Publishers Cooperative, 1981) with Harry Mattison and Fae Rubenstein. She was wounded during the Salvadoran fighting.

[25]*New York Times*, July 21, 1979, p. 1.

[26]*New York Times*, July 22, 1979, Sec. 4, 1E.

[27]For a full picture, see Paul Berman's "Nicaragua 1986," photos by Susan Meiselas, *Mother Jones*, December 1986.

[28]In April 1987 the author and colleagues Roberto Ceniceros and Phil Otis visited Palmerola Air Force Base, several hours outside of Tegucigalpa, one of the staging areas for U.S. training exercises in the region. U.S. National Guard units regularly made news by holding maneuvers. To Central Americans these were intimidating acts. Meanwhile the CIA and Contras used airstrips in Honduras, Costa Rica, and El Salvador for their supply and arms drops.

[29]*With the Contras: A Reporter in the Wilds of Nicaragua* (New York: Simon and Schuster, 1986). Bernard Diederich recalled how strange it was on one occasion to be

across the river on the Nicaraguan side with Ed Cody of the *Washington Post* and Juan Tomayo of the *Miami Herald*, while Dickey and a companion were on the Contra side.

[30]See "From Here to Eternity," *Rolling Stone* (May 24, 1984), p. 26.

[31]*Packaging the Contras*, pp. 31–33, and for additional insight see Dickey's opinions in *With the Contras*, pp. 232–34.

[32]Others earning respect of their colleagues were Chris Hedges of the *Dallas MorningNews*, Andrew Maykuth of the *Philadelphia Inquirer*, Dennis Volman of the *Christian Science Monitor*, and freelancers Bill Gasperini (*In These Times*, CBS radio, *Christian Science Monitor*), Nancy Nusser, Joel Millman, June Carolyn Erlick, Martha Honey and Tony Avirgan, the Costa-Rica based Lyle Prescot, and Mary Jo McConahay of Pacific News Service. Frank Wright of the Minneapolis *Star Tribune* authored a number of particularly insightful articles, as did Jean Hopfensperger, who spent considerable time in the region. It also should be noted that some less experienced freelancers embarrassed regular reporters by their open pro-Sandinista behavior, allowing the embassy to criticize the entire press corps.

One of the most difficult assignments was handled by Tracy Wilkinson, who opened UPI's Managua bureau in 1985 after three years in Peru and Bolivia. She covered Nicaragua, Costa Rica, and Panama while Doug Farah took El Salvador, Honduras, and Guatemala. Wilkinson held the Managua post until 1987 before joining the *Los Angeles Times*. She covered the Gulf War and in late 1992 returned to Central America as chief correspondent with an office in San Salvador. Louis Toscano also covered the region for UPI before heading to the Middle East. Farah joined the *Washington Post* and in 1992 welcomed Wilkinson to San Salvador, where he and Christian of the *New York Times* had regional offices. By that time the major newspapers had followed the lead of the networks and greatly reduced their Central American resources. Mexico City or San Salvador again became the journalists' base.

For the Associated Press, Joe Frazier was sent to San José as the region's first North American bureau chief in the 1981–82 period, to be joined shortly by Reid Miller. Frazier moved on to San Salvador in 1984 and was replaced by Bryna Brennan in 1986. In September 1987 she was assigned to Managua, becoming the first full-time North American staffer there, while Miller stayed in San José.

On the newsmagazine front, Charles Lane was a familiar figure for *Newsweek*, Laura Lopez was there for *Time*, and Carla Ann Robins, based in Miami, was a frequent contributor to *U.S. News & World Report*. Writers representing publications with clear viewpoints also made their appearances, from *The Nation*, *Progressive*, and *Village Voice* on the left to the *National Review*, the *New Republic*, and others on the right who supported all-out Contra aid. The classic argument for Congressional aid came from the *New Republic* in a March 1986, editorial essay, "The Case for the Contras, " 18 months after the same publication ran Robert Leiken's "Nicaragua's Untold Stories," a widely discussed piece of anti-Sandinista propaganda disputed by journalists living in Managua (*New Republic*, October 8, 1984; also see *The Nation*, December 28, 1985, p. 702).

[33]*Newsweek*, June 1 and June 8, 1987. Also see *The Nation*, June 13,1987, p. 790. While in Tegucigalpa in April 1987, Phil Otis, Roberto Ceniceros, and I had dinner with Nordland and Gentile, Marjorie Miller of the *Los Angeles Times* and Anne-Marie O'Connor of Reuters. There was plenty of talk about the Contra camps, but we had no idea that Nordland and Gentile were headed for a wild adventure.

[34]At an Ortega speech at Esteli in 1986 Collins, not knowing why I was there, asked me to comment on camera about the rather grim July 19 anniversary situation. I declined, saying that as a journalist I wouldn't feel comfortable giving my personal opinion to the public. But if given 10 minutes I might have told a story about the wildest presidential motorcade that I had ever seen. A few hours before our press bus had been pulled off the road by a policeman wailing his motorcycle siren. We were on the open highway about halfway between Managua and Esteli. Then helicopter gunships flew over at treetop level and circled the field alongside of our bus. We

thought Contras were up ahead. Then came a convoy of Land Rovers and other vehicles. Ortega was in the front seat and as they went by at about 75 miles per hour I couldn't resist saying loudly, "There they go, they'll be in Harligen, Texas in two days!" My reference, of course, was to President Reagan's claim that the mighty Sandinista army was only "two days away" from the Texas border.

[35]June Erlick, "Separating Fact From Fantasy," *Columbia Journalism Review* (January-February 1987).

[36]Interview with Dirk Vandersypen and Jan Van Bilsen, Los Angeles, November 14, 1992.

[37]Telephone interviews with Bernard Diederich, October 14 and November 13, 1992. After leaving his full-time post in 1981, he traveled to Central America from Miami off and on until 1983.

[38]Diederich interview, October 14, 1992. Edgar Chamorro, in his *Packaging the Contras: A Case of CIA Disinformation* (New York: Institute for Media Analysis, 1987), p. 36, describes conversations with both Kinzer and LeMoyne about the pressure to balance coverage to maintain access. He said he told LeMoyne that his coverage moved from "very critical" to increasingly "pro-Contra" over a period of time and that the journalist said this was because of the need to be with the Contra units. Finally, I attempted to arrange a trip to Contra camps in Honduras in 1987. The Contra contact in Miami, the well-known Bosco Matamoros, bluntly told me that I would have to be checked out first (presumably by the CIA). I did not pursue my request, so I have no idea if my freelance colleagues and I would have been admitted, but I have my doubts.

[39]Telephone interview with anonymous former press association reporter, November 13, 1992. For an early look at press association coverage of Latin American news, see Michael Massing's critical "Inside the Wires' Banana Republics," *Columbia Journalism Review* (November-December 1979), p. 45.

[40]Robert Parry, *Fooling America: How Washington Insiders Twist the Truth and Manufacture the Conventional Wisdom* (New York: William Morrow and Company, Inc., 1992). John Kenneth Galbraith first used the cynical term "conventional wisdom" in his *The Affluent Society*.

[41]Parry, *Fooling America*, p. 265.

[42]Parry spoke to the Los Angeles chapter of FAIR (Fairness and Accuracy in Reporting) on March 28, 1993, and discussed some of his points with the author after his formal presentation.

[43]Parry, *Fooling America*, p. 210.

[44]Parry, *Fooling America*, p. 288.

[45]For a concise description of these events, see "The Iran-Contra Scandal" in Michael and Edwin Emery's *The Press and America* (Englewood Cliffs, N.J.: Prentice-Hall, Inc., 1992), pp. 463–72.

[46]Telephone interview with anonymous former press association reporter November 14, 1992.

[47]As reported in E. Bruce Berman's "Closed Captions," *Lies of Our Times* (March 1990), p. 6.

[48]Joe Klein, "Our Man in Managua," *Esquire* (November 1986). The subtitle for this generally favorable piece was: "Meet Stephen Kinzer, a riddle wrapped in mystery inside a by-line in *The New York Times*."

[49]Klein, p. 106.

[50]Author's July 21, 1986, interview with Kinzer.

[51]Telephone interview with Kinzer, October 26, 1992. Kinzer was at the Intercontinental Hotel in Zagreb, Croatia. Assigned to Germany, he had just moved from Bonn to Berlin. His job in Yugoslavia was to provide overview analysis and as usual he wasn't very far from danger. Always the fatalist, he signed off with, "See you in the next war."

[52]Kinzer, *Blood of Brothers*, pp. 102–11.

[53]Ibid., pp. 363, 365.

[54]Interview with D'Escoto at his Managua home, March 1, 1990.

[55]Holly Sklar, *Washington's War on Nicaragua* (Boston: South End Press, 1988), p. 195. Also see Parry, *Fooling America*, p. 222, for details about NED activities paid for by taxpayers.

[56]Chamorro, *Packaging the Contras*, p. 6. For precise details about the CIA's activities, see Parry, *Fooling America*, pp. 223–45.

[57]President Ronald Reagan, speech to Conservative Political Action Committee, March 1, 1985.

[58]Chamorro, *Packaging the Contras*, pp. 26–27.

[59]Ibid., p. 6.

[60]Ibid., p. 3.

[61]Conversation with author, Managua party, July 18, 1985.

[62]Chamorro, *Packaging the Contras*, p. 38. Also see Wayne H. Cowan's "The Uses of Information," *Christianity and Crisis* (July 20, 1981). He traced how the State Department leaked information to *New York Times* reporter Juan de Onis in February 1981 that set off a chain of stories about alleged plans by the Soviet Union and Cuba to send tons of weapons to FMLN forces in El Salvador. A State Department White Paper on the subject also was widely hailed. But the story began to fall apart in June when Jonathan Kwitney scrutized the report for the *Wall Street Journal*. It later was widely discredited, but the damage had been done. Pacific News Service (John Dinges, March 14) and *The Nation* (March 28) criticized the government story but got little attention, as did *Christianity and Crisis*, which used the work of freelancer Anne Nelson in Central America. It is interesting to note how reporters from the *Times of London* and *Le Monde* were skeptical from the beginning, unlike the Washington regulars.

[63]Chamorro, *Packaging the Contras*, p. 2. (The stories appeared on February 16 and June 5.)

[64]"La Prensa: the CIA Connection," *Columbia Journalism Review* (July-August 1988), pp. 34–35.; also see Michael Massing's "Nicaragua's Free-Fire Journalism" on Nicaraguan newspapers in the same issue, pp. 34–35. And see Lawrence C. Soley and John Nichols, *Clandestine Radio Reporting* (New York: Praeger, 1987). This details CIA broadcasts into Nicaragua, Iran, and other nations.

[65]Martha Honey, "Contra Coverage Paid for by the CIA," *Columbia Journalism Review* (March-April 1987), pp. 31–32.

[66]Jacqueline Sharkey, "The CIA's Secret Propaganda Campaign," *Common Cause* (September-October 1986), cover story beginning on p. 28.

[67]*New York Times*, July 18, 1992, p. 5. The headline on the story by Neil Lewis brought memories of a few headlines from a decade earlier: "Wider CIA Role Seen in Nicaragua."

[68]Chamorro, *Packaging the Contras*, pp. 20–21.

[69]My account of this entire period is found in "Call Back If Anyone Gets Killed," *The Journalist* (University of Southern California), April 1986.

[70]*New York Times*, June 2, 1984, p. 3.

[71]*Los Angeles Times*, May 31, 1984, p. 16 of morning final edition and p. 1 of late final edition.

[72]*Los Angeles Times,* June 1, 1984, p. 1.

[73]Kinzer, *Blood of Brothers*, p. 233.

[74]Ibid., p. 234. The author spoke briefy about La Penca to an equally cautious Christopher Dickey in November 1987 while covering the Arab Summit Conference in Amman, Jordan. He had nothing to offer about the causes of the bombing or his opinion about the incident, no doubt rightfully so.

[75]Interview with Kinzer, July 21, 1986.

[76]The author visited Costa Rica a half dozen times while traveling in Central America during the 1985–91 period and wrote about aspects of the La Penca and Iran/Contra stories, including the first U.S. newspaper story about the La Penca investigation. This piece included allegations of drug-running and arms smuggling and a strong suggestion that people very close to then Vice President Bush were involved. See "Contragate: The Costa Rican Connection," *San Francisco Bay Guardian* (December 3,

1986); also see *San Francisco Bay Guardian* articles of Feb. 4, April 1, and May 27, 1987. Also, Martha Honey and Tony Avirgan, "The Carlos File," *The Nation* (October 5, 1985); Martha Honey and Tony Avirgan, "La Penca, Pastora, the Press and the CIA," (published in Spanish in Lima, Peru, 1985, later part of Christic Institute's packet of materials on La Penca); Joel Millman, "Whodunit: The Pastora Bombing," *Columbia Journalism Review* (March/April 1986); Jacqueline Sharkey, "Disturbing the Peace," *Common Cause* (September/October 1985); Robert Parry, Bria Barger, and Murray Waas, "The Secret Contra War, *New Republic* (November 24, 1986); script for June 25, 1986 segment of *West 57th St.* segment on Contra supply operations. Finally, see *Nicaragua vs. U.S.A.* (International Court of Justice: The Hague, The Netherlands (June 27, 1986).

[77]On one occasion a Los Angeles resident with experience in Central America called the *Times* foreign desk to inquire why the paper had not run an Associated Press story from San José telling how local agents had planted drugs in a book mailed to Martha Honey and Tony Avirgan—an awkward attempt to force the couple out of the country. Instead of being concerned about fellow journalists or at least about the story, the deskman made disparaging political comments about the couple to this total stranger and showed no interest in their plight. Journalists kid themselves when they say there is no political bias on the home desks.

[78]Nir's July 1986 meeting with then Vice President George Bush was scrutinized by Ted Koppel on ABC's *Nightline* show, October 2, 1992, and in the *New York Times* on November 4. While it became clear that Bush knew fully of the arms-for-hostages specifics earlier than he previously had said, no one brought out the Central American connection. Nir, after all, was active there as well. Bush continually said he knew nothing of the diversion of funds to the Contras.

[79]Kinzer interview, July 21, 1986.

[80]*Miami Herald*, August 8, 1993, p. 1; *San Francisco Chronicle*, August 9, 1993, foreign news section. For the La Penca story see Martha Honey's *Hostile Acts: U.S. Policy in Costa Rica in the 1980s* (Gainesville: University Press of Florida, 1994). This exhaustive 640–page work is based on years of research and her personal experiences while living in Costa Rica in the 1983–91 period. Without question it is the definitive description of U.S. government actions in Costa Rica, many designed to influence the war against Nicaragua.

[81]In late 1992 the author met T. J. Liggett of Claremont, California, a retired churchman with more than 40 years' experience of living in Latin America and observing Latin American affairs. Liggett had met Archbishop Romero in 1976. The archbishop asked Liggett if he should attend the swearing-in of Gen. Carlos Humberto Romero and bless the new military government. The archbishop said General Romero had paid a visit to ask him to do this, offensively bringing with him troops who surrounded the church. Liggett told Archbishop Romero that his nonattendance would be a signal of his opposition to the military. At the swearing-in, the archbishop was conspicuous by his absence. Four years later Liggett was asked to hurry to San Salvador to be a witness, because the archbishop had been threatened. He was forced to delay his trip by a few days, and in the meantime Archbishop Romero was murdered. "I would have been there," Liggett said.

[82]The bylines included those of Joanne Omang of the *Washington Post*, Laurie Beckland and Marjorie Miller of the *Los Angeles Times,* Lynda Schuster of the *Wall Street Journal*, Lydia Chavez of the *New York Times* , Shirley Christian of the *Miami Herald*, Beth Nissen of *Newsweek*, Geri Smith and Cindy Karp of UPI, Zoe Trujillo of CNN, and Hilary Brown of ABC. Anne Nelson was a stringer and wrote for *The Nation*, Magnum photographer Susan Meiselas was wounded in action.

[83]Shirley Christian, "Covering the Sandinistas: The Foregone Conclusion of the Fourth Estate," *Washington Journalism Review*, March, 1982; see May 1982 issue for Riding and DeYoung replies; also see *Reporters under Fire: U.S. Media Coverage of Conflicts in Lebanon and Central America,* edited by Landrum R. Boling (Boulder, Colo.: Westview Press, Inc., 1985), which contains verbatim transcript of panel

discussions of journalists and experts debating questions of bias and fairness, including mention of the effects of *Nicaragua: Revolution in the Family* (New York: Random House, 1985). Also see her reviews of two books on U.S. policy in Nicaragua, *New Republic*, August 29, 1988, p. 44.

[84]*New York Times*, September 19, 1992, p. 2.

[85]Raymond Bonner, *Weakness and Deceit: U.S. Policy and El Salvador* (New York: Times Books, 1984); Joseph Goulden, *Fit to Print: A. M. Rosenthal and His Times* (Secaucus, N.J.: Lyle Stuart, Inc., 1988).

[86]*New York Times*, January 11, 1982, p. 2.

[87]*New York Times*, January 27, 1982, p. 1.

[88]*New York Times*, January 27, 1982, p. 10.

[89]*Washington Post*, January 27, 1982, p. 1.

[90]*Washington Post*, January 27, 1982, p. 16. Dinges wasn't any higher on the embassy's list than Bonner. Bonner recalled that when Dinges was introduced to Col. John Waghelstein, the commander of U.S. advisers, at Ambassador Hinton's home, Waghelstein simply said, "Fuck you." Later he reportedly told another journalist, "I'd like to get Dinges and Bonner up in a plane." Bonner, *Weakness and Deceit*, p. 316.

[91]*New York Times*, January 29, 1982, p. 1.

[92]*New York Times*, January 30, 1982, p. 1.

[93]*Wall Street Journal*, February 12, 1982.

[94]Goulden, *Fit to Print*, pp. 340–41. See references to April 10, 1982, interview in *Editor & Publisher* where Rosenthal called AIM's criticism of the *Times* Central American coverage "pure agit prop, just as the communists use agit prop" and to his implicit endorsement of Bonner by including him on a panel at an American Society of Newspaper Editors' meeting in April. Actually, Goulden wrote, Rosenthal's private attitude was "a polar opposite."

[95]Bonner, *Weakness and Deceit*, p. 316, and Goulden, *Fit to Print*, pp. 334–38.

[96]Goulden, *Fit to Print*, p. 345; also see p. 333, where Goulden inaccurately reports that Bonner's first Mozote story was buried deep in the paper the day after the *Post*'s: "the next day, January 28, on page 12." This gave the impression that Bonner's editors had played down the story, which of course they had not, in placing his work on page one, three days in a row. Goulden also criticizes Bonner for not reporting that one of his sources, the Human Rights Commission, was pro-opposition (Marxist was Goulden's term). Goulden and others did not seem to mind that these so-called Marxists might have been telling the truth or if right-wing spokesmen came forth with details of "communist" killings.

[97]Bonner, *Weakness and Deceit*, p. 341.

[98]Michael Massing, "About-face on El Salvador," *Columbia Journalism Review* (November-December 1983), p. 42. Bonner said this was the most complete account of what happened to him.

[99]*New York Times*, October 22, 1992, p. 1.

[100]*New York Times*, October 26, 1992, p. A4.

[101]*New York Times*, November 1, 1992, p. 5.

[102]*New York Times*, October 22, 1992, p. 1.

[103]*New York Times*, October 22, 1992, p. 4.

[104]This information came from a highly placed journalist who covered both El Salvador and Nicaragua. It is used here to demonstrate how the State Department's disinformation campaign was effective and how journalists can hurt each other. The same journalist also substantiated statements made earlier in this chapter about journalists' collaboration. Correspondents for major print organizations went out together, for both physical and psychological security. Many were good friends. It was considered acceptable to share quotes with a colleague who arrived late; competition often ran second. This often was not the case for television and news magazine journalists.

[105]*The Marcoses and the Making of American Foreign Policy* (New York: Times Books, 1987).

[106]Mark Hertsgaard, *On Bended Knee: The Press and the Reagan Presidency* (New York: Farrar Straus Giroux, 1988), pp. 191 and 202, as quoted by Tom McCoy, "The *New York Times*' Coverage of El Salvador," *Newspaper Research Journal* (vol. 13, no. 3), Summer 1992. McCoy concentrated on coverage of the Bush years, concluding that "As the U.S. downplays the significance of developments in El Salvador, the *Times*' coverage reflects this marginalization" (p. 80). Also see Sydney Schanberg's October 27, 1992, column in *Newsday*. Important for the historical record is Mark Danner's *New Yorker* cover story, "The Truth of El Mozote," December 6, 1993, including photos by Susan Meiselas. The Bonner story comes at the end of a meticulously documented 74–page retrospective describing U.S. complicity and coverup. But the overall role of the press receives little attention. For more evidence that Washington knew far more than admitted, see Frank Smyth's "Green Berets in El Salvador," *Covert Action* (Fall, 1993), p. 20. Smyth's interview with former military adviser Greg Walker deals with U.S. government knowledge of Mozote and other killings. Walker placed the blame on Washington for covering up.

[107]Charles Clements, *Witness to War* (New York: Bantam, 1984).

[108]Part of fax from Bonner, then living in Nairobi, to author, November 14, 1992.

[109]Interview with Marc Cooper in Los Angeles, October 23, 1992.

[110]Cooper interview.

[111]Marc Cooper, "Whitewashing Duarte: U.S. Reporting on El Salvador," *NACLA Report on the Americas* (January-March 1986), p. 7.

[112]*NACLA Report on the Americas*, p. 10.

[113]Marjorie Miller of the *Los Angeles Times* was with Villalobos and his guerrillas in Morazan Province prior to this and talked with him, but he refused to sit for a formal interview.

[114]Marc Cooper, "The Mayan Revolution, the Zapatistas Fire the Shot Heard 'Round the Global Market," *Village Voice* (February 1, 1994); also see Open Magazine Pamphlet Series, February 1994 issue, and "Ten Days That Shook Mexico," *The Nation* (March 28, 1994), p. 408.

[115]*New York Times*, "U.S. Aware of Killings, Worked with Salvador's Rightists, Papers Suggest," November 9, 1993, p. 4.

[116]Chris Norton, letter to *Columbia Journalism Review* (July-August 1993), p. 7, in response to an article about Mozote in the January-February issue.

[117]As reprinted in the *Daily News* (Los Angeles), January 17, 1992, p. 1.

[118]*Los Angeles Times*, January 17, 1992, p. 1.

[119]"Out of the Jungle: El Salvador's Guerrillas," *New York Times Magazine*, February 9, 1992, p. 24 (cover story).

[120]"The Wounds of War," *Los Angeles Times Magazine*, p. 12 (cover story). Also see Villalobos interview, *Los Angeles Times*, September 22, 1992, p. H6.

[121]*New York Times Magazine*, February 9, 1992, p. 27.

[122]In these statements Ortega referred to the long economic involvement of the United States in the region and called for simple justice. He fully realized the importance of good relations with Washington. On one occasion Fidel Castro came to Managua and told Nicaraguans they should deal with the United States and avoid mistakes made by Cuba, reminding them that Nicaragua should not become "another Cuba."

NOTES FOR CHAPTER 7

[1]Perhaps the most creative presentation of the divergent viewpoints is found in Eric Black's *Parallel Realities: A Jewish/Arab History of Israel/Palestine* (Minneapolis: Paradigm Press, 1992). For another exploration of the two cultures and their religious roots, see Colin Chapman's *Whose Promised Land: Israel or Palestine?* (Oxford: Lion Paperbacks, 1992).

[2]*Los Angeles Times*, June 8, 1967, p. 22.

[3]*Chicago Tribune*, June 8, 1967, p. 1.

[4]*New York Times*, June 8, 1967, p. 1.

[5]Ibid.

[6]*Washington Post*, June 8, 1967, p. 14.

[7]For an understanding of the foundations of twentieth-century Palestine, see Alexander Scholch's "Britain in Palestine, 1838–1882: The Roots of the Balfour Policy," *Journal of Palestine Studies* (Autumn, 1992), p. 39.

[8]I. F. Stone, "Holy War," in Walter Laqueur and Barry Rubin (eds.), *The Israel-Arab Reader* (New York: Penguin Books, 1985), p. 313. The article originally appeared in the *New York Review of Books*, August 3, 1967. Also see Stone's *This Is Israel* (New York: Boni and Gaer, 1948), with photographs by Robert Capa, Jerry Cooke, and Tim Gidal. This was an eyewitness account of Israel's birth. Few noted Americans spoke in favor of the Palestinians in these early days, but one was columnist Dorothy Thompson, who said in 1951: "The partition of Palestine and the establishment of the State of Israel is an invasion of the Arab world, initially by European Jews, and therefore alien" (*Editor & Publisher*, February 10, 1961).

[9]Noam Chomsky, *The Fateful Triangle: The United States, Israel and the Palestinians* (Boston: South End Press, 1983), p. 97; Eric Black, *Parallel Realities*, p. 77; David McDowall, *Palestine and Israel: The Uprising and Beyond* (Berkeley: University of California Press, 1989), p. 67.

[10]Chomsky, *Fateful Triangle*, pp. 166–67.

[11]David Hirst, *The Gun and the Olive Branch: The Roots of Violence in the Middle East* (New York: Harcourt Brace Jovanovich, 1977), p. 124. For Haganah's role, Hirst cited stories in the April 13, 1948, *Palestine Post* and the April 13, 1948, *New York Times*. The respected Israeli journalist Benny Morris disclosed new information about Deir Yassin in 1986 when he revealed an IDF Intelligence Branch Report dated June 30, 1948 ("The Arab Exodus from Palestine in the Period December 12, 1947 to June 1, 1948") in the January 1986 issue of *Middle Eastern Studies*. He reported that most of the 300,000 to 400,000 who left their homes during this initial period had been attacked by the Irgun and Stern Gang. For complete details see his *The Birth of the Palestinian Refugee Problem, 1947–49* (New York: Cambridge University Press, 1993).

[12]See Simha Flapan, *The Birth of Israel* (New York: Pantheon, 1987), p. 196, where this Israeli scholar disputed his nation's official estimate (25,000 Jewish to 23,500 Arabs) and offered a detailed rundown of the manpower buildup on both sides. John Bagot Glubb, a senior British officer working with the Jordanians known as Glubb Pasha, said the totals on May 15 were 65,000 Jewish to 21,500 Arabs. The Jewish mobilization increased during the rest of the year; the most effective of the Arab units was the Arab Legion of Transjordan, with 4,500 men under Glubb Pasha. The British officers had pledged not to fight within lands ceded to the Jews in the Partition Resolution. From the outset the disorganized Arabs were on the defensive; the Jewish forces were not outnumbered, as reported by the press and future propagandists. The movie *Exodus* is a prime example of such distortions.

[13]For a complete discussion, see Bruce J. Evensen, *Truman, Palestine and the Press* (New York: Greenwood Press, 1992).

[14]The number of refugees varies, ranging from 500,000 to 800,000. Journalist Isaac Don Levine was one of those reporting 750,000 refugees. See his description of this period in *Eyewitness to History* (New York: Hawthorn Books Company, 1973).

[15]*Challenge*, September-October 1994, p. 34. This is an Israeli-edited, Jerusalem-based magazine devoted to the Israeli-Palestinian conflict.

[16]See Colin Chapman's *Whose Promised Land?*, p. 180.

[17]The precise quotation: "If I were an Arab leader, I would never sign an agreement with Israel. It is normal, we have taken their country. It is true that God promised it to us, but how could that possibly interest them? Our God is not theirs. There has been anti-Semitism, the Nazis, Hitler, Auschwitz, but was that their fault? They see but one thing: We have come and we have stolen the country. Why would they accept that?" As quoted by Nahum Goldmann in *La Paradoxe Juif* (no publisher listed, pp. 121–22) and

cited in Flapan's *The Birth of Israel*, p. 5, and *Al-Fajr*, an East Jerusalem newspaper, December 25, 1989.

[18]For a critical analysis of the U.S.-Israeli relationship see George W. Ball and Douglas B. Ball, *The Passionate Attachment: America's Involvement with Israel, 1947 to the Present* (New York: W. W. Norton Co., 1992).

[19]Michael Emery and Ibrahim Dawud, "Next Year in East Jerusalem," *Village Voice* (January 7, 1992), p. 15; also see Noam Chomsky's treatment and citations in *The Fateful Triangle* (see note 9) and the various writing of Walter Lehn and Uri Davis. A check of the *New York Times* index showed the Jewish National Fund to be almost invisible.

[20]His most notable effort was a multi-volume history of the 1948 war (in Hebrew).

[21]*Washington Post*, June 10, 1967, p. 10.

[22]Cited by G. H. Jansen, "The Shattered Myths," *Middle East International*, February 18, 1983, p. 13. William B. Quandt, senior analyst of the Brookings Institution in Washington, D.C., came to the same conclusion in his *Decade of Decisions* (Berkeley: University of California Press, 1977). Quandt says the distortion began in May 1967 when Israel tried to get Washington to believe that Egypt was preparing an attack. However, Secretary of Defense Robert McNamara said it was the judgment of three U.S. intelligence agencies that an Arab attack was not imminent. Nevertheless, when the Israeli act of naked aggression came, the United States gave open support and then covered up the Israeli attack on the U.S.S. *Liberty* communications ship. For other British and Israeli testimony to Israel's long-standing plans for launching the 1967 war, see Kenneth Love's writings (note 24).

[23]Eshkol, *Yediot Aharanot*, October 18, 1967; Rabin, *Le Monde*, February 29, 1968; Peled, *Ha'aretz*, March 19, 1972.

[24]Kennett Love, *Suez: The Twice-Fought War* (New York: McGraw-Hill Book Company, 1969), pp. 92–94. Nasser felt the February 28, 1955, Israeli raid on Egyptian-occupied Gaza was the turning point in his relations with Israel. He was furious when the *New York Times* failed to publish his interview in which he disclosed an offer to demilitarize the frontier. The Cairo press was given a statement from Nasser's office based on Love's final paragraphs in which Nasser warned that more Israeli attacks on Gaza would mean war; this story intended for local consumption was picked up by the United Press and spread throughout the United States and Israel: "Nasser Rattles Sabre at Israel" (*New York Journal-American*). The final irony came when the *Times*, after having dumped Love's exclusive work, published the UP story with the page-one headline "Gaza War Threat Voiced by Egypt."A series of incidents followed which climaxed with Israel's invasion of Egypt in November 1956.

[25]Love, *Suez: The Twice-Fought War*, p. 677. This is a well-balanced, fair-minded account.

[26]*Newsweek*, June 5, 1967, p. 43.

[27]*New York Times*, June 6, 1967, p. 20.

[28]Black, *Parallel Realities*, pp. 91–92.

[29]Some Jordanians believe that Israel fabricated radio reports from Egypt to the effect that Nasser was winning, I learned in a 1987 interview in Amman with a person who had high contacts during the 1967 crisis.

[30]*Challenge*, September-October 1994, p. 34.

[31]Morris died in 1979, killed by a sniper in Iran during the downfall of the Shah.

[32]*Los Angeles Times*, June 6, 1967, p. 1.

[33]*New York Times*, June 5, 1967, p. 1.

[34]*New York Times*, June 6, 1967, p. 1.

[35]*New York Times*, June 5, 1967, p. 1.

[36]*Washington Post*, June 6, 1967, p. 1.

[37]Ibid.

[38]*Los Angeles Times*, June 9, 1967, p. 26.

[39]*Los Angeles Times*, June 8, 1967, p. 26.

[40]*New York Times*, June 9, 1967, p. 18.

[41]*Los Angeles Times*, June 9, 1967, p. 1.

[42]*New York Times*, June 9, 1967, p. 1.

[43]James M. Ennes Jr., *Assault on the Liberty* (New York: Random House, 1979).

[44]The best overall source on this matter has been *The Washington Report on Middle East Affairs*. Richard H. Curtiss was executive editor.

[45]*Washington Post*, June 11, 1967, C3.

[46]*Los Angeles Times*, November 24, 1992, p. H1.

[47]*Los Angeles Times*, June 9, 1967, p. 23.

[48]See Caputo's *A Rumor of War* (New York: Holt, Rinehart & Winston, 1977).

[49]*Washington Post*, October 10, 1973, p. 1.

[50]For an analysis of the *New York Times* coverage of this turning point and a thorough description of the PLO organization, see Salwa Shtieh Rifai's *The Palestinian Guerrillas' Image in the New York Times during the Jordan Crisis* (M.A. thesis, California State University, Northridge, 1986).

[51]*Newsweek*, June 21, 1982, p. 23.

[52]See former correspondent Frank Gervasi's "The War in Lebanon," in Stephen Karetzky and Norman Finkel, eds., *The Media's Coverage of the Arab-Israeli Conflict* (New York: Shapolskyu Publishers, 1989). Chancellor and others are taken to task.

[53]Karetzky and Finkel, *Media's Coverage*, p. 217.

[54]*Time*, June 28, 1982, p. 9.

[55]For a detailed account of how American coverage of the Lebanon war convinced the American Jewish Congress that a *Hasbara*, or propaganda campaign, was needed in the United States, see Robert I. Friedman's "Selling Israel in America: The Hasbara Project Targets the U.S. Media," *Mother Jones* (February-March 1987). The campaign had mixed results.

[56]In visits to Israel and the Occupied Territories during the *Intifada* I saw tremendous interest in U.S. news coverage. Most Palestinians trusted U.S. correspondents more than they did our home editors and the public. Israelis tended to be more critical because, for "balance," human-rights abuses and other violent acts were reported—not enough to please Palestinians but certainly enough to make Israelis unhappy. The journalists, as usual, were in a no-win situation.

[57]*Washington Post*, September 17, 1982, p. 1.

[58]Chomsky, *Fateful Triangle*, p. 185. This is part of a long analysis of the war in Lebanon.

[59]*Washington Post*, September 17, 1982, p. 1.

[60]*New York Times*, September 18, 1982, p. 1.

[61]Thomas L. Friedman, *From Beirut to Jerusalem* (New York: Farrar, Straus & Giroux, 1989), p. 161.

[62]For the Israeli viewpoint, see Gervasi in *Media Coverage*, "The Massacres: Who Was to Blame?" p. 218. Also see Joshua Muravchik's "Misreporting Lebanon," *Policy Review* (Winter 1983), p. 11. Then see the extensive treatment of Lebanon in Landrum R. Bolling, ed., *Reporters under Fire: U.S. Media Coverage of Conflicts in Lebanon and Central America* (Boulder, Colo.: Westview Press, 1985). This contains transcripts of panel discussions.

[63]*New York Times*, September 19, 1982, p. 1.

[64]*Chicago Tribune*, September 19, 1982, p. 1.

[65]*Washington Post*, September 19, 1982, p. 1.

[66]Ibid.

[67]David Lamb, *The Arabs: Journeys beyond the Mirage* (New York: Random House, 1987).

[68]*Los Angeles Times*, September 19, 1982, p. 1.

[69]David Shipler, *Arab and Jew: Wounded Spirits in a Promised Land* (New York: Times Books, 1986). Shipler is another of the non-Arab, non-Jew observers who ended up seeing both sides.

[70]Friedman, *From Beirut to Jerusalem*, p. 160.

[71]Ibid., pp. 163–64. I met Friedman briefly at the 1987 Amman Arab Summit. I complimented him for recent stories wherein he had walked that delicate line where both sides might be offended by his observations. His modest reply was, "Thanks, it's not easy," reminding me of the conversation with Stephen Kinzer in Managua the previous summer.

[72]*Los Angeles Times*, December 12, 1987, p. 1. For a thorough look at the *Intifada* based on a personal investigation of the Palestinian community's inner workings, see Don Peretz, *Intifada* (Boulder, Colo.: Westview Press, 1990). Also see correspondent Michael Park's "Palestinians Can See a Future—and It Is Theirs," *Los Angeles Times*, November 24, 1992, p. H1.

[73]Eliyahu Tal, *Israel in Medialand* (Tel Aviv: Peli Printing Works, Ltd., 1988), p. 9. The study covers the period December 1987 to August 1988. For other views of the *Intifada* see Ze'ev Schiff and Ehud Ya'ari, *Intifada: The Palestinians and the Uprising—Israel's Third Front* (New York: Simon & Schuster, 1990); Geoffrey Aronson, *Israel, Palestinians and the Intifada* (London: Kegan Paul International, 1990); Alan Hart, *Arafat: A Political Biography* (Bloomington: University of Indiana Press, 1988; rev. ed. London: Sidgwick & Jackson, 1994); the various writings of Robert I. Friedman in New York's *Village Voice*, and analysis in other alternative publications such as Chicago's *In These Times*.

[74]See note 52.

[75]See Robert D. McFadden's story distributed March 5, 1988, by the New York Times News Service.

[76]Tisch made his opinion clear at a March 12, 1988, party hosted by Barbara Walters and attended by Kissinger and a number of political and media types including ABC's Roone Arledge. According to Ken Auletta in his *Three Blind Mice* (New York: Random House, 1991), pp. 488–91, Tisch argued that television should be banned from the Territories, and singled out ABC's Peter Jennings, while Arledge heatedly argued against blaming the messenger. *U.S. News & World Report* publisher Mort Zuckerman was there also. Following Mike Wallace's December 2, 1990, *60 Minutes* piece on the killing of Palestinians by Israeli border police, Walters and Zuckerman argued strongly with Wallace and his boss Don Hewitt, alleging an anti-Israel attitude.

[77]Jack Shepherd, "Middle East Surprise: How Enemies Talk to Each Other," *TV Guide* (March 5, 1988), p. 4. I recall one evening at Uri Milstein's Tel Aviv home where we watched television from the Soviet Union, Western Europe, Jordan, Egypt, and Israel.

[78]See Michael Emery, "An Endangered Species: The International Newshole," *Gannett Center Journal* (Fall 1989), p. 151. Note: In 1991 the Gannett Center for Media Studies became the Freedom Forum Media Studies Center. The study found that 10 leading American newspapers collectively devoted only 2.6 of their *non-advertising space* to news (*non-advertising* is everything, including crossword puzzles and comics). The figure was 6.0 in 1982. With the rush of foreign news in the 1989–94 period, the figure undoubtedly climbed back up. But with some exceptions U.S. dailies still consider foreign news something that readers do not want much of, unless there is an international crisis involving the United States.

[79]In early 1988 the Israelis claimed that about a thousand journalists, most of them freelancers, came to cover the action. By late 1988 the press corps was almost back to normal, with only a few freelancers roaming around. Among the wire service reporters gaining bylines in the United States were Louis Toscano, William Ries, and Carol Rosenberg of UPI and Nicolas Tatro, Marsha Hamilton, Jocelyn Noveck, Dan Izenberg, and Mary Sedor of AP. Foreign journalists were offered assistance by a growing number of Arab journalists, interpreters and "tipsters." Carefully accepting such help is normal; many Israelis assisted the journalists as well, often as members of television crews. The most prominent of the Palestinian journalists was Daoud Kuttab, who (among other things) authored op-ed pieces in major U.S. newspapers. See Daoud Kuttab's opinion article, "The Palestinian Time Bomb," *New York Times*, July 11, 1989.

[80]Apparently a new wave enters the region every four or five years, joining a few

diehards. In 1987 Dan Fisher, then in his third year in Jerusalem, when asked if he'd like to stay on, replied, "No, I'm a journalist" [Translation: I want to cover as many big stories as possible before I return to the home desk]. The *Intifada* broke out a few months later and he stayed into a fourth year before heading to London and eventually the home desk as editor of the nation's most comprehensive foreign news package, the colorfully illustrated *World Report* issued each Tuesday.

[81]For a wide range of information about the pros and cons of the television news controversy, see: *Israel in Medialand*, p. 11; newsletter of Committee to Protect Journalists (May-June 1988), p. 6; Peter Allen Frost's opinion section article, "Censorship of Palestinian Birth Pangs," *Christian Science Monitor* (April 5, 1988); Glenn Frankel, "The Camera Blinks as TV Crews Cover Israel's Troubles," *Washington Post* (March 14, 1988), p. 17; Dan Fisher, "Hate Mail Pelts Israeli TV for West Bank Coverage," *Los Angeles Times* (March 10, 1988), p. 8; Francis X. Clines, "In the U.S. TV, Israelis Find an Unflattering Mirror," *New York Times* (February 1, 1988); Anthony Lewis, "Anti-Israel Label for U.S. Press Based on Fallacies," *New York Times* (June 17, 1988); and Howard Rosenberg's View Section series, "The Other Middle East Conflict," *Los Angeles Times* (April 6 and 7, 1988).

[82]A transcript of the June 3, 1992, dinner remarks was obtained by Fairness and Accuracy in Reporting (FAIR), a New York–based media watchdog group. A syndicated column explaining the matter, written by Jeff Cohen, FAIR's executive director, and Norman Solomon, appeared in a number of newspapers. See *Seattle Times*, August 1, 1992; other newspapers covered the story, like the *Philadelphia Inquirer* on August 7. But many papers ducked it.

[83]These violations were reported when they occurred, by *Time* (April 11, 1988), the Associated Press (January 25, 1988), Reuters (May 1, 1988), and ABC News (Arledge complaint is in the *Los Angeles Times*, July 7, 1988, Part V).

[84]Reuters (November 22, 1988).

[85]The undercover activities received occasional attention; see a major story about special armed units "hunting" activists, by David Hoffman of the *Washington Post* (August 24, 1992), p. 1.

[86]A variety of organizations try to keep track of this data. The Israeli most quoted is human-rights activist Israel Shahak. Amnesty International has issued several scathing reports. The Palestine Human Rights Committee (PHRC), the North American Non-Governmental Organizations (NGOs), the Jerusalem Fund, and others issue periodic updates. In the Occupied Territories officials of the United Nations Relief and Works Agency (UNRWA) are sources; the most quoted Palestinian agencies are Law in the Service of Man (al-Haq) and the Independent Palestinian Commission for Human Rights. My most memorable interview on the subject of deaths and injuries was in Gaza. When I asked a Danish physician about the number of deaths recorded so far (May 1988), he responded with anger, "Why don't you ask instead about the number of beatings, the number of people who will never be able to sleep again because of tissue injuries, the number of people . . . " We also learned quickly that "rubber bullets" were simply metal balls covered with a thin sheath of rubber, and "plastic bullets" were made from an amalgam. Both were lethal; we saw X-rays of victims.

[87]See the full report, "Press Coverage of the Palestine Intifada," *Journal of Arab Affairs* (Fall 1988), p. 199. Several other studies of Middle East coverage and editorial opinion deserve attention, all from *Journalism Quarterly*. David Daugherty and Michael Warden (Winter 1979, p. 776) studied major newspaper editorials between January 1, 1967, and December 31, 1977. They discovered that while overall the press was "pro-Israeli" in "overall picture," the editorials had the predominant theme of urging a negotiated peace. The *Washington Post* was most supportive of Israeli positions; the *Christian Science Monitor* was most open to the Arab positions. V. M. Mishra discovered (*Journalism Quarterly*, Summer 1979, p. 374) that in 1971 the *New York Times* and *Washington Post* paid more attention to hard news items, but the *Los Angeles Times* had more interpretive news features and roundups. Daniel Sreebny (also Summer 1979, p. 386) discovered that the number of American journalists in the

Middle East jumped 50 percent between 1972 and 1975. Those sampled averaged 20 years' experience, 14 overseas and five and one-half in the Middle East. The majority felt there was insufficient religious, social, and cultural news, that stories were too "crisis oriented," and that there was a "pro-Israel" bias.

[88]The source must remain anonymous; the interview was in Amman.

[89]Those intrigued with proposals for settling the Jerusalem problem should see Adnan Abu Odeh's "Two Capitals in an Undivided Jerusalum," *Foreign Affairs* (Spring 1992), p. 183. Abu Odeh, Jordan's ambassador to the United Nations, called for the walled Old City to be administered by the various religious elements and retain the name Jerusalem. The western (Jewish) side would be Yerushalaim (Hebrew) and the eastern (Palestinian) side would be Al-Quds (Arabic for "Jerusalem").

[90]*Time*, October 6, 1980, p. 34.

[91]Anderson was released in 1992. Jerry Levin of CNN was seized in 1984 and held for 11 months. Sis Levin's *Beirut Diary* (Downers Grove, Ill.: Intervarsity Press, 1989) is the personal account of a hostage's wife, giving insight into the ordeal of all hostages and their families, with a focus on healing and reconciliation.

[92]See Tim Ahern's "White Smoke in the Persian Gulf: How the Press Pool Worked," *Washington Journalism Review* (October 1987). Ahern was an AP reporter with the pool. Also see Richard Pyle's "Sometimes the Pool Works," *Washington Journalism Review* (July-August 1988). Pyle, a veteran of numerous pools, was the AP's top reporter in the Gulf.

[93]While in London I had met with the foreign editors of the various press associations and television networks, to get an overview of the flow of news and to learn who their people were in the Gulf. Now I was at the other end, seeing the news flow from points of origin.

[94]The rest of the round-the-world trip doesn't fit into the specific chapters of this book. I flew from Dubai to Beijing, where there were very few Western journalists. The press associations had cramped two-to-three-person bureaus, including photographers, for covering all of China. Getting permission to travel within China was difficult. So were living conditions. There was an immense language barrier. The Xinhua people were as gracious as always, however. Then it was on to Seoul in early December, where I had the good fortune to meet David Holley, the *Los Angeles Times* Beijing correspondent, who was assisting with coverage of the presidential elections and the frequent street riots. Two Asian hands were there, Nick Williams Jr. and Sam Jameson. Clyde Haberman was the *New York Times* reporter. It was an exciting two weeks, with rallies of up to one million persons, numerous street battles, and allegations of vote fraud. My impression was that the U.S. journalists, most of whom "parachuted in" for this story, were as knowledgeable and aggressive as could be expected in their coverage of the election where Uncle Sam's man, Roh Tae-woo, emerged the winner over Kim Dae-jung and Kim Young-sam. By January I was in San José, Costa Rica, to cover the Central American peace talks. My main effort was to help secure exclusive statements from Costa Rican President Oscar Arias (whom I had interviewed twice on previous trips) and Nicaraguan President Daniel Ortega. Those statements and a full-length analysis co-written with Martha Honey filled page one of the *Times* Opinion Section in January 1988. The late Opinion Editor Art Seidenbaum commissioned the trip, and it was a joy to work with him. While going country to country I made several telephone reports to KFWB radio news in Los Angeles, a couple of which were heard by friends.

[95]See Elie Kedourie, "Reporting Islam," *Encounter* (February 1989), p. 74; also note the writings and films of Fadwa El Guindi, an Egyptian-born anthropologist who is director of El Nil Research in Los Angeles; and see correspondent Judith Miller's in-depth look at life in Syria, *New York Times Magazine* (January 26, 1992).

[96]Murray Waas and Craig Unger, "In the Loop: Bush's Secret Mission," *New Yorker* (November 2, 1992), p. 63. Two CIA sources confirmed that in July 1986 CIA director William Casey asked Bush to pressure Saddam Hussein for more bombing. Bush visited Jordan's King Hussein and Egyptian President Hosni Mubarak in early August, asking

them to pass the message to Iraq. The authors claim that Iraq responded and the arms-for-hostages deal continued.

[97] *Broadcasting*, January 21, 1991, p. 23.

[98] As quoted by CNN producer Robert Wiener in *Live from Baghdad* (New York: Doubleday, 1992), pp. 259–60.

[99] *Broadcasting*, January 21, 1991, p. 23; also see Patrick Mott, "New King of the Hill," *Quill* (March 1991) p. 14.

[100] *Daily News* (Los Angeles), January 17, 1991, p. 1.

[101] *Los Angeles Times*, January 17, 1991, p. 1.

[102] *Daily News* (Los Angeles), January 17, 1991, p. 1.

[103] *Daily News* (Los Angeles), Extra edition, January 17, 1991, p. 1.

[104] *New York Times*, January 26, 1991, p. 5.

[105] Also representing their papers at the daily briefings at the Dhahran International Hotel were such reporters as Guy Gugliotta of the *Washington Post*, Carol Rosenberg of the *Miami Herald*, Richard Willing of the *Detroit News*, Lawrence Jolidon of *USA Today*, Colin Nickerson and John Farrell of the *Boston Globe*, and George Rodrique of the *Dallas Morning News*—plus dozens of other well-known correspondents and legions of visiting columnists, commentators, and editors. *Time, Newsweek*, and *U.S. News & World Report*—in strict head-to-head competition—assigned from nine to 12 reporters each. Some British newspapers and correspondents commanding attention were Robert Fisk of the *Independent* (London), writers for the *Sunday Times* and *Financial Times*, and the *Telegraph*'s military historian, John Keegan. See column by Thomas Winship, *Editor & Publisher* (March 2, 1991), p. 5.

[106] See television critic Howard Rosenberg's "Missiles, Propaganda Fly Thick and Fast," *Los Angeles Times*, January 21, 1991, p. 12.

[107] *Los Angeles Times*, December 20, 1990, p. 1E.

[108] *Editor & Publisher*, September 1, 1990, p. 7.

[109] *Los Angeles Times*, March 4, 1991, p. 5.

[110] *Los Angeles Times*, August 17, 1990, p. 1F; *New York Times*, August 21, 1990, B1.

[111] See Howard Rosenberg, "Channel 7 Doesn't Hear the Voices," *Los Angeles Times*, January 26, 1991, p. 11; also see January 16, 1991, newsletter of Fairness and Accuracy in Reporting (FAIR), which said that from August 8, 1990, through January 3, 1991, television networks devoted only 29 of 2,855 minutes of Gulf Crisis news to opposition to the buildup.

[112] Everette E. Dennis, et al., *The Media at War: The Press and the Persian Gulf Conflict* (New York: The Freedom Forum Studies Center, 1991), pp. 52–63; one article cited was Gene Ruffini's "Press Fails to Challenge the Rush to War," *Washington Journalism Review* (March 1991), p. 20. The entire *WJR* was devoted to war coverage.

[113] *Washington Journalism Review* (January-February 1991), p. 14.

[114] *New York Times*, August 8, 1990, p. 1.

[115] *Los Angeles Times*, August 8, 1990, p. 1.

[116] U.S. Department of State Document—Policy No. 1298.

[117] Elihu Katz, "The End of Journalism? Notes on Watching the War," *Journal of Communications* (Summer 1992), p. 5.

[118] *New York Times*, January 11, 1991, p. 19.

[119] *New York Times*, "The Damage Was Not Collateral," March 24, 1991, p. 16E.

[120] The story circulating in New York was that NBC News President Michael Gartner made the negative decision after Tom Brokaw and producer Steve Friedman said they would like to air it. Alpert's video was shown on some local programs and used in college classrooms as an example of what the folks at home didn't see. As for Clark, he was next to invisible in the United States despite his tireless efforts to dig up the truth about the origins of the war and effects of the bombing. For details see *Extra*, the publication of FAIR (May 1991), p. 15.

[121] *Daily News* (Los Angeles), January 18, 1991, p. 1.

[122]Dennis, et al., *Media at War*, p. 27.

[123]Ibid., p. 28.

[124]See Author Lord's "The Flow of Combat News Was a Strangled Trickle," *Los Angeles Times*, January 23, 1990, p. B11. Also see Marc Cooper's eyewitness account and analysis, "The Press and the Panama Invasion," *The Nation* (June 18, 1990), p. 850.

[125]In June 1991, 18 news organizations complained to Secretary of Defense Dick Cheney about Gulf War restrictions. Prior security review, mandatory escorted pools, and delays in transmission were discussed in a September session. There continued to be disagreement about the need for prior security review, but some compromise was reached regarding pools. It remained to be seen if this agreed upon principle would be followed in the next conflict: "Open and independent reporting will be the principal means of coverage; pools, when necessary for early access, should be as large as possible and be disbanded within 24–36 hours" (*The News Media & the Law*, Spring 1992, p. 21). The reader is advised to follow these developments in this publication as well as in professional journals.

[126]*Los Angeles Times*, February 21, 1991, p. 5. Also see the excellent research of Michael Linfield, "Hear No Evil, See No Evil, Speak No Evil: The Press and the Persian Gulf War," *Beverly Hills Law Journal* (Summer 1991), p. 142. Linfield, an attorney and author of *Freedom under Fire: U.S. Civil Liberties in Times of War* (Boston: South End Press, 1990), offered a comprehensive historical background to the pool reports and a thorough look at domestic coverage.

[127]*Los Angeles Times*, February 11, 1991, p. 16.

[128]Dennis et al., *Media at War*, p. 28.

[129]David Lamb, "Pentagon Hardball," *Washington Journalism Review* (April 1991), p. 33.

[130]For the most comprehensive description of the media-military relationship in Saudi Arabia, filled with anecdotal material, see John J. Fialka's *Hotel Warriors* (Washington: Woodrow Wilson Center Press, 1992) (the author, *Wall Street Journal* reporter, was in Saudi Arabia); see also Jacqueline Sharkey, *Under Fire: U.S. Military Restrictions on the Media from Grenada to the Persian Gulf War* (Washington, D.C.: Center for Public Integrity, 1992); Peter Braestrup, *Battle Lines: Report for the Twentieth Century Fund Task Force on the Military and the Media* (New York: Priority Press Publications, 1985).

For newspapers accounts see Malcolm Browne, "The Military vs. the Press," *New York Times Magazine*, March 3, 1991, p. 26; Brown, "Conflicting Censorship Upsets Many Journalists," *New York Times*, January 21, 1991, p. 8; John Balzar, "Pool Reporting: There's Good News and Bad News," *Los Angeles Times*, January 21, 1991, p. 1; Balzar, "Reporters Wage Their Own Battles in the Gulf," *Los Angeles Times*, January 29, 1991, p. H1; Jason Deparle, "Covering the War," *New York Times*, May 5, 1991, p. 1 and May 6, p. 5; Anthony Lewis, "The Failing of the Press in the Gulf War," *New York Times*, May 6, 1991, p. 15; *Los Angeles Times* editorial, "It's Your Right to Know," September 14, 1991, p. B15.

Professional journal and alternative press articles include: Thomas Kleine-Brockhoff, Kuno Kruse, and Brigit Schwarz (*Die Zeit*, Hamburg), "Reporters in the Gulf Rally 'Round the Flag," *World Press*, April 1991; Theodore Draper, "The True History of the Gulf War," *New York Review of Books*, January 30, 1992, pp. 38; Debra Gersh, "Storytelling from the Persian Gulf," *Editor & Publisher*, October 20, 1990, p. 7; Gary Boulard, "Press Coverage of the Persian Gulf Conflict," *Editor & Publisher*, September 15, 1990, p. 13; Laura Fraser, "Everyone Out of the Press Pool," *San Francisco Bay Guardian*, February 6, 1991, p. 15; Pete Williams, "The Pentagon is Not in the Censorship Business," *Washington Post* (National Weekly Edition) March 25–31, 1991, p. 23; Peter Braestrup, "Censored," *New Republic*, February 11, 1991, p. 16; Nicole Volpe and James Ridgeway, "How to Win: 32 Examples of the Press on a Leash," *Village Voice*, March 26, 1991, p. 17; a number of Doonesbury cartoons; *Los Angeles Times* editorial of September 14, 1991.

131See the *New York Times,* February 22, 1991, p. 1, and *New York Times,* February 23, 1991, p. 1.

132Molly Moore, *A Woman at War* (New York: Charles Scribner's Sons, 1993), p. 135. This book is essential for anyone studying the nature of the war as well as the journalistic efforts. The author was given access to U.S. Marine documents in Washington. She recorded the many obstacles encountered as a woman in the field; she also noted the lack of cooperation of some of her own editors.

133*Los Angeles Times,* February 24, 1991, p. 1.

134*New York Times,* February 25, 1991, p. 1.

135*New York Times,* February 25, 1991, p. 1.

136Fialka, *Hotel Warriors,* pp. 23–24.

137Robin Anderson, "The Press, the Public, and the New World Order," *Media Development* (Special Issue, October 1991), p. 20. This is an extremely comprehensive analysis of the impact of press restrictions on coverage, with historical background. The entire issue, published by the World Association for Christian Communication, was related to the Gulf War coverage.

138Dennis et al., *Media at War,* p. 65.

139Ibid., p. 66.

140*New Yorker,* April 22, 1991, p. 27.

141See Alexander Cockburn, "The TV War," *New Statesman and Society,* March 8, 1991, p. 15; George Gerbner, "Persian Gulf War: The Movie," in H. Mowlana, George Gerbner and Herbert I. Schiller, eds., *Triumph of the Image: The Media's War In the Persian Gulf. A Global Perspective* (Boulder, Colo.: Westview Press, 1992). See also Douglas Kellner, "The Crisis in the Gulf and the Lack of Critical Media Discourse" in B.S. Greenberg and W. Gantz, eds., *Desert Storm and the Mass Media* (Cresskill, N.J.; Hampton Press, 1992). For a colorful firsthand journalistic report, see Nick Williams, Jr., *Los Angeles Times,* June 11, 1991, p. H2 (story on driving on Iraqi highways after the war while looking for damage).

142Ramsey Clark, *The Fire This Time: U.S. War Crimes in the Gulf War* (New York: Thunders March Press, 1992).

143Freelance journalist Larry Everest produced a video, *Iraq: War against the People,* providing some information missed by the mainstream media. Jordanian journalist Lima Nabeel went from Amman to Baghdad during the worst of the bombing and made a second trip after the war, writing poignantly about the war's effects on children and health care.

144Quoted by Christopher Hitchins, "Why We Are Stuck in the Sand," *Harper's Magazine* (January 1991), p. 74.

145For the historical record, the government of Jordan issued a white paper, "Jordan and the Gulf Crisis, August 1990–March 1991" in August 1991. When read carefully the Jordanian version is better understood. As a follow-up to King Hussein's fortunes, including his treatment for cancer and the outlook for Jordan's future, see Christopher Dickey's "Nobody's Invincible," *Newsweek,* November 23, 1992, p. 36.

146Alexander Cockburn, "Bombs, the Moral Tools of the West," *Los Angeles Times,* February 3, 1991, p. M7.

147Daniel Pipes, "The Media and the Middle East," *Commentary* (June 1984), p. 29.

NOTES FOR THE CONCLUSION

1Kenneth Stark and Estela Villanueva, "Cultural Framing: Foreign Correspondents and Their Work," a paper presented to the International Communications Division (AEJMC), Montreal, August 1992. Stark, a professor at the University of Iowa's School of Journalism and Mass Communication, taught journalism in China and has a longstanding interest in foreign affairs. His emphasis on "intercultural affairs journalism" fits the needs for the future.

²Danny Schechter, "A Failure of Journalism," *The Progressive* (April 1994), p. 27.

³Ralph L. Kliesch, "The U.S. Press Corps Abroad Rebounds: A 7th World Survey of Foreign Correspondents," *Newspaper Research Journal* (Winter 1991), p. 24; letter from George Krimsky to author, October 11, 1992; Michael Emery, "An Endangered Species: The International Newshole," *Gannett Center Journal* (Fall 1989), p. 151. The article summarizes the results of a six-month study of foreign news in leading newspapers during the 1987–88 period. The Gannett Center later was renamed Freedom Forum; its journal became the *Media Studies Journal* (Fall 1993). For earlier studies see Kliesch's "A Vanishing Species: The American Newsman Abroad," *Overseas Press Club Directory* (1975), and John Wilhelm's "The Re-appearing Foreign Correspondent: A World Survey," *Journalism Quarterly* (Spring 1963).

⁴Mark D. Alleyne and Janet Wagner, "Stability and Change at the 'Big Five' News Agencies," *Journalism Quarterly* (Spring 1993), p. 40. The article is both a qualitative and quantitative survey of the agencies. For an earlier period of press association activity, see International Press Institute, *The Flow of the News* (New York: Arno Press, 1972). Excellent on basic operations and statistics.

⁵As cited by Jacqueline Sharkey, an influential journalism professor and freelance journalist, in her "When Pictures Drive Foreign Policy," *American Journalism Review* (December 1993), p. 14.

⁶Sanford J. Ungar, ed., *Estrangement: America and the World* (New York: Oxford University Press, 1985), pp. 14–15. The author, Dean of the School of Communication at The American University and editor of this journalism series, joined with 11 others in writing essays around this theme. One of the contributors was Frances FitzGerald, a former Vietnam correspondent and author of one of the finest books on that period, *Fire in the Lake*.

⁷*Los Angeles Times*, September 21, 1994, p. 1.

⁸*Newsweek*, September 6, 1993, p. 26.

⁹Bernard Gwertzman, "Coverage of Foreign Affairs in the Post–Cold War Period," memo to foreign staff, November 30, 1992. For an overview of U.S. foreign news-gathering organizations, see Alicia C. Shepard, "An American in Paris (and Moscow and Berlin and Tokyo . . .)," *American Journalism Review* (April 1994), p. 22.

¹⁰*New York Times*, July 1, 1994, p. 1.

¹¹*Los Angeles Times*, August 7, 1994, p. 4. John Balzar, a throwback to foreign correspondents of the Jack London era, covered the Gulf War for the *Times*. He took his first journalism class from the author at Cal State Northridge after serving in a U.S. Marine medical unit during the Vietnam War.

Bibliography

This is a general bibliography for the foreign correspondence field. Please see the Notes section for references to books not listed here that were used specifically for one of the chapters.

Abbot, Willis J., *Watching the World Go By* (Boston: Little, Brown, and Company, 1933). The recollections of a veteran foreign correspondent.

Arnett, Peter, *Live from the Battlefield* (New York: Simon & Schuster, 1994). The premier war correspondent of his times relates his personal story, from Vietnam to Baghdad.

Associated Press, *The Instant It Happened* (New York: Associated Press, 1974). Collection includes numerous overseas photos.

Baillie, Hugh, *High Tension* (New York: Harper & Row, 1959). The overseas adventures of a United Press reporter and president.

Barnouw, Erik, *Tube of Plenty* (New York: Oxford Press, 1990). The condensed version of television history; see his three-volume *History of Broadcasting in the United States* (New York: Oxford University Press, 1966, 1968, 1970). Includes overseas developments.

Beasley, Maurine H., and Shelia J. Gibbons, *Taking Their Place: A Documentary History of Women and Journalism* (Washington, D.C.: The American University Press, 1993). A comprehensive history, including women foreign correspondents.

Belford, Barbara, *Brilliant Bylines* (New York: Columbia University Press, 1986). A biographical anthology of notable newspaperwomen in America, from Margaret Fuller to Georgie Anne Geyer.

Benjamin, Robert Spiers, *The Inside Story* (New York: Prentice Hall, 1940). Behind-the-scenes stories of 20 foreign correspondents, 1914 through the 1930s.

Bliss, Edward, Jr., *Now the News* (New York: Columbia University Press, 1991). A history of broadcast news written by a former CBS writer-producer that includes the highlights of foreign reporting.

Blum, Eleanor, and Frances Wilhoit, *Mass Media Bibliography: Reference, Research, and Reading* (Urbana: University of Illinois Press, 1990). The best single volume for mass communications; updates Price and Pickett (see below).

Blum, William, *The CIA: A Forgotten History* (London: Zed Books Ltd., 1986). A journalist's story of the CIA's intervention in more than 50 countries since WWII and the media's laxity in keeping the public informed.

Bolling, Landrum R., ed., *Reporters Under Fire: U.S. Media Coverage of Conflicts in Lebanon and Central America* (Boulder: Westview Press, 1985). Includes verbatim text of symposium involving foreign correspondents and media critics.

Bonner, Arthur, *Among the Afghans* (Durham, N.C.: Duke University Press, 1987). Excellent background for understanding the long conflict in that region.

Bourke-White, Margaret, *Portrait of Myself* (New York: Simon & Schuster, 1963). The photos and life story of *Life's* world traveler.

Bradshaw, Henry S., *Afghanistan and the Soviet Union* (Durham, N.C.: Duke University Press, 1985). A detailed account of a tortured relationship that brought years of violence.

Braley, Russ, *Bad News: The Foreign Policy of the New York Times* (Chicago: Regnery Gateway, Inc. 1984). A *New York Daily News* foreign correspondent looks at the opposition's coverage of the Kennedy-Johnson-Nixon years.

Brown, Charles H., *The Correspondents' War* (New York: Charles Scribner's Sons, 1967). The colorful story of the Spanish-American War.

Capa, Robert, *Slightly Out of Focus* (New York: Henry Holt, 1945). The work of the famed war photographer.

Carey, John, ed., *Eyewitness to History* (Cambridge: Harvard University Press, 1987). Collection of news stories across history, including foreign accounts.

Collier, *The Russo-Japanese War* (New York: Collier, 1904) and *A Photographic Record of the Russo-Japanese War* (New York: P. F. Collier, 1905). Magnificent photographs and maps accompanied by detailed battle explanations.

Considine, Bob, *It's All News to Me* (New York: Meredith, 1967). One of the great reporters for International News Service tells his story.

Cooper, Kent, *Kent Cooper and the Associated Press* (New York: Random House, 1959). Includes details of growth of the AP's foreign service.

———, *Barrier's Down* (New York: Holt, Rinehart & Winston, 1942). The AP's general manager describes coverage of major foreign events and the battles for press freedom.

Cooper, Marc, *Roll Over Che Guevara: Travels of a Radical Reporter,* (London–New York: Verso, 1994). A collection of in-depth articles that includes a number from Central America, the Soviet Union, Iran, and other foreign assignments for the *Village Voice*.

Creelman, James, *On the Great Highway* (Boston: Lothrop, Lee and Shepard Co., 1901). Life as a reporter for William Randolph Hearst.

Davis, Elmer. *History of the New York Times, 1851–1921* (New York: New York Times, 1921). Contains information about the early foreign news–gathering efforts.

Davis, Oscar King, *Released for Publication* (Boston: Houghton Mifflin Company, 1925). The *New York Herald's* star reporter tells his story.

Davis, Richard Harding, *A Year from a Reporter's Notebook* (New York: Harper and Brothers, 1903). The dashing correspondent was one of the best chroniclers of this period of foreign wars.

———, *Notes of a War Correspondent* (New York: Charles Scribner's Sons, 1912). Davis recounts personal experiences during the Spanish-American War, the Boer War and the Russo-Japanese War.

Deadline Delayed (New York: E.P. Dutton & Co., Inc., 1947). The stories of members of the Overseas Press Club of America, New York.

Desmond, Robert W., *The Press and World Affairs* (New York: Appleton-Century-Crofts, 1937). One of the important early books in the field. The late researcher's monumental and unfinished history of foreign correspondence (Iowa City: University of Iowa Press) included *The Information Process: World News Reporting to the Twentieth Century* (1978); *Windows on the World: The Information Process in a Changing Society 1900–1920* (1980); *Crisis and Conflict: World News Reporting Between Two Wars 1920–1940* (1982), and *Tides of War: World News Reporting 1931–1945* (1984). Excellent for reference and bibliographies.

Dubois, Jules, *Freedom Is My Beat* (Indianapolis: Bobbs-Merrill Company, Inc., 1959). The *Chicago Tribune's* Latin American correspondent describes three decades of covering the region's politics and violence and issues a strong call for press freedom.

Duncan, David Douglas, *Yankee Nomad* (New York: Holt, Rinehart and Winston, 1966). The photographic autobiography of the famed photojournalist.

Edwards, Julia, *Women of the World: The Great Foreign Correspondents* (Boston: Houghton Mifflin Company, 1988). McCormick, Schultz, Thompson, White, Higgins, and other major stars are profiled in separate chapters.

Emery, Michael, and Edwin Emery, *The Press and America*, 8th ed. (Englewood Cliffs, N.J.: Prentice Hall, Inc., 1995). The standard journalism history; extensive material on print and broadcast foreign correspondents.

Faber, John, *Great Moments in News Photography* (New York: Nelson, 1960). Fifty-seven photos, from Mathew Brady to Robert Capa.

Fenby, Jonathan, *The International News Services* (New York: Schocken Books, 1986). A Twentieth Century Fund study which includes data on the international flow of the news.

Fischer, Heinz-Dietrich, *Outstanding International Press Reporting* (Berlin: Walter de Gruyter, 1984). Pulitzer Prize–winning foreign correspondence from 1928 to 1945.

Gervasi, Frank, *The Violent Decade* (New York: Norton, 1989). Memoirs covering European fighting, 1939–45.

Ghiglione, Loren, *The American Journalist* (Washington, D.C.: Library of Congress, 1990). Oversized illustrated companion to the Library of Congress exhibit produced in cooperation with the American Society of Newspaper Editors and the Gannett [Freedom Forum] Foundation.

Gibbs, Phillip, *Adventures in Journalism* (New York: Harper & Brothers, Publishers, 1923). The famed British correspondent's story, including a section on the First World War.

Glenny, Misha, *The Fall of Yugoslavia* (New York: Penguin Books, 1992). Excellent background for understanding the crisis in Bosnia; written by a BBC correspondent.

Gramling, Oscar, *AP: The Story of News* (New York: Farrar & Rinehart, Inc., 1940). Includes development of the foreign service.

———, *Free Men Are Fighting* (New York: Farrar and Rinehart, 1942). Associated Press coverage, from the 1939 German attack on Poland to the 1942 Battle of Midway in the Pacific.

Hachten, William A., *The World News Prism: Changing Media, Clashing Ideologies* (Ames: Iowa State University Press, 1981). A thorough explanation of the New World Information Order arguments.

Halberstam, David, *The Next Century* (New York: Avon Books, 1992). The veteran correspondent assesses changes in the media and warns of an America isolated from the realities of the world.

Harriman, Ed, *Hack: Home Truths about Foreign News* (London: Zed Books, 1987). An irreverent and critical look at coverage of 11 world hot spots.

Harsch, Joseph C., *At the Hinge of History: A Reporter's Story* (Athens, Ga.: University of Georgia Press, 1993). The author worked for CBS and *Christian Science Monitor* at the start of WWII.

Hartwell, Dickson, and Andrew A. Rooney, eds., *Off the Record: The Best Stories of Foreign Correspondents* (Garden City, N.Y.: Doubleday and Co., 1952).

Head, Sydney, and Christopher Sterling, *Broadcasting in America*, 6th ed. (Boston: Houghton Mifflin, 1990). Best overall broadcast history; excellent for overseas broadcasting background.

Heald, Morrill, *Transatlantic Vistas: American Journalists in Europe 1900–1940* (Kent, Ohio: Kent State University Press, 1989). A survey that relates the personal experiences of the correspondents.

Herman, Edward S., and Noam Chomsky, *Manufacturing Consent: The Political Economy of the Mass Media* (New York: Pantheon Books, 1988). Two noted media critics include foreign events to show how "an elite consensus" structures many facets of the news in favor of governmental and big business interests.

Herr, Michael, *Dispatches* (New York: Avon, 1978). The grotesqueness and obscenity of war emerges from this tightly written and highly acclaimed account of combat in Vietnam.

Hersey, John, *Hiroshima* (New York: Alfred A. Knopf, 1946). The initial piecing together through interviews of the A-bomb's effect on the Japanese population. Originally in the *New Yorker*.

Hohenberg, John, *Foreign Correspondence: The Great Reporters and Their Times* (New York: Columbia University Press, 1964). A comprehensive analysis of foreign reporting with solid historical insight. One of the best overall books in the field.

———, *Free Press, Free People: The Best Cause* (New York: Columbia University Press, 1971). A broad survey of news challenges in U.S. history, ending with a plea for the press to make a more convincing case for its continued existence.

Hudson, Robert V., *The Writing Game: A Biography of Will Irwin* (Ames: Iowa State University Press, 1982). The definitive work on a discerning journalist.

I Can Tell It Now (New York: E.P. Dutton & Co., 1964). Another set of stories by members of the Overseas Press Club of America.

International Press Institute, *The Flow of the News* (New York: Arno Press, 1972).

Editors, news agency heads, and reporters based in 10 nations offer suggestions for improvement of news selection. One of a number of important IPI news flow studies.

Irwin, Will, *The Making of a Reporter* (New York: G. P. Putnam's Sons, 1942). The life story of one of America's favorite reporters; includes criticism of newspapers.

Jakes, John, *Great War Correspondents* (New York: G. P. Putnam's Sons, 1967). Brief chapters on 10 correspondents, from R. H. Davis to Walter Cronkite.

Jensen, Carl, *Censored: The News That Didn't Make the News—and Why* (New York: Four Walls Eight Windows, 1994). The 1994 yearbook of Project Censored, an organization begun by Jensen in 1976 to examine stories not covered by the mainstream news media.

Kaltenborn, H. V., *Fifty Fabulous Years* (New York: G. P. Putnam's Sons, 1950). The dean of radio news commentators tells of his adventures. He also was a foreign correspondent.

Kluger, Richard, *The Paper: The Life and Death of the New York Herald Tribune* (New York: Alfred A. Knopf, 1986). Includes the story of the paper's reknowned foreign service and its stars.

Knightley, Philip, *The First Casualty* (New York: Harcourt Brace Jovanovich, 1975). A critical look at war coverage from the Crimea to Vietnam, assessing the systems that often prevented the truth from emerging.

Laurence, William L., *Dawn Over Zero: The Story of the Atomic Bomb* (New York: Alfred A. Knopf, 1946). The *New York Times* reporter tells how he got one of the century's scoops.

Lee, Martin A., and Norman Solomon, *Unreliable Sources: A Guidebook to Detecting Bias in the News Media* (New York: Lyle Stuart, 1991). More than 400 pages documenting cases where ideology and self-interest prevailed over the reality of the news situation.

Lichty, Lawrence W., and Malachi C. Topping, *American Broadcasting: A Sourcebook on the History of Radio and Television* (New York: Hastings House, 1975). More than 700 pages of data; excellent resource for the early years.

Lyons, Eugene, *We Cover the World* (New York: Harcourt, Brace and Company, 1937). Sixteen famous reporters relate their favorite episodes.

MacNeil, Neil, *Without Fear or Favor* (New York: Harcourt, Brace and Company, 1940). A discourse about press freedoms and the art of reporting, with a chapter on the role of the foreign correspondent.

Marzolf, Marion, *Up From the Footnote: A History of Women Journalists* (New York: Hastings House, 1977). A pioneering book celebrating many unreported achievements, including those of women foreign correspondents.

Mathews, Joseph J., *Reporting the Wars* (Minneapolis: University of Minnesota Press, 1957). Final chapter is an overview of "The Literature of War Correspondence."

Mathews, Joseph W., *George Washburn Smalley: Forty Years a Foreign Correspondent* (Chapel Hill: University of North Carolina Press, 1973). The life of the famed nineteenth-century reporter.

Matthews, Herbert, *A World in Revolution* (New York: Charles Scribner's Sons, 1971). A *New York Times* correspondent, 1922–1967, the author gives his version of worldwide events that brought him into controversy.

Merrill, John C., et al., *Global Journalism* (New York: Longman, 1991). A survey of the world's media systems by one of the leading international communications specialists and five colleagues.

M.E.S. His Book (New York: Harper & Brothers Publishers, 1928). Melville E. Stone was founder of the *Chicago Daily News* and later the modern Associated Press.

Middleton, Drew, *Where Has Last July Gone? Memoirs* (New York: Quadrangle, 1973). A veteran correspondent examines his career with a special look at World War II.

Miller, Lee G., *The Story of Ernie Pyle* (New York: Viking, 1950). The biography of World War II's most well-known correspondent.

Miller, Webb, *I Found No Peace* (New York: Simon & Schuster, 1936). The veteran United Press correspondent covered a half-dozen wars before his death in 1940.

Mills, Kay, *A Place in the News* (New York: Dodd, Mead, 1988). Excellent description of the achievements of women in journalism.

Milton, Joyce, *The Yellow Kids: Foreign Correspondents in the Heyday of Yellow Journalism* (New York: Harper & Row, Publishers, 1989). A definitive study of the period.

Morris, Joe Alex, *Deadline Every Minute* (New York: Doubleday & Co., Inc., 1957). An exciting look at the history of the United Press, including the news agency's overseas triumphs.

Mott, Frank L., *American Journalism* (New York: The Macmillan Company, 1962). The final edition of a heavily detailed comprehensive journalism history. One of the classics.

Mowrer, Edgar Ansel, *Triumph and Turmoil: A Personal History of Our Times* (New York: Weybright and Talley, 1968). One of the finest correspondents offers his autobiography.

Mydans, Carl, *More than Meets the Eye* (New York: Harper & Brothers, 1959). The work of the famed *Life* photographer who became a World War II legend.

Nichols, David, ed., *Ernie's War* (New York: Random House, 1986). A valuable collection of stories.

Norback, Craig T., and Melvin Gray, eds., *The World's Great News Photos, 1840–1980* (New York: Crown, 1980). Includes memorable foreign events.

Nordenstreng, Kaarle, and Herbert I. Schiller, eds., *Beyond National Sovereignty: International Communication in the 1990s* (Norwood, N.J.: Ablex, 1993). Noted scholars examine the flow of ideas and images and their effects in this shrinking world.

Oestreicher, J. C., *The World Is Their Beat* (New York: Duell, Sloan and Pearce, 1945). The head of International News Service's foreign staff tells of INS's WWII coverage with marvelous anecdotes.

Palmer, Frederick, *With My Own Eyes* (Indianapolis: Bobbs-Merrill Company, 1932). One of the great correspondents of the early twentieth century tells of his adventures from Japan to Mexico to France.

Parenti, Michael, *Inventing Reality: The Politics of the Mass Media* (New York: St. Martin's Press, 1986). A slashing attack on major news organizations by a prominent media critic.

Pollock, John Crothers, *The Politics of Crisis Reporting: Learning to be a Foreign Correspondent* (New York: Praeger, 1981). A survey of journalists' life experiences led to a comprehensive look at their perspectives, responsibilities and dilemmas.

Price, Warren C., *The Literature of Journalism: An Annotated Bibliography* (Minneapolis: University of Minnesota Press, 1959). Contains nearly 300 citations in the Foreign Correspondence and War Correspondence category; supplemented by Warren C. Price and Calder M. Pickett, *An Annotated Journalism Bibliography, 1958–1968* (Minneapolis: University of Minnesota Press, 1970). See above, Eleanor Blum.

Pyle, Ernie, *Here Is Your War* (New York: Henry Holt & Co., 1943). One of the all-time favorites in the literature of foreign correspondence.

———, *The Best of Ernie Pyle's World War II Dispatches* (New York: Random House, 1986). Edited by David Nichols, who added a biographical essay.

Reston, James, *The Artillery of the Press: Its Influence on American Foreign Policy* (New York: Harper & Row, 1967). Reston warned that the executive branch would be more likely to abuse its power than the press.

Rosenblum, Mort, *Coups and Earthquakes* (New York: Harper & Row, Publishers, 1979). An Associated Press foreign correspondent from 1967 to 1979 digs thoughtfully into the system of foreign reporting, including government pressures, gatekeepers and making contacts.

———, *Who Stole the News? Why We Can't Keep Up with What Happens in the*

World (New York: John Wiley & Sons, 1993). How foreign correspondents battle political critics, hostile governments, and their own editors.

Rucker, Bryce W., *Twentieth Century Reporting at Its Best* (Ames: Iowa State University Press, 1964). Includes stories from Higgins, Bigart, Beech, and others.

Salisbury, Harrison E., *A Time of Change: A Reporter's Tale of Our Time* (New York: Harper & Row, Publishers, 1988). A personal look at America from the mid-1950s to the late 1980s, including foreign adventures. For the earlier years see his *A Journey for Our Times* (1983).

————, *Heroes of My Time* (New York: Walker & Company, 1993). One of the most respected correspondents recalls the famous people met in his 65–year career; this was his 29th and last book.

————, *The Long March* (New York: Harper & Row, 1985). The famed correspondent retraces the steps of Chairman Mao's retreat to the caves of Yenan.

Sanders, Marion K., *Dorothy Thompson: A Legend in Her Time* (New York: Avon, 1973). The story of a foreign correspondent who became a celebrated radio commentator and author.

Schiller, Herbert I., *Mass Communications and American Empire,* 2nd ed. (Boulder: Westview Press, 1992). One of the author's several critical reviews of the role of U.S. media in the battle for political and economic control.

Schwarzlose, Richard A., *The Rush to Institution, from 1865 to 1920* (Evanston, Ill.: Northwestern University Press, 1989–90). Volume 2 of definitive works on the history of the Associated Press.

Seldes, George, *Witness to a Century* (New York: Ballantine Press, 1987). The grand old man of newspaper criticism tells of his days as a correspondent.

Sheean, Vincent, *Personal History* (New York: Doubleday, Doran and Co., 1935). The first best-seller by a correspondent in this century, an introspective and romantic autobiography that set a standard.

Shirer, William, *Berlin Diary* (New York: Knopf, 1941); *20th Century Journey* (New York: Simon & Schuster, 1976); *The Nightmare Years, 1930–40* (Boston: Little, Brown, 1984); *A Native's Return, 1945–1988* (Boston: Little, Brown, 1990). An inside look at 50 years of history.

Smith, Howard K., *Last Train from Berlin* (New York: Alfred A. Knopf, 1942). The author, who became a legendary broadcaster, describes Germany in the 1936–41 period.

Snyder, Louis L., and Richard B. Morris, eds., *A Treasury of Great Reporting* (New York: Simon & Schuster, 1962). A fabulous collection of journalism history's classic stories, including many from overseas. Also see Snyder's *Masterpieces of War Reporting* (New York: Julian Messner, 1962), which deals with the great moments of World War II.

Stein, M. L., *Under Fire: The Story of American War Correspondents* (New York: Julian Messner, 1969). From Lexington to Vietnam, a lively anecdotal treatment of the war reporters.

Sterling, Christopher, *Communications Booknotes* (Columbus: Center for Advanced Study in Telecommunications, Ohio State University). This current annotated bibliography is published bimonthly.

Stevenson, Robert L., and Donald Lewis Shaw, eds., *Foreign News and the New World Information Order* (Ames: Iowa State University Press, 1984). A major study analyzing the content of news from and within 17 Third World nations.

Stone, Irving, *Sailor on Horseback* (Boston: Houghton Mifflin Company, 1938). Jack London, novelist and journalst.

Stone, Melville E., *Fifty Years a Journalist* (Garden City, N.J.: Doubleday, Page & Company, 1921). See above, *M.E.S. His Book.*

Stowe, Leland, *No Other Road to Freedom* (New York: Alfred A. Knopf, 1941). Veteran *Chicago Daily News* correspondent covers the opening of World War II. Also see his *Nazi Germany Means War* (London: Faber & Faber, 1933).

Sullivan, Mark, *Our Times* (New York: Scribner's, 1926 ff.) A reporter's six-volume story of America, 1900–29, with frequent references to the press. Poignant and highly descriptive.

Sulzberger, C.L., *A Long Row of Candles* (New York: Macmillan, 1969). This covers the 1943–54 period of his foreign correspondence work for the *New York Times*. His *The Last of the Giants* (1970) included observations to 1963.

Thomas, Lowell, *With Lawrence in Arabia* (New York: Garden City Publishing Company, 1924). The story of Great Britain's conquest of the Holy Land and the role of Col. T. E. Lawrence, as told by the future broadcast journalist.

Tregaskis, Richard, *Guadalcanal Diary* (New York: Random House, 1943). One of World War II's most intimate looks at the American soldier, by an International News Service reporter whose copious notes made him famous.

Voss, Frederick S., *Reporting the War: The Journalistic Coverage of World War II* (Washington, D.C.: Smithsonian Institution Press for the National Portrait Gallery, 1994). An oversized illustrated documentation of the print journalists, broadcasters, artists, photographers and editors who covered the war; includes chapter on women correspondents.

Wade, Betsy, ed., *Forward Positions: The War Correspondence of Homer Bigart* (Fayetteville: University of Arkansas Press, 1992). Covers the years 1940–71, with forward by Harrison E. Salisbury.

Wagner, Lilya, *Women War Correspondents in World War II* (Westport, Conn.: Greenwood Press, 1989). Includes interviews with 18 participants and names of accredited women reporters.

Wanniski, Jude, *The 1993 Media Guide*, 8th ed. (Morristown, N.J.: Polyconomics, Inc., 1993). An annual critical review of journalists including foreign correspondents.

Weiner, Tim, *Blank Check* (New York: Warner Books, 1991). A *New York Times* reporter tells about the Penatgon's "black budget" and the keeping of secrets from press and public.

White, Theodore, *In Search of History* (New York: Harper & Row, Inc., 1978). The fascinating story of the author's development as a journalist; the highlight is experiences in China while reporting for *Time*.

Wile, Frederic William, *News Is Where You Find It* (Indianapolis: Bobbs-Merrill Co. 1939). The life story of one of the most resourceful U.S. correspondents in Europe.

Willis, Jim, *The Shadow World: Life Between the News Media and Reality* (New York: Praeger, 1991). A detailed look at self-censorhip, manipulation, and agenda-setting, with a chapter dealing with foreign correspondence from the 1930s to the 1980s.

Index

Please see the Notes section for other names, terms and bibliographic entries related to the listings below